Sport and Spirituality

Sport science can quantify many aspects of human performance but the spiritual dimensions of sports experience cannot be fully understood through measurement. However, the spiritual experience of sport – be it described as 'flow', 'transcendence' or the discovery of meaning and value – is central both to our basic motivation to take part in sports, and to achieving success.

Sport and Spirituality: An Introduction explores these human aspects of the sports experience through the perspectives of sport psychology, philosophy, ethics, theology and religious studies. It includes discussions of:

*   spirituality in the postmodern era;
*   spirituality, health and well-being;
*   theistic and atheistic perspectives on sport and the spiritual;
*   nature and transcendence – the mystical and sublime in outdoor sport;
*   applied sport psychology and the existential;
*   spiritual perspectives on pain, suffering and destiny;
*   sport, the virtues, ethical development and the spirit of the game;
*   the Olympic Games and de Coubertin's idea of the *'religio athletae'*.

This groundbreaking theology and religious studies text will be a valuable resource for students of sport and exercise studies, sports coaching, physical education, and sport and health psychology. This book should be read by all those interested in the preparation, performance and well-being of athletes.

Foreword by Shirl J. Hoffman, author of *Sport and Religion* and *Introduction to Kinesiology*.

Jim Parry is Head of the School of Humanities and Senior Lecturer in Philosophy, University of Leeds.

Simon Robinson is Professor of Applied and Professional Ethics, Leeds Metropolitan University. He is also Hon. Fellow in Theology, University of Leeds.

Nick J. Watson is Senior Lecturer in Sport Psychology and Sociology in the Faculty of Health and Life Sciences, York St John University.

Mark Nesti is Reader in Sport Psychology, York St John University.

Sport and Spirituality

An introduction

Jim Parry, Simon Robinson,
Nick J. Watson and Mark Nesti

 Routledge
Taylor & Francis Group

LONDON AND NEW YORK

First published 2007
by Routledge
2 Park Square, Milton Park, Abingdon, Oxon, OX14 4RN

Simultaneously published in the USA and Canada
by Routledge
270 Madison Avenue, New York, NY 10016

Routledge is an imprint of the Taylor & Francis Group, an informa business

© 2007 Jim Parry, Simon Robinson, Nick J. Watson and Mark Nesti

Typeset in Goudy by
Prepress Projects Ltd, Perth, UK
Printed and bound in Great Britain by
TJ International Ltd, Padstow, Cornwall

British Library Cataloguing in Publication Data
A catalogue record for this book is available from the British Library

Library of Congress Cataloging in Publication Data
A catalog record for this book has been requested

ISBN10 0-415-40482-7 (hbk)
ISBN10 0-415-40483-5 (pbk)
ISBN10 0-203-93874-7 (ebk)

ISBN13 978-0-415-40482-2 (hbk)
ISBN13 978-0-415-40483-9 (pbk)
ISBN13 978-0-203-93874-4 (ebk)

Dedications

From Jim: To the memory of my mother.

From Simon: To the memory of Hardy Rhodes, grandfather and friend.

From Nick: To my mother and father, for nurturing the life my Father gave me.

From Mark: To my brothers Paul and Simon for our shared love of sport.

Contents

Contributors

Jim Parry is Senior Lecturer in the Department of Philosophy at the University of Leeds and Head of the School of Humanities. After a first degree in philosophy he trained and worked as a PE teacher and coach before returning to study. He then worked in teacher training and graduate programmes for 12 years before moving to his present position, where he teaches political philosophy and applied ethics. He is Founding Director of the British Olympic Academy, and a collaborator with the International Olympic Academy in Ancient Olympia for the past 22 years. His publications include the co-edited *Ethics and Sport*, and the co-authored *Olympic Games Explained*.

Simon Robinson is Professor of Applied and Professional Ethics, Leeds Metropolitan University, and Assistant Director of the Centre for Business and Professional Ethics. Educated at Oxford and Edinburgh Universities, Simon Robinson became a psychiatric social worker before being ordained into the Church of England priesthood in 1978. He entered university chaplaincy at Heriot-Watt University and the University of Leeds, developing research and teaching in areas of applied ethics and practical theology. In 2004 he joined Leeds Metropolitan University. Ongoing research interests include religious ethics and care, and spirituality and healthcare. His books include *Agape, Moral Meaning and Pastoral Counselling*; *Living Wills*; *Spirituality and Healthcare*; and *Spirituality, Ethics and Care*.

Nick Watson is a Senior Lecturer in Sport Psychology and Sociology within the Faculty of Health and Life Sciences at York St John University and is the co-founder and Director of the Centre for the Study of Sport and Spirituality. He holds degrees in Sport and Exercise Science and Theology and Religious Studies and teaches on both undergraduate sport programmes and the Sport Psychology Masters degree at York St John, which includes modules on spiritual and religious issues in sport. Nick serves on the editorial board of the *International Journal of Religion and Sport* and is a reviewer for various sport and religious studies journals. He is the author of a number of scholarly articles on the sport–religion interface and is currently writing a book titled *Relating to the 'Other' in Sport: Theological Reflections*. Nick was a junior gymnast and footballer and now enjoys golf, snowboarding, hiking and coaching football.

Mark Nesti is a Reader in Sport Psychology at York St John University and has been a BASES accredited sport psychologist since 1990. He has just finished his sixth season as counselling sport psychologist at Bolton Wanderers Football Club and has worked with a range of sports and with different levels of performance from club to Olympic standard. His main interest is in the relationship between existential psychology and sport and how this approach can assist those working in applied contexts. Mark is the Executive Director of the Centre for the Study of Sport and Spirituality at York, and is editing a book on sport psychology support in professional football in addition to being on the editorial board of the new *International Journal of Religion and Sport*.

Foreword

The fascinating aspects of the hyper-kinetic world of sports – the acrobatics of the goalkeeper, the ballet moves of the basketball player, or the golfer's precision shot to the green – have the regrettable tendency of diverting our attention from what may be the most important thing about them. Statistics may precisely denote all of the athletes' accomplishments, photos may underscore their aesthetic brilliance, and science may clarify their biological concomitants, but none is able to capture sport's essence: its capacity for touching us in deep, mysterious and difficult-to-explain ways. The essence of play, the social historian Johan Huizinga reminded us in his seminal work *Homo Ludens* (1938), is far removed from the physical and the psychological; its primordial quality lies in its 'intensity, absorption, and power of maddening'. 'Play', said Huizinga, 'casts a spell over us; it is "enchanting," "captivating".' And in case his readers had missed the point, he added: 'In play we may move below the level of serious, as the child does; but we can also move above it – in the realm of the beautiful and sacred.' Sport may manifest itself in slam dunks, touchdowns, goals, takedowns or in record-breaking dashes or marathons, but at its core it is fundamentally an expression of the human spirit.

Scores of books and articles have explored this third dimension of sports, but this is the first to do so within the conceptual framework of 'spirituality'. As such it is fitting that its release should coincide with the Inaugural International Conference on Sport and Spirituality sponsored by the recently established Centre for the Study of Sport and Spirituality (see http://sportspirituality.yorksj.ac.uk) at York St John University. Among the strengths of the volume are its broad range of perspectives and the diversity of disciplinary backgrounds of its authors. Readers will find penetrating insights into the intersection between spirituality and sports ranging from the humanistic to the theological.

Simon Robinson's brave attempts in Section I to define, explain, and classify this ambiguous term highlight anew the enormous breadth of formal and implicit definitions that accompany its use in contemporary discourse. To some, perhaps most, 'spirituality' connotes transcendence; a journey into a 'spirit world' that is beyond words, description and systematization. Others find it impossible to imagine spirituality divorced from the context of religion which, for them, is the only true source of meaning, myth and symbol. Still others think of spirituality as a human rather than transcendent quality: a way of being in the world and relating to others that can be organized and manipulated to the benefit of others. Unrestrained by qualifying definitions, spirituality can easily take on the characteristics of tapioca pudding: an amorphous blob of syntax that can be put into the service of myriads of shades of meaning. Happily the authors in this book have been careful to avoid this trap.

Those whose understanding of 'spirituality' is inseparable from religion will find Nick Watson and John White's contributions to Section II particularly informative. The Western church's relentless accommodation of popular sports over the past century hasn't been accompanied by a great deal of thought about the axiological implications of such an admixture. The authors help fill this gap by advancing our understanding in such matters. Mark Nesti's thought-provoking series of chapters (Section III) on existential psychology chart a new path for sport psychology: away from mind-numbing reductionism and toward a more holistic understanding of sport in which pain, suffering, hope, passion, spirit and other unquantifiable affections are recognized as central issues. In Section IV, Jim Parry, in a new and thought-provoking way, explores the values and virtues that underscore our highest aspirations for sports. In a sports world where nihilism, more often than Aquinas' virtue of *misericordia*, rules the day, Parry's astute recommendations for cultivating virtuous dispositions deserve a broad hearing.

These varied inquiries into sport all suggest, directly or indirectly, that the richest experiences of sport await those who are reflective, even contemplative in their approaches to competition. Simply put, sport contests go best when participants are able to appreciate them as products of our artistic and imaginative impulse and to remain sensitive to their impact on the human spirit. Sportspersons talk a lot about 'heart' – that unidentifiable place within us from which stem acts of courage, perseverance and unfailing will. In the context of this book 'heart' assumes a much broader meaning: it is the human spirit that encompasses our hopes, aspirations, choices and actions. Along with movies, media, literature, drama, advertising, television and other agents of popular culture, sport, for better or worse, adds form and texture to our hearts. It shapes our spirits and creates alternative realities and states of consciousness. As such this cultural phenomenon – and particularly its spiritual dimension – deserves the serious treatment given it in this important book.

Some might find all of this too heavy a baggage to load onto sport, something most of us do simply for fun. Others, for whom sport seems little more than muscles and sweat, might think sports are too trivial an enterprise to launch deep thoughts about one's place in the universe. This book will disabuse readers of such thinking. Perhaps it will even convince them that among the various offerings on the menu of contemporary popular culture, sports are the most organically suited for offering glimpses into their souls, or that, in their own way, sports can be a means of grace.

Professor Shirl James Hoffman
Greensboro, NC, USA
March 2007

Introduction

The idea of spirituality has been going through something of a revolution in the late twentieth and early twenty-first centuries. It has begun to break loose from the meaning structures that held it together for centuries, not least the framework of formal religion. Mapping the spiritual terrain, however, is not a straightforward or simple task.

To begin with, since there is no settled view of what spirituality is, we have to grapple with the object of our enquiry. One part of the field is taken up by a generic view of spirituality, one that is gaining in strength. Such a view looks to the development of life meaning that is based in the experience and practice of the person or group. Increasingly, this view is informing enquiry in professional life and the experience of work. The question is asked, for instance, what work means (Randolph-Horne and Paslawska 2002). Is it simply a means to an end, or is there a purpose or meaning that might give value to the work, the work place and the workers? These questions are asked increasingly of education, healthcare and other professional areas, so that this view of spirituality is both transdisciplinary and interdisciplinary, and is rooted in and focused on practice. It also seeks to make connections between the experience of different professions and practices.

This, then, will be our first focus – seeking to explicate this 'new' account of spirituality. One way of making a start on understanding this 'generic' view is to construe 'life meaning' in two broad ways, doctrinal and existential (see Robinson 2007, chapter 2). On the one hand, there is the development of doctrines or philosophies that attempt to encapsulate something about the nature of life, including the social and physical environment. So, theological, psychological and ethical doctrines (for example) provide the basis of how we might make sense of the world and so respond to it.

On the other hand, however, life meaning in the light of the holistic and community perspective cannot be simply confined to conceptual beliefs. It is also located in and understood in two major ways: *holistic meaning*, which involves existential whole person awareness; and *value-based meaning*, which is discovered in the value the person recognises in herself and others through, for example, acceptance from the other, a sense of the worth of the other, a contribution to the other and the wider community, or a sense of purpose in relation to self, the other or the community.

Even this view of spirituality, however, is not univocal but involves many different perspectives, from New Age thinking to positive psychology. But this new and extended view of spirituality relates to sport in its widest sense and scope, from the individual sportsperson's or team's experience to the organisation and management of sports institutions, and to the wider community of stakeholders in sport – media, spectators, fans and so on.

A second important focus is that of the formal religions. The formal religions, and especially Christianity, have often been linked to sport, both historically and theologically. Religions continue to argue that they provide a distinctive view of spirituality that must be taken into account in today's pluralist society. Some theologians even go so far as to suggest that the spiritual and theological narrative of their faith has a claim to unique and powerful forms of integrity, and is thus superior to secular narratives (Reader 1997). In all this, at least it is clear that religion has a great deal of light to shed on applied spirituality but that, like the area of generic spirituality, it involves an ongoing debate inside, between and beyond the religions.

A third focus in terms of applied spirituality is that of particular disciplines, none more than psychology. Psychology provides important insights into personal and social identity and experience, and health and well-being in different contexts. Given this, certain parts of psychology have enthusiastically embraced the development of spirituality in practice, not least in therapy and sport. The positive psychology school has focused on modern manifestations of the virtues that have brought to life a range of spiritual practices, from Buddhist to Aristotelian. The focus has often been on the instrumentality of these virtues and related techniques, but also includes broader concerns about purpose and life meaning. Once again, of course, it must be noted that this interest of psychology is not uniform. There are many questions from different schools of psychology that contest these approaches, fuelling ongoing debates.

Finally, there is that most intriguing relationship between spirituality and other related areas, especially ethics. For the religions there is the claim that morality has to be based in spirituality, both in terms of doctrine (conceptual statements about reality that form the basis of any view of purpose) and existential relations (what or whom one puts one's faith in). Clearly, both doctrinal and existential truth can be discovered beyond religions, and much modern philosophy from Iris Murdoch onwards looks to the vision and imagination that might underlie an ethical response, taking us beyond straightforward ethical theory. This moves us into the world of virtues and ethos, the character or spirit of the person or group. Once again there are many different perspectives within this area, ranging from virtue ethics to the ethics of care, and it is worth considering what they might have to say in the context of sport.

In writing a book about spirituality and sport it would be tempting to give the reader an easy ride, in which all the connections between these different areas are smoothed out. We believe, however, that this would be to ignore the reality of the ongoing debate around reflective and meaningful practice. It would ignore the energy of that debate and the importantly different lenses through which spirituality and sport can be viewed.

Hence, we offer the reader four sections to this book, which reflect both the different areas discussed above and the expertise of the authors.

Section I provides an introduction to spirituality, and to spirituality and sport. It provides a working definition of the term 'spirituality', centrally involving the holistic development of meaning.

Section II addresses the relationships between religion and sport, perhaps for the first time bringing to bear a robust theological grounding in serious reflection upon sport.

Section III shows how sport psychology could begin to consider the spiritual dimensions of sport, and how research might develop with an acceptance of the idea of the person as an embodied spiritual being.

Section IV explores the connection between the development of the virtues and the spirit of the game, foregrounding the ethical core of sport as exhibited by its rule structures and by the notion of ethos.

When these four sections are taken side by side we hope that the richness of the modern debate about spirituality and sport will become apparent. This includes the different theoretical approaches. But just in case the intellectual plurality should provide an excuse for not taking spirituality seriously, it also includes ways in which the integration of spirituality in practice makes a difference: in the practice of sport, in its management, and in the relationship of sport to the wider community. And in the end there is a remarkably simple point that recurs throughout these different perspectives: spirituality is not simply about fine ideas and aspirations, but about the embodiment and the lived experience of beliefs and values that inform and provide the backdrop to people's lives. Hence, the real exploration of spirituality in sport is in the reflection, the dialogue and the practice.

Section I

Sport and spirituality

This section of the book provides an introduction to spirituality, and to spirituality and sport. In Chapter 1 the gradual rise of spirituality in the twentieth century is charted. Spirituality had been associated exclusively with formal religion, but the postmodern era and rise, albeit briefly, of the New Age asserted the right of anyone to develop their own spirituality. Perhaps even more significant was the way in which core services, such as education and healthcare, claimed spirituality as a part of their practice. Both have a long history of associating religion with their services, and so in one sense it is not surprising that they should want to keep that. What is different is the stress on a more generic spirituality. Neither area has always been clear about what this meant in practice, but the debate between practitioners and academics is very much alive. In the light of such concerns the association of spirituality and sport makes sense. Like those services, sport has long been associated with religion, and now as with them there are attempts to understand how a broader view of spirituality relates to sport.

Chapter 2 attempts to develop a working definition of the term 'spirituality'. Some philosophers and theologians delight in arguing that spirituality is impossible to define. Of course, this largely depends what you mean by definition. If it means an exhaustive and precise description then spirituality might well be hard to define. But much the same is true of most really interesting words, such as psychology, philosophy, theology. All of these have many different meanings which are being continually debated. Moreover, without at least a working definition it is hard to see how this term could be related at all to practice. The development of such a definition is related to the experience of a footballer. It looks at the holistic development of meaning through terms such as faith and hope. Finally, this definition is compared to other terms such as religion, ethics and psychology.

Chapter 3 examines the reflective context of spirituality, beginning with the example of Barcelona football club. The context of spirituality in reflective practice is then drawn out and the underlying dynamic examined. In the light of that it is suggested that spirituality relates closely to a holistic view of health and well-being. Such a view of spirituality is contrasted with negative spiritualities, involving attempts to find significant meaning through asserting an identity which denies the rights and even the presence of others. The Olympic rallies are contrasted with the Nuremberg rallies – both focusing on sport, well-being and value and belief systems. One, however, looks beyond itself, whereas the other could not see beyond itself, or even see difference within itself. The chapter concludes by setting out a range of different ways in which spirituality can relate to sport.

1 Spirituality

A story so far

Simon Robinson

With four miles to go you can see the Thames, and you know that you are going to make it – if you stay focused. And that is the problem. The legs are telling the brain 'Stop, we can't go another yard.' That demand is quite easy to shrug off. It's when your feet try the more subtle approach that you start to wobble: 'You've made it, no need to push yourself – you could walk it from here and still have a respectable time.' The lungs join in the chorus, 'Nothing left in the tank, gasp, got to stop,' and the mind offers an anxious counterpoint, 'What's that pain in the left side of the chest – am I having a heart attack?'

And then you see Big Ben – one mile to get there and just over one mile beyond, and the crowd is even bigger, almost overwhelming. The wave of support lifts you, and it is speaking to you directly. Now the thousands of people lining the street are pushing *you* on. Of course they have been doing it for the last 24 miles, from people outside their front gardens, to those outside the pubs, to the bands every few miles. And what bands! Jazz bands, brass bands, steel bands, drumming bands, even mini orchestras, all with an insistent rhythm that both cushions and focuses the tread, and lifts the heart. But now, with two miles to go, it's all bigger and better. St John's ambulance volunteers who have been hovering like beneficent vultures, just waiting for the first touch of a stagger, are now cheering. The last thing they want is to treat someone this close to the end. It seems like every few yards there are the charity supporters, with their colourful balloons. They're not just cheering for their runners now but for everyone. What's that – a big banner saying 'False start – will you please return to the start in an orderly fashion.' Humour can raise the spirit, even at this stage – but only just.

And all of this helps you feel and get in touch with your spirit, who you are and why you are doing this. So as Big Ben looms large you think of the people who have been behind you for months, the group you are raising funds for, the colleagues and friends who have pledged money, your family, especially if you know that they are going to be at the end. Just looking forward to their faces takes you back to why you are doing all this.

One mile to go. You're turning right at Big Ben and into the last mile. How can you feel so good when the legs ache so much? But you do feel good. In fact you feel so good that you are getting a second and third wind. Feels like you are sprinting now – only pausing to encourage some of the guys who have slowed down to a walk. By the time you have reached Buckingham Palace all the old aches are back but it doesn't matter any more. It's like you have been released from your body. Its more than a runner's high, it feels as though you are outside yourself, but at the same time truly yourself. All these things connect you with your spirit, your real self.

(Jon Green, London marathon 2003)

The experience of running any marathon is amazing, but especially so in one of the big ones – such as London, New York, Chicago or Paris. Thousands of runners come together to experience what professional runners experience on a regular basis. Pushing themselves to their extreme, they compete with themselves and sometime others, and each one feels like a winner. But Jon's story involved more than just the glory; it involved getting 'in touch with the spirit'. The experience was something special, and included:

- A sense of holism, with mind, feelings and body stretched together.
- A sense of being part of a greater community or entity.
- A sense of transcendence, being taken beyond the self.
- A sense of common and significant purpose, even of service. The vast majority are running to raise money for people in need, often known to them personally.
- A connection to the runner's core community, from family to colleagues.
- A sense of ritual in the great public event, even of sacrament. Sacrament is an action which represents or embodies an underlying reality and meaning.
- A sense of transformation and development.

This represents for many people a spiritual experience, or as some would have it a religious experience. I will explore in more detail later the meaning of spirituality. For now it is worth at least reflecting on the etymology of religion. The Latin *religionem* refers to respect or care for what is sacred. There is also in *religiare*, attested by Augustine, the meaning 'to bind fast, to place obligation on' (Chambers 2004). At the heart of the term then is commitment to something, be it a way of life, an idea, a belief. There is no doubt that for the marathon runner there is that sense of commitment. Without this, it is hard to see how one can get to the end. And the commitment is expressed not just in the marathon event itself but in the months of training, 'religiously' pounding the pavements. For many there is also a sense of the transformative experience, perhaps attached to the loss or illness of a loved one, whom you are running for. For many the decision to run the marathon is not taken lightly, and for many it is just such a major incident in their lives that motivates them, or a sense of the need to find something new in their lives. So by the time the runner hits the last straight this is the culmination of something that has become a habit, a good habit. It is a wonderful moment of achievement, but it is also the endpoint of the commitment of six months or more. As the runner crosses the line, aware of the spent self, another ritual cry goes up, 'Never again!' But because the experience has been so all-encompassing, because for many it held a sense of awe, and because the experience had brought so much together,

the majority are soon anxiously scanning the papers for when next year's applications are out. There is about the marathon something that is liberating, allowing
every runner to experience what was seen until only decades ago to be the domain
of a super-fit elite. Here is the priesthood of *all* believers, with silver foil blanket in
place of the priest's alb.

For a moment, however, return to the start. There on the green at Blackheath is
all the pent up excitement, the nerves, the hopes. All this is accompanied by other
rituals: the stretching; the aerobics, led by some celebrity; even the interminable
queues for the portable loos. Trivial in themselves, they all contribute towards a
sense of solidarity or belonging, all pointing towards the big event. Not far from
all this is a small Anglican church, which provides early morning worship time for
the runners. Here the picture is rather different. Only a small number partake of
communion, in an atmosphere which is quiet and subdued, though nonetheless
special.

Contrasting the energy of the larger 'congregation', families and friends alongside the runners, with the tiny service, you might be forgiven for wondering which
was the 'national religion'. The one seems to bespeak shared public meaning, the
other a private club. None of this is meant as a judgement, academic or otherwise,
on the state of formal religion. It is simply a reflection which raises the question
just what has happened to this idea of spirituality. Has the 'spirit' left the churches,
to be embraced by the population at large in events such as the marathon? Or is
something a little more complex going on?

In the rest of this chapter I will develop a brief review of spirituality during the
twentieth century, noting how it was dominated by the Christian church in the
West, and how the postmodern era and the New Age movement led to a very
different view. I then look at a second crucial development, which has focused on
spirituality and practice, picking up the stress on spirituality as a human, rather
than a transcendent, dimension. The chapter then focuses on the attempts of
different professions to integrate the new insights about spirituality into practice,
in particular education and health. Emerging from this are a number of tensions
which I note have not been addressed either in the numerous books on spirituality
and professional practice, or in practice. These tensions involve the different professions and different views of spirituality within the professions. I end the chapter
with a note on how the concern for spirituality in health, well-being and education
naturally moves to a focus on spirituality and sport.

Spirituality

In the Western world the Christian church has dominated spirituality, relating it
directly and exclusively to religion. Spirituality was not about a reflection on, or
development of, the human spirit, whatever that might be, but rather a reflection
on the Holy Spirit, the third 'person' of the Christian godhead, and attempts to
develop that relationship. Hence, the term 'spirituality' is often defined by the
Christian churches as the practice of worship, devotion and prayer which enables
an awareness of the Holy Spirit (James 1968). Such spirituality was dominated

by the clergy, part of whose task was 'spiritual direction', guiding lay persons into how they might develop their religious faith. In Western society, where the church was the centre of learning and care, this led to the church taking responsibility for healthcare and education and for any underlying spiritual meaning. Hence, for instance, Anglican clergy have always held 'the cure of all souls', that is, responsibility for pastoral and spiritual care for all within the parish area. Despite the presence of other denominations it was accepted that, even if not an active church member, each person was part of a system of care which gave shared meaning, value and purpose at times of personal development or crisis, not least through the rituals of baptism, wedding and funeral.

But as Bruce (1995, 35) points out, now it is not at all clear, even within the Christian traditions, what it means to be a member of a particular church or group. Moreover, Christian church membership (Protestant and Roman Catholic) fell during the last century from 7.4 million in 1900 (30 per cent of the adult population) to 5.6 million in 1990 (12 per cent of the adult population). There began a breakdown of what might be termed traditional spirituality with the emergence of the postmodern era and the New Age movement when a very different perspective on spirituality was ushered in.

The new spirituality

Scholars argue fiercely about whether we are in so-called postmodern times and if so how such a world might be characterised (Connor 1989). It is, however, possible to distinguish between postmodernism as a theory and the experience of the postmodern era. In the first of these, new ways of understanding language and social constructs are argued for. Baudrillard (1973), for instance, sees the division between art and life as breaking down. There is no objective sense of reality and each person has to create their own reality and underlying life meaning. Whether or not we agree with such theory it is hard not to accept something of the postmodern *experience*, in which old certainties have broken down. Such an age is characterised by:

- An explosion of scientific and technological progress, making resources available that were undreamed of even 50 years ago. At the same time this has led to a stress on rights and choice, often expressed in legislation, and also to new attitudes and value perspectives. The feminist movement, for instance, would not have grown in the way that it did without the technological means to freedom, such as contraceptives.
- An increasing influence of theories which stress relativity, indeterminacy or chaos. These began with Freud and his stress on the unconscious, culminating in the postmodern thinkers such as Lyotard, Baudrillard and Derrida (Reader 1997). The French theorists, in particular, rejected any natural foundations to knowledge, or any correspondence between language and reality. Even the human person is no longer seen as autonomous, but rather as the effect of discourse or power systems.

- A breakdown of patterns of behaviour and institutions such as marriage and the family, caused partly by the increase in wealth and mobility, but also by changes in attitude towards the sanctity of marriage and the notion of securing a partnership for life.
- A greater development and awareness of cultural and religious diversity within society, caused by increased migration and global awareness (Markham 1994).

All of this has led to a breakdown of any sense of objective knowledge and in particular of adherence to the so-called 'grand narratives' of the last century which had gone before. Grand narratives are those 'stories' which claim some universal truth (Lyotard 1979). They range from views about the person – characterised after the Enlightenment as autonomous rational decision maker – to views about the purpose of humanity – dominated in the West by the Christian ethic. Such grand narratives might exist in the minds of the great thinkers or they might give meaning and purpose to whole nations that help to sustain them through times of crisis. The grand narrative of the British Empire, for instance, gave meaning to the people of Britain and beyond, undergirding the initial acceptance of the sacrifice of so many in the First World War. We no longer buy into those narratives in quite the same way. So many of the cultural and economic underpinnings have gone. Major conflagrations such as the First World War raised questions about the underlying assumptions, leading eventually to a greater stress on individualism and the values of the free market. The grand narratives have been replaced by many different narratives, both local and national. There are still major narratives, including national loyalty, consumerism, the free market and the more communitarian views (with a stress on the importance on the development of community). However, these are either in competition or in dialogue (Brueggemann 1997, 718–719). None of these narratives are more acceptable than the other and there are no privileged interpreters of any meaning.

Spirituality in the West had been seen as directly expressed in the Christian narrative. Many do still view it in that way. However, with the breakdown of the acceptance of the grand narratives three things began to happen:

- The emergence of a spiritual vacuum. Spirituality had become so identified with the churches that if the churches were no longer a critical part of the life of the majority then it followed that for the majority there was no 'spiritual life', and nowhere to engage in spiritual practice or dialogue.
- The privatising of 'things spiritual'. If the public language of spirituality, as practised in the churches, was no longer accessible to the majority, then the world of the spirit was seen as private. In one sense the privatising had already begun. The power structures of the churches tended to discourage reflection within churches, seeing the priest or minister as the 'expert' or 'guru' who had the orthodoxy and spoke for the community. This is well demonstrated by Hull (1991) in relation to religious attitudes to learning. The individual believer would often see his or her faith then as private. This was however

reinforced by elements in the postmodern world, not least with the stress on individual taste and freedom.
- An attempt to reclaim the spiritual life in a way that anyone could be part of it. Here the postmodern era intersects with the New Age movement.

The New Age

The so-called New Age movement, which began in the 1960s, is really a loose collection of many movements and ideas which asserted different spiritualities. It generated a real sense of excitement and inspiration focused on the idea that each person can discover, control and develop his or her own spirituality in his or her own way. A common theme throughout the movement is asserting freedom from a view of spirituality that had been imposed by patriarchal institutions and authorities.

Other central themes include:

- Spirituality as acceptable, whatever the form, unless it harms another. Hence there is a tolerance of a great range of spirituality. Indeed, all existence is seen as a manifestation of some greater Spirit. All religions are seen as an expression of this same reality.
- Everyone is free to choose his or her own spiritual path.
- Spirituality as to do with the 'other worldly', stressing the mystical and even magical. This seems a conscious attempt to locate spirituality in the numinous, that which is beyond and greater than oneself.
- Spirituality as largely anti-rational. Feelings and experience are paramount.
- All life is interconnected and human beings work together with the Spirit to create reality.
- At the source of all this is a form of cosmic love which enables all human beings to be responsible for themselves and for the environment (Perry 1992).

Underlying much of this was a strong sense of the intrinsic goodness of humanity and a sense of a continued evolution towards spiritual enlightenment, both for the individual and for the community. Although there is a sense of novelty about this movement it is also concerned to recapture something of the past. Hence, paganism, for example, claims a history extending back well before the Christian era (Perry 1992). The movement is also concerned to chart the connection between spirituality and well-being and health, leading to a proliferation of complementary therapies (Watt 1995). Hence, New Age elements have developed views on spirituality and medicine.

The New Age movement is not without criticisms. The optimism about human nature and society, for instance, has little sustained empirical support. Since the flowering of the movement, there have been many examples of conflict and disasters, in the Middle East, the Balkans, southern Africa and so on, which do not indicate spiritual evolution. Second, the movement by definition lacks critical rigour. If all forms of spirituality are acceptable then there can be no common criteria for how to judge the claims and the worth of any particular spirituality. Third, the movement is not as inclusive as it would claim. On the contrary, the majority of New Agers are, in fact, articulate, middle class and middle aged. They have no more success in connecting with the vast majority of the population than the main line faiths (Perry 1995).

Despite such criticisms the movement remains important to any understanding of spirituality in the West in recent years. Perry sums it up in this way:

> In general . . . it demonstrates a high degree of social and ecological aware-ness; it demonstrates a particularly useful attitude in understanding that life can be led as a self reflective process of growth and transformation; and liber-ates spirituality from the confines of religious dogma and empowers direct personal experience.
>
> (Perry 1992, 36)

In all this it is fair to say that it offered a new paradigm for spirituality.

Secularisation?

The ideas surrounding both postmodernity and the New Age suggest that there is no simple move away from a religious to a secular society, defined as a society which lives explicitly without religious faith. This is confirmed by the work of Grace Davie (1994). Davie's research, much of it confirmed by subsequent work (Davie 2004), suggests that, although the decline of formal religious observance has meant that the majority of people do not belong to such a community, they nonetheless still believe.

> For most, if not all, of the British retain some sort of religious belief, even if they do not see the need to attend churches on a regular basis. In contrast secularism, at least in any developed sense – remains the creed of a relatively small minority.
>
> (1994, 69)

What is more evident then is a mixture of different views and practices, formal and informal, with some Christians, for instance, able to assimilate pagan practices and beliefs (Kemp 2001). Reader (1997, 8) notes the more difficult example of the Nine O'Clock Service in Sheffield as trying unsuccessfully to assimilate New Age worship techniques into a Christian service. In one sense little of this is surpris-ing, given that formal religions throughout history have always related to popular alternative spiritualities.

Beckford accepts the view that, apart from the rise of more fundamentalist religions, there is a decline in church-based practice. However, he stresses the importance of religion to a sense of belonging, suggesting that 'religious forms of sentiment, belief and action have survived as relatively autonomous resources' (Beckford 1989). These emerge especially at times of crisis such as the death of Princess Diana or the Hillsborough disaster. On these occasions there is the expression of both formal religious and informal spiritual rituals which try to articulate common feelings about the events (Nathanson 1999). The stress here is less on belief, in the sense of assent to ideas, such as a belief in a God, and more on the means of affirming shared feelings, solidarity and belonging at such times. Hence, the stress is more on rituals and symbols than creeds as such. Here then there may be complexity but with greater stress on belonging, in a broader sense, than believing.

Connected to this view of religion, as the focus for shared meaning, is the way in which formal religion and other social movements can become sites for resistance (Reader 1997, 12). Liberation Theology and the feminist movement, for instance, have become focuses for change in local communities. Even institutions such as universities are seen by some as means of focusing meaning in change, standing out against injustice (Robinson and Katulushi 2005, 256–257).

There needs to be more research to develop these different perspectives. As Davie (2004) herself notes, the distinction between believing and belonging should not to be held too rigorously. She attempts rather to point to a 'space' within which there are many different ways of framing belief. Ultimately this research raises as many questions as answers, about the nature of the belief or belonging. At first sight it might seem that the belief is largely about ideas, and it is not clear that such belief, e.g. in a benign power, focuses on a fundamental belief that makes a difference to the lives of those interviewed. In other words it is not clear that belief is the same as faith, i.e. putting faith in some being or idea that is the basis of life, such that the belief informs everyday decision making. Similarly, it is not clear that belonging is central to the life of the community or the person so much as connected to a particular challenge or trauma. There is little evidence that the particular ritual responses to crises radically affect subsequent patterns of behaviour. Grainger (2003) suggests then that any sociological perspectives on spirituality or religious patterns of behaviour do not reflect the complexity of the individual of social experience, and thus need to be supplemented by psychological insights. This in turn raises questions about how spirituality relates to personal development and autonomy, and I will return to these in Chapter 3 below.

Alongside the concern for spirituality in the broad sense noted above there has been concern for spirituality focused not in relation to belief systems per se, but in relation to practice.

Spirituality of practice

A very different focus has attempted to locate spirituality not so much in the experience of the numinous as in the everyday experience of the person, as a member of different organisations, as a learner, as experiencing different crises. A report from the Leeds Church Institute, for example, examined spirituality in work organisations, focusing in particular on how members of these organisations relate their work to life meaning, and how the organisation of work might enable this (Randolph-Horn and Paslawska 2002). Intriguingly, amongst other things, this suggests that those with a religious background often do not relate this to their experience of work. Those with a non-religious background tend to develop a spatiality of work, in the sense of consciously finding significant life meaning there.

Reader (1997, 11; see also Ashley 2000) also notes how personal development resources, initially developed through the human potential movement, are increasingly used in commerce and industry, as well as formal and informal religious settings. These range from the Myers–Briggs Personality Indicator to the Enneagram. Amongst others, these seek to enable reflection on purpose and character, and how they interact with practice. This reflective approach is further stressed in professional developments which stress the importance of the organisation reflecting on value and purpose. This moves further into the identity of the professions, from nursing to even engineering. Carter (1985), for instance, locates 'spiritual qualities' at the centre of the skills and qualities needed by the professional engineer, alongside personal and moral qualities.

However, spirituality in practice has been focused most securely in education and healthcare. In one sense this is hardly surprising, as the development of both areas has been intimately linked to the institution of the church. Only in the nineteenth century did the church begin to let go of responsibility for education, passing it on to the state. In healthcare, the title Sister, which still largely exists today, is a throwback to the sisterhoods which developed in the nineteenth century. Titles such as Almoner, which disappeared in favour of social workers in the late 1960s, represented a link between almsgiving, the church and the much earlier infirmarian brothers within religious houses.

However, the focus of spirituality in both areas has become wider than simply the religious. Spirituality is not something which is brought *to* the practice of learning or caring but something which is bound up in it, with spiritual meaning emerging from reflection upon the experience and the practice. Hence, there is a great deal of research into practical spirituality (George *et al.* 2000; Miller and Thoresen 2003).

Spirituality and education

Education has had the concern for spirituality and spiritual development enshrined in legalisation and codes. The 1988 Education Reform Act, for instance, requires schools to promote 'the spiritual, moral, cultural, mental and physical development of pupils' (Alves 1991). The 1944 Education Act extends the idea to the community:

> and it shall be the duty of the local education authority for every area, as far as their powers extend, to contribute to the spiritual, moral, mental and physical development of the community by securing that efficient education . . . be available to meet the needs of the population of their area.
>
> (HM Government 1944, 4)

However, not far beneath this concern for the spiritual there are tensions. In the midst of the postmodern era, religion, and in particular the Christian religion, still wants to be involved in defining the spiritual dimensions of practice. Beck (1999, 153–154) charts the way in which religious thinkers have been involved in the developments of spirituality in the curriculum and suggests that part of this involvement is an attempt to smuggle in a very particular view of spirituality, once more connected to a formal religious view. Such an approach tends to identify spirituality with religion, and argues that religion-based spirituality is the basis of moral meaning and behaviour. The argument, however, simply assumes necessary connections between spirituality, religion and morality. Hence, it does not provide any way in which different approaches to spirituality can be included in any educational process. Often this comes down to an attempt to include different *religious* approaches, thus once more moving away from an examination of what sense spirituality might have for the majority of people who are not involved in organised religion.

The contrasting approach is that being developed by researchers such as Peter Doble and Chris Meehan at the University of Leeds. They aim to develop spirituality in education that would be essentially school centred. The staff and pupils are invited to reflect on underlying values and beliefs about their purpose and to develop a reflective spiritual framework for their school (Meehan 1999). Spirituality is seen in this sense as developing significant life meaning and the framework of community which can be the basis for that meaning. In this sense the community becomes the basis for values and faith, faith in a generic sense (Fowler 1996).

There is then a real concern for spirituality in the practice of education. However, just what spirituality means is debated and there are underlying issues of how the whole can be worked through.

Spirituality and healthcare

As in education, there are strong drivers which encourage focus on spirituality in healthcare. Also as in education there are underlying tensions. These reflect once more the complexity of the term 'spirituality' but also the concerns of the different stakeholders in this area: chaplains, nurses, doctors and patient or family. I will briefly examine the debate from their different perspectives.

Healthcare chaplaincy

The chaplain's identity is based around spiritual care and therefore he or she has a real interest in trying to define what is meant by this and to work closely with others. For some the question is about delivery of spiritual care in a postmodern health service. For others there is the key question of integrity. How does the chaplain provide effective person-centred spiritual care for patients and staff, without losing his or her identity as a leader/member of his or her faith community? Many chaplains seem to be questioning their own identity and authority, looking to acceptance through registration as healthcare professionals. If the chaplain were seen primarily as religion centred this might cause some, including healthcare and medical staff, to be unsure of his or her motivation. The implication for some is that the chaplain would be there to care for patients in an instrumental way, to care for them in order, ultimately, to convert them to religious practice. Behind this is the fear that the chaplain cannot be both patient centred and God or church centred. Pattison (2001) goes further and argues that modern healthcare chaplaincy is in danger of 'dumbing down the Spirit', and thus essentially losing its religious identity. Others argue that spirituality is essentially connected to reflectivity and that therefore the central role of the pastor/chaplain is to enable that reflection and the person's ownership of her own spirituality (Robinson *et al.* 2003).

The nursing profession

In the past two decades there has developed a real sense of ownership by the nursing profession of the concept and practice of spirituality and spiritual care, leading to many publications. There are several reasons for this. First, a good deal of the history of nursing is based in some understanding of spirituality (Bradshaw 1994). Second, the concern for holistic care evidenced in recent years inevitably seeks to include all aspects of care. Indeed, for many holistic care is tantamount to spirituality, connecting mind, body and spirit (Papadopoulos 1999). Third, the nurse, in general, spends more time with the patient than other healthcare professionals, and thus can actually get to know the patient better than a doctor or chaplain. Hence, some nurses argue that they are in the best position to be aware of and to respond to the spiritual needs of the patient (O'Brien 1998).

This concern for spiritual care is also 'driven' through a number of Professional Codes or educational recommendations. One recommends that nurses should be able to 'Undertake and document a comprehensive, systematic and accurate nursing assessment of physiological, social and spiritual needs of patients, clients and communities' (UKCC 2000, 13). The American Association of Colleges of Nursing takes this a stage further. The nurse should be able to 'Comprehend the meaning of human spirituality in order to recognise the relationship of beliefs to culture, behaviour, health and healing . . . and to plan and implement this care' (AACN 1986, 5).

Such professional codes are reinforced by the revised Patient's Charter which assures the patient that 'NHS staff will respect your privacy and dignity. They will be sensitive to and respect your religious, spiritual and cultural needs at all times' (Department of Health 2001, 29).

Like the concern within education, then, spirituality is enshrined in official health-related documents. As in education, references to spirituality are both generalised and unclear. There are no guidelines on how these aims might be achieved. Moreover, within the different references there seem to be different emphases. Some see religion as the same as spirituality. Others, such as the Patient's Charter, can distinguish religious from spiritual needs, though do not say what the distinction is. In some ways the most interesting is the AACN code. This looks to the way in which beliefs, not simply religious ones, relate to different aspects of the patient's life meaning and experience. Intriguing though this is, however, there are again no indications of how such comprehension might be achieved.

It is perhaps not surprising that the actual practice of spiritual care is very variable (Oldnall 1996). The very different approaches and the lack of clear direction about the nature of spirituality also reveal a lack of clear aims and objectives in nurse training, and difficulty in determining how the different professions might work together around this theme.

The medical profession

The response of the medical profession to the question of spirituality has been variable. In one respect it has been quite the opposite of the nursing profession. There have been few writings on the subject in general medicine, other than in areas such as care of the dying and cardiology (Cobb 2001; Thoresen and Hoffman Goldberg 1998). There has also been great interest in the use of spiritual techniques. Often this has been in the part that prayer or meditation might play in actually affecting therapeutic outcomes (Koenig 1997). Concern for spirituality has also led to major developments in mental health, especially in the USA. Part of this has been in the development of so called 'positive psychology' by Martin Seligman (Gillham 2000). This movement has focused on the development of positive personal qualities, especially what have been characterised in philosophy and religion as the virtues. Such qualities have included hope and faith, and the capacity to forgive. In all cases the writers have looked to establish on an empirical basis how the development of such qualities actually affect therapeutic outcomes, in general as well as psychological medicine (Miller 2003).

The patient

The spirituality of the patient is at the centre of healthcare. It has generated a considerable amount of research, examining attitudes and therapeutic outcomes. However, similar tensions to those above exist in this area. As research in spirituality of work shows, the ordinary person is not clear him- or herself about the meaning of spirituality (Randolph-Horn and Paslawska 2002). This can lead to some patients ignoring questions about spirituality, or trying to say what they think the health worker wants to hear. Researches into patient spirituality range from examination of a generic view of patient spirituality (Ross 1995; Ross 1997) to work on the efficacy of formal religious acts such as prayer (Koenig 1997).

What is clear is that concern for spirituality does emerge in many patients faced by severe illness which in some way questions their value and belief systems and identity. It is part of making sense of such severe illness (Robinson et al. 2003; Robinson 2007).

Sport

Sport does not have any of the drivers, professional or legal, that motivate the integration of spirituality into education or healthcare. Nonetheless, in several contexts there are real overlaps. The concern for personal development is traditionally linked to sport, with the idea that the practice of sport can enable transformation, liberation and character development (Cooper 1998, 121). By extension, the stress on educational development that is holistic increasingly takes in sport. The ideas of health, well-being and human activity are intimately connected to spirituality that stresses a holistic perspective (Miller and Thoresen 2003). This concern for holism in sport can be seen as both means and end. Saint Sing (2004), for instance, stresses the balance of mind, body and spirit and how important this is in enabling the person to develop the best performance. There may be several different approaches to this, from the overtly religious, as lived out by the triple jumper Jonathan Edwards (Folley 2001), to the development of positive psychology, expressed through techniques such as meditation. Meditation in this context aims to create mindfulness, an awareness and centredness (Marlatt and Kristeller 2003; see also Bernardi *et al.* 2001). As I will note below, however, the technique aspect of spirituality is only one aspect of a broader reflection on meaning. Positive psychology looks to deeper developments, such as resolution and forgiveness (Worthington 1989), and this includes how to handle failure.

If the holistic techniques enable better performance then there is a sense also in which sport itself can lead to the holistic experiences. 'Runner's high' is that experience of awareness, akin to a mystical or transcendent experience, that the runner finds when the body and mind work together. Saint Sing (2004, 12) relates this to the Greek concept of *areté*, a state both of grace and excellence. I will return to this virtue below.

Sport also acts as a centre of meaning and purpose. For the sportsperson this is about the development of individual purpose. This is not necessarily simple. Many sportspersons see their identity as connected to successful practice, with a deep sense of pride which goes with that. Others see their identity in the way that sport and community intersect. Lucas Radabe, for instance, sees his identity as football player (Leeds United) as tied in with how he can affect underprivileged communities both in Britain and in South Africa. At the level of the wider community a sense of shared meaning emerges. There are different ways in which this might be expressed in sporting terms. For some the meaning is about acceptance, the sense of community. For others it is conditional, i.e. support and sense of identity with the club depends upon the continued success of the club. For others there is something of the 'worship' of heroes. As Grimshaw (2000, 90) notes, this can easily be seen in terms of the worship of perfection. He suggests that in fact sport might better be seen in terms of fallible heroes, enabling the fan to focus more on reality, and to accept the less than perfect. This ties in closely with the idea of spirituality seen as awareness of the self and others, and thus an awareness and acceptance of the limitations of the self as well as potential.

In all these ways sport can represent and embody meaning, and act as the ground of significant meaning. Such meaning can extend from personal fulfilment to the more complex community meaning, including the idea of serving society. Sport itself can act as the basis of value systems. In a recent day for local school children, organised by the Leeds Metropolitan University, one boy suggested that he found his values and sense of ethics through the golf club. There he found rules of behaviour and a strong sense of respect and fairness communicated by those rules. Hence, sport as a social organisation communicates significant meaning. It is not surprising that Grimshaw (2000, 95) can write of different kinds of epiphanies (revelations) that can be communicated in experience of different aspects of sport.

Meaning and purpose and personal and educational development come together in the development of virtues, and so to the identity of the sportsperson, organisation or community. The virtues of the individual sportsperson are the strengths of character that enable excellence (Saint Sing 2004, 110). The virtues of sport in community might involve, for instance, collaboration and empathy. This suggests a possible tension between self and other centred spiritualities in sport, something I will address later in terms of eros and *agape*.

Spirituality has often been seen in terms of energy and power (Aldridge 2000, 41; Goddard 1995). This be might in terms of a transcendent model, with external power being given to the sportsperson (Boyd 1995). Or it may be seen as energy that comes from holism and from positive relationships (King and Dean 1998). Either way this is relevant to the spirituality of sport, bringing us back for a moment to that painful experience of the last marathon mile, and that search for 'something extra', and to the way in which the marathon, in all its relationships, empowered the participants.

Conclusions

Spirituality through the late twentieth century broke free of the simple identification with religion. With the postmodern era and the New Age there has been:

- greater awareness of spirituality as a human dimension, not exclusively expressed in formal religion;
- increased concern for spirituality which both respects and embodies autonomy;
- greater awareness of spirituality in the context of community and institutions;
- increased awareness of spiritual diversity;
- greater exploration of spirituality, in organisations and in the experience of the individual, through the social sciences;
- increased focus on spirituality, well-being, health, and personal development.

Spirituality and sport takes up many of these themes, in the organisation and in the experience of the individual sportsperson. As we shall see in more detail, however, it also develops insights into the nature and purpose of sport. Before that, given the tensions described above, it is important to focus on a more detailed definition of spirituality itself.

Study questions

1 How do you perceive spirituality in practice? Was there any sense of underlying value and belief systems in the school(s) you went to?
2 How might spirituality relate to higher education? What values and beliefs are expressed in the colleges you have been in? How were they expressed?
3 From your experience of sport, first as a spectator and second as a participant, what meaning does it communicate?

2 Spirituality
A working definition

Simon Robinson

Geoff collapsed in the middle of a championship soccer game, and was rushed to hospital with a suspected heart attack. Apart from the intense pain he remembered three things. First was the huge sense of shock. One minute he was focusing on the ball being returned to him by the right full back, as well as on the attentions of the opposition centre half, and the next minute he was on the floor, and all of the things he expected to happened had suddenly stopped. The second was an unexpected sense of shame. He was a fit 27-year-old, with 17 goals behind him that season, in control of his destiny, and the destiny of his family, and suddenly he had no control, and was being carried through the swing doors of the hospital like a baby. The third was a sense of fear, fear that grew as the hospital staff confirmed that there was something wrong with his heart.

By the middle of a sleepless night he felt that he was going mad. His whole purpose in life was in question and he could not do a thing about it. What kept him going through that night was not any words of comfort, but holding firmly on to the soccer scarf that a fan had passed him as the stretcher went by in the ground. 'Hanging on to that scarf was like hanging on to my self.'

It may seem odd to begin this chapter with a disaster. However, it is almost self-evident to say that we tend not to examine our life meaning with any real attention until we hit a challenge to the meaning, leading to transition or potential transition. Bridges (1980) notes that transition is a part of growth and development, for persons and groups, and suggests four characteristics of this experience that lead to questioning and developing spiritual meaning:

- *Disengagement.* This involves a breakdown of relationships and shared meaning that helped constitute a sense of the self.
- *Disidentification.* The person tries to rediscover her identity in the old patterns of faith but cannot identify with them.
- *Disenchantment.* This involves a loss of faith in the old perceptions of reality. This often brings with it feelings of anger resentment, grief, loss, guilt and confusion. It can also bring with it a sense of liberation and new possibilities.
- *Disorientation.* This is the cumulative effect of the previous three experiences, involving a loss of direction, energy and motivation, and much time and energy put into trying to grasp any meaning.

That holds true for individuals and for organisations, such as Manchester United and the Munich disaster. It is often at that point that one most clearly sees what gives meaning to life and whether that meaning is sufficient to carry one through. Hence, this is one very clear way into exploring a working definition of spirituality.

There are those who would argue that it is wrong to define a term like spirituality. Bellamy, for instance, notes, 'Definition is a tool of rationality, an instrument which seeks to enclose. The term spiritual however, needs to remain elusive if it is not to betray its very identity' (1998, 185). However, not to describe the term more closely runs the risk of it becoming one of those 'slippery words' that everyone interprets in their own way, and it would be hard to see how this could be of use in or to practice. In any case many of the very best words, such as equality, freedom and community, are quite as slippery, and that does not, and should not, stop attempts to establish a working definition.

In this chapter I will first look at the meaning of spirit and then develop a three-fold definition of spirituality. I will then look behind this definition to the dynamic of spirituality, and note how spirituality relates to religion and other areas.

Spirit

As Geoff lay there he needed to lock into his very self – the essential self, often associated with 'spirit'. There are different views as to what the spirit might be, including a transcendental or essential dimension of life (Reed 1987; Highfield 1992), a force or energy (Sims 1994; Boyd 1995; King and Dein 1998), and life meaning and purpose (Hiatt 1986; Doyle 1992; Joseph 1998). However, rather than involving distinct models, all of these indicate important aspects of the human spirit, which, as described, was central to Geoff coping.

The term spirit comes from the Latin *spiritus* (Hebrew *ruach*, Greek *pneuma*), meaning breath, wind and even life principle. It is that which is vital to and animates the self. As such the spirit is not primarily about ideas but about lived experience. Hence, the spirit is evidenced not so much in doctrines but in practice, attitude and experience through being embodied. Doctrines, understandings of what that spirit is, may be developed, not least to help maintain that spirit, but they are not the spirit as such. This view of the spirit has a strong sense of holism – involving the integration of affective, cognitive and physical elements, making it impossible to isolate the spiritual from the physical. The spirit is a dynamic reality that expresses itself in the body, the organisation or the team.

The holistic view of the spirit is well supported by empirical evidence that charts the relationship between feelings, thoughts, the body and the social and physical environment (Swinton 2001, 16–17). Importantly, the term 'spirit' refers to the sense of life (that which animates), the identity (that which particularly characterises the person or group) and the qualities of that person or group. By definition it is something which is to be admired, and which has important meaning and value.

This holistic view of the spirit contrasts sharply with the more dualistic view of the spirit as quite separate from the body (often referred to as the soul). This arose from the philosophy of Plato and ultimately led to the view that the 'spirit' was that which was incorruptible, hence immortal, and of the highest value, and the body was that which was corrupting and corruptible, and of the least value (Edwards 1999, 86–89). Although such dualism has been very influential and continues in many, popular, ways of thinking, it has little in empirical terms to support it. Moreover, it tends to lead to a fragmentation of human experience.

At another level, for Geoff, the spirit was about something beyond the self. It was difficult to hang onto his spirit without reaching out beyond the self and being aware of the *other*, be that another person, including his colleagues, or the community of the soccer club and his family. Hanging on to his spirit meant hanging on to himself in relation to all the people who gave him a sense of purpose, all the practice that gave him meaning, and all the things that he could depend on, the things he believed in. In them he found energy that could be built upon as he began to work through his illness. In this view the spirit is not then some external force which animates, but is rather that essence of the self which is experienced in relationships, leading to the development of energy (Goddard 1995). These relationships enabled Geoff to be more aware of his essential self, reducing anxiety and increasing a sense of well-being and thus empowerment.

The spirit in all this is strongly connected to the development of significant meaning. Ellison (1983, 331) describes the connection in this way:

> It is the *spirit* of human beings which enables and motivates us to search for meaning and purpose in life, to seek the supernatural or some meaning which transcends us, to wonder about our origins and our identities, to require morality and equity.

Spirituality

Spirituality is about the practice and outworking of the spirit and the ways in which it is developed, with its different aspects and relationships connected, sustained and understood. As we shall see, this may involve the spirituality of an individual or that which is developed in and through the disciplines and practices of a group or team. It is often a combination of both. Essentially then, spirituality is relation and action centred, and about making connections with these different aspects of life.

A working definition of spirituality then involves three parts:

- Awareness and appreciation of the other (including the self, the other person, the group, the environment and, where applicable, deity).
- The capacity to respond to the other. This involves putting spirituality into practice, embodying spirituality, and thus the continued relationship with the other.
- Developing significant life meaning based upon all aspects of awareness and appreciation of and response to the other.

Awareness and appreciation of the other

Each 'other' might be deemed to be of ultimate value and could be the ground of a person's faith.

The self

It is reasonable to speak of the self as other (Ricoeur 1992). In one sense the self is indeed simply one amongst others and so is an other to someone else. In another sense we can speak of the person moving beyond the self, and thus being able to relate to the self, including dialogue with the self, important to self-development (van der Ven 1998, 108–110). Freeman calls this a process of reflective distanciation (Freeman 1993). Hence, we can speak of self-transcendence. This self-transcendence enables, first, some awareness of the whole person, including thoughts, feelings, physical experience, practice and relationships. For Geoff this meant connecting, in his pain, to the significant people and groups in his life, and beginning to look at himself and his meaning as a footballer. Second, it can involve the experiencing of centring the person – the experience of being at one with the cognitive, affective and somatic side of the self. Third, it can lead to an awareness and acceptance of the limitations of the self. For Geoff the ultimate limitation that he was all too painfully aware of was his mortality. Finally, it can lead to an appreciation of the ambiguity of the self, as good and bad, dependent yet independent, free yet constrained.

In much tradition the self has been fragmented and polarised, a good example of these being sexuality. The spirit was often seen as not simply distinct from but antipathetic to the body and thus to sexuality. Sexuality is by definition ambiguous, both a wonderful experience and expression of the embodied person and also something fraught with risk and moral challenge. The easiest way to handle this culturally was often to simply separate the spirit (good) from the sexual (bad). As Avis notes, the result was to devalue the physical and sexual and thus to retreat from real awareness of the self and other, in all its ambiguity and risk (Avis 1989). Spirituality rather involves the integration of sexuality with the self and looks to find meaning in relationships which include this (Helminiak 1998).

Interpersonal relationships

Awareness of the other person, like awareness of the self, involves recognition of difference and sameness. For the other to be simply different means that there is no point of common humanity through which to relate to him or her. Hence, the person who is seen purely as different is often literally dehumanised, seen as enemy as well as stranger. This is the dynamic at the heart of racism, expressed ultimately in the Holocaust (Bauman 1989).

Equally, to see the other as purely the same can lead to loss of identity, that which makes the other unique. Hence, Gibran notes the importance of distance and space within even marriage (1995, 5).

This means that the spirituality of the interpersonal relationship must be dynamic. The sameness that is recognised in the other provides the basis for trust and collaboration; it enables the person to see the other. The difference provides the basis for continued learning, disclosure and discovery.

The personal and interpersonal are then connected in this context. It is not possible to be aware of the holistic and distinctive nature of the self without developing awareness of the other. Equally it is not possible to see the other without seeing something of the self in the other (Buber 1937).

The greater group

Beyond the one-to-one relationship is that of corporate or cultural spirituality. For Geoff the corporate identity of the football club provided him with both a sense of belonging and security, and also a sense of active participation and contribution.

John Mbiti writes in the context of African spirituality:

> A person cannot detach himself from the religion of his group, for to do so is to be severed from his roots, his foundation, his context of security, his kinship and the entire group of those who make him aware of his own existence.
>
> (Mbiti 1990, 2)

This element in society is increasingly lost under the stress of consumerism and individualism, which tend to emphasise the contract nature of groups, i.e. groups formed from individual choice and with no historical or moral claim on the person beyond a mutually agreed contract. Groups, as a result, can easily become instrumental, simply used by the person for his or her own ends.

Increased awareness of any group reveals complexity and ambiguity, with different voices within and different functions of the group. The group, for instance, might be both administrative institution and community, each with different purpose and value. Geoff reflections on the football club were not just of football but also of the community programme and his developing relations with local schools and hospitals. Taylor (1996) can then speak of the multiple person, and of the need to relate to the many different areas of meaning in one's life, many of which have had influence over time. One group may be more central than others, with the person placing more faith in it, yet all are part of the meaning structures of the person.

Moreover, being a member of more than one group can help to clarify both the wider meaning of the group or groups and the identity of the person. Van der Ven refers to intertextuality, the dialogue which the self develops with the narratives or texts of all the different groups and through which personal moral and spiritual meaning is developed (van der Ven 1998, 258–260). In other words there is rarely simply one narrative alone that provides life meaning. Life meaning arises out of the different narratives in dialogue. This is stressed in the work of Kelly, who is able to reflect not simply upon the spirituality centred round different groups but also upon that of a nation itself, in his case Australia (Kelly 1990).

The environment

The term 'transcendent' can be applied to all the above categories, moving beyond the self, aware of that which is beyond the self, the person or the group. The term, however, is most often used with the last two categories, those of the wider environment and the divine. The environment has a wide definition, from the physical and social environment which surrounds us each day, through the environment that is created through art, to nature itself. The environment, of course, can be so vast that the sense of otherness is overwhelming. Standing at the foot of the Bridal Veil Falls at Niagara, for instance, it is difficult not to feel a part of the greater whole, a literally breathtaking experience, which can lead to a momentary loss of the sense of the self as separate. However, there are boundaries there, not least for safety, and without boundaries, and thus a knowledge of the self over against the other, there could be no actual conscious awareness of the other.

Awareness of the environment as another presence again is not simply about difference. The spirituality of the Lakota Native Americans, for instance, perceives the environment in terms of its own familiar social networks of belonging. Hence, a Lakotan can pray 'for all my relatives', including animals, birds, plants, water, rocks and so on (Lartey 1997, 121–122). In the same way St Francis of Assisi was able to refer to 'dear mother earth' or 'brother sun and sister moon'.

Once again a genuine awareness of the environment reveals ambiguities and complexities. Humans depend upon the environment for sustenance, and it depends upon mankind for protection and responsible stewardship. At the heart of this is an interconnectedness that sees humans as not existing as separate from the environment, and as affecting it whatever they do (McFague 1997). It can also be very threatening, not least when out of control. Hence, Rudolf Otto (1968/1923) pinpoints the ambivalent response of fascination and fear.

Deity

For many, the divine is the epitome of the transcendent. Any deity tends to be seen as totally other, with the idea of him or her as all-powerful, perfect and so on. This sense of otherness informs common views of the concepts 'holy' or 'sacred', meaning 'set apart'. Characteristically the more that the otherness of the divine is stressed the more he/she is seen as a figure to be feared, and thus to be placated with sacrifices and the like. It is critical then to see the sameness in any divinity as well as the difference. This is expressed well in the Hebrew *imago dei* doctrine – that man was made in the image of God (Genesis 5:1). It is also expressed in Christian spirituality through the idea of God becoming man in Christ. The human face of God is the way in which the presence of God can be expressed, making that which is the experience of God immanent, and lifting the relationship, from the tyrannical God who is to be feared, to one who identifies with his people. It is precisely such imminence that a Christian sportsman such as Jonathan Edwards expresses (Folley 2001).

There are, of course, many different expressions of the spirituality of the divine, but all seek some sense of the divine in the present 'known' experience, and all have some sense of the complexity of the divine. Ascribing human qualities to the divine has, of course, been common in many religions, from Ancient Greece to Hinduism.

Summing up so far

Even at this stage it is clear that spirituality in this view is essentially relational and reflective. It cannot be static, or simply be a set of meanings forced upon experience. Moreover, it is well suited to the idea of a postmodern time, precisely because it recognises that anyone's spirituality may involve relationships with many different groups. Hence, by its very nature spirituality is not likely to depend on a meta-narrative, one story that gives meaning to experience.

In slightly different ways in each of these areas, awareness involves knowledge of:

- the holistic other, involving cognitive, affective and somatic elements and as connected to and affecting a network of others;
- the other as both same and different, and hence ambiguous;
- the interdependence of the different others;
- the nature of the other as always emerging, as always learning and therefore never totally knowable;
- the other as involving both immanence, awareness of the self, and transcendence, a movement beyond the self.

The capacity to respond to the other

Response to the other is essentially about the articulation of spirituality in practice. It involves roles that express something of the relationship to others, and the contribution towards these relationships. The working out of these roles involves the expression of the uniqueness of the person and their particular part in any relationship.

The response to the other can be seen in terms of *vocation* (calling), or response to the *calling*, or needs, of the other, and in terms of placing *trust* in the other. The idea of vocation has tended to be restricted either to particular purpose or professions or in practice to the Christian spirituality, with God calling the Christian. However, in terms of a broader human spirituality all the different others 'call' the person in some ways. The environment calls the person or group to be aware of the complexities and interconnectedness and to respond with responsible stewardship. The group calls the person or other groups to be aware and to respond to need with a particular contribution. The other person calls for response as his or her needs are disclosed. McFadyen (1990) argues that such a call is the basis of personhood. Any calling, of course, has to be tested, and, as will be seen below, it also involves negotiation about how responsibility is to be shared.

The response to the other may be one of accepting need *for* the other in some way. We need the environment for our continued existence and different groups for social and physical well-being. Acknowledging that need, and the way in which the other fulfils it, enables us to begin to trust the other. Placing trust in the other is a clear response to that person, group or environment.

The response of the person to the other then becomes an embodiment of spirituality, life meaning in action. In this sense the response is another aspect of transcendence, with action going beyond the self. The embodiment may be individual or collaborative. Importantly, the embodiment of this spirituality is in itself a working out of the life meaning, not simply the applying of a set meaning to the situation. Indeed, it is not possible to fully understand any life meaning other than in and through the practical testing and outworking of it (Ricoeur 1992).

Developing life meaning

Life meaning can be seen in two broad ways, doctrinal and existential. First there is the development of doctrines or philosophies that attempt to encapsulate something about the nature of life, including the social and physical environment. These form the basis of belief about how the world is and how we might best operate within that world. Scientific doctrines provide a clear view of the limitations and possibilities of our human context. Philosophical and theological doctrines provide the basis of how we might make sense of that world and so respond. Hence, ancient religious doctrines, for instance, set out how God related to the world and therefore how we might respond. In sporting terms such doctrines relate to the nature of sport, its effect on community and well-being and so on.

However, life meaning in the light of the holistic and community perspective cannot be simply confined to conceptual beliefs. It is also located in and understood in two major ways:

- *Holistic meaning*. This involves existential whole person awareness.
- *Value-based meaning*. Meaning here is discovered in the value the person recognises in him- or herself and others. Such value may be based on a sense of acceptance from the other and a sense of the worth, and or any contribution to the other and the wider community, a sense of purpose, and hope.

Holistic meaning

Knowledge and awareness involves four levels of meaning: cognitive (to do with ideas about the world), affective (to do with emotions), somatic (to do with 'body language', including tactile communication) and interpersonal. This can involve awareness of all of these aspects of the other and how these affect each other. Once again this cannot be a complete awareness. In most situations the person reflects and discovers different aspects of the self that may have been previously not recognised or accepted. Such awareness is mediated through one or more of the routes of knowledge. In Geoff's case the somatic knowledge – provided by holding the scarf – was able to mediate the interpersonal knowledge and affective knowledge which gave him a sense of security. Later cognitive meaning was worked through as he thought about what the experience had meant to him. The experience was made sense of not simply in terms of doctrinal truths but rather in terms of how he retained his holistic identity in the light of the intense feelings of fear, loneliness, isolation, anger and frustration. At the same time it caused him to review just what his life in that club meant to him, in particular the value it had for him.

Meaning and value

Life meaning is attached to value. It is not simply about interesting ideas, or consciousness per se, but rather meaning that is central to the life project and reflects the value of the person and her identity. Indeed the formation of an identity that connects to these factors provides the ground of value.

At one level this is about the acceptance of the self as valuable in him- or herself. This demands acceptance based on unconditional value, an inclusiveness that emerges from an awareness of the other as part of common humanity. This is ultimately the basis of *faith*. Faith is developed in response to that which gives value to life. Hence, Fowler defines faith in two ways:

> (i) the foundational dynamic of trust and loyalty underlying selfhood and relationships. In this sense faith is a human universal, a generic quality of human beings;
> (ii) a holistic way of knowing, in which persons shape their relationships with the self, others and the world in the light of and apprehension of and by transcendence.

> (Fowler 1990, 394–396)

Fowler refers to two other views of faith that are specifically religious: the response to the gift of salvation; obedient assent to revealed truth.

Faith, in its generic sense, is very much belief *in* an other. This is in contrast to belief *that* or belief *about*. It is possible, for instance to believe in the concept of God, or *that* God exists, without making the belief *in* him the basis of life. Belief in may involve any of the others noted above, or ideas related to them. Clearly, such faith will vary from complete trust in the other to partial or working trust. The latter can build faith on the other whilst being aware of its limitations.

Such belief directly affects practice. Fowler argues that faith develops through discernible stages. Each of these stages is about the development of the self and the relationship of the person to the different others.

Stages of faith

Fowler proposes seven stages of faith which he locates at different ages. These were very much based upon the work of Kohlberg (1984), who developed Piaget's work in the development of moral meaning and judgement into three phases each with two stages.

Fowler proposes seven stages in the development of faith (Fowler 1996, 54):

Undifferentiated or primal faith (infancy)

This is a pre-linguistic and pre-conceptual stage in which the infant begins to form a disposition towards an environment which is gradually being recognised as distinct from the self. This stage forms the cradle of trust or mistrust and of self-worth based on unconditional or conditional grounds.

Intuitive–projective faith (ages 2–6)

This stage builds upon the development of language and the imagination. With no cognitive operations which could test perceptions and thus reverse beliefs, children grasp experience in and through powerful images. The child is thus attentive to ritual and gesture.

Mythic–literal faith (7–12)

This sees a reliance on stories and rules, and the narrative that is implied in the family faith experience. The lived faith of the family, through practice, ritual and belief, is valued in a concrete and literal sense. This can also involve some testing of the story meaning.

Synthetic–conventional faith (12–21)

The child in this stage moves on to search for 'a story of my stories'. This looks to the development of life meaning and the person's particular life meaning. At one level this is a product of the development of new cognitive abilities referred to by Piaget as 'early formal operations'. At the same time the developing life meaning is built up of the original faith system, and thus compiled of conventional elements.

This faith is often accompanied by a strong sense of the need to keep together the faith group as a priority.

Individuative–reflective faith (21–30)

Faith meaning is more personally chosen and believed. There is an awareness that one's view is different from others, and can be expressed in abstract terms. The faith developed at this stage is for the sake of the person and of making sense of her life in family or community. It is not developed primarily for the unity of the family.

Conjunctive faith (31–40)

In this, many of the different ideas and perspectives, and the resulting tensions and paradoxes, are worked at. Previously not examined, these are now held together in balance, with an openness to the perspectives of others. This sees a deepening of appreciation of the complex nature of faith and life meaning.

Universalising faith (40 and beyond)

This not so much a stage of faith as a category of individuals who have developed a coherent faith which is grounded in the 'Other', and which enables them to live unfettered by self-concern. Membership of this group is very rare and includes, for example, Ghandi and Martin Luther King.

Criticisms of the Fowler stage approach include arguments that it is too cognitive/intellectual and too individualistic. Others argue that the stages are normative, with the later stages seen as superior to the early ones. Others question the adequacy of the research (Parks 1992).

However, first, though Fowler sees the stages, like Kohlberg, to be invariant, sequential and hierarchical, i.e. they have to be gone through in turn, he does not advocate that they be taken too rigorously. They are a useful tool for noting characteristics of faith development, and can help the practitioner to be aware of needs. Second, Fowler does argue for a broader rational view of faith including affective knowledge. The intellectual component of spirituality does not make it a superior form. Third, he argues that the needs expressed in the earlier stages are not left behind.

Moreover, as noted above, these spiritual needs may be most apparent in times of crisis or transition. Someone who has suffered a major crisis, for instance, may need the safety of a simple childlike faith to carry him or her through the pain, or even to express the pain. Later a more complex view of faith may emerge as the complexity of relationships in the crisis is worked through. Fowler also suggests that the faith of the earlier stages is carried over and reworked into the new faith. Indeed, without this any sense of affective continuity is gone.

Geoff found that he had several relationships that had such meaning for him: the manager, the fans, the chairman, the club and its history, the community, and his family. He found that he placed faith in different ways in all of them, and needed that to work through what turned out to be a long-term injury. He found in particular that much of his faith up to this point had been placed in himself and his body. The injury dented that faith, especially when, at one point, he thought he might not play again. Part of his recovery involved both rediscovering a faith in himself, and also placing more faith in others.

Other critical aspects of meaning in spirituality include hope, purpose and resolution.

Hope

Hope has often been seen as a theological concept based upon future promises. Hence, some expressions of spirituality see hope as based upon the promise of life after death (Edwards 1999). Hope, however, is better seen as a virtue and may be defined as 'the capacity to envision a meaningful and significant future' (Robinson 1998). This differs from optimism, the unspecific belief that things will be all right. A meaningful future depends upon capacities, resources and the attitude of hopefulness. Hope will depend upon a person's present ground of faith as much as any future promise. In Geoff's case one of his critical grounds of faith was his own physical capability. Without that it looked as if he was without hope. In broader terms each new season brings hope for fans and sportspersons alike, with mutual support providing the grounds.

Purpose

Critical to the underlying meaning is purpose, and purpose once more connects to significant relationships. Geoff's initial view of purpose was contained in his skills to entertain and give meaning to others. However, as he reflected about the community links that the club had with schools and hospitals, he felt very much a part of that, and could see purpose that was connected to sport but went beyond sport. The relationship that he had begun to form in this area broadened the understanding of his purpose. This in turn enabled him to feel that he was valued for his primary purpose of playing football, but also for how he enabled the club to relate to the community, and for how he could relate those in need in the community.

Resolution

The ideas of resolution are summed up in the Hebrew concept of *shalom*, meaning peace and justice. At one level this may be reconciling with the self; accepting limitations. At another level it involves reconciling relations with others. In certain contexts this may involve simply working through how one relates to the other, involving perhaps negotiation of responsibility. In more extreme situations it may involve the capacity to forgive. This meaning is central to a relational view of spirituality, the end point of responding to the other. Hence, it is difficult to confine spirituality to the personal realm. Selby even suggests that spirituality can be expressed in relationships in wider society and politics (Selby 1983).

The development of meaning in spirituality then is focused on holistic, existential and value meaning, which relates to the different relationships. In particular, it focuses on the development of *faith* in the other, and *hope* which is generated through significant purpose and function, leading to resolution of conflict and possibly reconciliation and forgiveness.

One element in this is about finding meaning through transcendence. Hence, Reed sums up spirituality as 'the human propensity to find meaning in and through self-transcendence; it is evident in perspective and behaviours that express a sense of relatedness to a transcendent dimension, or to something greater than the self, and may or may not include formal religious practice' (Reed 1998, 50).

Spirituality and . . .

But what makes all that has been described so far spirituality and not religion or ethics or psychology? Here are some distinctions.

. . . *religion*

Whereas formal religions are examples of spirituality, spirituality is not exclusive to religion. The relationship is summed up as follows:

- Religion is focused in social institutions. As such it is concerned with maintaining the boundaries of that institution, not least through defining orthodoxy and orthopraxy. Spirituality has no concern for boundaries, indeed it moves beyond them in the search for meaning.
- Religion has tended to be prescriptive, with meaning transmitted through doctrine and the stories of the community. Spirituality is more about discovery of meaning in the context of the person.
- Although religion may provide an important motivational and disciplined framework for spiritual development it is not necessary for it. As we noted above, the New Age points to the possibility of self-directed spirituality.
- Religions are founded upon experience of and faith in the divine – the transcendent other. Spirituality finds significant meaning in a much broader way, including experience of and faith in other people and the environment.

In terms of sport this means that the study of spirituality and sport can both look at the major generic sense of spirituality embodied in sports meaning and practice but also examine how the major religions, with their particular spirituality, have related to sport.

. . . *ethics*

Much of ethics is about developing and testing underlying theories or applications, such as codes. Both of these are quite distinct from spirituality. However, some schools of philosophy have argued that ethics can only make sense if viewed in terms of the community and culture which provide the meaning context to any values, and the basis of ethical identity (McIntyre 1981; Murdoch 1993). Philosophers such as Taylor (1996) and Ricoeur (1992) see ethics in terms of overall meaning-making and as arising directly from the insight and experience of spirituality. Hence, like religion, ethics can involve spirituality but spirituality cannot be confined to ethics. The relationship is summed up as follows:

- Spirituality can provide a metaphysical base for ethics. This is about beliefs that begin to define something about a present and ultimate reality that informs practice. Murdoch (1993) sees these as providing the vision within which ethical imagination can develop.

- Spirituality provides motivation. This motivation might be positive or negative. The religious person, for instance, might be concerned above all to serve God, a relationship sustained through prayer. This commitment to the higher being then acts as a continual reminder to attend to ethics (Frankena 1986, 402). This can be expressed negatively through saying that unless one pleases the divine the person will not achieve salvation.
- Spirituality provides an unconditional and transcendent perspective for ethics. This is partly a perspective that goes beyond narrow or self-interest. Hence, the prompting of religion urges us to look beyond those narrow perspectives.
- Spiritual experience and ritual can provide an awareness that enables better moral practice. Typically religious experience, in the sense of an experience of the numinous, heightens awareness, and can have the effect of heightening awareness of the self and others, including the environment. This in turn is important in any ethical decision making.
- The spiritual community can play an important part in the moral formation of the person. This is partly about modelling good practice in the ethos and practice of the community, and in and through the associated stories and texts of the community. This is tied to the development of the character and thus of the virtues that might be central to community life. The gifts of the spirit set out by St Paul (1 Corinthians 12) are a good example of this. That very idea of the gifts of the spirit suggests that virtues are not just learned by imitation of any model, but in and through the relationship in the community.

. . . psychology

It is possible to suggest that spirituality, which is essentially about relating to different groups or areas, is better dealt with under the heading of psychology. However, although is possible to have those relationships analysed by a psychologist, it is not clear that the relationships themselves are the exclusive domain of psychology. In all this, spirituality does not pretend to be an academic discipline as such. It is about the existential experience and the development of meaning, including belief, and how this works out in the practice of the person or group. As such, spirituality cannot pretend to be about a neutral scientific exercise. Nonetheless, spirituality does have much in common with therapeutic psychology, not least the focus on enabling relationships to be developed. Hence, there is an increased concern from counsellors and psychotherapists to include attention to spirituality in treatment (Miller and Thoresen 2003). Spirituality can be an area for many different disciplines to examine, not least theology, sociology and philosophy. It can also be accessed in literature and the arts.

Conclusion

Spirituality is focused on practice, experience and belief. It is mediated through physical and psychological presence, and is located in experience. It is not simply knowledge *about* the other but existential awareness of the other. Hence, meaning is learned in that direct experience and from subsequent reflective dialogue with different narratives. To develop that spirituality demands faith in an other and in the self – a faith which provides both the basis of personal identity and also the ground from which the continual discovery and disclosure can be achieved. It also requires hope, the capacity to envision a positive future. The development of hope and faith depends upon both a sense of acceptance and a sense of purpose.

At the core of this spirituality is the capacity to appreciate the other in all its ambiguity, not least the central ambiguity of being the same *and* different. Such a spirituality demands both a commitment to the other and also a distance, one which respects the independence of the other.

I have offered in this chapter a model of spirituality. It may be asked why this model should be accepted rather than any other. Indeed it is not clear at first sight what might be the criteria for judging such a model. There are no obvious empirical tests of inclusion, and many different groups lay claim to different perspectives as the truly spiritual ones.

However, there are certain key strengths to this model:

- *Inclusive.* The model is based in human spirituality whilst also recognising institutional religions as particular expressions of spirituality.
- *Person centred.* Fundamental to this spirituality is the autonomy of the person. Spirituality cannot be imposed upon a person.
- *Other centred.* Balancing autonomy is the recognition of the need for and challenge of others. Hence, it is hard to see spirituality as individualistic or simply created by the individual in a consumer, 'pick and mix' way. A good deal of spirituality is about the givenness and discovery of the other, not least the communities in which one is or has been based, and what they give to the person and how he or she might respond.
- *Dialogic.* Meaning is essentially developed through dialogue.
- *Holistic.* The model takes account of the cognitive, affective and somatic aspects of the person and how these relate. It also shows how all the different views of spirituality fit together, including spirituality and its relation to energy, transcendence, an inner essence, and life meaning and purpose.
- *Practical.* This view of spirituality focuses on practice and response to experience rather than on theory. As such it offers something which is not a bolt-on extra to the practice of sport and does not require the development of a separate set of skills or knowledge.
- *Risk related.* A runner reported coming across a wolf as he ran in the Rockies. For the two weeks he was there he reported that the effect on his awareness of the environment was profound. Awareness of the dangers in the environment was directly related to his experience and appreciation of it. Sport itself is played out in a context of risk, winners, losers (as business and team), which is partly why there is so much emotional investment in it. Faith in that context is tied to action and commitment.
- *Dynamic.* Spirituality in this model is interactive and dynamic, not a static concept imposed on the other. As such it is about learning and developing.

- *Realistic.* Spirituality is not about fantasy worlds where everything is resolved and all are happy. It starts from the reality of relationships and seeks to find significant meaning in this those relationships. The context of this can be tragedy and loss, as much as celebration.
- *Transdisciplinary.* Spirituality cannot be confined to any one profession or discipline. Because it is focused in holistic experience and meaning it focuses on both doctrinal concepts and existential meaning, and different disciplines and different relationships can inform both of these.

For Geoff spirituality was also about coping, finding a life meaning that would carry him through an experience that had challenged his faith and hope. Bill Shankly, the great Liverpool football manager, was right – football, and any sport, is more than a game . . .

Study questions

1 Reflect on your own spirituality. Is it explicit or implicit?
2 What is important to you? Who or what do you put your faith in?
3 How do you articulate hope? What are the key purposes in your life? How does all that relate to your practice of sport?

3 The spiritual journey

Simon Robinson

If sport is more than a game then it involves commitment and meaning that goes beyond contract or rules. Something of this spirit is contained in this letter from Barcelona FC to its fans.

Open Letter to Barça Fans

Av. Arístides Maillol s/n 08028 Barcelona Tel 902.1899.00
oab@club.fcbarcelona.com www.fcbarcelona.com

Dear Barça Fan, The Great Challenge FC Barcelona has set itself for the immediate future is to consolidate our place amongst the best and biggest football clubs in the world. All the top clubs base their growth and success on one differentiating feature or another. Some exploit the fact that football was invented in England. Some operate in football markets that are bigger or more highly developed than our own. Some engage in other business areas as well as in football. But what differentiates FC Barcelona is an absolutely extraordinary fact. No other sports club in the world has so many loyal members. We are running the club as efficiently as possible to reduce costs as we apply the best managerial methods in order to increase income. All this is indispensable to achieve the greatest sporting success. But it is not the most important thing. Our Great Challenge is to develop and build on what differentiates us from the rest. Imagine what would happen if every Barça club member brought along one new member and there were suddenly 200,000 of us. Just think what we could do if all Barça fans were club members. Imagine how we could transmit our values (public spirit, sportsmanship, solidarity and integrating Catalan nationalism) all over the world. We need all Barça supporters and fans to join the club as members. Then, together, all those that love our club could decide its future. Now is the time: becoming a member costs less and offers greater benefits than ever. Building the best and biggest sports club in the world is not a dream; it is the Great Challenge that awaits all those who truly love FC Barcelona.

The FC Barcelona Board of Directors

The open letter to the fans of Barcelona Football Club is replete with the spirituality outlined in the last chapter. First, it stresses the role of fans as members. The status of the club as a cooperative, with members able to be an effective part of the democracy and vision building of the club, underlines this. Second, it assumes that members 'love' the club. Of course, it does not define what this means, but it clearly includes an attitude of loyalty, care and commitment. Third, there is a strong sense therefore of the fan identifying with the spirit of the club. Finally, it gives us clear pointers about what that spirit involves, and it is more than simply solidarity with the club itself. At its heart are:

- public spiritedness;
- sportsmanship;
- solidarity;
- Catalan nationalism.

The first of these is about the corporate responsibility of the organisation. It goes beyond 'green washing' and simply trying to manufacture reputation, to the idea of shared responsibility (Robinson 2007). It involves an attitude of openness to society.

The second acknowledges that there are in sport values that are more than the local values of an organisation. There is an overarching view of value and practice that is included in the identity of the club and its members. Players and fans alike share this vision of character and conduct. The third focuses on the experience of belonging to the club itself. The last reminds the membership that they are part of a wider, national identity. Again this looks beyond the club and to how the members and the club relate to and find meaning in not simply society, but that very particular identity of that part of Spain.

This underlines that spirituality in sport is not simply about consciousness or awareness, but about relationships. As such, it is ongoing, with meaning gradually developing. Hence, the Barça member can contribute towards the ongoing vision and stated purposes of the club. It is also about plurality, different persons and groups that the club and members relate and respond to. Each contributes towards meaning. It is also very much about shared commitment to the vision of the club but also to the club itself and to the other stakeholders.

The dynamic of spirituality then, seen as the development of awareness and meaning, involves a reflective, relational process. In the history of different spiritual traditions, it is often seen as in itself a journey or a quest. There is no arriving, only travelling and the constant searching, learning and development. This state of continual journeying is inevitable in a relational view of spirituality. The person can never know the other fully, and in any case is faced by many challenges to life meaning that are posed by experience. The process can be best seen as a recurring learning cycle involving several phases, summed up by Kolb's (1984) learning circle:

- *articulation* of narrative in response to experience;
- *reflection* on and *testing* of meaning;
- *development* of meaning;
- *response*, leading to new experience.

This applies to the club, the fan and the professional sportsperson.

In this chapter, I will look at how the spiritual process or journey relates to and can be drawn out from the reflective practice of the professional. Then I will examine the spiritual dynamic that underlies spiritual journey.

Reflective practice

Donald Schoen (1983) famously argued against a simplistic view of the professional development. Traditional professional education assumed that there was a standard body of knowledge that would be learned in professional schools. This knowledge would be applied to a range of issues. The problem with this approach is that:

- it can encourage a view of professional practice which is largely about achieving targets;
- it can lead to the attempt to apply knowledge in an unreflective way, hence to impose expertise.

Schoen noted through observation of a range of different professions that in practice there was a response which led not to an imposition of knowledge but rather to a 'reflective conversation with the situation'.

What emerged was a process like this:

- the analysis of the situation in order to work out what the problem might be and what issues are involved;
- 'appreciative' or value systems which help to find significant meaning in the situation;
- overarching theories that might provide further meaning;
- an understanding of the professional's own role in the situation, both its limits and opportunities;
- the ability to learn from 'talkback', which involves reflective conversation about the situation;
- the professional also treating clients as reflective practitioners.

In a sense Schoen is simply developing the idea of what it is to be a professional. He builds on the work of Ivan Illich (1977), who questioned the role of the professional in society, not least in the way that society has become dependent upon professions such as doctors. Such dependence was negative, partly because it led to the individual not taking responsibility and partly because it led to personal and public disasters. The technical skill of the professional could not be exercised without taking into account the relational context.

Reflective practice is at the heart of professional and amateur sport, as well as sport management and support.

For spiritual meaning to emerge from reflective practice at corporate or individual level demands a process of articulation, reflection, meaning development and creative response.

a. Articulation

The key vehicle for spirituality is the person's or group's story or narrative. The story brings together experience and all levels of meaning: cognitive, affective, somatic and interpersonal. A good example of this is the spirituality of the psalms in the Old Testament (Brueggemann 1984). The psalmists articulate their story, often one involving hardship or trauma, and how they feel about their situation. A critical part of this story is previous experience and belief systems, as they try to make sense of experience that does not easily fit with views of morality and justice. Generally, it eventually makes sense in terms of those belief systems, but not always. This is the place where so many sportspersons and supporters have been. Those who are not weaned on success try to make sense of ending last, of being demoted to a lower division, of ending just outside the top three, of missing out on a medal and so on.

Several things happen in this phase. First, it enables the person to gain distance from the self, and so begin to be aware of the effect of experience upon the self and the meaning and feelings which are shaping that experience. Freeman refers to a phase of *distanciation*. This leads to a sense of differentiation: 'a separation of the self from the self, such that the text of one's experience becomes transformed into an object of interpretation' (Freeman 1993, 45). This is important for the development of empathy for the self.

Second, it is a means not simply of expressing but of discovering meaning. Until an idea has been articulated it is not fully understood. Articulation is not simply a bilateral communication. The self can hear what it being said and itself becomes both a learner as well as an interpreter or commentator, shaping and reshaping the story. Articulation then becomes a three-way conversation, raising the story to a level of publicness, and opening it to examination. This enables the development of self-criticism and by extension the capacity to critique others (van der Ven 1998).

Third, with the act of articulation the person begins to take responsibility for that spirituality, without which there is no effective integration of meaning and experience.

Articulation may occur in different ways, individually or in large groups where feelings and ideas are expressed through ritual. A classic example of this is the ritual at the beginning and end of the Olympic Games. This sets out through displays, ritual and speech several things:

- The core values of the Olympic movement.
- The sense of solidarity, in which very different identities and hopes of the different nations come together in one movement. Hence, one can speak of a movement transcending any particular group's interests, concerns or needs.
- The sense of diversity, in which the distinctive identity of the different national teams is valued and respected.
- The pride of the home nation, who in effect have been chosen to embody the values and practice of the Olympic movement.

None of this takes away from the edge of competition which occurs within this framework of meaning, nor from the sense of risk which surrounds any attempt to achieve. It rather gives both of them a context of meaning and value.

b. Reflection

Once the story is told this provides the basis for a more systematic reflection on the meaning it embodies. This focuses on the different relationships noted above, their significance, and how far they provide faith and hope in the person's life.

1 *The self.* This involves identifying feelings, and clarifying ideas, including beliefs and values or principles. This inevitably leads on to reflection on how the person sees him- or herself, not least whether he or she is someone of value.
2 *Significant others, and their stories.* This examines how the person perceives significant others and how he or she feels and thinks about them, and what demands they make of him or her. What meaning do they give to him or her, and how does that meaning affect his or her life?
3 *Communities.* Relationships to communities are examined, identifying the core communities which give significant meaning to his or her life. Do they supply rules for living? a place of comfort? an opportunity for service or success? Such reflection allows feelings and thoughts about such groups to emerge.
4 *The environment.* Is the person aware of the environment? How does he or she feel about it, and respond to it? What does the environment give to him or her?
5 *Deity.* Reflection on this may focus on 3 or 4 above, with many things, ranging from a football team or the environment providing the 'ground of being'. It may centre on one of the religious grounds of faith. In that case reflection should be on the person's image of, and feelings for, the divine.

Each of these reflections is interconnected and involves dialogue between the different parts of the network. Dialogue enables an increased awareness of the values and beliefs of the other. In turn this leads to the clarification of spiritual and moral meaning and greater awareness of the other – hence the development of empathy. With the development of such holistic awareness, the person is then faced by the truth of the other and the inevitable complexities, difficulties and occasional conflicts.

Once more the Olympic experience offers a good example of these things. Reflection may occur during the times of ritual or be ongoing during the event, or between the different games. At any time there may be reflection that begins to test the underlying values of the movement, exemplified by any expression of political values from oppressed groups or nations. At other times the values of the movement will be tested by attitudes of participants who value competitiveness and winning above the Olympic community, something which may move into illegal acts such as drug taking. The whole experience then can be underpinned by intertextual dialogue, dialogue between different value narratives (van der Ven 1998), which tests the meaning of the event and any underlying conflicts. This stresses that, although there may be settled spiritualities, there are always many different voices in any community. The dialogue from these will always test and cause the community to re-examine beliefs and values.

At the heart of these reflections emerge the fundamental questions such as:

- What purpose and function does the person have in his or her life?
- Who or what is the person's ground of faith?
- What is the person's basis and content of hope?
- How should the person respond to the other?

Such questions can be asked directly, but emerge more naturally as part of the reflection. Many people have built up belief systems without being fully aware of whom or what they put their faith in, what is the cognitive as well as affective ground of their faith, or that they may have several grounds of faith.

c. Developing meaning

The next phase continues the learning process for whoever is involved. Having tested life meaning, the person may be unhappy with contradictions or inconsistencies that have emerged. This may lead to a development of life meaning in a different way, perhaps developing the cognitive or affective aspects or focusing on the value of the self as much as the value of others. It may lead to a re-evaluation of faith and hope and to a conscious development of faith in other areas. A good example of this is where the person may move from a conditional faith – one based upon personal achievement of some kind – to a more unconditional one, based upon acceptance of the other. Freeman (1993), using the life of Augustine, notes this as a point of recognition, involving both a recognition of need, because of limitations, and a recognition of the need to change.

d. Creative response

This naturally moves through to an embodying of the spirit in some way. At one level this might involve the negotiation of responsibilities. Finch and Mason (1993) argue that such negotiations not only lead to real changes in relationships, they also develop the moral and spiritual identity of the person and the group. In their work with families they noted that the majority did not have a predetermined set of beliefs or values which informed the setting of responsibility for different members of the family (especially for the elderly). Instead there was a process of negotiation. This was a way of developing 'moral reputation' and literally involved the 'creation and recreation of moral identity' (Finch and Mason 1993). Such negotiations depend on but also enable the acceptance of mutual limitations and awareness of the possibilities in terms of individual and collaborative contributions.

At another level this response moves into reconciliation of some kind, as noted above. This may be a reconciling with the self, accepting limitations, summed up well in the Alcoholics Anonymous prayer of St Augustine:

> God grant me the serenity to accept the things I cannot change,
> the courage to change the things I can,
> and the wisdom to know the difference.
>
> (quoted in Clinebell 1968, 152)

At another level it moves into acceptance of and reconciliation with the other, summed up in the Hebrew term *shalom*, involving justice and peace. At its heart is the recognition of common humanity in the other, breaking down the barriers of enmity. This in turn may lead to action which looks for justice or which leads to some appropriate form of reconciliation (Smedes 1998). For sport this moves into the continual tensions between different purposes and relationships, from commerce to community, and how they can be creatively resolved.

With each aspect of the spiritual process there is both a recognition of the limitations and a move out to the creative possibilities.

The dynamic of the spirit

As noted above, the dynamic of awareness is not passive or fixed. It involves transcending the self, enabling a perspective on the self and dialogue with the self. It involves an awareness of the other as transcending the self yet also part of the self, both different and the same. With that sense of the other comes often the sense of the holiness, sacredness or specialness of the other, or a sense of being 'out of the self'. This has often been associated with experience of the divine but is not exclusive to it. Similar experiences can be discovered with the environment and also with other people or groups (Aldridge 2000, 38). Central to this dynamic and the resultant development of meaning are care, empathy and *phronesis*.

Care

The Barcelona letter was suffused with ideas of care and commitment. A wide variety of social thinkers suggest that this itself is core to spiritual awareness. At one level one could see awareness as a neutral activity about gathering data so that we can be fully aware of the situation. Then we can be in a position to make an ethical decision. However, as Spohn (1997, 116) suggests, there is no value-free awareness of any situation: 'We make choices in the world that we notice, and what we notice is shaped by the metaphors and the habits of the heart that we bring to experience.'

Levinas (1998), Bauman (1989) and Baird (2002) take this further, suggesting that ethical commitment, that is responsibility, to the other precedes awareness. In this view ethics would be at the heart of, and indeed precede, spirituality. These three writers develop spirituality in different ways in response to the experience of the Holocaust. For them it is not simply a matter of developing spirituality so that we can achieve transcendence, to see the situation and thus respond better. Instead they propose that it is not possible to develop that spiritual awareness without an ethical commitment to the other. Spirituality begins with a sense of responsibility to the other. Without that sense of prior responsibility we cannot begin to see the other in an inclusive way. This means, however, genuinely seeing the other in his or her ambiguity, same and different, good and bad. For Levinas this even applies to the oppressors, the perpetrators of the Holocausts. Unless we begin with responsibility for all, then some will, by omission or commission, be excluded from our view of humanity, and that way lies the Holocaust. For Levinas this places the face of the other at the heart of the ethical obligation. It is the face in all its vulnerability that calls forth my responsibility, without any reference to rights or even to rational grounds for why we should be ethical. As Baird puts it 'I am called to be responsible for the other before understanding who the other is or why I should engage with him or her ethically' (2002, 70). There is a similar stress in McIntyre's later work (1999) around the idea of ethics being built upon the vulnerability of the other. Self-transcendence in this occurs not through reference to some *idea* of the good but rather through the openness and response to the unique irreplaceable other.

At the heart of a genuine openness to, and thus awareness of, the other, then, is commitment to and responsibility for him or her.

This sense of care or responsibility for the other, expressed in various ways, is fundamental to religious and non-religious traditions (Rogers 1983; Bauman 1993; Robinson 2001). It is well summed up by the Greek word *agape*, a form of love. Care is central to response, involving not simply a way of relating but also a way of knowing and empowering (Robinson 2001).

A way of relating

Agape is an acceptance of the self and other that sets no conditions. All are equally valuable. Core to this is commitment to the other and service of the other. In sport this occurs at many levels, not least in the commitment of fans to a club, often regardless of the success that the club has.

A way of knowing

Agape is critical to the dynamic of empathy. The truth about the other, in particular about the other person, will not be disclosed, not least to the self, without an awareness of being accepted. Weil can thus argue that 'love sees what is invisible' (quoted in Gaita 2000, xvi), in others and in the self. Invisibility of the true nature of others is often created by our own stereotypes and judgements. Equally, the person can only begin to see his or her self, including difficulties and flaws, once he or she feels accepted. In this sense then truth and acceptance come together.

Because of this it is precisely *agape* that enables the ambiguity of the other to be held together – to see the other in all his or her ambiguity and still remain committed to him or her. Hence, *faithfulness* (fidelity) and *honesty* (veracity) operate closely together. *Agape* enables the other to be seen both as the same – part of common humanity – but also as quite unique. Indeed, as Gaita argues, the common humanity of the other person, and therefore any sense of the universal, is only known through the awareness of the particular other, something revealed as he or she develops and crafts his or her own story (Gaita 2000, xxix).

A way of empowering

Agape does not attempt to manipulate or control but precisely gives the other freedom to develop awareness of the self and others, and the freedom to respond. Hence, as W.H. Vanstone notes, this involves giving power to the other:

> The power which love gives to the other is the power to determine the issue of love – its completion or frustration, its triumph or tragedy. This is the vulnerability of authentic love.
>
> (Vanstone 1977, 67)

Spirituality may relate to the narratives and traditions of history but ultimately it can be achieved only through the person freely working out his or her own meaning in relation to others.

Agape thus points to a response that remains committed over time, accepts the other, not simply on the basis of attraction or success, and empowers the other. One can see startling examples of this in sports clubs that have rarely achieved major success, but have maintained a strong fan base expressing their commitment through the ritual of being there every weekend.

Empathy

Scheler defines empathy as 'a genuine reaching out and entry into the other person and his individual situation, a true and authentic transcendence of the one's self' (quoted in Campbell 1984, 77). The idea of moving beyond the self has its problems, not least because it assumes fixed boundaries to the self that are being transcended. It is better expressed as a movement beyond the concerns of and for the self, and with this an expansion or reaching out of the self. This involves moving away from the things that cause the person to attend in an exclusive way to the self, such as fears or guilt, and which block any openness to the other. It also involves not taking the self and self concerns too seriously. Hence, Scheler writes of abandoning 'personal dignity'. Empathy, then, fosters an attitude of humility, humour and playfulness, developing a wry openness and appreciation of the ambiguity of the human condition.

With humour is also wonder and awe, precisely because the openness to the other is constantly revealing something new, and because, as Berryman (1985) suggests of children, transcendence involves living 'at the limit of their experience'. Myers (1997) argues that this is the case in spirituality of all ages. Hence, Phenix (1964) argues that 'human consciousness is rooted in transcendence, and that the analysis of all human consciousness discloses the reality of transcendence as a fundamental presupposition of the human condition'. Michael Jacobs (1998) suggests then that spirituality is precisely found in the 'margins', the places between each other.

We would further argue that such transcendence is not static but is a continual to-ing and fro-ing between the self and the other, each time learning a bit more about the self and the other and the self reflected in the other. This is also an awareness which is not self-conscious but rather one which is 'unmindful' of 'individual spirituality', allowing 'the instinctive life to look after itself'. This simple letting go of the self is contrasted with a self-conscious concern for the other, in which the calculated concern itself tends to dominate. This may be compared with the classical pianist whose technique can actually get in the way of the music. The pianist who is really aware of the spirit of the music allows the music to shine through naturally. This reaching out to the other applies in all the categories set out above. Hence, Scheler bemoans the way in which an awareness of nature has been increasingly lost (Campbell 1984, 78).

As empathy reaches out, so the person becomes more open to the other and in turn the other begins to disclose more of him- or herself. This moves to an interactive view of empathy, involving mutual disclosure, albeit not symmetrical. Hence, Swinton (2001) suggests the term 'interpathy'.

The dynamic of empathy is essentially one of risk. To see the other, the person has to reach out. He or she cannot stay in the safety of the narrow self and thus has to lose that security. Hence, for empathy to flourish there must be courage to reach out, imagination to see the possibility beyond the self, and above all acceptance of the person.

Empathy has often been associated, through the work of Carl Rogers (1983), with counselling and counselling skills. However, Scheler and others would argue that it is a basic human capacity, enabling awareness of the other. It can thus best be seen as an affective virtue.

It is also important to note that empathy is effectively based in *agape*. Empathy, as simple awareness of the other, is value neutral. One can be aware of the other, their feelings and needs, without being concerned for them or committed to them, as shown by Iago in *Othello* (Robinson 2007). Hence, empathy needs prior concern if it is to be beneficent.

Phronesis

Empathy provides the means of developing awareness of the other, and of noting affective meaning. It might be called an affective virtue. *Phronesis* is more an intellectual virtue which enables the person to reflect on underlying values and views of the good, and especially ideas about purpose (Robinson 2005). This has been associated mainly with Aristotle and with virtue ethics, but is equally comfortable in a broader spirituality. This capacity enables the person or group to understand and articulate the underlying concepts of value.

Although it is deemed an intellectual virtue it also has to relate to the affective level of meaning, not least because any view of purpose may have a strong affective content that keeps that in place. Equally, because there may be many different views of purpose arising from the related groups that give life meaning to any person, *phronesis* is important holding those together or deciding between purposes that conflict. This is a virtue that is often thought of as being simply to do with philosophy, but actually is necessary in practice, as the professional works through any significant decision.

Accompanying the journey

If spirituality involves continual reflection and development, both person-led and in response to unexpected challenges, it raises the question of how the person or group maintains continued identity.

First, even where change occurs there is usually some element that remains familiar such as relationships or values. Fowler (1996) refers to the 'tent pegs', the coping mechanisms or activities which maintain a sense of identity. Second, the very act of reflective process provides critical continuity, so that the person can chart a journey and see how he or she has developed. At the centre of this is the development of integrity, with the person taking responsibility for the change. Such responsibility enables him or her both to see where he or she has come from and, even if there has been radical change, to know that it has been caused by him or her. This sets up the spirituality of sameness and difference, noted above, over time. The person is the same but different from his or her previous history, but because it is his or her *own* history there is continuity in that change.

Third, there is the need for a 'holding environment', a relationship which keeps faith with the person, enabling faithful change. This might be a community, or it might be simply another person. The identity of that person may differ from context to context. In systematic religious approaches this is sometimes focused in the idea of the spiritual director. Leech (1997) offers a less formal and more interesting view of the *soul friend*, literally someone who will keep faith and maintain the person's sense of continuity. Such support may come from persons, the environment or divinity. It may come from a formal relationship or one that springs up in a moment of crisis, such as tutor, nurse or doctor. It is something about the focused and attentive presence of the other which enables the person to begin to develop spiritual meaning. Vanier (2001, 128) views this in terms of an accompanier.

As intimated above, this is not a linear process but cyclical. The development of meaning comes around new each time, as new challenges are faced, and old belief systems and awareness challenged. Sometimes the old beliefs are tested and make sense, sometimes they don't. Sometimes the perceptions which have been relied on for decades break down. More fundamentally this means that the very life meaning and underlying faith is continually being tested by experience and by relationships. Hence, there is no presumption that the spiritual experience will be either easy or comfortable.

It is not fanciful to see something like a football club as providing this kind of environment. Indeed, the vision of Barcelona sets up a similar dynamic, encouraging reflection, dialogue and creative response.

Ritual and meaning

Another anchor for continued identity can be ritual. As Erikson (1977) notes, ritual is a key part of each stage of personal development, not least because it enables the development and celebration of shared meaning. Rituals can enable shared *attention*, signalling presence there for the other, *intention*, be that long- or short-term purpose, aims and objectives, and *affect*, how we feel about each other or certain issues (Stern 1985, 129). Hence, ritual can lock creatively into awareness and appreciation of the other, cognitive, affective and somatic. As such the ritual can be a key part of the reflective process. It can be part of the experience which the person or group reflects upon, and as such is open to criticism and change. It can sum up the embodiment of personal or group spirituality, as regular meals together might do for a family. It can also provide part of any continuity over time, acting as a reminder of purpose and hope.

The process

The characteristics of the spiritual journey then can be summed up as follows:

- It is dynamic and responsive, not about imposing meaning on a situation.
- It is a learning experience. Belief systems are tested and challenged and may lead to development or confirmation of old views.
- It is a relational experience. The simple act of articulation sets up a dialogue, even with the self, and thus develops a relationship.
- It stresses the responsibility for the person of group for developing significant life meaning; hence it is built upon the autonomy of the person or group.
- It also values tradition and community as the base of belief systems. Such valuation is not uncritical; on the contrary, any belief system is tested by reflection on experience and practice. Diversity is also valued.
- It needs a supporting community or environment within which to grow and develop.
- It leads to creative response which embodies the vision and purpose of the person or group, and shares responsibility.

Challenging spirituality

Although it is important to accept faith at whatever stage, we are left with the question whether there are examples of spirituality which might actually be wrong or need to be challenged. Two examples focus on this.

The first parallels the Olympic vision and rituals but takes us to the Nuremberg rallying fields prior to the Second World War. At the rallies there was a strong emphasis on spiritual well-being connected to physical activity and sport. As Burleigh (2000) notes, Hitler developed a belief system as the basis of the Third Reich, one which connected ancient myths and modern martyrs. The belief system was precisely one which denied the presence or value of the other, of any group that was different from the Aryan race. All of this came together in the Nuremberg rallying fields with massive public rituals and huge support. Combined with the oratory of Hitler it produced an ecstatic response form the crowd – a feeling of purpose and hope, and of transcending their situation. All this would suggest two things. First, sport cannot be of itself a fundamental ground of faith. It is rather a means to expressing more fundamental relational values. This means that sport can be abused, or used for ends that are not acceptable. Second, attention has therefore to be paid to the ends of sport, and what makes spirituality in sport acceptable. The reflective process above would suggest that some spiritualities are not healthy, including:

- those which deny the presence of others;
- those which encourage dependency and discourage mutual reflection or critical autonomy;
- those which lead to fragmentation and alienation, including the denial of responsibility for their own thinking and the denial of responsibility for the other;
- those which are not open to the learning process.

Spiritual experience

The second area that raises issues is that of ecstacy, often seen as the spiritual experience.

In this the person is taken out of him- or herself. It is often characterised by a strong sense of the other, which overwhelms. Rudolf Otto refers to this as the experience of the numinous, the other which is greater than the self, characterised as *mysterium et tremendum* (Otto 1968/1923). There is a letting go of the self into the other. Once again this is not something which can be restricted to the religious. The search for ecstasy can be through dance, drugs, group practices and so on (Biggar 1997).

There are major dangers with this view of spirituality, taken by itself:

- Its whole approach is one which is disembodied. It seeks release from bodily constraints. To concentrate on that as the focus of spirituality actually takes away from the whole point of embodying spirituality in practice. Moreover, spirituality as outlined above is aiming to live *with* the constraints of the body, not be released *from* them.

- It can lead to a stress on the experience itself, and thus the danger of the experience becoming the end in itself. This leads to greater and greater efforts to maintain the intensity of the experience, with dangers of addiction to the experience itself.
- The stress is very much upon affective knowledge. However, affective knowledge which has no link to the cognitive, or to the process of planning and commitment to a larger life plan or project, does not develop any richness of life meaning.
- Stress on affective experience can lead to a loss of the distinctiveness of the self, over against the other.

The terms 'holy' and 'sacred' are often associated with such experiences, and many spiritual practices, such as meditation or worship, are meant to put one in touch with the 'other'. Places, people and literature are deemed to be holy, sacred – literally set apart from others. Hence they have the feeling of being special and in certain contexts pure. Spirituality as we have defined it above invites us to experience this sense of specialness not simply in the numinous but in all relationships, in that all relationships viewed empathically involve a sense of other and difference. This does not deny the importance of spiritual experience. It can enable the person to let go and so begin to involve the affective and somatic in reflection as well as the cognitive. Positive spirituality then is formed round the balance of these many aspects.

Spirituality, well-being and health

The relationship of spirituality to health and well-being is complex. Health can be viewed in an analytic perspective or a holistic perspective (Nordenfelt 1987). The first of these defines illness in terms of biomechanical problems – analysing factors such as tissue damage, the normal or abnormal function of organs. Health is then defined in terms of absence of disease. The emphasis in this approach is on evidence of damage which can be empirically verified.

The holistic approach to health focuses more on a state or lack of well-being, asking how the person feels and how he or she is functioning in his or her social network. Health in this context is more than the absence of disease, and focuses on subjective factors and upon the empowerment of the person.

It would be foolish to favour only one of these views. It is better to see health as a latent construct, like personality, character or happiness, i.e. 'a complex multi-dimensional construct underlying a broad array of observable phenomena' (Miller and Thoresen 2003, 4). Miller and Thoresen suggest that health be viewed under three broad domains: *suffering*, *function* and *coherence*.

Suffering

Suffering takes a variety of forms, from physical pain to anxiety, affective disorders and distress. Health under this head is categorised as an absence of suffering, and suffering is a common ground for seeking medical help. However, suffering has a subjective element and awareness, and understanding of suffering can be affected by many different things. Hence, 'many healthy people have lived with chronic pain' (Albom 1997). Miller and Thoresen note the possibility of seeing the suffering 'continuum' as involving not merely absence of suffering but also presence of certain qualities, such as energy or enthusiasm.

Function

Health in this domain involves functional ability over against impairment. Miller and Thoresen note physiological functions such as 'immune competence, neurodendocrine function, blood pressure, muscle strength, physical flexibility, and blood cell count, judging an individual's functioning relative to norms of previous performance' (2003, 5). Other functions include cognitive, emotional, sexual and psychomotor. Clearly the effect of the loss of different functions will be felt differently. Cognitive impairment, for instance, would greatly affect a teacher. Once again it is possible to view a person with great impairment as in other respects healthy. In this sense the impairment becomes an acceptable impairment. What makes impairment, or for that matter suffering, acceptable is a function of meaning. This meaning can be generated in different ways:

- socially, with illnesses which are socially acceptable or not;
- interpersonally, with the illness involving guilt or moral stigma, such as HIV.

Coherence

Miller offers several definitions of this term, from an 'inner peace', to 'a global sense of predictability of one's internal and external environment', to 'resilience', or 'learned optimism' (Miller and Thoresen 2003, 5). This focuses very much on the category of the person and thus upon the spirituality which we have been exploring in the previous chapters. Strong coherence could clearly affect how the person deals with suffering or loss of function. A lack of this inner peace could involve in itself direct suffering or affect how the pain and suffering are experienced.

All three domains interact in any particular context, leading to a much broader view of health and well-being. Jurgen Moltmann (1985) suggests a view of health as 'the strength to be human'. This means the maintenance or development of humanity whatever the experiencing of suffering or impairment of function. He contrasts this view with one which sees health, defined as a general state of well-being or absence of illness, as the supreme value in life. In a similar vein Alastair

Campbell (1995) argues that health can be seen as liberation. The liberation can be seen as from different aspects of illness from impairment to lack of coherence or domination by a meaning structure which oppresses or denies humanity.

Spirituality and healing

Attempts to make the connection between spirituality and healing fall into three categories:

- holistic perspectives on therapy;
- the effect of spirituality and spiritual beliefs on therapeutic outcomes;
- spiritual techniques which affect health.

Holism

There is an increasing amount of work on the holistic view of the person and how this affects health. David Benner, for instance, notes the development of *psychoneuroimmunology*: the study of the effects of stress on the functioning of the immune system. Research in this area has found that depression, anxiety and repressed emotions play a part in suppressing the immune system (Benner 1998). Strong correlation has been shown between particular diseases and psychosocial factors, including:

- rheumatoid arthritis (associated with suppressed emotions and perfectionism);
- cardiovascular disease (associated with repressed hostility);
- cancer (associated with non-assertiveness and the inability to express emotions, hopelessness and depression) (Benner 1998, 60).

The effect of traumatic experience has been shown to have an effect on the immune system (Siegel 1986, 148). Several studies, for instance, have noted the suppression of the immune system after bereavement – an effect seen at two months after the experience but not at two weeks (Benner 1998, 60).

Other studies point to the effect of emotional states, lifestyles and life views on the development of disease as well as the maintenance of health (Thomas 1982). It is difficult to pinpoint precise disease vulnerabilities. However, research suggests that certain characteristics or experiences make individuals prone to 'immunosuppression'. These include conformity, sensitivity to criticism, restricted emotional expression, denial of dependence, and major stress (Benner 1998, 60).

There is sufficient evidence of the holistic nature of the person to confirm that attitudes and states of mind do affect therapeutic outcomes. 'Life-coherence' in turn contributes to the development of such healthy attitudes. This reflects a distinction between holism per se and spirituality. Spirituality is holistic and enables holism, but is not holism as such.

Spiritual beliefs

Many attempts have been made to measure the importance of spiritual and religious beliefs in therapy. Results are surprisingly consistent and show:

- Religious groups with rigid belief systems and practice were linked to greater health and lower mortality than less religious groups or non-believers (Idler and Kasl 1992; Kark *et al.* 1996; Strawbridge *et al.* 1997).
- The greater the religious intensity (measured by church attendance and attitudes) the better the health and the lower the rate of illness. These findings were very pronounced in hypertension and colorectal cancer (Comstock and Partridge 1972; Medalie *et al.* 1972; Larson *et al.* 1989; Levin and Vanderpool 1989).

Similar finding were discovered in wider views of spirituality, including scoring on spiritual and existential as well as religious well-being (Frankel and Hewitt 1994; Shuler *et al.* 1994). Religious practices were also associated with increased tolerance of pain and a higher quality of life (Landis 1996).

Religious involvement may also influence the course and eventual outcome of illness. Research suggests an association of religion with better recovery from illness including survival after heart transplants (Harris *et al.* 1995), reduced mortality after other cardiac surgery (Oxman *et al.* 1995), reduced risk of repeat heart attacks (Thoresen 1990) and reduced mortality in breast cancer patients (Spiegel *et al.* 1989).

Perhaps more interesting were the findings of King, Speck and Thomas, that patients who expressed strong spiritual belief were *less* likely to do well (Speck 1998, 29).

Speck suggests several possible reasons for these findings, from strong belief leading to a reduced fear of death, to patients with a poor prognosis developing a stronger belief system. However, more importantly, the measurement of strength of belief is in itself problematic. A *strong* belief may well be a limited or brittle belief, i.e. one that has not been tested empirically, or an essentially cognitive belief whose congruence with affective awareness has not been tested. Such a professedly strong belief may well be more liable to lead to spiritual meaninglessness when faced by the illness experience. Research of this nature might more usefully use the stages of faith model, distinguishing, as it does, between different kinds of faith and transition experiences.

Despite difficulty with the third area of evidence there is sufficient basis to indicate the potential importance of spirituality to health outcomes, and thus the clear impact that it can have. Because of this many healthcare texts now draw attention to 'spiritual distress' and 'inner resource deficiency' and how they might adversely affect therapeutic outcomes (Hay 1989). The first of these might involve spiritual suffering, such a sense of hopelessness or lack of faith. Inner resource deficiency might include questioning of previously held belief systems. Such distress may not be a negative thing but simply part of the process of coming to terms with a challenge.

In that case the spiritual needs of the person are to have someone who will enable them to work through the distress. Other therapeutic assessment of spirituality focuses on the positive, some measurement of spiritual well-being (Cohen *et al.* 1997).

Spiritual techniques

The use of spiritual techniques has received increased attention and research, especially around the area of meditation, and is associated with twelve-step self-help groups, in particular Alcoholics Anonymous. I will focus briefly on the first of these, which will later be noted in relation to sporting practice. Meditation has a long history in Western and Eastern religious spirituality. Used in more recent times in the health context it is often associated with relaxation, and therefore a useful technique for patients who suffer anxiety. In the mental health context it is now increasingly being used to develop 'mindfulness'. Mindfulness is the capacity for the human mind 'to transcend its preoccupations with negative experiences – with fears, anxiety, anger and obsessions – and to become more comfortable with the experiences of compassion, acceptance and forgiveness' (Marlatt and Kristeller 2003, 68).

It involves a focusing on the present experience, and acceptance of that experience, including negative feelings, and thus development of an observing self. Teasdale (1997) notes that this aims not to change the content of thoughts but rather to enable the patient to alter his or her attitude to or relationship with that thought.

Meditation then is associated with two main processes. First, it leads to an experience of and acceptance of 'impermanence', the way in which perceived reality is constantly changing. Second, it enables the capacity to monitor the self from the perspective of a detached observer. Involved in most meditation practice is the heightened but detached awareness of sensory and thought experience. This fits in well with psychotherapy, which is aiming to free the patient from the effects of negative emotions.

Glasser (1976) suggests that meditation can also be seen in terms of a 'positive addiction' which is intrinsically rewarding. Such an addiction has six characteristics:

- it is non-competitive;
- it can be done without self-criticism;
- it has positive value;
- it can be done alone;
- it is a simple process, easily accomplished;
- improvement needs to be judged by only one person.

Research has shown a wide constellation of physical and psychological effects including:

- Reduced oxygen consumption and carbon dioxide and lactate production.
- Reduced adrenocorticotropic hormone excretion. This produces the opposite effects from stress.
- Reduced heart rate and blood pressure.
- Reduced activity in the sympathetic branch of the nervous system.
- Changes in electroencephalographic brain wave activity and function. These are consistent with slowing down of brain and body activities (Benson 1996).

The use of meditation then can range widely, including work with anxiety and depression; some severe psychiatric disturbances, such as obsessive–compulsive disorder; and heart conditions (Marlatt and Kristeller 2003, 76). Such meditation also relates directly to sports performance, and the focusing in the 'zone'. Although as a technique this can be divorced from wider spiritual meaning, it can connect to that wider meaning.

Transcendence

Transcendence has been a key concept in writings on spirituality and now it is possible to sum up just what it might involve. Transcendence is not about a separation for the world but rather is an engagement with it. Through *agape* and empathy, the person transcends him- or herself, reaching out towards the other, and is able to clarify and reflect on presence, thoughts and feelings, of the self and other. Hence, there is the capacity to transcend both rationality and emotions through relating to the other.

The idea that one might transcend the 'world' through reaching out to the divine, as it were escaping from the world, seems difficult to sustain in this model. If the spirituality involves God then reaching out to him is in itself engaging with another. When such a God also engages with the world, as in the Judaeo-Christian tradition, then the dynamic reinforces engagement with reality, rather than taking one away from it. Articulation is the first moment of this transcendence, enabling distanciation and thus allowing the person to hear his or her self.

Second, the ensuing dialogue and critique enables the person to transcend the groups that have been the source of beliefs and values and may have held them in place. Transcendence, again, does not demand a separation from the group. On the contrary, the very dynamic of *agape* is about acceptance and thus the capacity to remain belonging to the group and to see the group in its ambiguity.

Third, in those moments, the person also transcends the present. He or she becomes aware of the self as a person with a history, experiencing growth and development. As the present experience is transcended, so the idea of a future, of possibilities, not least the possibility of change, begins to develop.

Fourth, there is the transcendence of the limitations of the self, something about enabling the person to go beyond limitations. Parry (1988) suggests the centrality in ancient Greek culture and sport of *areté*. Translated as 'virtue', it is closer to 'being the best you can be', or 'reaching your highest human potential'. Of course, if spirituality is about awareness of the self and others this includes limitations. Such awareness, however, is partly developed through testing those limitations in striving for the best. Enabling the transcendence of limitations can also be achieved through acceptance of shared responsibility, the negotiation of responsibility and the development of creative partnerships.

Finally, there is transcendence through transformation, through finding new meaning, new purpose and new practice and partnership. This is the transcendence of creative imagination and response.

Conclusions

I have suggested that spirituality can be seen as a journey, one which involves the continual making of significant meaning and one which needs support. It is not enough to say that any spirituality should be accepted, not least because some can be very negative, both personally and socially. Hence, it is important that through reflection and dialogue all significant meaning should be challenged. Such challenge is there in all organised religions (Robinson 2007). Spirituality in all this is closely related to physical and psychological well-being. Moral meaning then is at the heart of spirituality, both in the sense of the connection of awareness and responsibility, and in the challenge of the values of any relationship and in the attempt to embody a creative response. This will emerge more fully in the consideration of virtues.

The experience of sport interweaves throughout this in several ways:

- Sport as a ground of faith which enables supporters and players to find significant meaning. Nick Hornby (2000) sums this up well in relation to football in what he characterises as an 'obsessive' relationship. In effect, though, he describes a faith relationship in which supporters experience the emotional highs and lows of the season, express their hopes through ritual, and find new hope with each new season. The ultimate expression of this is in football supporters' cooperatives. These embody that sense of shared ownership already felt by most supporters.
- Sport as a spiritual community which points beyond itself to significant life meaning. The Olympic movement sees sport as embodying certain fundamental values and beliefs which are universal – they do not just apply to sport, but sport embodies them. The campaigns for racial equality and tolerance in sport exemplify how unthinking spirituality can be challenged in and through sport.
- Sport as embodying existential pleasure, and enabling existential engagement, for player and supporter alike. In all this the practice of sport is tied to risk, and therefore sense has to be made of failure as much as success.

- Sport as linked to and in dialogue with other communities of meaning, not least through links to education and local community.
- Sport as linked directly to well-being in a holistic sense.
- Spirituality as having a functional relationship with sport, including the use of spiritual techniques to focus the performer.
- Sport as bringing together many different perspectives on spirituality and enabling dialogue between them. Again this is exemplified in the intercultural nature of the Olympic movement.

In all this sport is polyvocal, embodying very different expressions of spirituality, some with little reflection and some with a great deal. However, the plurality at the heart of sport, expressed through different clubs, different professional bodies and organising institutions ensures continuing dialogue.

Study questions

1   Choose two major clubs from different sports and visit their websites. What do they tell you about the beliefs and values of those clubs? Is this explicit or implicit? How do they compare?
2   Go to the websites of the Football Association and the Olympic Movement. What do they tell you about the values and beliefs of these institutions? How do they compare, and how do they compare to the clubs?

Section II

Religion and sport

This section addresses the relationship between religion and sport that is a central topic in the much broader field of spirituality and sport, as articulated by Simon Robinson in the first three chapters. There is an already well-established literature base that examines the sport–religion interface, although it is not yet well-developed. Drawing on this literature and a range of Christian theological, literary and psychological sources, the authors analyse in successive chapters three distinct but interrelated topics.

Chapter 4 examines the 'win at all costs' culture of modern sport, arguing that it requires 'wholesale spiritual rehabilitation'.

Chapter 5 follows the historical and theological development of Victorian Muscular Christianity and the birth of Modern Sports Ministry, and explains how this has impacted upon the relationship between sport and Christianity in twenty-first-century Britain and America.

Chapter 6 explores the nature of the mystical and the sublime, and discusses the application of those concepts to reported experiences in extreme sports.

Perhaps the defining and original characteristic of this section is its robust theological grounding. Whereas many past studies have identified and basically explained the links between religion and sport, they have for the most part failed to provide a rigorous analysis of what Professor Robert J. Higgs has called a 'semantic abuse' of theological terms and concepts, such as 'spiritual', 'holy' and 'mystical'. This has, in part, been owing to the seeming reluctance of theologians and religious studies scholars to reflect seriously upon *sport*, which is surprising, since sport is arguably the West's most popular cultural pastime, now surpassing other previously dominant cultural expressions such as art and music.

The chapter themes closely link with those tackled in the following section by Mark Nesti, who discusses various aspects of sport psychology consultancy in relation to traditional religious ideas and broader understandings of spirituality, which again reflects the truly interdisciplinary nature of this text.

4 'Winning at all costs' in modern sport

Reflections on pride and humility in the writings of C.S. Lewis

Nick J. Watson and John White, PhD candidate (Theological Ethics), University of Edinburgh

Introduction

The late Pope John Paul II fully understood the cultural significance of sport, calling it a 'paradigm of mass psychology' (John Paul II 1995/1986, 80). In one of many addresses to Olympic Committees, he championed the role of sport as a vehicle that 'contributes constructively to the harmonious and complete development of man, body and soul' (John Paul II 1995/1979, 60). The Vatican has also recently identified the need to provide theological reflection on sport, which is arguably the most pervasive cultural phenomenon at the beginning of the twenty-first century, and thus has established an office for Church and Sport within the Pontifical Council for the Laity.[1] Their vision is to foster 'a culture of sport' that is 'an instrument of peace and brotherhood among peoples' (Glatz 2004, 12).

Unfortunately, the reality of big-business competitive sport in the Western world, especially America,[2] is a far cry from such a utopia. Ladd and Mathisen (1999, 93) note that 'problems in the sports culture (cheating, rule violations, ego exaggeration) came to fruition in the 1920s and affected sport for the remainder of the twentieth century'. This corruption and perversion that sport readily exhibits has been highlighted in recent scholarship on sport ethics (Volkwein 1995; Grace 2000; Spencer 2000), the socio-theological status of sport (Hoffman 1992; Ladd and Mathisen 1999; Higgs and Braswell, 2004) and cultural critiques of sport in periodicals, such as *Christianity Today* (Galli 2005). The ethicist Professor Albert Spencer (2000, 143) identifies one of the main thrusts of these writings, commenting:

> There is a growing belief that sport [in America], rather than encouraging moral virtue and spiritual values, promotes just the antithesis: man's inevitable fall from grace through egotism, cynicism, nihilism, an obsessive focus on money, and win at all costs mentality that fosters disrespect for competitors and society. There are frequent news reports about athletes who violate both civil and moral behavioral codes through alcohol and drug abuse, gambling, theft, promiscuity, violence, and even murder.

There exists for many a deep underlying belief system in sport that is laden with values that John Paul II reminded us 'may be used for other purposes, with the danger of corruption and decadence' (John Paul II 1995/1980, 64). According to Piltz (1995), the reduction in fair play and sportsmanship is rooted amongst other things in a philosophy of 'winning is the only thing' or to 'win at all costs'. In terms of this popular dictum, most notably attributed to Vince Lombardi,[3] it is a conviction that the sport world adopts this view in order to make sense of the many dimensions of the 'sport reality'. When winning becomes the principle of 'being' for competition (and for life), it may have a baneful effect on the experience and personal identity of the athlete, coach or fan.

A major reason for this is that 'for professional players, naturally, sports are no longer pure. Sports are business, a craft, a way to earn a living, a specialization' (Novak 1994/1967, 164). A Catholic lay theologian and renowned social theorist, Michael Novak has identified and discussed five dimensions of winning that all professional athletes wrestle with in varying degrees. Arguably, the most important reason they are 'no longer pure' is the over-emphasis on winning, at the cost of the playful and joyful elements of sporting activities.[4] As Tony Campolo (1988, 126), professor of sociology and well-known Christian speaker, observes, 'from little league on up, American sports have become far too regimented to allow for much spontaneous fun'.

There exists a significant sports ethics literature, addressing moral issues such as sportsmanship, cheating, doping and the nature of competition; however, very little has been written applying Christian ethics and theology. There are however promising signs. For example, the philosopher Mark Hamilton (2003) presented a theological paper at the 2003 annual International Association of Philosophy of Sport conference, critiquing our relationship to modern sport using an Augustinian framework.[5] He suggests that 'maybe we should forget about attempting to solve its [sport's] problems through piecemeal solutions and attempt to determine whether there is something much greater, more profound, or even metaphysical which lies at the core of our current moral failures in sport and work to correct this' (2). We agree, and argue with Mathisen (2002, 30) that there is a real need to start to 'think biblically and theologically about sport' if we are to uncover the roots of the ethical and moral dilemmas in modern sport.

This chapter will provide a Christian ethical and theological analysis of the 'cult of winning' that is embodied in the beliefs and practices indigenous to competitive sports. Our goal is to imaginatively read and place the sport reality (competitive reality) within the world articulated by the gospel, with a specific focus on the 'wrongs of the system', while acknowledging that sin ultimately stems from individuals' hearts. At times our discussion is highly critical of the modern sport world. Therefore, from the outset, we would like to clearly articulate that as lifelong sport competitors, coaches and teachers in the field we champion the good of sport in a balanced theology of leisure.

We will propose that the foundational source of 'alienation' and the 'win at all costs' attitude can only be fully understood through an examination of underlying spiritual issues, in particular the sin of pride.[6] Although we will not be critiquing sport competition per se,[7] some preliminary discussion will be necessary as 'questions about the importance of winning are closely tied to but not identical with questions about the value of competition' (Simon 1991, 13). Our first task is then to briefly examine the nature of sport and competition and the reasons for the *distortion* of competition and pursuit of winning in modern professional sport.

Modern sport: competition and 'winning at all costs'

Sport, as defined by many sport philosophers, 'is a form of play [or should be], a competitive, rule-governed activity that human beings freely choose to engage [in]' (Clifford and Feezel 1997, 11).[8] Furthermore, since this is a competitive activity, inherent in its structure are the exercise of skills and strategies directed toward meeting a goal(s) in which athletic performances are evaluated and assessed by the particular standards of a specific sport (Sherif 1976). In short, competition involves a serious challenge or contest, in the original Greek the *agon*,[9] between players, resulting in a winner and loser – a *zero-sum* situation. From this, some scholars have seriously questioned the moral value of competition in sport and other institutions per se (e.g. Kohn 1992), arguing that it usually has negative consequences for the loser(s). Nonetheless, there seems to be a general consensus among sport philosophers, psychologists and theologians that competition in most human endeavours, when correctly understood, provides the opportunity for self-discovery, experiencing excellence and building social and national relations.

Etymologically, the word 'competition' derives from the Latin *com-petito*, to strive or question together (Hyland 1988). Idealistically, competition in sport can then be conceived as a 'mutually acceptable quest for excellence', in which opponents *cooperate* to bring the best out in one another. On a positive note, Simon (1991, 33) believes, as we do, that competition in sport is ethically defensible and that the 'meeting of the demands athletes place upon their talents often involves beauty, courage, dedication, and passion'. This said, the finely balanced dialectic of sport competition, which often involves 'intense passion', also carries the ever-present risk that 'such intensity will devolve into alienation and violence' (Hyland 1988, 177). Or, as Robert Nye (1973, 88) comments in his psycho-social account of competition, 'any type of competition . . . contains the seeds for mutual hostility', at personal, group and national level. This is clearly articulated by Professor Brian Aitken (1992, 239), in his oft-cited essay, 'Sports, Religion and Human Well-Being':

> In contemporary sport we are confronted with a perverted or alienated form of winning. Today winning does not involve just the desire to demonstrate a superiority of skills which is the normal goal of any game; rather, it involves an inordinate desire to win in an absolute sense.

One does not have to trawl the sports ethics literature for evidence of this. A cursory glance at the sports media and advertising will suffice. The world of child and youth and professional competitive sport is replete with dubious messages and stories of corruption and nationalistic fervour. For example, for those athletes whose identities are embedded in sport, the prophets of modern media herald, 'You are nothing until you are number one,' 'You don't win silver, you lose gold' (Nike ad), 'Nice guys finish last, there's no such word as chicken, and every time you lose you die a little' (Kohn 1992, 118) and 'Second place is the first loser'.[10] For some, these are merely hyperboles. But for others, these transform sport into more than a game and invoke fear, anxiety and the potential for experiencing a loss of identity and self-worth through failure in sport. Reports of physical and psychological abuse, especially in child and youth sport, further demonstrate the moral morass that exists.

A recent story in *U.S. News and World Report* describes how children across America are sometimes subjected to ridiculous and ugly situations with coaches and parents. In this special report, Fred Engh, founder of the National Alliance for Youth Sports, describes a father telling his kid, 'You little bastard, you could never get anything right' and another father who yells, 'I am gonna get you tonight because you let me down, buddy' (Carey 2004, 45). In addition, Peter Carey of *U.S. News* records a survey in South Florida in 1999 in which 82 per cent of 500 adults indicated that parents were too aggressive and 56 per cent said they observed overly aggressive actions.

Similarly, in elite professional sport this life view often results in alienation and violence, masquerading as athletic prowess. Violence may become a means to justify and validate in sport.[11] Of course, there are the infamous examples like Tanya Harding, Vinny Jones, Mike Tyson and Latrell Sprewell, but violence and alienation are expressed in a myriad of ways. The following are examples, many of which can be applied to children's and youth sports as well, of how certain actions and values have institutionalised this cult of victory:[12]

- A willingness to mistreat (acts of violence and aggression) and even 'hate' the opponent for they are the main obstacles to winning. The warlike rhetoric of annihilation used by many coaches acts as a form of arousal or motivation so that the opponent is objectified as the enemy. What is valued is more of a military style victory (might makes right) by the different soldier–athletes, rather than a joint moral quest for fair play and respect for human relationships.
- From this, we are left with a competitive ethic that stresses survival at virtually all costs not only at the expense of the opponent but also at the expense of the athlete's body. Performance-enhancing drugs, surgical enhancements, injured players competing through pain and assuming serious risks to body and mind, unhealthy eating habits (and disorders, e.g. bulimia and anorexia nervosa) and drastic weight reduction among some women gymnasts, wrestlers and jockeys, and extreme training regimens among endurathon-type athletes, exemplify the kind of action of this life view.[13]
- The practice of deceiving officials, bending rules, looking for loopholes in rules and the ritual of trash talking, along with other purposeful intimidation, are forms of negative and potentially damaging behaviour.[14] For example,

psychological antics like showboating/strutting, or trying to take an opponent out, would appear alien and inane without this belief because these practices are not a necessary condition for sport to exist or flourish. Moreover, the loser is belittled and booed (withheld praise), and sometimes given extreme workouts for his or her failure to win, and other negative reinforcement, such as verbal and physical abuse, thus ritualising the importance of this doctrine.

In his book *Games and Empires: Modern Sports and Cultural Imperialism*, the sports historian Allen Guttman (1994) has defined the formal structures of 'modern sports', which undoubtedly imbibe the 'win at all costs' doctrine and often lead to the consequences outlined above. He describes in detail how the character of modern Western sports has evolved from the industrial, scientific, capitalist, imperial and cultural developments of the nineteenth and twentieth centuries.[15] He identifies seven defining characteristics of 'modern sport'. Six of these, especially the 'secularisation' of modern sport, are particularly helpful in illustrating the structural foundation of the 'win at all costs mentality' and in turn reasons for the gradual decline in the non-utilitarian play ethic in modern sport (Guttman 1994, 2–3):

- *Secularism*. Despite their tendency to become ritualised and to arouse strong emotions, modern sports are not related – as pre-modern sports often were – to some transcendent realm of the numinous or sacred.
- *Bureaucratisation*. Modern sports are typically governed neither by priestly conclaves nor by ritual adepts but rather by national and transnational bureaucracies (of which the United States Olympic Committee and the Fédération Internationale de Football Association are examples).
- *Specialisation*. Many modern sports have evolved, like rugby, soccer, baseball and American football, from earlier, less differentiated games, and many, like cricket, baseball and football, have a gamut of specialised roles and playing positions.
- *Rationalisation*. The rules of modern sports are constantly scrutinised and undergo frequent revision from a means–ends point of view; athletes train scientifically, employ technologically advanced equipment, and strive for the most efficient employment of their skills.
- *Quantification*. In modern sports, as in almost every other aspect of our lives, we live in a world of numbers; the 'stats' have become an apparently indispensable part of the game.
- *The obsession with records*. The unsurpassed quantified achievement, which is what we mean by 'record' in this uniquely modern usage, is a constant challenge to all who strive to surpass it and thereby to achieve a modern version of immortality.

It can then be legitimately argued that, for some athletes and fans, modern sport, especially the dimension of winning, with its many potential extrinsic rewards, has become a 'ritualised obsession', and even a vehicle for 'immortalising the self'.[16] In his paper, aptly subtitled *The Religious Aesthetics of Sport as Postmodern Salvific Moments*, the religious studies scholar Michael Grimshaw (2000) has provided a thorough examination of this notion. He maintains that 'sports provides a post-Christian "pagan mythology" of "fallible gods"', through which athletes and fans can experience the mystical 'yet without the other-worldly connotations of a traditional understanding' (87, 92). Like that of the Buddhist scholar Charles Prebish (1993), Grimshaw's understanding of athletes' and fans' aesthetic–mystical experience, or what he calls a 'total now-ness of being',[17] can be understood as a 'postmodern salvific experience'.

Unlike Prebish, however, who suggests that aesthetic experiences in sport can provide 'redemption into a new type of reality ... permeated with ultimacy and Holiness' (1993, 70), Grimshaw recognises the need for the theological deconstruction of this pagan mythology. It is worth quoting at length from his discourse, as his comments provide the evidence base for our discussion of the deeper spiritual problems that we will argue drive the modern world of sport:

> It is increasingly obvious in today's market-driven world that the promotion of sports people as role models results in their commodification. This occurs because we misinterpret what occurs in sports, positing sports stars as liminal figures between modernist dualistic assumptions of the real and unreal of the secular and religious and of the sacred and profane. In doing so we deny and negate their humanity – and, in an uncritical acceptance and worship, we denigrate our own ... sports stars have become promoted and commodified as objects of veneration and an anticipatory end in themselves, for, fundamentally, who they are (or at least appear to be) and not for what they can achieve. The result of this is they become what is termed the hyper-real. This refers to the situation where the symbol of something (in this case the sports star) replaces and negates any actual reality of that person in popular understanding. This results in a media-driven and perpetuated scenario whereby the consciously fabricated image of symbol is believed to be expressing a truth and an experience that is "better than the real" ... In one sense this reflects the crisis of belief experienced in Western post-Christian society and especially the problems for belief after Nietzsche proclaimed and the 1960s confirmed the "death of God". For if "God is dead", then who are we who were supposedly created "*imago dei*" (in the image of God)? Even if for many God is not so much dead as either absent or irrelevant, does not the overwhelming commodification of contemporary life entice into idolatrous hyper-real longing, where it is the image of the image of the (sporting) god that so many strive to attain and achieve? Do we now abase ourselves at the Nike-shod feet of a new pantheon of gods, whereby worship is undertaken and achieved by ritualistic acquisition? Are we led to believe that by buying their uniform, wearing their shoes, drinking their drink and eating their burger we can achieve symbolic unification with our idol, who is often never more than a pixilated image on a screen, a flat image on a poster? ... For while our "idolatry" in sport is an attempt to present our "fallible gods" as

perfect, in fact it is their very fallibility that results in our giving them special status, for what they (though recognizably fallible) can still achieve it is this that is important. It is what they can achieve (if only for the most fleetingly temporal moment), that is of the ultimate importance and value, not who they are. At heart the issue is one of what a religious reading of sport might entail. The first, most familiar and traditional reading is what I would call a functionalist and ritualistic view. This argues that sport contains elements of religion and so within sport can be recognized sacred sites, sacred rituals, sacred festivals, sacred songs, sacred texts, saviour and heretical figures, times of persecution, reformation and so on. It is from such a reading that I could claim that "Rugby is New Zealand's national religion".

(Grimshaw 2000, 89–91)

Grimshaw's closing comments highlight what is a major theme in past writings on the sport–religion interface, that is, how scholars have in varying ways attempted to demonstrate the similarities and parallels between modern sport experience (both for participants and spectators) and primordial and modern religious rites, rituals and symbols. In turn, they have championed a 'religion of sport', in the guise of sport *as* a 'natural religion' (Novak 1994/1967) or 'popular religion' (Price 2001). In a post-Christian culture, this 'ritualizing of culture' and the resultant 'theologies of society', Grimshaw observes, are symptomatic of the modern tendency to perpetuate 'the notion of universal religious archetypes' (2000, 95).

Following the critique of Higgs and Braswell (2004),[18] we would argue sport is *not* by definition formally a religion. Nonetheless, worldviews operate from the heart and thus a human being can conscript a cultural activity like sport to try and answer these most fundamental questions. In this case when sport is *inflated* or *substituted* for religion then it has become an idol.[19] At a theologico-ethical level, this means that the idea and application of the 'win at all costs' ethic becomes the soil in which the personal (of athlete, coach, parent or fan) and structural sins (of institutions) of pride and idolatry are borne. Our next task is then to provide a theological analysis of competition in sport and discussion of these points. A particular focus will be on the sin of pride, which the great twentieth-century scholar C.S. Lewis (1997/1952, 100) called the 'Great Sin', the 'essential vice, the utmost evil . . . the virtue opposite to it, in Christian morals, is called humility'.

Pride and humility in competitive sport

While acknowledging that studies in sport philosophy, psychology (Walker 1980; Nye 1973), anthropology (Mead 1937) and religious studies (Newman 1989) have greatly contributed to our understanding of human competition, we propose there is something far darker and more insidious at the root of the problems in modern sport. Although Western culture has largely rejected the notion of an evil force in the universe that is diametrically opposed to a supernatural God and his purpose in the world, this is a fundamental part of the Christian story.[20] As Hamilton (2003, 7) notes in his theological critique of modern sport, we must recognise that 'the [root] cause of evil in the limited microcosm of sport is the same as that which is the cosmic cause of evil'.

Theologically, because of the spiritual crises we all share with Adam, Reinhold Niebuhr (1964, 178) declared that 'man is insecure and involved in natural contingency; he seeks to overcome his insecurity by a will-to-power which overreaches the limits of human creatureliness'. In sport, when winning is the primary aim of the athlete or coach, we see the desperate and even bizarre attempts by athletes and coaches to address the angst of their human predicament by doing anything and everything to reach their goal and bolster their identity and sense of significance. It is this driven, single-minded striving to 'win at all costs' that often leads to boasting of achievements, alienation of others (e.g. opponents and family members) and violence and cheating in sport, which we maintain flows from a prideful heart.

Considering that the postmodern consciousness is characteristically self-centred and self-sufficient and the world of sport is a naturally competitive environment, the potential for pride to corrupt and alienate is ever present. 'Pride is *essentially* competitive above all other vices', wrote C.S. Lewis (1997/1952, 101), that is, any human endeavour that involves competition also presents the *temptation* for individuals to become prideful. Nowhere is this temptation more prominent than in American culture,[21] in which the quest to be 'better than' has reached 'exaggerated, often ludicrous proportions' (Kohn 1992, 2–3). Lombardi himself once stated 'The zeal to be first in everything has always been American, to win and to win and to win'.[22] In his most well-known book, *Mere Christianity* (1997/1952), Lewis illustrates the often subtle dynamics of human pride that can be applied to competitive sport:

> It was through Pride that the devil [an external evil force] became the devil: Pride leads to every other vice: it is the complete anti-God state of mind. Does this seem exaggerated? If so, think it over. In fact, if you want to find out how proud you are the easiest way is to ask yourself, 'How much do I dislike it when other people snub me, or refuse to take any notice of me, or shove their oar in, or patronise me, or show off?'[23] The point is that each person's pride is in competition with every one else's pride. Two of a trade never agree [consider bitter rivals in sport or academia] . . . Pride gets no pleasure out of having something, only out of having more of it than the next man . . . people are proud of being richer, cleverer, or better looking [or better at sport] than others . . . It is the comparison that makes you proud: the pleasure of being above the rest . . . for of course, power is what pride really enjoys: there is nothing makes a man feel so superior to others . . . It is a terrible thing that the worst of all the vices can smuggle itself into the very centre of our religious life . . . as pride is direct from hell, it is purely spiritual, consequently it is far more deadly and subtle . . . Pride is spiritual cancer: it eats up the very possibility of love, or contentment, or even common sense.
>
> (101–104)[24]

In concluding his discussion of pride, Lewis (1997/1952) makes a number of qualifying statements that are important in our examination of pride in sport. Not all forms of pride are evil and unhealthy. Pertinent examples he gives include the 'pleasure of being praised' (e.g. by a parent, friend, coach, fan, teacher etc.), as long as this feeling does not result in self-adulation and vanity, and parents' pride in their children (e.g. for sports performance or achievement), which Lewis describes as a 'warm hearted admiration for'. This healthy admiration can, however, easily dissolve into parents living their life vicariously through their children's sport, academic or musical achievements – a prideful and damaging scenario that Overman (1997) and many others argue is rife in American sport. 'Parents relive personal successes and failures in their children. They use children as an extension of their own ego needs, seeking reassurance of their own sense of self-worth in their children', remarks Overman (1997, 244). In light of Lewis's call for moderation in how we understand pride, it is vital not to 'throw the baby out with the bath water' and demonize competitive sport and physical activity altogether, as for example did some sections of the medieval Church and the seventeenth-century English Puritan reformers.[25]

In remaining true to our thesis though, we maintain with Bud Williams (2004, 7) that in modern sport 'the real battlefield is not the game, the playing field, but in us, in our hearts and minds, ultimately our will to right or wrong. It is a battle for control of self – to play toward excellence and control of self to play fairly within the rules and the spirit of the contest'. This is, as the psychologist Paul Vitz (1994/1977, 91) states in his trenchant critique of humanistic psychology, the struggle between the 'relentless and single-minded search for and glorification of the self [rooted in pride]' which 'is at direct cross purposes with the Christian injunction to lose the self [to seek humility]'.[26] From a theological perspective, the principal enemy in this battle in sport is the often deeply seated and unconscious vice of pride; deeply seated in that pride is something that most people, including Christians, fail to see in themselves but hate in others (Lewis 1997/1952). We must however guard against simplistic arguments that attribute all moral wrongs in sport, or everyday life, to pride that is induced by an external evil force.

Hinting at this, Lewis, in his clever and imaginative work *The Screwtape Letters* (1942, 9), famously warned against the 'two equal and opposite errors' into which our race can fall concerning evil. These are for people to 'disbelieve in its existence' or to have an 'unhealthy interest in it' (rather than focusing on, and trusting in, the goodness, love and grace of God) and in turn often attempt to relinquish their responsibility (i.e. their free will to choose) for wrong behaviour by blaming this external evil force. We concur with Kohn (1992, 97), who states 'the reasons for trying to be successful at the price of other people's failure are numerous and multilayered', but we would also point to the spiritual dimension. Thus, we hold to the idea that pride is at the root of much wrong in sport and that humility, 'the virtue opposite to that in Christian morals' (Lewis 1997/1952, 100), is the principal remedy.

For those within the Christian tradition the ultimate act of humility was that the God of the universe should enter the world by sending his son to reconcile us to himself through the crucifixion and resurrection (2 Corinthians 5:18–19).[27] Humility was the very essence of Jesus' character: 'learn from me, for I am gentle and humble in heart' (Matthew 11:29). He exhibited the 'fruits of the spirit' described in Galatians (5:22–25), 'love, joy, peace, patience, kindness, goodness, faithfulness, gentleness and self control', in his very being and in his relations to others. Consider, are these virtues normally found, or easily practiced, in modern sporting contests? In comparing and contrasting the fruits of the 'Holy Spirit' with the modern 'sporting spirit', scholars, Higgs and Braswell (2004, 262) suggest not:

> How do you prepare for an agonic [contest] event for months by rigorous training, defeat a worthy opponent in public contest for a worldly prize and glory, and still be an example of "gentleness" and "meekness," to name only a couple of the famous "fruit"? Is this also as difficult to do as a camel going through "the eye of a needle"? To make matters more complicated, what if the winning athlete in question makes a quarter of a billion dollars per decade?[28]

We are in agreement with the authors in so much that the modern professional sporting arena is perhaps not a place where humility and love are common currency and the 'system of competitive sport' certainly does not encourage these virtues. However, we do feel along with others (Lofton 2004)[29] that Higgs and Braswell (2004), while explicitly adopting a metaphorical approach in their scholarly and thought provoking book, at times overstate and dichotomise various aspects of the relationship between sport and religion. For example, they contend that 'it is not realistic (or fair) to expect sports to build the fruits of the spirit defined by Paul' (2004, 262). To be sure, sporting contests should never replace the well-worn paths of prayer, study, fellowship and worship as methods for gaining intimacy with God and developing the fruits of the spirit (only by grace). But we do see them as potential places of learning and virtuous character development,[30] in which athletes can learn about different forms of love,[31] patience, compassion and self-sacrifice. This potential is of course predicated on whether or not the athlete or coach is 'actively seeking the good', that is, a humble, gracious and respectful approach to others when engaged in sport contests and in relations with others.

On this note, Andrew Murray, in his classic devotional text *Humility* (1982), describes below how it is 'insignificances of daily life' (we are not suggesting that sport is insignificant), especially in our relations with others, that reflect our true character. It is relationships, in particular with people who 'irritate and trouble us' (Murray 1982, 63), that are often the 'crucible of sanctification', that is, the means to developing virtues listed in St Paul's letter to the Galatians (5:22–25):

> It is in our most unguarded moments [in the heart of a sporting contest] that we really show and see what we are. To know the humble man [or woman], to know how the humble man behaves, you must follow him in the common course of his life . . . Humility before God is nothing if not proved in humility before men [or woman] . . . It is in our relationships to one another, in our treatment of one another [in sporting contests], that the true lowliness of

mind and the humility of heart are to be seen . . . Amid what are considered the temptations to impatience and touchiness, to hard thoughts and sharp words [trash talk, verbal abuse and intimidation] . . . the humble man [or woman] shows it in his [her] life.

Following this and recent empirical work (Schroeder and Scribner 2006)[32] it could then be argued that in sporting contests, *including those of a physical and aggressive nature*, there is a possibility of nurturing virtues in an athlete's character, rather than engendering pride. For male athletes, John Eldridge's book, *Wild at Heart: Discovering the Secret of a Man's Soul* (2001), lends support to this view in arguing that 'authentic masculinity' (like that of Jesus and the prophets) in a domesticated Western world is rare and that men have become emasculated, particularly Christian men, principally through a church that often advocates the need for men to be 'nice'.[33] He suggests that men are to varying degrees intrinsically competitive (which directed in the right way is responsible for much of the good in the world), desire adventure and relish physical challenge, but that these dimensions of masculinity are scarce in the modern world.[34]

For the most part, we endorse Eldridge's view, but also grant along with Higgs and Braswell (2004) that the 'acid test' for the athlete in any competitive sporting encounter is whether he or she come away having learned something about him- or herself and others and with a commitment to change and grow in humility and virtuous character. This is in contrast to an athlete's prideful quest for 'victory at all costs' that leads to the alienation of others and, paradoxically, often physical, psychological and spiritual harm to themselves.[35] Building on this theme, our next task is then to examine the 'direction' and 'underlying motivations' of the institutions of sport that are largely responsible for cultivating and nurturing the 'win at all costs' motto.

Institutions, heroes and idols in modern sport

In her challenging and thought-provoking paper 'Kierkegaard and Sport: Willing One Thing in Competitive Sports', Cindy White asks the question, 'could sports be one of those powers that have such a grip in our corporate consciousness that we are forgetting what is good?' Following Søren Kierkegaard (1813–55), who castigated the lukewarm domesticated Danish church in the nineteenth century, she suggests that 'the game is being spoiled and it is happening so slowly that few can see the disintegration because our identity as a nation [America] and as individuals is so wrapped up in sports culture' (2004, 1). This is of course the obsessively competitive sports culture that has its 'ideological roots' in the Protestant work ethic, which dominated the evolution of 'American religion along with other national institutions' (Overman 1997, 93).[36]

In his influential book *The Influence of the Protestant Ethic on Sport and Recreation*, Steve Overman demonstrates that 'the emphasis on achievement pervades virtually every American Institution, but nowhere is the need to achieve more pervasive and compelling than in sport' (1997, 217). He adds weight to Lewis's argument for the essentially competitive nature of pride, by identifying how endemic is the idea that 'status and achieved success equate to salvation'. Ultimately, the sin of pride in sport competition operates through the thoughts and actions of individual men and women, although of course this often manifests itself in societal institutions.

Margaret Mead's (1937) famous anthropological field work showed that individual competitiveness is conditioned by the dominant social philosophy of that society, what she called 'enculturation'. Of course, any one society or sports team is not exclusively competitive or exclusively cooperative and the dialectic between these two is complex (Newman 1989). It is though clear that the West, in particular America, is predominantly competitive and we should not underestimate how deeply this idiom lies in the American psyche. A 'predatory' and 'consumerist' culture, as the social economist Thorstein Veblen (1970/1899) called it, which is based upon the mutually beneficial alliance of sports, religion, government and warfare. As both 'athletic and economic competitions are highly institutionalised' (Newman 1989, 31), there is a constant temptation for sportsmen and -women and institutions to sin.[37] Remember, the sin of pride is in essence competitive and 'people are proud of being richer [better at sport] or more powerful', which is unashamedly a characteristic of the American collegiate system.

As early as the 1960s recruiting 'star athletes' for colleges, and high schools even, had become highly competitive. 'Aggressive recruiters' allegedly using 'bribes of money, automobiles, privileges, and sexual favours [often illegally] to secure their services' (Overman 1997, 230), what Carroll (1983) calls 'blue chip athletes'. A well-known problem of this deeply corrupted system, however 'seldom expressed', is how many American universities, including so-called Christian institutions, exploit young, often black athletes, providing very little in the way of a worthwhile academic education (Campolo 1988). Institutions commonly 'have little regard for them [athletes] beyond how many points they score and how many ticket buying fans they can lure through the gates' (1988, 124).[38] As Schmitt and Leonard (1986, 1104) observe, when sports become a means of immortality (i.e. idolatry) for the masses, 'the production of sport heroes, in turn, serves the political economy of sport'. To be sure, excluding a Nobel laureate on the academic faculty, nothing comes close to possessing sporting stars or highly ranked teams for attaining status and worth (Hollander and Zimmerman 1967, quoted in Overman 1997, 222). This frequently obsessive and prideful quest for status and economic gain in the American educational system predictably also operates on a national level.

History has clearly shown that 'whether communist, democratic, or fascist, modern governments have one thing in common – a reliance upon sports to help define and bolster national pride' (Higgs 1982).[39] In the build-up to the 2008 Olympics in Beijing, the host nation, China, epitomises this in the 'abusive' and disturbing elite child Sporting Academies that have recently been exposed. The list of examples is of course endless, with the 1936 Nazi Olympics perhaps being the most well-known from recent history. One thing is certain though: humility is 'not a virtue conspicuous in any national character' (O'Connor 1970, 35), especially when it comes to the use of national sporting heroes.

'Sporting heroes' are more often than not the vehicle for nationalistic tendencies. They 'serve as symbols of group and national pride . . . International sporting events such as the Olympic games often serve as symbolic conflicts between nations' (Carroll 1983, 47). An example that Carroll gives is the 'national pride' accrued by the American hockey team who defeated the Soviet Union in the 1980 Winter Olympics. Although this is so, we agree with Hager (2002, 10) that athletes can be seen as heroic if their actions on and off the field are virtuous and 'contribute to the good of society or our humanity'. Virtues in sport such as fair play, honour, self-sacrifice, courage, respect and love toward opponents have often been 'ignored or forgotten in the blind pursuit of victory' (Hager 2002, 10). It is then the 'type' of sporting heroism that is esteemed in the modern world that needs to be discerned (Higgs 1982), to see whether it is prideful or may lead to unhealthy nationalistic fervour and idolatry.

Perhaps the most important point to glean from this brief discussion of the archetypal modern sports hero is that conceptions of the heroic are wholly dependent on the dominant worldview of any given society.[40] In his incisive and award winning book *The Denial of Death* (1973, 82), Ernest Becker nicely summarises this in stating, 'the social hero-system into which we are born marks our paths for our heroism, paths to which we conform [often uncritically], to which we shape ourselves so that we can please others, become what they expect us to be'. Arguably, Western culture, especially American, is at present dominated by 'the religion of the godless celebrity' (Thompson 1997, 40), in which the high priests are often global sports stars. Sports heroes more often than not have become 'saints', even 'gods' to others (Prebish 1993) and are objects of worship institutionalised in Sporting Halls of Fame. Without a doubt, 'the specialist appears to be the man of the hour . . . favourites of today whose appeal consists of one thing (often trivial): pinups and profiles; movie and television stars; . . . the athlete . . . and other splendid performers', remarks Orrin Klapp in his book *Heroes, Villains, and Fools: The Changing American Character* (1962). Klapp compares modern heroes to the archetypal 'renaissance man', those such as Leonardo, Franklin, Churchill and Bacon, and bemoans the denigration of the heroic in the modern world. Great men, and heroes of sorts maybe, but let us not forget the most distinguishing characteristic of the heroic is the sacrificial, that is, sacrificing your needs, wants, desires, and even life itself, for the good of others.

From the perspective of a Christian believer the ultimate act of heroic sacrifice is when God himself entered the world in the form of his son Jesus, and 'humbled himself and became obedient to death . . . even death on a cross' (Philippians 2:8), so that we might know his love. Humans, including Christians, can never fully comprehend the magnitude of this heroic sacrifice, nor are we called to *directly* imitate it. Nonetheless, we are all called to 'take up their cross and follow him' (Luke 9:23)[41] in every aspect of our life, including sport. C.S. Lewis, in his magical allegorical tale *The Great Divorce* (2001/1946), provides an illustrative example of the heroic in Christian terms. The writer, in a dream, embarks on a journey into the heavenly spiritual realms. On this voyage he meets a variety of supernatural beings that convey to him how the 'daily insignificances' of life have eternal consequences. The story of 'Sarah Smith' challenges us to consider how, and why, we classify celebrities and sports stars as great and heroic in the truest sense of the word. The narrative starts with the writer asking his spiritual guide, or teacher as to the identity of 'one of the great ones':

'Is it? . . . is it?' I whispered to my guide.

'Not at all,' said he. 'It's someone ye'll never have heard of. Her name on Earth was Sarah Smith and she lived at Golders Green.'

'She seems to be . . . well, a person of particular importance?'

'Aye. She is one of the great ones. Ye have heard that fame in this country and fame on Earth are two quite different things.'

'And who are these gigantic people . . . look! They're like emeralds . . . who are dancing and throwing flowers before her?'

'Haven't ye read your Milton? *A thousand liveried angels lackey her.*'

'And who are all these young men and women on each side?'

'They are her sons and daughters.'

'She must have had a very large family, Sir.'

'Every young man or boy that met her became her son – even if it was only the boy that brought the meat to her back door. Every girl that met her was her daughter.'

'Isn't that a bit hard on their own parents?'

'No. There *are* those that steal other people's children. But her motherhood was of a different kind. Those on whom it fell went back to their natural parents loving them more. Few men looked on her without becoming, in a certain fashion, her lovers. But it was the kind of love that made them not less true, but truer, to their own wives.'

[. . .]

'In her they became themselves. And now the abundance of life she has in Christ from the Father flows over into them.'

I looked at my Teacher in amazement.

'Yes,' he said. 'It is like when you throw a stone into a pool, and the concentric waves spread out further and further. Who knows where it will end? Redeemed humanity is still young, it has hardly come to its full strength. But already there is joy enough in the little finger of a great saint [hero] such as yonder lady to waken all the dead things of the universe into life.'

Of course, Sarah Smith is a hero of a different caste from that we usually see in modern sport, but we cite this analogy in the hope of challenging the reader to examine our distorted conceptions of the heroic, or what Becker (1973, 82–83) calls the 'standardized hero-game' that we all blindly play. Although it is important to note that 'taking up one's cross' has *deep spiritual meaning*, in sport it is perhaps demonstrating 'the moral strength to follow the correct path when easier routes are available' (Birrell 1981, 368). This is something that would help rectify what Higgs (1982, 154) calls the 'youthful idolizing of sport heroes and the subsequent disappointment[s]' that often ensue, when their heroes are caught taking drugs or attacking an opponent. Do we value and even worship sportsmen and -women because of their virtuous actions and character, *as well as* their physical performance and displays of aesthetic beauty? Or is it *primarily* for the winning and results that we transform them into fallible gods and live vicariously through their performances? For those who prize victory above all else, Higgs (1982, 137) suggests 'the athlete comes back from this mysterious adventure with the power to bestow boons on his fellow man, that is a sense of identity and self-worth'. As we have argued throughout, realising one's identity principally through sport, as an athlete and perhaps to a lesser degree as a fan or parent, does, however, often come at a price.

Concluding remarks

The aim of this chapter was to reflect theologically on big-business competitive sports, in particular the 'win at all costs' ethic that dominates modern sports. Within a balanced theology of leisure, sport competition can be an immensely positive endeavour for individuals and even a potential means of reconciliation and friendship between nations. Too often, however, these ideals are marred by the sin of pride, which we have argued has a metaphysical source and is the foundational but not exclusive cause of much of the wrong in professional and youth sport. Dr Bud Williams (2004, 18) encapsulates the finely balanced dialectic that exists in sport in stating that sport 'has the potential to bring out the best or worst. It can tempt one to be extremely proud or bring one to the point of humility. It can easily arouse anger and hatred or evoke deep respect and even self-sacrificing love'.

It seems that pride, which as C.S. Lewis advocates is competitive in its essence, has significantly contributed to the 'win at all costs' attitude and concurrently idolatry in modern sport. This is a system that we maintain requires 'wholesale spiritual rehabilitation' and a good starting point for change would be the promotion of the virtues such of humility, love, self-sacrifice, respect and honour. At present, however, the evidence strongly suggests that, for many involved in big-time professional sport and children and youth sport (especially parents and coaches), pride and its frequently damaging consequences hold court. What then is the answer to this dilemma, as 'affecting change within the world of big-time, competitive sport . . . is a daunting prospect' (Mathisen 2005b), but one that it is argued needs urgent attention.

Those in evangelical circles claim that Christians should 'protest loudly against such abuses' and seek to reclaim 'sports to be what God intended them to be' (Campolo 1988, 20). To be sure, Jesus' teachings clearly instruct us to protest against injustices in all aspects of life and work together to redress what is not right, including the moral and ethical problems in sport. In addition to the scholarship and research of pioneers and leading thinkers in the field (Hoffman 1992; Prebish 1993; Novak 1994/1967; Higgs 1995; Ladd and Mathisen 1999; Price 2001; Higgs and Braswell 2004; Van Andel *et al.* 2005) there are promising signs that individuals and groups are beginning to recognise the widespread damage that is being done within the confines of what is arguably the most popular form of recreation in the Western world.

Two new university research centres have recently been established that seek to examine the spiritual and religious dimensions of sport and exercise and provide taught modules on the topic.[42] An academic peer-review journal, the *International Journal of Religion and Sport* (Mercer University Press), has also recently been launched to promote interdisciplinary scholarship and research in the field. Additionally, a diverse group of individuals, comprising theologians, philosophers, sports philosophers, ex-professional athletes and sports chaplains/ministers recently met in Dayton, Ohio, USA, for a 'think-tank' that explored the relationship between sport and Christianity.[43] These relatively new initiatives have, however, been preceded by the excellent work of the Christian Society for Kinesiology and Leisure Studies (CSKLS),[44] which is an American organisation that was established in the late 1980s. The CSKLS forum seeks to integrate faith, sport and leisure through the sharing of scholarly work and fellowship, principally through the society's annual conference. This has resulted in the publication of two books in the field (Byl and Visker 1999; Van Andel *et al.* 2005) that are composed of selected papers from past conferences.

New 'projects' and writings will no doubt lead to some positive change in sport, as has previous sports ethics research and the excellent work of initiatives such as the Sports Ethic Institute and the Positive Coaching Alliance. This may especially apply to analysis and change in the structures of sporting institutions, based on the premise that it is 'impossible to manage the ambiguity of competition at the local face-to-face level unless the ruthless competition at the highest level' is first addressed (Hull 2001, 273). Nonetheless, any radical and lasting change in the modern sporting arena we maintain will only evolve from the spiritual transformation of the hearts of individual men and women, which begins as Lewis tells us in 'taking the first step' of humbling ourselves (1 Peter 5:5–6)[45] and acknowledging that sport occupies a number of floors in our 'modern Tower of Babel'. 'If anyone would like to acquire humility, I can, I think, tell him [her] the first step. The first step is to realise that one is proud. And a biggish step, too. At least, nothing whatever can be done before it. If you think you are not conceited, it means you are very conceited indeed', Lewis (1997/1952, 106) notes.

The philosopher of sport Mark Hamilton (2003, 8) believes, as we do, that the competitiveness and the pride and shame that are often its life source 'reaches into every nook and cranny of our life', including sport at all levels. Have we so 'lost our moral compass', as Hamilton suggests, that we are blind to the 'myth of progress' that is deeply embedded in postmodern culture?[46] This modern 'myth of progress' has been compared by theologians to the story of the Tower of Babel (Genesis 11:1–9), the primordial quest to build 'a city with a tower reaching to the heavens' (Middleton and Walsh 1997). There is little doubt that the multi-billion-dollar business of sport is a major edifice in this 'modern Babel', along with other cultural idols such as scientism, healthism[47] and intellectualism. In the academy, where 'arid scholasticism, crass careerism' and 'pompous posturing' are arguably rampant (Steele 2000, 90), this manifests itself in the 'publish or perish' ethos that is just as destructive as the 'win at all costs' attitude in modern sport.

At the heart of this modern myth is the belief that humanity can save itself and does not need a saviour in the form of a transcendent God. Prophetic voices, such as Blake, Dostoyevsky, Kierkegaard, Pascal and, in the twentieth century, C.S. Lewis and G.K. Chesterton, have all given dire warnings about the modern myth and our prideful and idolatrous quest to create, and to be, our own Gods. Perhaps it is time for those involved in sport, especially those in positions of power and influence, to accept that the 'false myths', as Lewis called them, have all proved ineffective in combating the moral and social fragmentation in wider society (Walker 1996) and sport. False myths that have lead to what the social anthropologist Clifford Geertz (1973, 99) calls the 'gravest sort of anxiety'. A deep anxiety that plagues the young hearts and minds of 'the little boys in grey flannel uniforms' (Campolo 1988, 126–127) and leads sporting gods like the England Rugby Union player Johnny Wilkinson to be 'wracked with anxiety' and feeling 'incredibly depressed, demoralised, even bitter' with his life during a long injury lay-off (Jackson 2006, 80).

What is perhaps most worrying is that for the 'self-sufficient modern' who 'has it all together' and is 'competent' is that this anxiety, or dread, is often buried in the caverns of the mind, an unconscious denial that Kierkegaard (1989/1849, 74) called the 'worst form of despair'. A 'spiritless sense of security', Kierkegaard suggests, underlies this dread, a despair that will be only uncovered 'when life begins to quake' or what Martin Buber called the 'shudder of identity' and the 'illusion is broken'; then we will see what 'lies beneath' (Agassi 1999, 74). As individuals and as a nation(s), are we prepared to peer beneath the corrupt and damaging 'popular mythology' (Kohn 1992) of 'winning at all costs' in modern sport? Echoing the thoughts of Kierkegaard, Kohn suggests not, as 'it would be painful and might force us to make radical changes in our lives, so instead we accept rationalizations' (1992, 114) for the damage that is being done all around us in sport. Perhaps it is these superficial rationalizations that prevent us 'breaking through the bounds of cultural heroism' and 'fictional games being played in . . . society' (Becker 1973, 91) and lead to what Kierkegaard called a 'fictitious health'. The provocative and challenging words of the writer John Eldridge (2001, 90, 150) make this a little more personal and perhaps uncomfortable for us all:

> The world [the Western system] offers man a false sense of power and a false sense of security . . . the world cheers the vain search on . . . Be brutally honest now – where does your own sense of power come from? Is it . . . how well [you] play sport? . . . Is it how many people attend your Church? Is it *knowledge* – that you have an expertise and that makes others come to you, bow to you? Is it your position, degree, or title? A white coat, a Ph.D., a podium [?]

Then getting right to the very 'heart' of the matter, Eldridge (2001, 150) asks, 'what happens inside you when I suggest you give it up? Put the book down for a few moments and consider what you would think of yourself if tomorrow you lost everything that the world has rewarded you for.' For those embedded in the postmodern world of sport, which is constructed from socio-cultural norms and reinforced and manipulated by the mass media, Eldridge's words may be a little too piercing and thus quickly dispatched to the caverns of the mind, and consequently they will continue to 'travel with the carnival' (Middleton and Walsh 1999, 61). This is the 'herd mentality' that Kierkegaard wrote extensively on. 'The crowd *is* untruth. It either produces impenitence and irresponsibility or it weakens the individual's sense of responsibility by placing it in a fractional category' (Moore 1999, 243). We do hope, however, that all those involved in sport may search their hearts and perhaps consider what C.S. Lewis famously called the 'Deep Magic', 'the Myth that became Fact' (Lewis 1988/1944, 31) – the story of a God who humbled himself in the most unimaginable way that we might know his love and guidance in every dimension of our lives, including sport.

> "But what does it all mean?" asked Susan when they were somewhat calmer. — "It means," said Aslan, "that though the Witch knew the Deep Magic, there is a magic deeper still which she did not know. Her knowledge goes back only to the dawn of Time. But if she could have looked a little further back, into the stillness and the darkness before Time dawned, she would have read there a different incantation. She would have known that when a willing victim who had committed no treachery was killed in a traitor's stead, the Table would crack and Death itself would start working backwards."
>
> (Lewis 2001/1950, 176)

Study questions

1   In your experience of playing, officiating or watching sport, consider times when you have witnessed alienation and violence of others. What was the effect on those involved and on you? What does this tell you about modern competitive sport, and your values and motivations in sport?

2   In light of the 'win at all costs' ethic, discuss the ethical and theological implications of genetic performance enhancement in sport, the topic of an important book by the philosopher of sport Andy Miah (2004).

3   In your own experience of playing or watching sport, consider times when you have experienced or witnessed virtuous actions, e.g. sportsmanship, self-sacrifice, correcting officials' judgements in favour of the opposition. What was the effect on those involved? How did it make you feel about yourself or others?

4   The theologian Michael Wittmer (2005) suggests that to think biblically/ theologically about sport it would be helpful to use a three-point conceptual framework of Creation, Fall and Redemption. Adopting one or more of these philosophical start points should help spark group debate and systematic thinking for writing projects on a wide range of topics. Examples of questions are: What is the nature and meaning of competitive sport? What are the

potential positive and negative outcomes of sport competition? How should Christians involved in sport think and behave? What is God's will for sport?

Acknowledgements

First, Nick would like to thank my friend and co-author John White, Director of Athletes in Action (USA), who provided the original idea and inspiration for this work. In this regard, some small sections of this chapter are taken from a previous publication: White, J. and Watson, N.J. (2006) 'Exegeting Homo Sportivus', *World of Sports*, 22 (1–2). Second, I would like to express my thanks to Scott Kretchmar, Professor of Sport Philosophy (Penn State University, USA) and Mark Hamilton, Associate Professor of Philosophy (Ashland University, USA) for their most helpful comments on our first draft. Third, I would like to thank Kate Hutchings and Dr Chris Bell for their invaluable assistance with proofreading, and the library staff at York St John University, especially Claire McClusky, for help with sourcing literature.

5 Muscular Christianity in the modern age

'Winning for Christ' or 'playing for glory'?

Nick J. Watson

Introduction

The development of Muscular Christianity in the second half of the nineteenth century has had a sustained impact on how Anglo-American Christians view the relationship between sport, physical fitness and religion. It has been argued that the birth of Muscular Christianity in Victorian Britain forged a strong 'link between Christianity and sport' that 'has never been broken' (Crepeau 2001, 2). The emergence of neo-Muscular Christian groups during the latter half of the twentieth century (Putney 2001) and the promotion of sport in Catholic institutions such as the University of Notre Dame can be seen as a direct consequence of Victorian Muscular Christianity. Modern evangelical Protestant organisations (i.e. Sports Ministry) such as Christians in Sport (CIS) in the UK and the Fellowship of Christian Athletes (FCA) and Athletes in Action (AIA) in America, have resurrected many of the basic theological principles used to promote sport and physical fitness in Victorian Britain.

The basic premise of Victorian Muscular Christianity was that participation in sport can contribute to the development of Christian morality, physical fitness and 'manly' character.[1] The term was first adopted in the 1850s to portray the characteristics of Charles Kingsley's (1819–1875) and Thomas Hughes' (1822–1896) novels. Both Kingsley and Hughes were keen sportsmen and advocates of the strenuous life. Fishing, hunting and camping were Kingsley's favourite pastimes, which he saw as a 'counterbalance' to 'education and bookishness' (Bloomfield 1994, 174). Hughes was a boxing coach and established an athletics track and field programme and cricket team at the Working Men's College in London where he eventually became principal (Redmond 1978). Not just writers but social critics, Kingsley and Hughes were heavily involved in the Christian Socialist movement and believed that the Anglican Church had become weakened by a culture of effeminacy (Putney 2001). Kingsley supported the idea that godliness was compatible with manliness and viewed manliness as an 'antidote to the poison of effeminacy – the most insidious weapon of the Tractarians – which was sapping the vitality of the Anglican Church' (Newsome 1961, 207). From this, the doctrine of Muscular Christianity was adopted as a response to the perceived puritanical and ascetic religiosity of the Tractarians, later known as the Oxford Movement.

Aside from the religious motivations for the evolution and advancement of Muscular Christianity, the Victorians' preoccupation with health is arguably the most significant factor. 'No topic more occupied the Victorian mind than Health ... they invented, revived, or imported from abroad a multitude of athletic recreations, and England became in Sir Charles Tennyson's words, the *world's game master*' (Haley 1978, 3). Haley suggests there were three main reasons for the prominence of the concept of the healthy body in the mid-nineteenth century.

First, the Industrial Revolution, which in time brought about a Leisure Revolution within the working-class population (Cunningham 1980) and played a major role in focusing the Victorian psyche on health, although, paradoxically, the automation of industry had led to sedentary lifestyles and as a consequence an exponential rise in cardiovascular and respiratory disease. In addition, poor conditions and long, arduous working hours in the factories resulted in many contracting occupational diseases. Second, the nineteenth century witnessed a number of major developments in medical science. The founding of physiology as a distinct discipline separate from biological science, and the emergence of physiological psychology, engendered a holistic understanding of health and an emphasis on the mind–body connection. Third, and often less publicised, there was a real threat of war from a number of European countries and the Americans. Responding to this, the intelligentsia saw the need to protect the British Empire and produce leaders that were well educated and 'manly' (Haley 1978). Kingsley and Hughes, amongst other members of the Protestant elite, saw Muscular Christianity as an appropriate vehicle for advancing British imperialism and increasing the health and well-being of the nation (Putney 2001). Through the medium of sport, Kingsley saw the potential for spiritual, moral and physical development:

> in the playing field boys acquire virtues which no books can give them; not merely daring and endurance, but, better still temper, self-restraint, fairness, honour, unenvious approbation of another's success, and all that 'give and take' of life which stand a man in good stead when he goes forth into the world, and without which, indeed, his success is always maimed and partial.
>
> (Kingsley, quoted in Haley 1978, 119)

The aim of this chapter is to provide an understanding of the historical and theological development of Muscular Christianity in Victorian Britain and how this has contributed to the evolution of Modern Sports Ministry. Discussion will primarily focus on the historical and theological roots of the movement from a British perspective[2] and then will broaden to an analysis of modern Sports Ministry in both Britain and America.

Historical, theological and philosophical roots of Muscular Christianity

The origins of Muscular Christianity can be traced back to the New Testament, where St Paul and others used athletic metaphors to help describe the challenges of the Christian life (e.g. 1 Corinthians 6:19, 9:24–25; 2 Timothy 4:7).[3] However, the explicit advocacy of sport and exercise, in the guise of Muscular Christianity, did not evolve until the mid-nineteenth century in Britain, and the source of the idiom has been a point of debate amongst scholars (Redmond 1978). It is commonly accepted that a review of Charles Kingsley's *Two Years Ago* (1857) for the *Saturday Review*, written by a cleric, T.C. Sandars, was the first place the term appeared (Simon and Bradley 1975). Ironically, Kingsley abhorred it and wrote a vitriolic response to the author, who had used 'that painful, if not offensive term, "Muscular Christianity"' (Haley 1978, 109). Thomas Hughes, a friend and supporter of Kingsley, then used the concept in a follow-up to *Tom Brown's Schooldays* (1857), called *Tom Brown at Oxford* (1861). In contrast to Kingsley, who seemed worried about the negative connotations that may have been attached to the secular expression 'muscular', Hughes used it to promote the athleticism that was so pervasive in his novels (Winn 1960). This said, Rosen notes that he was careful to clearly distinguish the concept of 'muscular Christians' from the 'musclemen' (athletes without Christian beliefs): 'the only point in common between the two being, that both hold it to be a good thing to have strong and well-exercised bodies . . . Here all likeness ends'. The Christian belief is 'that a man's body is given him to be trained and brought into subjection and then used for the protection of the weak, the advancement of all righteous causes' (Hughes 1861, 99).

Interestingly, Redmond (1978) has noted that a closer examination of other children's literature long before the birth of the concept in Kingsley and Hughes shows that the general thesis of Muscular Christianity was implicit within works published between 1762 and 1857. The work of writers such as J.-J. Rousseau, William Clarke, Dorothy Kilner, William Howitt and S.G. Goodrich all possess glimpses of the Christian muscular gospel that flowered in the literature of Kingsley and Hughes. In his classic *Emile* (1762), Rousseau emphasises the importance of physical education in the development of moral character: 'Give his body constant exercise, make it strong and healthy in order to make him good and wise . . . The lessons the scholars learn from one another in the playground are worth a hundred fold more than what they learn in the classroom' (quoted in Redmond 1978, 9). In conclusion, Redmond suggests neither Kingsley nor Hughes can be accredited with the original 'athletic gospel' but they 'reaped the harvest' that gave birth to the Muscular Christian movement during the Victorian period.

Their personal lives, education and political and theological affiliations heavily influenced Kingsley's and Hughes' ideas. The period between 1850 and 1900 was characterised by social unrest and political instability, in the form of labour unrest in the working-class population and serious problems with public health (Clark 1996). Both Hughes and Kingsley had been sympathisers with Chartism, a political movement that developed in response to the social injustices suffered by the working classes. As a rector and author of social novels such as *Yeast* (1848), *Westward Ho!* (1855) and *Alton Locke* (1850), Kingsley became widely known as the 'Chartist clergyman' (McGlynn 1999). Following the House of Commons' decision to reject the Chartist Petition in 1848 and the subsequent demise of Chartism, Kingsley and Hughes continued to support the grievances of the working classes as leading proponents of Christian Socialism. They joined forces with other Christian Socialist thinkers such as F.D. Maurice (1805–1872), J.M. Ludlow (1821–1911) and Thomas Arnold (1795–1842). It was Ludlow who convinced Kingsley and Maurice that Christianity and socialism could be integrated to offer an antidote to the political doctrine of Chartism (Bloomfield 1994).

Although the Christian Socialist movement had a similar goal to Chartism, its primary focus was on providing solutions to social ills through educational and moral change, not change in political legislation (Norman 1987). At the time this was a radical idea. Prior to the late 1840s the Church of England's attitude to implementing social reform was conservative with leading evangelicals emphasising the hierarchical class system, thus marginalising the poor and downtrodden. They saw poverty as being self-inflicted through various sins such as self-indulgence and intemperance (Parsons 1988). The class system was also reinforced during the late nineteenth century by the fashionable concept of social Darwinism. In short, the primary concern of the Victorian Church of England before the mid-nineteenth century had been to 'save the lost' (i.e. to win converts), with concern for social welfare often coming a poor second.

The Christian Socialists heavily criticised the Church's advocacy of the classic political economy and hierarchical class structure, which had contributed to the dehumanising and neglect of the working-class population during the early nineteenth century (Norman 1987). In respect to Muscular Christianity, Kingsley had stressed the social benefits that accrue from participation in athletic activities, especially in terms of demolishing class divisions. Nevertheless, the Christian Socialist idea of a classless society often concealed 'a deeper belief in the class system and in the bourgeois hegemony' which is personified by the middle-class boys depicted in Hughes' *Tom Brown's Schooldays* (Allen 1994, 120). And, although implicit, there seems to be what Allen calls a 'conceptual dilemma' in Hughes' classic work, between 'the classless democracy of the athletic body and the hierarchical structure of the class system' (1994, 120–121). This tension was also evident in what Hargreaves (1986) calls a 'leadership cult', which existed in middle-class public schools where society's leaders were being nurtured.

The Christian Socialists, a small but very influential group of academics and Protestant clergy, disseminated their ideas primarily through two journals, *Politics of the People* (1848–1849) and *The Christian Socialist* (1850–1851). Maurice, who is recognised as the movement's most influential and leading thinker, also founded the Working Men's College in London in 1854, which ran evening classes, thus acting as a vehicle to educate the working-class people. The theology that underpinned the Christian Socialist thesis and which complemented Muscular Christianity can be mainly attributed to F.D. Maurice. Heavily influenced by the idealism of Coleridge, he believed that the Kingdom of God should be accessible to all members of society, a theology of universal brotherhood (Norman 1987). In Maurice's book *The Kingdom of God* (1838) and in a later controversial publication *Theological Essays* (1852), he championed an incarnational theology, which provided an elevated view of humanity with a stress on the importance of educating the masses to recognise their place in God's Kingdom.

During the first half of the nineteenth century there had been an emphasis on the Atonement within theological circles. Nevertheless, the advent of the Christian Socialist movement, especially in the work of Maurice, saw a shift 'to promote the study of social and political questions in the light of the Incarnation' (Norman 1987, 30). This, it was argued, has a sound biblical basis in the teachings of Jesus (e.g. Mark 3:20–30; Matthew 12:25–32; Luke 4), and provided the basis for Kingsley's theological position, which recognised the significance of the embodied soul, and in turn the goodness of athleticism and physical strength in the formation of character. Hall (1994) has noted that the frequent reference to the body in *Politics for the People* and other Christian Socialist literature provides evidence that 'the metaphors and pedagogical goals of the Christian Socialists and muscular Christians are inextricably linked' (1994, 48). This highlights the importance and significance of Hughes and Kingsley's work within the Christian Socialist movement, and its impact upon social and cultural change during the Victorian period. Of the two, Kingsley has written more on the Muscular Christian ethic and deserves the credit for providing Muscular Christianity 'with a cohesive and conscious philosophy, consisting equally of athleticism, patriotism, and religion' (Putney 2001, 12).

It can be argued that the most significant idea to evolve from Kingsley's corpus of writings is 'Christian manliness'. His doctrine of masculinity had been originally based upon his 'instincts which told him that the life of a clergyman was compatible with married life and with that of a sportsman' (Haley 1978, 111). From this, he sought to provide philosophical and theological justification for his feelings and borrowed from a diverse group of thinkers. The philosophical lineage of Kingsleyan masculinity is derived from Plato's concept of *thumos*, which he interpreted as a primal manly force involved in sex, morality and fighting (Rosen 1994). Although Bloomfield acknowledges that it is speculative, she suggests Kingsley's work may have also been influenced by the mystical and occult philosophy of Emanuel Swedenborg (1688–1772). There are a number of clear parallels in their work and perhaps most significantly their 'desire – to seek the relationship between soul and body' (Bloomfield 1994, 173). Due to the influence of Plato's mind–body dualism[4] and the liberal philosophy of Swedenborg in his work, his more orthodox contemporaries frequently accused Kingsley of Neoplatonism and pantheism, an accusation that he angrily refuted. These philosophical roots were formed during his time reading Classics at Cambridge University, where he gained a first class degree. He then developed and focused his ideas into a doctrine of social action and reform through reading the works of, and collaborating with, the essayist and social historian Thomas Carlyle (1795–1881) and the theologian F.D. Maurice.

Carlyle had been influenced by the German Romantic thought of Herder and Goethe. In trying to synthesise what Kant had described as the *noumena* and *phenomena*, Johan Gottfried von Herder (1744–1803) had promoted the 'veneration of the body as being natural, beautiful manifestation of life and vitality, a vehicle through which, by means of gesture, the soul could speak' (Bloomfield 1994, 180). Hence, it is possible to trace certain elements of German Romanticism in the thought of Kingsley. Haley (1978) proposes that Kingsley's notion of the Muscular Christian or 'healthy hero' was primarily based upon three of Carlyle's ideas: the body is an expression of the spirit and therefore the obedience to healthy impulse is a sign of constitutional harmony; the state of health is acknowledgment of the laws of nature and compliance with these laws; and heroism is a life of action made possible by observing the laws of health (1978, 111–112). In light of this, neither Kingsley, Maurice nor Hughes accepted the entire 'vague theistic gospel' of Carlyle but nevertheless it had a significant impact upon their work. Primarily, it was the 'angry Old Testament rhetoric of Carlyle's social criticism,' which was a 'brutally direct stimulus to social action and intervention' that most significantly influenced the Christian socialist theology of Maurice and his associates (Vance 1985, 59).

In Alderson's (1996) analysis of Christian manliness in Kingsley's novel *Alton Locke* (1850), he contends that 'the imperatives of a counter-revolutionary and Protestant culture . . . enabled the Kingsleyan sense of the ideal male body to be-come so central to the masculine self-definition of Britain's rulers' (1996, 43–44). In addition to the fears within the Protestant elite of the feminisation of the Vic-torian church,[5] the rise of evolutionary theory and, in the late nineteenth century, Freudian and Jungian psychologies also helped strengthen Kingsley's notion of masculinity (Rosen 1994). The doctrine of masculinity has been absorbed into the 'deep structure' of society, often specific subcultures, and continues to have a pervasive influence in athletics, religion and men's movements within modern Anglo-American culture (see Randels and Beal 2002). For example, twentieth-century men's movements that 'seek to rid men of the problems of pre-sixties' macho and post-sixties' sensitivities' owe much to Kingsley (Rosen 1994, 39–40). And in relation to sports participation, Harris (1990, 11) proposes that 'the mus-cular novel according to Kingsley and Hughes contributed to the immense vogue of athletics from the late sixties onwards'.

In light of the widespread and prolonged influence of Kingsley's notion of the Muscular Christian, there were notable Victorian and post-Victorian writers, such as Gerard Manley Hopkins (1844–1889) and E.M. Forster (1879–1970), who strongly disagreed with Kingsley's ideas (Putney 2001). Forster suggested that those educated within the movement ended up with 'well-developed bodies . . . and underdeveloped hearts' (Forster 1936, 5). Likewise, in a contemporary analysis of values, sport and education, Grace (2000, 17) suggests that 'the irony of muscular Christianity is that it elevated sport more than the Gospels'. There were also staunch criticisms from a number of leading professors within American academia, especially before 1880. A major reason for this was the American Civil War. Soldiers hardly needed to prove their manliness on a playing field after dem-onstrating it on the battlefield and thus often derided the concept of Muscular Christianity (Putney 2001).

The fruits of Muscular Christianity: socio-cultural developments in Victorian Britain

Following the rise of Chartism and Christian Socialism, and shifting theological perspectives during the mid-Victorian period, a significant number of the Protes-tant elite, especially Kingsley and Hughes, advocated the use of sports and exercise to promote the harmonious development of mind, body and spirit (Hall 1994). Mathisen (1994) identified four models of Muscular Christianity that had developed from the ideas of Hughes and Kingsley by the end of the nineteenth century. These are the classical model, the evangelical model, the YMCA model and the Olympic model.[6] The promulgation of sport and physical pursuits in English public schools such as Rugby, Eton and Uppingham was arguably the most significant socio-cultural development to evolve from 'classical' Muscular Christianity.

During the late 1850s, the tenets of Muscular Christianity became an integral part of the public school educational system. The primary reason was to encourage Christian morality and help develop the character of the future captains of industry and political leaders, and in turn strengthen the British Empire (Wilkinson 1964). Edward Thring (1821–1887), headmaster of Uppingham between 1853 and 1857, sums this up when he states, 'the whole efforts of a school ought to be directed to making boys manly, earnest and true' (Rawnsley 1889, 12). The main impetus for the integration of the Muscular Christian ethic into public schools was Thomas Hughes' book[7] *Tom Brown's Schooldays* (1857), a story of a boy whose character was shaped playing sport at Rugby School. Hughes had been heavily influenced by the Revd Dr Thomas Arnold, his headmaster at Rugby during the 1830s, who instilled in him 'a strong religious faith and loyalty to Christ' (Brown 1880: x). Although it is Arnold that is most frequently cited in the literature as the driving force behind sports in public schools, it was the Revd George Cotton who had masterminded the sports programme at Rugby School under Arnold. Cotton was perhaps the prototype of what Mangan (1982, 23) called 'a novel kind of school master – the athletic pedagogue'.

The Muscular Christianity movement within public schools relied heavily upon the notion of Kingsleyan manliness. The sport of rugby was particularly popular as it gave plenty of opportunity to 'take hard knocks without malice',[8] a desirable trait in possible future leaders of industry and the military. Rugby, Dobbs suggests, was almost the perfect game for the promotion of Muscular Christianity and if it had not already existed leaders of the movement would have invented it:

> If the Muscular Christians and their disciples in the public schools, given sufficient wit, had been asked to invent a game that exhausted boys before they could fall victims to vice and idleness, which at the same time instilled the manly virtues of absorbing and inflicting pain in about equal proportions, which elevated the team above the individual, which bred courage, loyalty and discipline, which as yet had no taint of professionalism and which, as an added bonus, occupied 30 boys at a time instead of a mere twenty-two, it is probably something like rugby that they would have devised.
>
> (Dobbs 1973, 89)

Dobbs' reference to rugby as an activity that would distract boys from vice and idleness was closely associated to the two unmentionables of the Victorian period, masturbation and homosexuality (Dobre-Laza 2003). It was hoped that 'games

and religious worship [would] offer the Muscular Christian substitute gratifica-
tions for sexual desire' which might otherwise be expressed in the perceived vice
of masturbation (Harrington 1971, 50). Homosexuality was also a major concern
of public school masters. Holt (1990, 90) has commented that 'at precisely the
moment when the new norms of maleness were coming into force, the incarnation
of the opposite of "manliness" was defined in the form of homosexuality, which for
the first time was generally designated a crime in 1885'. Thus, Kingsleyan masculinity acted as the antithesis of homosexuality and aesthetics during the Victorian
age (Dobre-Laza 2003).[9]

A number of modern sports historians are sceptical about the motivations behind the original Muscular Christians and the implementation of these ideas in
nineteenth-century public schools. Baker (2000) for example, argues that the ideologies behind the promotion of sport in Victorian schools were primarily related
to class, the Protestant work ethic and the idea of manliness that was peddled
as an antidote to the feminisation of the church. As Grace has argued, Baker
presents a purely functionalist thesis, which has some merit but is a rather narrow
and simplistic analysis of a movement that has offered much to our understanding
of sport and Christian values. In summary, the birth of Muscular Christianity in
nineteenth-century public schools has been one of the most significant factors in
the development of sport and physical training in our modern educational systems
(Mechikoff and Estes 2002).

A form of Muscular Christianity was also adopted as an evangelical tool by
a number of individuals and groups during the Victorian period. C.T. Studd
(1860–1931), a world-renowned cricketer and leader of the so-called Cambridge
Seven, and the American Presbyterian clergyman and evangelist Dwight L.
Moody (1837–1899), both recognised the compatibility of sport and Christianity. However, their philosophy was not directly in line with 'classical' Kingsleyan
Muscular Christianity, which was largely a liberal and high church phenomenon.
As evangelicals, they emphasised that sport, although a valid recreational activity,
was unimportant compared to gospel ministry. The story of the Scotsman Eric Lid-
dell, Olympic athlete, international rugby player and Christian missionary in the
early 1920s, powerfully depicted in the Academy award-winning film *Chariots of
Fire* (1981), closely resonates with the type of Muscular Christianity advocated by
Studd and Moody. Liddell's decision not to race on a Sunday, due to his Christian
faith (Exodus 20:8), so missing the 100 metres final of the 1924 Olympics, and
his decision to give up a distinguished athletics career to become a missionary in
China (Liddell 1985), demonstrate many of the virtues of the Muscular Christian
ethic. Vance highlights that Liddell was a popular speaker at evangelical rallies
and in universities where students were keen to listen to the testimony and ideas
of the 'flying Scotsman'. Additionally, he points out that that Liddell has 'carried
the neo-evangelical version of what was essentially Victorian Christian manliness
into the middle of the twentieth century' (Vance 1985, 172), which has undoubtedly had some influence on modern understandings of Sports Ministry.

The legacy of Muscular Christianity in the modern world

Many Catholic colleges and universities, such as the University of Notre Dame in America, have emphasised the importance of a holistic education that includes sport and athletic activities. Notably, Lawrence Dallaglio, the English rugby union captain who is often venerated for his leadership qualities and who many would argue epitomises 'manliness', is a former pupil of Ampleforth College, an English Catholic boarding school.[10] Following the tradition of the nineteenth-century public schools, the college is renowned for its sporting prowess, especially its 12 rugby teams (Ampleforth College 2004). Their mission statement is imbued with the ideals of Victorian Muscular Christianity:

> To share with parents in the spiritual, moral and intellectual formation of their children . . . to work for excellence in all our endeavours, academic, sporting and cultural . . . to help Ampleforth boys and girls grow up mature and honourable, inspired by high ideals and capable of leadership, so that they may serve others generously.

In a similar vein, the University of Notre Dame and Neumann College formed a Sports Ministry Partnership 'with the goal of bringing a faith-based approach to Catholic youth sports programs in parishes across the country . . . a renewal of Catholic youth sport organisations . . . in the 1920s and 1930s' (Mendelson Center and Neumann College 2003). A key part of this venture has been the establishment of the Center for Sport, Spirituality and Character Development at Neumann College[11] and the Mendelson Center for Sports, Character and Community at the Notre Dame campus, which offers taught modules. Similarly, the British Protestant evangelical organisation Christians in Sport (CIS)[12] has recently established a one-year course at All Nations Christian College, called Sports and Intercultural Leadership Studies, which is validated by the Open University as a Certificate of Higher Education. Modules offered on the course are Theology of Sport, Sports Mission and Sports Leadership. Graham Daniels, General Director of CIS, suggests the course will allow graduates to view the world of sport as a mission field. With around 25 million people participating in sport in England during April 2003, Daniels sees it as imperative not to 'take Christians out of this mission field!' (Saunders 2003, 7).

As sport is a major socialising agent in the Western world, evangelical groups such as CIS have been quick to pick up the mantle of the original Muscular Christians. Many Protestant evangelical organisations have been founded in America. The Fellowship of Christian Athletes (FCA), Athletes in Action (AIA) and Pro Athletes Outreach (PAO) are three of the largest, and are active in nearly all intercollegiate athletic programmes (Crepeau 2001) – an approach wholeheartedly sponsored by the famed evangelist Billy Graham. Graham's regular use of famous sportspeople in his crusades became a significant mode of evangelical Muscular Christianity from the 1940s until the 1990s (Ladd and Mathisen 1999). Organisations such as the CIS, FCA and others are active worldwide, sending 'Sports

Ministers' to third world countries such as Africa, Latin America and south-east Asia to deliver the gospel message while providing fun and healthy activities.

In Britain, the triple jumper Jonathan Edwards is perhaps the most well-known Christian sportsperson and has often been portrayed as a modern-day Eric Liddell (Folley 2001). As the British trials for the 1988 Seoul Olympics were on a Sunday, Edwards bravely decided to follow in the footsteps of Liddell and not compete. The media created a furore, much to Edwards' surprise, but some writers clearly saw virtue in Edwards' actions:

> A religious athlete is a contradiction in terms in our psyched up, hyped up, drugged up days of sport. Eric Liddell, of *Chariots of Fire*, was already an anachronism when he refused to compete on a Sunday in the Paris Olympic games. But that was 1924 when there were still a few Christians left in Britain. They have become an endangered species who surprise the rest of us with their eccentric belief in God and the soul and other such things you can't buy with a credit card. Jonathan Edwards might as well be a time traveller, hundreds of years old, who's come along in his personal Tardis to shake things up a bit.
>
> (Rafferty, quoted in Folley 2001, 56–57)

Edwards clearly saw his Christian beliefs as more important than sport and money. He admitted at the time that his decision had not been directly influenced by the story of Liddell and that he was flattered at the comparisons that had been made to the great Scot. He had much respect for Liddell, 'an exceptional man . . . who won Olympic gold, but we remember him as a man of faith . . . He committed himself to serve God and, though he could have used success by staying in Scotland and sharing the gospel, he bravely went as a missionary to China' (Folley 2001, 61). Nevertheless, in time Edwards had a change of heart and decided to compete on what he had previously viewed as the one true holy day in the week. Using Romans 14:15, which states that 'one man considers one day more sacred than the other; another man considers every day alike', he argued that modern-day Christians are not under any requirement to observe the Old Testament law of the Sabbath (Exodus 20:8). This decision provoked a mixed response from family, friends, media and the sporting world.

Through the example of his life in sport and beyond, Edwards and other Christian athletes provide a welcome response to the 'egotism, cynicism, nihilism . . . obsessive focus on money, and win at all costs mentality' (Spencer 2000, 143)[13] that is so pervasive in modern sport. Paradoxically, past scandals surrounding athletes at Texas's explicitly Christian Baylor University, 'who have been pursuing a very public quest to become America's Protestant Notre Dame' (Armstrong 2003, 1), emphasise the disparity between the Muscular Christian ideal and today's dominant sports ethic, especially in America. Revelations of under-the-table scholarships and drug use have caused much embarrassment. In America it is commonplace for 'coaches and players to make the sign of the cross and spew references to their faiths during post-game jubilation . . . and from their celebrity pulpits . . . encourage their followers to subscribe to their faiths' (Elliott 2004, 1–2).

However, it is legitimate to ask how much of this outward witness is demonstrated in athletes' personal lives. Although a high percentage of Americans assert a belief in God, this is not reflected in 'ethical conduct inasmuch as many sense that the nation is in moral discord' (Spencer 2000, 145). Writing in *Christianity Today*, Armstrong suggests a need for a twenty-first-century Thomas Arnold to resurrect the genuine Muscular Christian message in American sport and education:

> the darker side of the 'athletic ethic' [in America] . . . has little to do with an excess of evangelistic zeal, and everything to do with the usual muck of life in a country too rich and self-indulgent for its own good. Perhaps the memory of the original ideals will spark some modern reformer to usher school athletics, as a prodigal son, back to the father.
>
> (Armstrong 2003, 4)

In the hope of fulfilling this ideal, neo-Muscular Christian organisations in Britain and America still endorse some dimensions of the Victorian Muscular Christian ethic, such as manliness, morality and health, perhaps at times with a little too much 'evangelistic zeal' (especially American models). On this theme, Professor James Mathisen (2002, 15), in his commendable attempt to provide a biblical foundation for sport and Sports Ministry, has raised some concerns about what he sees as a 'hermeneutical disaster' in the absence of a clear theology of sport:

> Well-meaning muscular Christian speakers who are more familiar with the rhetoric of Sports World than with the New Testament text, but who care passionately about evangelism, often take unwise hermeneutical liberties in seeking to make connections among these three elements – the text of New Testament, the rhetoric of Sports World, and the task of evangelism.

Primarily, Mathisen is referring to the liberal use of mainly Pauline athletic metaphors[14] that are often used in the mission statements and training resources of sporting evangelical organisations, at times it seems with limited exegesis.[15] I agree with Mathisen (2002) that conservative evangelicals' (whatever that means!) 'high view' of scripture frequently results in a high degree of knowledge but with limited textual interpretation and, may I add, a lack of openness to the creative, aesthetic and mythical dimensions of faith and sport. But I am convinced that there is much good done by sport ministers, especially if they do not fall into the trap of 'crass hard-nosed evangelism' and a utilitarian and 'works'-based approach to sport, i.e. that of not *valuing* sport itself but *using* it to win converts. While urging modern Sports Ministry organisations to be open to critical scholarship and to 're-evaluate past models' (Mathisen 2005a), scholars should also be very careful not to disparage or alienate those working 'in the field'[16] but rather, offer encouragement and support through collaborative projects, sound biblical exegesis[17] and systematic theological study of their work.

In developing the beginnings of a biblical theology of sport beyond what I would argue is an appropriate and valuable critique of modern sport ministry, Mathisen (2002) has argued that modern Muscular Christian movements have five essential elements,[18] which have become a 'folk theology'. Perhaps the most important to consider is *pragmatic utility*: the worth of sport is essentially determined by its utilitarian effectiveness as a means of conversion. The American Muscular Christian model, in comparison to its origins in Victorian Britain and modern British Sports Ministry, is arguably far more 'evangelical', that is, more utilitarian and extrinsic in its attitude toward sport, which is of course rooted in the Protestant work ethic that has shaped all American institutions, especially religion (Overman 1997). The fact that the 'evangelical Protestants in the 1940–50s initially had little interest in sports and athletics per se, until they realised the power of sport to attract an audience of potential converts to the faith', further supports this notion (Mathisen 2002, 10). This has also long been a bugbear of Professor Shirl Hoffman (manuscript in preparation), who suggests:

> the evangelical community prefers to think of sport in concrete terms of muscular activity, perspiration, momentary escape, and as a method for achieving more respectable ends than in the more abstract terms of meanings, symbolism, and ritual . . . evangelicals [need to be] more open to symbolism and mystery, unfamiliar territory for people who like their worship literal, concrete, down to earth. Making sport a part of the expression of Christian faith means ridding evangelicalism of the "winning a championship for Christ syndrome,"[19] substituting an excellence of doing with an excellence of being and approaching sport with an eye toward what Rahner[20] called the Spiritual essence of play.

Supporting Hoffman's concerns, Wenzel and Allison (1998) acknowledge that evangelicals in sport have a tendency of to be so ' "heavenly-minded" that they neglect or even disparage the body [and thus often sport itself as intrinsically valuable activity]' and 'both extremes are to be avoided'. Clearly, this propensity to 'dichotomise' seems to be deeply embedded in the American evangelical mind. There are of course complex historical and cultural reasons for this that go beyond the fact that all American institutions are founded on the Protestant work ethic (Overman 1997), not least the church's general drift away from its Hebraic roots and in turn a *holistic* understanding of human beings and life, including participation in sport and exercise. As the Hebrew scholar Professor Marvin Wilson (1989, 131) suggests, 'the American Church has struggled vainly to support itself by a variety of artificial roots. Consequently, its growth has been stunted, its fruitfulness impaired', mainly because it has been 'severed from its biblical Hebraic roots'.

The widespread influence of the dualistic Greek philosophy of Plato[21] on Christian doctrine in the early centuries of the church, especially in the writings of the church father Origen (182–c. 251), is the principal reason for this, argues Wilson (1989). Platonism advocates that there are two distinct realms, the visible material world and the invisible spiritual world, which results in the material world, including the body, being viewed as inferior. In correction of this, Wilson (1989) comments on the Jewish and Pauline understanding of life and the sacredness of the body that he wholeheartedly supports in the realms of sport and exercise:[22]

> To the Hebrew mind everything is theological. That is, the Hebrews make no distinction between the sacred and secular areas of life. They see all of life as a unity. It is all God's domain . . . The Psalmist states clearly this aspect of Hebrew thought: "I have set the Lord always before me" (Ps. 16: 8). It is also taught in the Proverb, "In all your ways acknowledge him, and he will make your paths straight" (Prov. 3: 6) . . . As King and Creator of the universe, God's presence is acknowledged at all times and in every sphere of activity in the world [1 Corinthians 10:31, 3:17; 1 Peter 4:11] . . . In Hebrew thought, a person is a soul-body. He is viewed as a unity, a single entity, an indivisible whole . . . "soul" or "spirit" refers to the whole person or individual as a living being . . . Often Christians become too focussed on enjoying the never-ending pleasures of the spiritual world to come, they also minimize the importance of the present, short-lived opportunity to glorify God in their bodies right now (1 Cor. 6: 20) . . . One's body (i.e., entire being) is to be offered daily in joyful obedience as a "living sacrifice" (Rom. 12: 1). On the one hand, pleasure and satisfaction are not ends to be pursued in themselves; on the other hand, enjoyment of the material and physical aspects of this life is far more than mere preparation for higher things. To enjoy is an opportunity to bring blessing to one's Creator, "So whether you eat drink or whatever you do, do it all for the glory of God" (1 Cor. 10:31).[23]

'There are no ordinary acts', C.S. Lewis was fond of reminding his students at Oxford (Yancey 2003), when trying to illustrate the sacredness of every dimension of life, including sports. In what has been described by many as Lewis's most celebrated essay, 'The Weight of Glory', he clearly illuminates that 'the body was made for the Lord' (2001/1949, 45) and that we should delight in the physical pleasures, *as well as* seek His face through the inner spiritual journey, the path of childlike humility: 'To Please God . . . to be loved by God, not merely pitied, but delighted in as an artist delights in his work or a father a son – it seems impossible, a weight of burden of glory which our thoughts can hardly sustain' (2001/1949, 39). 'But so it is', Lewis tells us. Can evangelicals, can *any* of us, really *believe* it in our daily lives, in the beauty and creativity of athletic performance, as has been the case with dance for thousands of years (Savage 2000)?[24] To be sure, it just 'seems impossible', perhaps a little too romantic for some in a 'win at all costs culture', but I would venture that this conception of sport and physical activity is closer to the 'biblical' truth, far more enriching and enjoyable for all involved than any striving to 'win a championship for Christ'.[25]

Concluding remarks

The principal aim of this chapter was to examine the historical and theological development of Muscular Christianity particularly in Victorian Britain and how this has impacted upon the relationship between sport and Christianity in twenty-first century Britain and America, particularly in the guise of 'Sports Ministry'. Some comparative reflections were offered between modern conceptions of American and British Sports Ministry and, although it is clear that on both sides of the Atlantic the original ideals of manliness, health and morality remain, the force of American protestant revivalism has reshaped and redirected its modern counterpart. This has resulted in a utilitarian 'work-based ethic' that seems to characterise *some* of what sporting evangelical organisations do. I would agree with Mathisen (2005a) that all those involved in neo-Muscular Christian endeavours, that is, modern Sports Ministry, need to construct and practice a theology that considers the following: doing our textual homework, bringing systematic insights to bear, practising a careful hermeneutic, and thinking and practising in less material and utilitarian terms. As Sport Ministers, and those leading them, frequently have a 'background in sport but often . . . little formal biblical or theological preparation' (Mathisen 1998, 9), addressing the points noted above would seem to be a priority. It is hoped that there could be greater collaboration between practitioners and scholars in the form of symposia and writing projects and a real openness by all involved to accept constructive critiques and develop Sports Ministry further.[26]

Some more conservative evangelicals may however be sceptical and can notoriously become 'defensive' against anything that is not in their eyes 'biblical' or 'theological', as it seems they did with sports, until they realised its potential as an evangelistic agent. Indeed, the church at large has long held a deep suspicion of the arts even though 'the arts have played a massive part in the story of Christianity' and have 'been recognised as powerful theological interpreters' (Begbie 2000: xii). For example, 'non-Christian literature and fiction' has been one of the most recent enemies of the faith according to the evangelical community, a fact which Markos (2001) argues has in part led to an inability to identify and connect with the deep spiritual needs of this age.

One of the intellectual giants of the twentieth century, Christian apologist and mythologist C.S. Lewis, certainly was not guilty of this, emphasising that 'we must not be ashamed of the mythical radiance resting on our theology' (1988/1944, 37). This was of course something that was illustrated in his magical series of tales, the Chronicles of Narnia, which allowed him to ' "smuggle" Christian principles into a post-Christian age' (Markos 2001, 10) and in turn to touch the hearts of minds of millions of children, and adults. Maybe it is time for Sports Ministry organisations, and indeed the wider American evangelical church, to more fully[27] recognise and promote the mythical, beautiful and even poetic side of faith and sports; to reconnect to the beautiful prose and poetry of the Old Testament narratives, to see them, as Wilson (1989, 131) suggests, as 'the bedrock upon which the Christian faith rests' and thus to view the body, sport and life itself through a more holistic lens.

Sports Ministry does not however take place 'on a cloud', if readers were thinking me a little over-romantic (!), and it is important to recognise that sports ministers do not typically spend their days doing exegetical analysis of Pauline passages or reciting poetry from Isaiah! 'On the ground', camps, clinics and overseas mission trips need organising, bible studies need preparing, and leaders need equipping with the knowledge and skills to effectively lead, nurture and disciple others (see Williams 2005a,b; McGown and Gin 2003; Mason 2003).[28] Nonetheless, for those involved in Sports Ministry and all Christians involved in sport, I would argue that by far the most important concern is the testimony of their *life* that includes how they *play* sport. 'Preach the gospel', said St Francis, 'and when necessary use words'.[29]

Study questions

1   In short, the Christian life is a journey of becoming more like Jesus in character and enjoying the blessings of his love (1 John 4:7–21; John 3:16, 10:10) and peace (Philippians 4:6–7) in all situations (Philippians 4:11; 1 Thessalonians 5:16). Consider some passages in the Bible that demonstrate Jesus' masculinity and courage (Matthew 21:12–13, 26:36–45), humility, love, joy and gentleness (Galatians 5:22–24; Matthew 11:29) and self-sacrifice (Philippians 2:5–8) and reflect how these qualities may be understood for yourself and others in a competitive sporting situation.

2   C.S. Lewis suggests 'that there are no ordinary acts' in life. Reflecting on Lewis's maxim, how might sport participation or spectatorship have a spiritual or religious dimension?

3   Christians believe the body is the temple of the Holy Spirit (1 Corinthians 3:16) and the Ancient Greeks advocated the role of sport in maintaining a sound mind in a sound body – *mens sana in corpore sano*. Adopting these ideas as a start point for discussion, consider the importance of personal health attainment and maintenance and the often extreme stress and/or abuse of the body in elite sport.

4   As a Christian coach, sports minister or parent, how can you most effectively nurture, teach and witness to children and youth? Consider St Francis' maxim, 'Preach the gospel and when necessary use words'.

Acknowledgements

First, I would like to thank Stuart Weir, Executive Director, Verité Sports, and Stephen Friend, Senior Lecturer in Religious Studies at York St John University, who were the co-authors of an article from which some small sections are included in this chapter. See Watson, N., Weir, S. and Friend, S. (2005) 'The development of Muscular Christianity in Victorian Britain and beyond', *Journal of Religion and Society*, vol. 7, available online. Second, I am most grateful to James Mathisen, Professor of Sociology, Wheaton College, IL, USA, for his helpful comments on my first draft.

6 Nature and transcendence

The mystical and sublime in extreme sports

Nick J. Watson

Introduction

Over the past thirty years there has been a marked increase in writings that have identified the potential of sport to act as a vehicle for experiencing the religious and mystical dimension of life. The ex-athlete and philosopher of sport Howard Slusher (1967, 127) was one of the first to suggest that 'within the movements of the athlete a wonderful mystery of life is present, a mystical experience that is too close to the religious to call it anything else'. Indeed, modern athletes often describe self-transcendent experiences using 'religious and spiritual metaphors' that *seem* to point to a supernatural origin. This is personified by the Catholic priest Thomas Ryan (1985, 115), who recounts what for him was an ecstatic 'moment of prayer' while skiing in the Canadian Rockies:

> On one occasion I took the lift up to the very peak and crossed over the top, gliding down into the back bowl. Within seconds I discovered myself completely alone in the vast expanse of space, with the jagged peaks towering above me, no other skier in sight not a sound to be heard. I stood transfixed for a while. The scriptures use the word "theophany" for such moments when the divine is experienced breaking through and transfiguring natural events with a sense of the sacred. When I finally pushed off with my poles, I did so slowly and deliberately, with a sense of one touched by the Holy and visited with awe. Even now, months later, I can recall that experience and those feelings with astonishing clarity. I have no other word for it than mystical – a level of experience I am convinced we are called. It is primarily a question of refining our inner and outer senses to the presence of the Holy, daily in our midst.

Although Father Ryan's religious vocation has undoubtedly offered the framework to contextualise and interpret his experience, there are thousands of testimonies by athletes from both 'mainstream' and so-called 'extreme sports',[1] with no religious affiliation, that have been regarded as 'mystical, occult, or religious' (see Murphy and White 1995, 4). As Higgs and Braswell (2004, 195) suggest, 'the language of athletes "in the zone" or maybe even transcending the zone is convincing and often extremely spiritual in tone, almost evangelical'.

Psychologists and sport theorists have conceptualised athletes' experiences of the mystical and 'being in the zone' as peak experiences (Maslow 1962; Ravizza 1984), states of flow (Csikszentmihalyi 1975, 1990), moments of deep play (Ackerman 1997) and, in the Eastern tradition, Zen states (Herrigel 1999/1971). These positive psychological states can be legitimately grouped together with mystical and religious experiences and broadly understood as altered states of consciousness (ASCs). The psychologists of religion Ralph Hood *et al.* (1996, 198) have defined an ASC as an 'introspective awareness of a different mode of experiencing the world'. Following this, it is clear that an ASC does not require a religious (supernatural) source and may be derived entirely from the psyche of an individual. Nevertheless, taking athletes' ASCs that are frequently rich in religious and mystical language at face value, a number of contemporary authors have made the questionable leap of suggesting that sports can provide an avenue to mystical and religious experience per se.

Although this small corpus of writings on mysticism in sport is commendable, with some interesting and insightful commentary, there is at times a lack of theological rigour and most pointedly an etymological naivety in the scholarship. Theological terms, such as the 'mystical' and the closely related concept of the 'numinous' (Otto 1968/1923), are frequently applied to sport experience with a liberality that would have no doubt alarmed their original proponents.

On this note, Higgs and Braswell (2004, 183) in their recent book, *An UnHoly Alliance: The Sacred and Modern Sports*, observe that 'the extraordinary things that occur in them [sports] in the flow of performance are admittedly "uncanny," that is, "*seeming* to have a supernatural character or origin, that is, eerie and mysterious'. While acknowledging this, the authors, and I, are deeply suspicious about the suggested supernatural root of, and validity of, so-called mystical sport experiences. As a lifelong sport participant and enthusiast, I do not in any way wish to diminish the immensely positive intrinsic worth of sporting experience. A critical analysis of the oft-cited symbiosis between sport and religious and mystical ideas is however warranted.

From the outset, it is important to recognise that mystical and numinous experiences are by nature subjective and deeply personal and thus any empirical verification of their occurrence or source is impossible. 'Your criticism is about as valid as a teetotaller who vainly tries to understand the pleasures of drunkenness without ever having tasted wine', retort the Islamic Sūfis to their critics![2] For this reason, any attempt to theorise about the validity of *others*' experiences in sport must be done so in a spirit of humility, recognising that this side of heaven 'we know in part' (1 Corinthians 1; 2; 13:12–13).[3] This should not, however, restrict us from critical scholarship, based upon a clearly defined philosophical and anthropological start point. Unfortunately, this foundation has been lacking in past work that has suffered from 'a general weakness in the quality of "conceptual tools," especially "definitions" and "distinctions"', the foundation of Higgs and Braswell's (2004, 17) polemic.

What follows is in no way an attempt at such a broad-ranging and nuanced analysis, as Higgs and Braswell (2004), who gazing through a Christian theological lens, 'took to task' a group of scholars they aptly call the 'sport apologists'. While implicitly also challenging *some* of the sport apologists' overarching assumptions, the focus of this chapter will be to examine the authenticity and validity of mystical and numinous experiences in sport, specifically extreme sport. As the extreme sports discussed are conducted in 'wilderness' settings, an additional aim is to explore the possibility of sublime experience through the nature–person interaction. Considerable past research and scholarship exists that has investigated spiritual and transcendent aspects of sport participation, using Eastern religious paradigms, especially Zen Buddhism. Conversely, very little has been written on the mystical in sport from a monotheistic[4] perspective, in particular adopting a Christian theological framework.

In the hope of adding something to this small body of writings, a mainstream Christian theological worldview[5] and anthropological understanding of human beings forms the basis for my analysis of mysticism in extreme sport. Discussion is therefore predicated on the biblical position that *all* human persons are made in the image of God – *imago Dei* (Genesis 1:27) and comprise soul, body and spirit (1 Thessalonians 5:23).[6] The following section provides the reader with some background information on the evolution of extreme sports and their defining characteristics.

Setting the scene

Although having its roots in the 1960s counter-cultural movement, during the past decade there has been an exponential increase in the popularity of what have been variously called 'extreme sports', 'lifestyle sports', 'action sports', 'adventure sports' and 'whizz sports' as an alternative to mainstream sports (Wheaton 2004). The launch of the Extreme Sports Channel, with an estimated audience of 20 million in Europe alone and the worldwide proliferation of extreme sports as mainstream 'tourist activities' (with extravagant safety regulations!), especially in New Zealand, Australia and South Africa, is evidence of this challenge to the previous dominance of 'mainstream sports'.

The global nature of this phenomenon is also demonstrated in the evolution of the X Games, birthed as a parallel event to the modern Olympic Games. In 1997 the X Games had over 500 competitors from 20 different countries (Rinehart 2000). Predictably, this new generation of sports, and in particular the term 'extreme', have been exploited by media and marketing moguls who have created a very lucrative sporting subculture. This has led to virtually any alternative sport form being falsely classified as extreme. Following Russell's (2005) noteworthy philosophical analysis of 'The Value of Dangerous Sports', the term 'extreme' will be used herein only to define sports that may lead to *serious injury or death*. In a further attempt to maintain clarity and focus, only those activities that are undertaken in wilderness environments will be addressed; specifically, big-wave surfing, mountaineering and back-country skiing and snowboarding, as the role of the natural environment in triggering mystical experiences has been shown to be an important variable.

One of the mostly commonly cited reasons for the shift towards these alternative sport forms is people's urge to escape from the increasingly materialistic, paternalistic and utilitarian Western lifestyle. Implicit in this movement is the 'anti-mainstream [sport]' impulse (Rinehart 2000). As the sport sociologist Rebecca Heino (2000, 183) states, 'the Zen of snowboarding is far removed from the competitive nature and bureaucratization of contemporary sport'.[7] This is concurrent with the wider cultural revolution that has seen a gradual shift away from organised religion towards a much more inclusive and eclectic understanding of 'spirituality' (see Tace 2004). Both leisure theorists (Heintzman 2003) and theologians have acknowledged that a distinguishing facet of many new spiritualities is the re-emergence of the relationship between religious and spiritual notions, the wilderness, and recreational activities. 'Today . . . forests, oceans, mountains . . . rivers, deserts and the wilderness are appreciated as natural cathedrals, sacred places and sanctuaries for humans to commune with the Holy', acknowledges Valerie Lesniak (2005, 12).[8]

Besides the well-documented role of the wilderness, there are a number of other distinguishing features of extreme sports. Risk-taking and thrill-seeking, a generally non-competitive ethic, periods of isolation that lead to the opportunity for contemplation, and varying degrees of suffering and discomfort have been suggested as catalysts for encountering the spiritual and mystical (Lester 1983, 2004; Murphy 1995; Price 1996). Extreme sport enthusiast and writer Rob Schultheis, after experiencing a mystical state of transcendence during a life-threatening experience alone on a mountain, believes there are clear parallels between extreme sports and Shamanistic and Zen Buddhist rituals and initiations. 'Many of the Shamanistic training rituals were really nothing more than extreme games, like mountaineering, distance running, trekking, engineered to deliberately induce the kind of power and ecstasy I had accidentally stumbled upon on Mount Neva' (1996, 50). Differentiating between 'nature mysticism' (natural) and 'theistic mysticism' (supernatural), will be a key aspect in attempting to clarify the source and authenticity of the 'power and ecstasy' experienced by Schultheis and others. The next section will explain different theories of mysticism and offer definitions of key terms and concepts offering a foundational understanding of the topic and how it may be applied to extreme sport.

Towards understanding mysticism in extreme sport

Overview

Scholars from the psychology of religion have studied and written about mysticism in a number of different contexts. Music, art, significant life events (birth and death), religious worship, mind-altering drugs, psychosis, artificial stimulation of the right temporal lobe, solitary nature situations, the practice of meditation and prayer, sex and stressful situations are some of the activities and states that have being shown to trigger mystical states. A review of the psychology of religion literature revealed only one text (Fontana 2003, 127–129) that made a passing, and uncritical, reference to sport as a potential medium for mystical experiences. This is surprising, as sport has become arguably the most popular Western cultural pastime in the twenty-first century, even surpassing other previously dominant cultural expressions such as music and art. The first task then will be to analyse the legitimacy of claims by scholars about the spiritual and mystical nature of positive psychological states often experienced in sport.

Accounts of psychological states, such as peak experiences and flow[9] in sport are often tinged with mystical or religious undertones. Hence, boundaries between the operational definitions of peak experiences and flow and theological concepts, such as the mystical and numinous, are easily confused. Maslow's (1968) 19-point characterisation of peak experiences, for example, contains a number of dimensions that clearly allude to religious and mystical concepts, such as awe and reverence, feeling godlike and ego-transcendence.[10] In relation to the experience of flow-states, Csikszentmihalyi (1990) does not attempt to *equate* flow experience with mysticism or the Holy Spirit. Others, however, have done so liberally, but with little accurate theological exposition or reference to primary sources. Although beyond the limits of this chapter, there is arguably a historical connection between 'flow' and the 'Holy Spirit', but only at a conceptual and, in part, experiential level.[11] The important distinction to make is that flow in sports can be more closely aligned, on an ontological level, to the experience of 'nature mysticism' that emerges from the psyche. This theme is central to my thesis and will be examined in more depth. First, however, some key definitions and explanation of concepts are required and a brief historical background to the study of mysticism.

Mysticism is to some degree inseparable from the related concepts of religion and spirituality and the fact that the terms are often used interchangeably further clouds conceptual boundaries between them. Religion has been defined as 'a system of beliefs in divine or superhuman power, and practices of worship or other rituals directed toward such a power' (Argyle and Beit-Hallahmi 1975, 1). Examples are Christianity, Judaism, Islam and Buddhism. Spirituality is a term that Spilka (1993, 1) suggests is a 'fuzzy' concept that *now* 'embraces obscurity with passion'. It can be defined from a religious or humanist perspective, in which personal meaning is derived from *whatever people deem to be ultimate*, and valued in and of itself. This has led to a widespread 'semantic abuse' (Higgs and Braswell 2004, 185), in the world at large and modern sport, with very questionable parallels being drawn between popular terms such as 'sporting spirit' and 'team spirit' and the biblical understanding of the Holy Spirit, Christian spirituality and mysticism.[12]

Mysticism is not to be regarded as a religion itself, but the highest expression of all true religions and a means of *directly experiencing* the supernatural.[13] 'The immediate feeling of the unity of self with God . . . in which the self and the world are alike forgotten, the subject knows himself to be in the possession of the highest and fullest truth' (Woods 1980, 20) is one among 25 definitions that have been proffered down the ages.[14] Any worthwhile discussion of mysticism must then begin with clear definitions of terms and concepts. Historically, the tradition of Eastern mysticism is much better established than that of Christianity (Stace 1960), thus I in no way wish to belittle the enormous contribution of this rich school of thought.

Theologians suggest that all authentic Christian mysticism flows from 'Jesus Christ as the mediator, the God-man as we call him, the person in whom the incomprehensible Deity is communicated to us; translated so to speak, into a form accessible to our minds' (Macquarrie 2004, 243). Following Jesus' ascension to the Father on the day of Pentecost (Acts 1:1–11), it is of course the 'spirit of Jesus' or the 'Holy Spirit' that is the *relational source* of any mystical encounter in the soul of the believer (1 John 4:12–16). The theologian John Macquarrie has suggested ten characteristics of Christian mystical experience, which include a direct relation to God, enhanced self-knowledge through cognitive elements of the encounter, a sense of awe, states of ecstasy or rapture and, perhaps most characteristic, and important here, a feeling of unity with God.[15] For the Spanish mystic St John of the Cross (1542–1591), this 'state of divine union consists in the total transformation of the will into the will of God' (1922, 2).

Accordingly, the Christian tradition has always taught that the only way to authenticate mystics' claims is through inner transformation and the fruit shown in their lives (Galatians 5:22–26). The Christian mystic, the German Dominican Meister Eckhart (1260–1327), stresses this point in stating 'those who are out for "feelings" or for "great experiences" and only wish to have the pleasant side: that is self-will and nothing else' and 'what a man takes in contemplation he must pour out in love'.[16] Do so-called mystical athletes undergo anything remotely resembling 'the soul's purification from vices' that has been the benchmark of Christian mysticism for the past two millennia? Do extreme athletes come away from these experiences with a conviction of the consequences of the encounter and 'a new commitment to humility', the essence of Christian discipleship?[17] I strongly suspect not. More likely, as Professor McGinn indicates in the introduction to his encyclopaedic commentary on mysticism, 'in common parlance, the word is often taken to refer to anything that is strange or mysterious' (2005, 19), including it seems, 'uncanny' and 'meta-normal' sport experiences (Murphy and White 1995).

This eclecticism in the sports mysticism literature generally stems from a pluralistic understanding of mysticism. For example, William James's and Abraham Maslow's psychological theories of religion and mysticism and the psychical research of Fredrick Meyers provide the bedrock of much of Murphy and White's (1995) work. Because mysticism is a form of spirituality 'ideally suited to the postmodern age: experiential, individualistic and progressive' (Barnes 2003, 278), it is not difficult to see why some authors have tried to 'mystify', even 'deify', sport experience. One aspect of this has been a resurgence of interest in Jamesian thought in both academic and popular writings.

William James (1842–1910), in his classic *The Varieties of Religious Experience* (1902), was the first to seriously examine the phenomenology of religious and mystical experience and to consistently use the term 'mystical' in modern psychology. Often overlooked though is that this theme was implicit in the liberal Protestant theology of Fredrich Schleiermacher (1768–1834). Having been heavily influenced by German romanticism, Schleiermacher constructed an experience-based theology that had 'all the ingredients of the theory of a mystical core of religion in its primary sense' (Jantzen 1990, 60). In his magnum opus *The Christian Faith* (1928/1830), Schleiermacher contends that religion is not to be found in doctrines, moral codes or institutions, but in humans' immediate 'feeling of absolute dependence' on God. Following this in part, James (1902, 401) advocated that 'personal religious experience has its root and centre in mystical states of consciousness'.

Through his research, which is often cited by those advocating sports mysticism, James identified four defining factors of mystical experience: *Ineffability* – the experience is inexpressible, and it cannot be transferred to others; *Noetic Quality* – the experience offers insight or knowledge beyond the intellect; *Transiency* – mystical states cannot be sustained for long; and *Passivity* – a sense of being acted upon by an outside force (1902, 402–404). Talk of an *outside force* and absence of reference to a transcendent object (i.e. God) indicates that James clearly could not swallow the core message of Schleiermacher's theology, however liberal his interpretation of the Christian story. His definition of religious experience as 'the feelings, acts and experiences of individual men in their solitude, so far as they apprehend themselves to stand in relation to *whatever they may consider divine*' (James 1902, 53, emphasis mine), clearly reflects his lack of sympathy for monotheism.[18] Despite this, James's classic work has been foundational to the phenomenological study of mysticism, in both Western and Eastern religious traditions. Further clarification of a yawning abyss that exists between the experiences of religious pilgrims and modern sporting mystics can be found in Rudolf Otto's (1869–1937) landmark work on religious experience, *The Idea of the Holy* (1968/1923).

Otto's phenomenological analysis of religious experience, in which he coined the term 'the numinous', describes the primal form of religious experience which is characterised by non-rational and ineffable feelings of 'awe', 'mystery' and 'fear'. Numerous scholars have drawn comparisons between the 'numinous' experience and the 'mystical' experience, and have noted that they are two poles of religious experience that are ultimately united (Spilka *et al.*, 2003). There are conceptual differences, however. The numinous is based upon an awareness of the 'holy other' *beyond nature* that the subject feels in communion with, whereas mystical experiences tend to engender a sense of unity or oneness with God, and/or with self, objects in the environment and/or the world.

The word 'numinous' is a derivative of the Latin term *numen*, describing the power within the sacred and transcendent object (God, Allah or Yahweh) that evokes the response from the subject. The transcendent object is what Hood (1995) calls the 'foundational reality' of a faith tradition. Often overlooked is that Otto recognised the holy as both a *rational* and a *non-rational* (not irrational) aspect of human nature, but clearly sees the numinous as the 'innermost essence of religion'. He richly described the complete experience of a human–divine encounter as the *mysterium tremendum et fascinas* (the awe-inspiring and fascinating mystery), drawing on powerful extracts from the Old Testament (e.g. Genesis 18:27; Exodus 23:27; Job 9:34, 13:21), to illustrate the fear and 'ontological nothingness' that is felt when confronted by the transcendent God – *the numinous object*. This fear is *not* solely negative, as the well-known proverb (Proverbs 9:10) tells us: 'The fear of the Lord is the beginning of wisdom'. 'Awe' is perhaps a better word to express this Godly fear, a 'realisation of one's own littleness and apparent insignificance in the face of that which is truly great' (Maquarrie 2004, 242). Jonathan Edwards (1703–1758), the American theologian and revivalist leader of the 'Great Awakening', describes such an experience (Simpson 1970):[19]

> The person of Christ appeared ineffably excellent . . . which kept me the greater part of the time in a flood of tears, and weeping aloud. I felt an ardency of soul to be what I know not otherwise how to express, emptied and annihilated; to lie in the dust, and to be full of Christ alone: to love him with a holy and pure love . . . to serve him and follow him; to be perfectly sanctified and made pure.

Reflecting on Edwards' vivid encounter with the holy, biblical revelation and the abundance of ancient and modern mystical writings, it is legitimate to ask whether the scores of anecdotal accounts from athletes reported as having a 'numinous dimension' bear any resemblance, if any, to Otto's monotheistic model? After selectively presenting elements of Otto's thesis, Murphy and White (1995, 29; emphasis mine) state that:

> The athlete knows that being in perfect control of the football, or the puck, or the bat may be a matter more of grace than of will, and that one can only "do it" by letting it happen, *by letting something else take over*. And it is the awareness and the closeness to that "*something else*" that can lead to terror.

Similarly, Tom Faulkner (2001, 186), professor of comparative religion, seems to teach his students that in attending an ice hockey match they can experience 'fandom as a way of being religious' and even encounter the *mysterium tremendum*. Presumably because of the 'fear and terror' that may ensue in the combative sport of ice hockey? In his chapter 'Training into Transcendence', the Buddhist scholar Charles Prebish (1993, 223) in a similar fashion suggests that 'in the religious breakthrough in running, in which ultimate reality is truly manifest, *time is transcended altogether*. By that I mean to say that time has no function whatsoever for the duration of the apprehension of what Rudolph Otto has called the "wholly other".' I find it baffling after reading Otto and the Old Testament narratives of Abraham, Moses and Job that he points to how these authors find these parallels. I would agree with Professor Maquarrie (2004, 243), who remarks that for 'over-enthusiastic believers in the spiritual marriage, Otto's stress on the *tremendum* is a justifiable corrective'. The experiences of athletes and fans therefore, although highly valuable in themselves, when accurately interpreted are *far from* an experience of Otto's 'wholly other' transcendent object (God, Allah or Yahweh).

Building on the work of Schleiermacher, James and Otto, a number of twentieth-century thinkers such as Huxley (1954), Stace (1960), Zaehner (1961) and Underhill (1955/1911) have provided reflection on mystical experience across the world's religions. Predictably numerous models for mysticism have been developed. The typology of Professor Richard Zaehner is useful here, enabling some clarity in the distinction between natural and supernatural mystical experience in sport.

Nature mysticism and supernatural mysticism in extreme sport

In his well-respected study, Zaehner (1961) notes that only theistic-based mysticisms are recognised as including union or oneness with a monotheistic God (as with Otto's numinous). Monistic mysticisms are those that involve feelings of union or oneness with 'self', objects in the experients' perceptual field (e.g. in extreme sport, with the mountains or the ocean) and/or with God.[20] For example, nine rock climbers in Csikszentmihalyi's seminal study of flow categorised their experiences as a state of deep flow, describing them as 'transcendent, religious, visionary, or ecstatic' (1975, 88). One participant reported, 'you don't feel like you're doing something as a conscious being; you're adapting to the rock and becoming part of it' (1975, 86). Another experienced 'the Zen feeling, like meditation or concentration. One thing you're after is the one-pointedness of mind . . . somehow the right thing is done without ever thinking about it' (1975, 87).

Similarly, in other extreme sports such as big-wave surfing, participants often attest to their 'communion with nature' during participation, reporting feelings of 'oneness with the environment' and 'loss of self in the activity'. Often, this is experienced through the 'Holy Grail of surfing', that is, the surfer getting 'barrelled' inside a cylindrical shaped wave. For example, one 'soul surfer' contends that 'man and board are as centaur riding the waves, so that for a short spell they are indistinguishable, and all three unite with that sense of oneness and identification' and that it is a 'complete integration of man's natural body and spirit with the violent forces of nature in the most total and satisfying way possible' (Muirhead 1962, 52). Surfers often use this type of flowery language to capture the beauty of the activity (Farmer 1992), which can be traced back to the anti-establishment counter-culture of 'soul surfing' in the 1960s (Booth 2004).[21] Arguably, this informal 'folk speech' that characterises the sporting subcultures of surfing, snowboarding and perhaps to a lesser degree mountaineering is one of the main reasons behind the trend of describing sport experience in a spiritual or mystical tenor (Segrave 1997). This aside, we should not discredit the idea of mystical experience (in its broadest sense) in extreme sport just yet, as 'nature mysticism exists and is widely attested is not open to serious doubt', concludes Professor Zaehner (1960, 199).

The crux of Zaehner's comparative model, which seeks to differentiate theistic and nature mysticism as clearly as is possible, is his critique of Aldous Huxley's famous book *The Doors of Perception* (1954). Huxley, a novelist and social critic, had in his later years personally experimented with the hallucinogenic drug mescaline, a clinical drug used to evoke a state similar to schizophrenia, or more accurately the manic state of manic-depressive psychosis. Huxley's superficial interpretation, that his ecstatic experiences were equatable with those of religious mystics of all religions, was the chief reason for Zaehner's embarking on his comparative study of mysticism. Unfortunately, like others who have stepped outside their field of expertise – William James and Freud are noteworthy examples – Huxley's arguments were ironically utilised by Zaehner to buttress his argument for theistic mysticism. Arguing that nature mysticism is merely an 'expansion of the personality', Zaehner concludes that:

> By making the confusion one is forced into the position that God is simply another term for Nature; and it is an observable fact that in Nature there is neither morality nor charity nor even common decency. God then is reduced in sum-total of natural impulses on which the terms of 'good' and 'evil' have no meaning. Such a god is sub-human, a god for animals, not for rational creatures; and to experience such a god has rightly been termed 'downward transcendence' by Mr. Huxley.
>
> (1961, 200)

Taking into consideration the 'moral relativism' that may ensue from Huxley's philosophical position, it is interesting to note that his ingestion of mescaline was generally 'washed down with bourbon'[22] and that he was a pioneer of recreational drug use in the 1960s. There are undoubted links here to the drug-taking that was a 'source of counter-culture enlightenment' in the 1960s surf scene, a subculture that was deeply wedded to 'philosophical environmentalism and eastern mysticism' (Booth 2004, 97). Hence, surfers' anecdotal accounts such as 'when I surf, I dance for Krishna', and 'claimed journeys to "inner truth"' often 'degenerate, on inspection, into puddles of vomit' (Caute 1988, 40). Warning that 'though sports and play may provide aesthetic pleasure, natural delight, and rest for the mind and soul, they are not inherently divine and should be watched over very carefully lest they show signs of corruption', Higgs (1992, 101) would then seem to have a valid point.

I would like to venture the thesis that these seemingly very positive experiences in extreme sport are more likely a form of 'nature mysticism', or what Zaehner (1961) termed 'pan-en-hen-ism',[23] i.e. they occur in the psyche of the athlete and are more accurately understood as flow-states, peak experiences or Zen states. He defines such mind-states as 'a unifying experience in which the sense of individuality is lost and merged in a blissful sense of unity of all nature' (1961, 180). In this vein, Prebish's (1993, 69) observation that 'very often the mystical [in sport] is described in terms consistent with Asian religion', as are modern renderings of the peak experience in sport, brings to the fore one of the key aspects of my argument, the doctrine of 'pantheism' – a belief that, as Maquarrie (2004) notes, still haunts the Christian mystics' doctrine of God.

Nature mysticism is intimately linked to the theological idea of pantheism. Pantheism states that God infuses the entire universe, therefore 'all things', including humans and nature, are inseparable (as in Hinduism and Buddhism).[24] This theme is clearly evident in the results of Lester's (1983, 38) qualitative investigation of the psychological dynamics of high-altitude mountain climbing on a Mount Everest expedition. One climber said that he 'always felt a very close spiritual association with the mountains. I love to be free completely free. I firmly believe that God exists . . . as I climb I begin losing contact, in a physical sense, with the world below . . . I feel an extremely intimate oneness with the universe.' Distinguished Christian mystics, such as the German Dominican Meister Eckhart (1260–1327), advocated a creation-centred pantheistic theology, of sorts. Some twentieth-century theologies, such as that of the existentialist Paul Tillich, have also been *in part* accommodating to pantheistic ideas (Macquarrie 2004), which considering the long history of theological debate around this issue may hold *some* credence. This said, this should not lead us to make the common mistake evident in many pantheistic writings, i.e. suggesting that theism proposes God's transcendence as distance between God and the world, whereas the true meaning of transcendence is difference between God and the world (Bauckham 2003, 182). Whether legitimately so or not, however, pantheism in all its guises is widely accepted as a dissent from Christian theological orthodoxy.

The reason for this is because it eradicates the qualitative distinction between creature (human persons) and the creator (God): the creature–creator distinction that Otto and others, such as the eminent twentieth-century Protestant theologian Karl Barth (1969/1933), were keen to emphasise as fundamental in appreciating the 'Otherness' and majesty of God. Heavily influenced by Hasidic mysticism and that of Nicholas of Cusa and Jacob Böhme, the topic of his doctoral dissertation, the great Jewish philosopher Martin Buber (1952) is not convinced by Barth and others of a similar ilk.[25] He argued they had overplayed divine transcendence (a sovereign God 'out there') at the cost of divine immanence (opportunity for 'intimacy' and mystical encounter with God) in their quest to put Christ back at the centre of the theological project, following the liberal theology of the nineteenth century. Buber's moderate voice is perhaps wise in 'so difficult a field' where, Stace (1960, 7) cautions, 'we cannot expect "proofs", "disproofs", "refutations", or "certainties"'.

On this theme, Professor Ninian Smart (1978) reminds us that a natural mystical experience may also include a supernatural dimension. Indeed, many of the most notable Christian mystics, such as St Theresa of Avila, were never completely certain whether their mystical experiences originated from God or Satan (St Theresa 1930). What, then, are we to make of sporting mystics who suggest 'I sought God and found him there *easily*, there in the waves and people of surfing' (Quinn 1965, 82, emphasis mine).[26] Following Higgs and Braswell (2004, 219), I doubt that mystical experience with the 'other' 'is as uniform and handy as Prebish and other sport apologists make it appear'.

Although this is so, it is important to note that *all* persons (Genesis 2:7) have the potential of spiritual awareness as they are made in the image of God. And through active contemplation on, and interaction with, the beauties of creation everyone can undoubtedly glean something of the spiritual. Paul writes in his letter to the Romans (1:20), his most noted theological treatise, 'for since the creation of the world God's invisible qualities – his eternal power and divine nature – have been clearly seen, being understood from what has been made, so that men are without excuse'. There is something of the recognition of the 'sublime' in this verse from Paul's letter to the Romans, which is preceded of course by many poetic accounts of the majesty and mystery of creation in the Psalms and Job.

The beautiful and sublime: sporting experiences in the wilderness

In Professor Higgs' well-argued critique of 'sport *as* religion', he argues 'sports belong to the realm of the beautiful, play the natural, and religion to the sublime' (1992, 94). Although this may be so for traditional sports, the beauty and awe-inspiring characteristics of the wilderness may provide an opportunity for experiencing something of the religious sublime in extreme sports. 'Passive appreciation of natural beauty or in the active merging with the mountain through the dynamics of climbing' is how Mitchell (1983, 147) describes what he sees as the religious and sublime qualities of mountaineering. This human capacity to encounter a deeper reality through the beauty of creation is something that has long entertained philosophers and theologians.

In the twentieth century beauty in all its guises has been a major theme in the allegories and metaphors of literary giants, such as C.S Lewis and J.R.R Tolkien, and theologians and spiritual writers, such as Hans Urs von Balthasar and Thomas Merton.[27] 'Every experience of beauty points to infinity', and 'the beautiful brings with it a self-evidence that enlightens without meditation' Balthasar tells us in volume I of his magisterial work, *The Glory of the Lord*.[28] Empirical studies by psychologists of religion (Hood 1977, 1978) and data from Greeley's (1974, 141) well-known survey study, in which 45 per cent of a national sample reported the 'beauties of nature' as a trigger of mystical type experience, support these literary and theological reflections. There are then 'underground connections between the mystical and aesthetic' (Stace 1960, 81), in which one may be confronted by a mysterious 'otherness'. This provides one potential root of the sublime encounters of extreme athletes amongst mountain peaks and raging seas.

A small number of sports scholars writing on the sublime in surfing (Stranger 1999), skydiving (Ilundain 2002), mountaineering (Mitchell 1983) and single-handed sailing (Hutch 2005, 2006) have also discussed the role of fear and risk-taking. The Enlightenment philosopher Immanuel Kant (1952/1790, 110–121) seems to express something of this in his famous discourse on the sublime: 'The *astonishment* amounting almost to terror, the awe and the thrill of devout feeling, that takes hold of one when gazing upon . . . mountains ascending to heaven', can provoke a 'a state of joy'. Kant's allusion to the awe and terror evoked *by contemplation* of nature identifies what I see as a weakness in the past literature. That is, the confusion between exciting or even neurotic fear experienced by athletes taking risks of their own volition (e.g. climbing the north face of Everest) and Kantian feelings of astonishment and awe when gazing upon 'boundless oceans rising with rebellious force' or 'mountains ascending to heaven'.[29] In discussing what he calls states of 'soul-stirring delight', Kant (111–112) alludes to this difference:

> External nature is not estimated in our aesthetic judgement as sublime as far as exciting fear, but rather because it challenges our power . . . therefore nature is here called sublime merely because it raises the imagination . . . and gives us the courage to be able to measure ourselves against the seeming omnipotence of nature.

Therefore, traditionally, the sublime has been used in a religious manner to name objects that inspire awe, feelings of joy and an elevation of the soul, *not* feelings evoked through volitional risk-taking.[30] This is derived from eighteenth-century and Romantic aesthetics, primarily in the philosophy of Kant and Edmund Burke (1990/1757), although as Fludernik (2001) notes the idea can be traced back to the 'rhetorical sublime' in neo-classical poetics of the seventeenth century. Interestingly here, it was from the poetry of Alpine travellers during this period that the idea of the sublime gained access into literary theory. This is reflected in the following definition of the sublime by Fludernik (2001, 2):

> The sublime . . . is closely linked to the experience of God in nature [*not* pantheism], its main effect being an elevation of the soul (the ethical and aesthetic component) and a feeling of being overwhelmed by the majesty of divine nature (the ideological component: man is nothing in contrast to God!).

This definition is based upon the Kantian understanding of the sublime, which comprised two elements (Kant 1952/1790, 94–121).[31] First, the 'mathematical sublime' relates to the overwhelming feelings of the magnitude (size/height/depth) and mere vastness of an object or thing in nature, e.g. the size and power of large waves in surfing and sailing and the beauty and magnificence of the landscape in mountaineering. The second element of the Kantian sublime is the terror-inducing 'dynamical sublime', which has an ethical impact upon the subject who is awed by the power and immensity of the thing in relation to us, i.e. experience of fear and risk in relation to the wave, mountain or ocean. Both these dimensions of the sublime have been implicitly identified in writings and testimonies in the extreme sports literature. Although within Kant's conception of the dynamical sublime there are elements of awe and reverence, it was Edmund Burke (1990/1757, 53) who explicitly emphasised the role of fear and terror as one way of experiencing sublimity:

> The passion caused by the great and sublime in nature . . . is Astonishment; and astonishment is that state of the soul, in which all its motions are suspended, with some degree of horror. In this case the mind is so entirely filled

with its object, that it cannot entertain any other, nor by consequence reason on the object which it employs.

A big-wave surfer in the cult video *Metaphysical: Surfing on a Higher Level* (1997) encapsulates both something of the role of terror and fear in the Burkean sublime and Kant's mathematical sublime:

> When you paddle out and see a [10 meter high wave] staring you in the face, it's like 'Oh my God' . . . Being a surfer and being involved with nature all the time gives you a different understanding of where you might find God.

It is then plausible that the *combination* of the awe (dynamical sublime) and the physical features of the natural environment (mathematical sublime), which are characteristic of most extreme sports, may engender the religious sublime to some degree, i.e. an awareness of something 'wholly other' than themselves (Romans 1:20). Some readers may object to the tentative links made between biblical creation narratives and the two dimensions of the Kantian sublime. However, Kant himself, although acknowledging distinctions between the beautiful and the sublime, also recognised that 'in experience' the two are inseparable (1952/1790, 90–93).[32] Maybe one reason that athletes and recreationalists have repeatedly gone 'back to nature' during historical eras of materialism and rationalisation, such as ours, is this primal 'aching need for the infinite' (Dubay 1999), whether they are conscious of the fact or not.

My next task is to try and offer some clarity on the theory that *volitional risk-taking* can induce mystical encounters with 'ultimate reality', and how this has been confused with Kantian feelings of sublime (i.e. astonishment and awe) on contemplation of beauty and majesty of nature.

Risk-taking: a doorway to the mystical and sublime?

A number of researchers have suggested that volitional risk-taking and thrill-seeking are inherently linked to experiences of self-transcendence and the mystical in high-risk sports. 'From the vantage point of embodied consciousness, death provides us with our clearest connection with the eternal', Leonard (1974, 224) notes in his discussion of risk in sport. The majority of past literature, however, has centred on the psychology of risk in high-risk sports (sensation-seeking and personality traits) and the physiological stress response of the neuroendocrine system in high-risk sports.[33] Athletes commonly describe an 'adrenaline rush' or a 'euphoric high' (e.g. the runner's high)[34] during participation from the release of neurotransmitters, such as dopamine, endorphins and serotonin. Although these lines of enquiry are of some value, there is a danger that an athlete's experience is explained away through the identification of biochemical markers, reducing human experience to the chemicals that cause specific mood-states. This ignores the existential dimension of participation in high-risk sports, something that has sparked the interest of a small group of thinkers.

Scholars from the fields of sports philosophy (Reid 2002; Slusher 1967), n
stream philosophy (Wyschogrod 1973) and religious studies (Hutch 2005, ?
have provided excellent existential analyses of meaning and risk in sport, primarily
adopting a humanistic stance. A major theme of this work has been to highlight
how taking risks in sport, and in turn confronting our personal limitations and
sense of mortality, can often lead to self-growth and enhanced sense of being or, as
athletes often report, 'feeling fully alive'. The mountaineer Maurice Herzog (1953,
12) captures how this existential anxiety born of the risk that is often present in
extreme sports may offer a route to a state of 'self-transcendence' or 'being':

> In overstepping our limitations, in touching the extreme boundaries of man's
> world, we have come to know something of its true splendour. In my worst
> moments of anguish, I seemed to discover the deep significance of existence
> which till then I had been unaware.

Existential and humanistic psychologists, such as Erich Fromm, Rollo May, Victor Frankl and Abraham Maslow, also claim that facing one's finiteness can promote personal growth and a liberation of our creative powers. What is important
to recognise about these psychological musings on death is that they are describing
a 'symbolical transcendence of individual finiteness' (Moraglia 2004, 337), not a
literal transcendence and experience of the supernatural (as in theistic mysticism
and Otto's numinous).[35] The philosopher of sport Howard Slusher nicely summarises this in his classic work, *Man, Sport and Existence* (1967, 207), explaining
how when confronted with one's own mortality, as described by Maurice Herzog
above, one commonly experiences meaning and authenticity:[36]

> Facing death makes the man of sport available to an awareness of authentic
> existence. Performance, faced with such extreme stakes, will tend to represent
> authentic being. Putting it another way, man is rarely as moral as when he is
> facing death. Death tells man to "face up" to life. Meaning comes to the per-
> former when he becomes aware of the end. The totality is taken into account
> . . . Now he faces ultimate reality. Is Man capable of passing the test? It is *real*
> ability that counts. It is rather paradoxical that man needs to escape the 'real'
> world (which might not be so *real* after all) and enter into the artificial realm
> of sport in order to determine authentic self. He now must admit real exist-
> ence of the self, something he usually can manage to avoid. To this degree,
> the man of sport is closer to truth. He learns his potentiality. He realises what,
> perhaps, he has already and always known – namely, who he is.

It is argued that this existential 'finding self' ('who he is') and the meaning and
authenticity found through risk-taking are primarily a *humanistic* idea, which is
closely related to previous research of peak experiences and flow-states. Risk and
adversity in extreme and challenging sports, such as sky-diving (Lipscombe 1999),
high-altitude mountaineering (Della-Fave *et al.*, 2003; Lester 1983, 2004), English
Channel swimming (Hollander and Acevedo 2000) and ultra-marathon running

(Acevedo *et al.* 1992), have been suggested as catalysts for self-transcendence in the form of peak experiences and flow-states. These findings are supported by studies in the psychology of religion.

Administering the Mysticism Scale (M Scale)[37] and Subjective Stress Scale (SSC), Hood (1977) examined the impact of stressful activities, such as rock-climbing (the first time, for many students) and white-river rafting (river difficulty high), and also the experience of staying alone in the woods at night in a week-long outdoor adventure programme for adolescent males. Findings suggest that nature and the stressful activities experienced *together*, and periods of isolation and sensory deprivation (see also Hood 1978),[38] triggered various depths of mystical experience, especially states of 'unity' (oneness). It is interesting that subjects anticipating and experiencing less stress scored higher on the M Scale, as one of the key prerequisites for experiencing flow-states is task-mastery, i.e. a balance between perceived challenges/risks and skills. This again adds weight to the thesis that extreme athletes are *mostly* experiencing 'nature mystical experiences' (flow-states and peak experiences) that are accentuated by the 'adrenaline rush',[39] but which *may* also include something of the religious sublime.

I do, however, agree with past writings that suggest engaging in challenging sports can stretch us to our physical and mental limits, and may well open the door to self-actualisation, character development and *spiritual* insight, *humanistically* conceived.[40] This is further highlighted by Shvartz (1967) and Mechikoff and Estes (1998), who have acknowledged how the search for maximal physical and mental development in extreme sport can be likened to aspects of the nineteenth-century nihilistic philosophy of Friedrich Nietzsche. Nietzsche advocated living dangerously, 'saying yes to life'; testing oneself both physically and mentally, so to 'become who you are', i.e. living by the basic values of adventurousness, aggressiveness, creativity, individuality and honesty.

In a similar vein, the French existentialists Sartre (1956) and Camus (1955) believed that if we want to *live* in the face of the 'absurdity' of human existence without belief in a supernatural being, we must '*choose* an authentic life'. For Sartre, the passionate engagement and risk-taking in extreme sport would then be just another 'secular life-world/project', amongst many others (e.g. work, family, other recreational activities etc.), that provides a source of meaning and authenticity in our 'meaningless' universe.[41] A reflective surfer captures something of Sartre's notion in stating, 'I sought a *meaning for life* and found it when I ventured helplessly among the towering waves of Makaha . . . I got a brief glimpse of glory' (Quinn 1965, 82, emphasis mine).

Sartre (1956, 585) does not explicitly discuss flirtations with death in what he calls 'open-air sports', but concedes that wrestling with elemental forces, such as 'enormous masses of water, of earth, and of air', can be a vehicle to a more 'authentic' life. Building on Sartre's ideas, the philosopher Edith Wyschogrod (1973, 169, 196) has argued that:

> It is not only for the sake of this experience that one dares to die, but the risk of death itself is a component in the hedonic quality of these sports . . . the

pleasure experienced is the pleasure of freedom, of a struggle with death on man's terms rather than on the terms of destiny.

To a degree, Wyschogrod points us to what Reid (2002) and Mechikoff and Estes (1998) see as a primary reason for the ever-increasing popularity of high-risk and alternative sports, a cultural resurgence of the Socratic dictum of 'Know thyself'. This is played out in the 'testing of the athletes' personal will and limitations', what Reid calls 'pushing the envelope'. She illustrates this by citing the following quote from 'adventure racer' Jonathon Senk: 'Our society is so surgically sterile. It's almost like our socialization just desensitizes us. Every time I'm going out doing this I'm searching my soul . . . to find what your limitations are.'[42] Athletes' exploration of personal boundaries and quest for euphoric highs and ultimate meaning, however skilled they maybe, can cost dearly.

Wyschogrod and the results of recent empirical studies suggest that the experience of altered states of consciousness and the sublime in high-risk sports can lead to the subjugation of rational risk assessment.[43] 'The pleasurable loss of identity [via nature mystical experience: flow-states and peak experience], of sensed separateness from the world, sublates the sense of responsibility for one's life . . . the same force which sustains pleasure turns with alarming suddenness into a power of death and destruction', comments Wyschogrod (1973, 168). Or, as the mountain skier Hans Castrop more concisely puts it, 'the fear of death cast out by oneness' (Mann 1954, 476).

Sadly, the high-profile deaths of a number of big-wave surfers (e.g. Mark Foo) and mountaineers (e.g. Alison Hargreaves) support this notion, and point to a 'selective fatalism' (Reid 2002) that seems to be a belief of *some* in the extreme sport community. Likewise, Thomas (1996, 498) alludes to this, suggesting that often when 'injury and death are serious possibilities . . . calculations of risk are coupled with a belief in a guardian angel', for some sporting daredevils. Although beyond the scope and focus of this work, these findings raise a whole host of moral and religious dilemmas for participants (see Olivier 2006; Palmer 2004). Not least, in relation to the *level* of risk-taking that is deemed appropriate in any activity, if you believe that life and family are God-given gifts (James 1:17).

I am sympathetic with the ideas of scholars such as Slusher (1967) and Reid (2002) to a point, recognising the real worth of these sporting activities and endorsing their concerns about inappropriate paternalistic limitations (John 10:10), as have others. In his thought-provoking book, *Wild at Heart* (2001), John Eldridge persuasively argues that 'true masculinity' is a rarity in our domesticated world, especially in the church (a high percentage of extreme athletes are men). As a Christian writer, counsellor and avid outdoorsman, he maintains that many men have a 'deep spiritual longing' to experience *some* danger and wildness, which is seldom available in our paternalistic society. To be sure, Jesus and the Old Testament prophets, such as Moses, Isaiah and John the Baptist, were all 'Men' in the truest sense of the word, who sought inspiration from God in the wilderness. It is often said that the solitude and loneliness of the wilderness is 'God's university', a place of testing and preparation (e.g. Luke 4:1–13). Indeed, 'Moses does not encounter the living God at the mall' and often 'the geography around us corresponds to the geography of the heart', notes Eldridge (2001, 5).

Tentatively, I would then suggest that athletes' 'scrapes with death' and powerful 'nature mystical experiences', when mingled with aesthetic experiences of the wilderness, *may* start athletes wondering about the 'significance of existence', as the mountaineer Maurice Herzog put it.[44] Writing from a Christian standpoint, I must however depart from past authors (Slusher 1967; Reid 2002) when they talk of volitional risk-taking in itself as a potential medium for extreme athletes to experience 'ultimate reality', 'the authentic self' and 'truth'.[45]

Borrowing from the humanistic psychology of Abraham Maslow and Carl Rogers, the twentieth-century monk and spiritual writer Thomas Merton reminds us that self-actualisation for the Christian is the abandonment of the *illusion* of the 'false self', an identity based largely on 'life projects'. From a Christian perspective, Sartre's 'life projects', which include family, work, sports and any other form of recreation, are *God-given gifts* to provide meaning, enjoyment and well-being for his creatures. But, as the biblical story of Job (1:6–22) so painfully demonstrates, they do not provide 'ultimate meaning'. This is only accomplished through finding the 'real/authentic self' (Romans 8:9–17; Matthew 14:6, 16:24–26), which is inseparable from our search for the ground of our being, a Father God (Morea 1997); not through the construction of *our own* meanings and ideas of personal authenticity. As Slusher (1967, 159) himself notes, 'in a way, the sportsman is truly a representative of Nietzsche's *Superman*', the archetype of the fragmented postmodern self.[46]

This leads me to conclude that *volitional* risk-taking is independently *not* a means of encountering theistic mystical or numinous experience. Professor Shirl Hoffman (1992a, 72) also doubts whether it is the risk-taking properties of these experiences that infuse them with religious meaning for participants. He asks whether perhaps it is 'the isolated non-interactive character of these sports' that 'fosters religious experiences by providing an especially supportive spiritual ecology for contemplation'. I would agree and point to the sublime encounters, or what Merton calls moments of 'active contemplation', in the wilderness that are *like* a 'mystical experience' but on a 'natural level' (Morea 1997, 82, 87) that perhaps provides an 'intimation of God' for extreme athletes. The absence of spiritual and religious metaphors in the literature from high-risk sports that are not undertaken in wilderness environments, such as indoor extreme moto-cross, Formula One or motor racing, boxing and in-line ramp skating, perhaps goes some way to supporting this conjecture.

Concluding remarks

In holding true to my philosophical start-point, I am sure that I have perhaps at times 'infuriated some readers', as Professor Prebish (1993: xix) himself remarked about the potential response to his own chapter, 'Training for Transcendence'. However, the aim of this chapter was to examine the legitimacy of claims that athletes in extreme sports may encounter the mystical and numinous, when examined though a Christian theological lens. As to whether extreme sport experience provides access the realms of the holy that Otto, St Paul, Jonathan Edwards and St John of the Cross are referring to, my answer is an emphatic no.[47] I am also quietly confident that Judaic and Islamic scholars (e.g. Odibat 1989), representing the other monotheistic faiths, would be sympathetic to my thesis. To reiterate, however, the interpretative lenses through which we scrutinise others' experience are far from perfect (1 Corinthians 13:12–13), and I do not wish to propose a 'false dichotomy' between this world and the next.

We are *all* spiritual creatures (Genesis 2:7), made in the image of God, and therefore have 'a tendency toward mystery and the infinite' (Berdyaev 1947, 62). Mountaineers' and surfers' sublime encounters in the bosom of God's creation may then be what Professor Peter Berger (1970, 52) called 'signals of transcendence . . . within the human condition', a primal longing for something infinitely greater than self, a yearning, however, that is oft buried deep in the caverns of the mind. Although this is so, we need to steer clear from any idealistic pantheism, recognising that all Christian experience of the transcendent, is an inward spiritual experience that manifests in the depths of the soul. 'The kingdom of God is within you', Jesus told his disciples (Luke 17:21), pointing to the crucifixion, the event in which God through his sacrificial love reconciled humanity to himself. As the German theologian Jürgen Moltmann emphasised in the opening sentence of his classic work, *The Crucified God* (1974), the inner criterion of any Christian theology that 'deserves to be called Christian' is the centrality of the cross.

Thus, talk of sport offering '*redemption* as well as *rebirth* into a new type of reality, separated from ordinary reality by its sense of being permeated with *ultimacy* and *holiness*' (Prebish 1993, 70, emphasis mine) cannot be accommodated in a Christian worldview (John 3:3–8; 1 Peter 2:24). It is this type of speculation, which Prebish himself acknowledges is 'somewhat fanciful', 'anecdotal' and 'irreverent' (xix), that particularly concerns me. When scholars suggest that sports can *offer* 'redemption', 'rebirth' and *easy* access to God's throne of grace, it is at this juncture I feel they have done a grave disservice to both believer and non-believer.

Not to be misunderstood, I again wish to clearly articulate my enthusiasm for sports such as mountaineering, surfing and snowboarding. Within a balanced theology of leisure, they can be seen as forms of 'deep play', even spiritual expression in an aesthetic, creative sense that provides opportunities for meaningful, therapeutic and exhilarating activities in the wilderness. Perhaps St Irenaeus captures something of what extreme athletes experience in famously suggesting 'the glory of God is man fully alive'. The pursuit of the 'adrenaline rush' and concomitant states of flow and peak experiences must, however, be carefully weighed against the *motivations* for (often unconscious) and *level* of risk and potential losses that may ensue, none greater than the gift of life itself. I would agree with Shirl Hoffman (1992b, 158): let us not *erroneously* 'burden a fascinating human experience – made all the more fascinating for the freedom and lightness of spirit it entails – with some weighty cosmic baggage'.

The pillars of my argument and conclusions have been first biblical revelation, supported by a rich tradition of biographies and scholarly writings on the mystical, and – dare I say it? – personal experience.* This said, no amount of 'epistemological ingenuity' will reveal the incomprehensibility and deep simplicity of divine nature in subjective experience (in extreme sport), warns Professor Nicholas Lash (1988). At the same time, he does not disparage our attempts to explore religious and mystical experience, suggesting that it can 'enlarge our understanding of ourselves and the world in which we live' (1988, 234). In this spirit of scholarship and discovery it is hoped that for those, sportsmen and -women, students and scholars, wishing to delve further into this challenging and complicated field of study, the questions below may help stimulate your thinking.

Study questions

1   Some suggest that risk-taking sports, which may lead to serious injury or death, allow the athlete to live a more authentic and abundant life through facing death. What are the implications of this seemingly fatalistic outlook for those who hold religious beliefs and view life and family as gifts from God? Consider the potential impact on significant others (especially family) and mountain and sea rescue teams who often risk their lives to save others.

2   In mainstream sports the cliché is often heard (and certainly practised) that 'winning is the only thing'. Explain in a single sentence or paragraph what is the purpose and meaning of extreme sports.

3   The purpose of art, according to Joseph Conrad, is 'to make us see'. What are the purposes of mainstream sports, risk-taking sports, and private prayer and meditation with regard to art and the quest for glimpses of the 'Other'? Consider the role of the sublime in the wilderness in extreme sports.

4   Pick two mainstream sports governed by time and two risk-taking sports that are not and compare and contrast them with regard to time, setting and purpose or other areas of your own choosing.

5   From your own experience in meditation or prayer on the one hand and sports and play on the other, which way, stillness or movement, has been more effective in providing 're-creation' of the soul for you or a linkage with something Wholly Other that provides inspiration, hope, meaning?

6   Discuss the difference between developing 'intimacy' with God (the title of a book by Alex Aronis) and seeking 'ultimacy' (e.g. peak experiences) of experience through sports.

Acknowledgements

First, I would like to thank my friends and colleagues, Professor Andy Smith and Dr Mark Nesti, for supporting me and giving me free rein to explore this area of study, on a 'British Sports Science Degree'(!), which provided the impetus for writing this chapter. Second, I am most grateful to Robert (Jack) Higgs, Professor Emeritus of English Literature at East Tennessee University, and the Revd Professor John Macquarrie, formerly Lady Margaret Professor of Divinity and Canon of

Christ Church College, University of Oxford, for their challenging and helpful comments on my first draft. Third, my thanks go to the author of the Foreword of this book, Professor Shirl Hoffman, University of North Carolina at Greensboro, who has provided feedback on this and other work and encouraged me to pursue this sometimes 'isolating' area of study. Finally, I would like to thank my friend and golfing partner, James Joyce, a rock-climber and tree surgeon, who offered some 'real world' pantheistic insights!

* I am sure it struck some readers as highly unoriginal that I used the same quote to open my chapter as Shirl Hoffman (1992) in the introduction to the *Sport as Religious Experience* section, within his landmark book. This was not, however, without purpose. Although I was blissfully unaware of it at the time, the roots of this chapter were planted some eight years ago, while I was coincidentally snowboarding in the Canadian Rockies, like Father Ryan. After snowboarding alone down a virgin powder run, I clearly remember sitting at the bottom of the descent, rather like Father Ryan, 'completely alone in the vast expanse of space, with jagged peaks towering above me', still awash with feelings of joy and exhilaration and a sense of awe at my surroundings. Unlike Father Ryan, however, I had no religious framework in which to interpret my experience (I am not questioning the authenticity of Father Ryan's personal experience). As far as I can recall, I thought something like 'that was awesome', picked myself up and headed back to the chair lift hoping for another dose of the same.

Three years later, during research for my undergraduate dissertation, which explored religious and mystical experience in extreme sport, I stumbled on the mystical writings of Michael Murphy and Rhea White, George Leonard and other devotees of sports mysticism. Suffice to say my snowboarding experience in the Rockies was swiftly transformed in *my mind* into a 'divine encounter'. All I can say is that it was fortunate that my supervisor was an 'exercise physiologist', as I had become a true disciple of those I have critiqued! Rather like Professor Zaehner (1961, xiii), however, who had a 'nature mystical experience' during his undergraduate days and then later became a Christian, I came to realise that what I had experienced snowboarding in the Rockies was certainly *not* a direct revelation (i.e. ecstatic/theistic mystical experience) of a Holy God, through the Holy Spirit, but rather, in line with my original thoughts, an 'awesome experience', in which I sensed a *very real* 'expansion or transcendence of *self*', great joy and a real urge to repeat it (i.e. nature mysticism/peak experience). And I am sure I perhaps experienced something of what Kant called a 'soul-stirring delight' (the sublime) in the bosom of creation, that is, a *spiritual* intimation of the creator, as from a Christian standpoint we are all spiritual beings.

Following Professor Zaehner, I hope that those who come to the text with an 'open mind', while 'detecting my biases (for bias there is bound to be)' (xiii), may view the inclusion of my testimony as an 'authentic' contribution to the academic argument.

Section III

Existential psychology and sport

This section shows how sport psychology could begin to consider the spiritual dimensions of sport, and how research might develop with an acceptance of the idea of the person as an embodied spiritual being.

Chapter 7, on existential psychology and sport, begins with the experience of athletes, coaches and others who claim that the spiritual is an important element in their identity. It argues that we should take their experience and self-descriptions seriously and try to investigate the notion of spirituality and its place in the lives of sport performers. The existential perspective is contrasted with the dominant approaches in sport psychology and discussion is directed at how phenomenology could provide the methods to access the meaning that athletes ascribe to spiritually related terms such as responsibility, anxiety and flow.

Chapter 8 acknowledges the fact that sport psychologists have long been interested in the relationship between personality and sport performance, and enjoyment of the sporting experience. However, they have very rarely considered the concept of *person* which underlies their research. In ordinary language, 'person' is usually understood as referring to an individual made up of mind, body and spirit. This chapter examines the implications for sport psychology and the work of applied sport psychologists where there is acceptance of the idea of the person as an embodied spiritual being.

Chapter 9 further develops this focus on embodiment in relation to suffering and sacrifice. The sport experience is usually seen as something associated with fun and joy. However, it may be nearer the truth to say that it is equally about difficulties, pain and personal sacrifice. These terms can be understood from a spiritual perspective and may even be valued in themselves because of this, which is something considered in this chapter.

Acknowledgements

I would like to thank some very important people who have been a source of inspiration and support for me during the past few years. To Sam Allardyce, formerly manager of Bolton Wanderers Football Club, for encouraging me to make the idea of spirit a key part of my work as a sport psychologist at the club. To Mike Forde,

Performance Executive at BWFC, for giving me the opportunity to learn so much about the real world of professional football. My academic growth has been hugely stimulated by these two individuals from the non-academic world.

The work of the centre, this book and our university modules on sport and spirituality would have been quite impossible tasks without support from the resilient spirit of Professor Andy Smith. As my colleague and head of school in Sports Science and Psychology at York St John University, Andy provided the ideal environment to allow us to challenge the new orthodoxies and to convert our abstract ideas into something of substance.

Finally to Sarah my wife and our children, Beth, Vincent and Catherine, for providing the ballast so necessary to keep the passionate academic grounded! You have, as always, shown me that the family is the most important home to encounter daily the spiritual quality of love.

7 The spirit of sport

An existential psychology perspective

Mark Nesti

Introduction

It is important to consider how the discipline of psychology has viewed the idea of spirituality to understand why sport psychology has largely been unwilling to accept this topic as a legitimate area of study. Despite recent work arguing for greater attention to the importance of spirituality in applied work (Ravizza and Fazio 2002) and sport research (Watson and Nesti 2005), most journals and text books in sport psychology do not include anything on this subject. This is very surprising in many ways, not least because of the burgeoning interest in different forms of spirituality in contemporary society and the increase in research investigating its links to health (McCullough 1995) and medical practice (Firshein 1997). Beyond the academic community and empirical research there is an even more remarkable fact that seems to have been overlooked. A survey of the reports of sports journalists, interviews with top coaches and athletes, and the conversations of the fans would reveal that alongside reference to character, 'guts' and 'bottle', the term 'spirit' is frequently used. Often mentioned in relation to team spirit, spirited fight-backs and individual performers showing great spirit, this word is one of the most used in the world of sport. When asked to justify the limited references to the spirit in sport psychology it is common to hear the argument that concepts like confidence, self-belief and motivation fully capture this term. The general view of most within academic sport psychology is that the world outside is still reluctant to let go of their belief in empirically false and dated notions like spirit and the spiritual. Apart from the incredible arrogance that this position conveys it also suffers from one very important weakness. Some of the most famous scientists ever, such as Leonardo Da Vinci, Newton, Einstein and current world leading figures, such as the physicist Professor John Polkinghorne and Dr Peter Hodgson, fellow of the Oxford Institute of Physics, are in agreement with the sports fan, coach and performers that the spiritual dimension exists. This should be very embarrassing for academic sport psychology, particularly when the advocates of the reality of the spiritual are not just 'woolly' social scientists and those from the Arts and Humanities, but are a group of eminent natural scientists! It seems that the everyday language of the people has found some support from the work of scientists, researchers and scholars of the very highest standing. As will be discussed later in this section, this connects very closely with the idea of phenomenology which is the preferred research method in existential psychology. Phenomenology is a method that is used to access individual consciousness of an event or experience. It does this by attempting to go directly to the phenomenon as described by the participant in the research study.

Although there are competing views on notions of spirituality and how this topic can be investigated, there is little evidence that this debate has touched on the work of researchers in sport psychology. A history of the discipline arguably reveals that it eventually follows developments in psychology and other sciences and that there is much strength in this. However, there are those such as Martens (1987) and others who have proposed that sport psychology should begin to develop its own theory and approaches where these are warranted. One such area where this might be helpful could be in relation to the concept of spirit and spirituality in sport. Beyond the confines of the university, many people involved in sport, including those at the highest levels of performance and a diverse group of highly educated commentators, are clearly convinced that success in sport is given to those with appropriate physical and mental attributes combined with spirit. Indeed a current manager of a very successful football team in the English Premiership is so convinced of this that he has claimed that character and spirit are the most important qualities he looks for when buying new players (personal communication). When asked about his understanding of 'spirit', he replied that it is the relation between the mental and physical qualities of the person, and that it is not a thing as such but a process. He suggested that although it is very difficult (impossible) to measure directly, it can be seen and felt in everything someone does, and is most clearly evident in their eyes! This last observation has of course a long and distinguished history outside of psychology and sport. The expression that 'the eyes are the mirror of the soul' is arguably a more theologically derived account of a similar phenomenon. These utterances from the world of elite professional sport are unlikely to convince sport psychologists that spirit is a valid and identifiable concept. Some of the reasons for this have already been touched upon earlier. A deeper level of analysis suggests that ultimately sport psychology has not been able to accommodate terms like 'spirit', 'spirited' and 'the spiritual' because the discipline is mostly based on materialist, positivist and reductionist paradigms. The overwhelming majority of studies and scholarly publications in sport psychology draw on social learning, cognitive behavioural and trait approaches in psychology. When researchers have used psychoanalytical and humanistic psychology paradigms these have not included the work of Jung (1964) or Erikson (1964). Jungian psychoanalytical psychology built on Freud's work but, unlike the position adopted by his mentor, Jung acknowledged that human beings have spiritual needs. He argued that mankind:

> has freed himself from 'superstition' (or so he believes), and in the process he has lost his spiritual values to a positively dangerous degree. His moral and spiritual tradition has disintegrated ... As scientific understanding has grown, so our world has become dehumanised.
>
> (Jung 1964, 94)

Erikson's (1964) theory rejected Freudian dogma which asserted that religion and spiritual belief were the result of collective neurosis based on childhood fears. He viewed religious belief as evidence of a human need to find meaning in life and fulfil our capacity for the transcendental.

However, existential psychology is the clearest example of an approach that welcomes meaning, spirituality and religion as central to human *being*. In sport psychology there have been a number of researchers and writers who have drawn on existential–phenomenological psychology in their work in exercise settings (Fahlberg *et al.* 1992) sport performance (Dale 1996, 2000) and applied contexts (Nesti 2004). Watson and Nesti (2005) and Czech *et al.* (2004) have highlighted that existential psychology can be used to examine sources of personal meaning in sport. For many athletes these include religious belief and life philosophies that encompass spiritual dimensions.

Why existential psychology?

The existential psychology perspective provides a number of different conceptualisations of spirit. Some of these relate closely to religiously grounded accounts whereas others focus on more secular and postmodern notions of spirituality. However, the most clearly psychological definition is found in the theologically informed writings of Kierkegaard's (1989/1849) work *The Sickness unto Death*, which he called a 'Christian Psychology Exposition'. Kierkegaard is considered by many to be the founder of existential psychology. His work predates that of Freud and the experimental psychology research carried out by Wundt in the nineteenth century. In contrast to psychoanalysis and experimental psychology, Kierkegaard's existential approach places the notion of human spirit at the very centre of any account of our psychological life. This can be seen in the following statement that would be rejected outright by both Freud and experimental psychology albeit for quite different reasons:

> The human being is spirit. But what is spirit? Spirit is the self. But what is the self? The self is a relation which relates to itself, or that in the relation which is its relating to itself . . . . A human being is a synthesis of the infinite and the finite, of the temporal and the eternal, of freedom and necessity. In short a synthesis. A synthesis is a relation between two terms. Looked at in this way a human being is not yet a self.
>
> (Kierkegaard 1989/1849, 43)

Although the ideas and language used in this quotation may appear strange and unfamiliar to the modern reader, there are several clear points which are easy to discern. First, this approach claims that the core of who we are, our self, should be conceived in spiritual rather than psychological terms. Second, the self is dynamic and active. It is not (and never can be) a static and finished entity. This links in with more modern accounts such as Maslow's (1968) idea of striving towards self-actualisation. Finally, it seems that, despite the high profile Premiership manager's never having heard of Kierkegaard (let alone read him), his description of spirit as ultimately a *relationship* connects well with Kierkegaard's view of human *being* as a synthesis! Related to this, Kierkegaard has pointed out that most people are afraid to acknowledge that they are spiritual beings who have spiritual needs, and would rather conceive of themselves as material entities whose aim in life is to satisfy physical and psychological demands only. This is powerfully expressed in arguing that:

> Every human being is the psycho-physical synthesis planned as spirit; this is the building, but he prefers living in the basement, that is in the categories of sensation.
>
> (Kierkegaard 1989/1849, 74)

Existential psychology has been put forward as an alternative to the prevailing reductionist and natural science paradigm in psychology. One of the most lucid accounts of this is contained in the work of Giorgi (1970), who argued that psychology should be conceived as a *human science*. Giorgi (1985) has argued that psychology should acknowledge that it is closely related to philosophy. He argues that it needs to reject the idea that the discipline of psychology is a natural science in the same way as physics. There are many reasons behind this; however, the most important is that, whereas physics deals with inanimate matter, psychology is about the study of human beings.

Existential psychology is very explicit about its links to the philosophy of existentialism. This has undoubtedly led to objections that existential psychology is more a kind of philosophy, and as such is a threat to the independence of psychology that the discipline attained in the mid-nineteenth century. In sport psychology there has been an uncritical acceptance of the natural science foundations of the discipline, although some researchers (Andersen 2005; Sparkes 2002) are beginning to challenge this. However, it is only within the work of sport psychologists drawing on existential approaches that in-depth accounts examine the philosophical roots of the dominant reductionist paradigms of Freudian and behavioural psychology, and the opposing reaction of subjectivist approaches such as humanistic psychology and postmodern perspectives. Existential sport psychology literature contains reference to Cartesian dualism, epistemology, metaphysics and the transcendental (Fahlberg *et al.* 1992; Dale 1996; Nesti 2004). These terms are rarely mentioned and discussed in other approaches to sport psychology, being seen as beyond the concerns of psychology. This is very unfortunate because, as Giorgi (1970) and others have stated, *all* scientific methods and even science itself rest on particular philosophical assumptions. Knowledge of these does not in itself interfere with the enterprise of science and scientific research. However, it does assist scientists and psychologists to recognise the limitations of the methods they use and consider how these can be adapted to *correspond more closely to reality*, that is, to become *more empirical*.

The following extract picks up on some of these themes in commenting on existential principles and the idea of phenomenology, which is the preferred research method of this approach to psychology. The main aim of existential–phenomenological psychology has been to attempt to reconstitute psychology as the science concerned with the study of how human beings, as *persons* rather than as *things*, make sense of situations and experiences. The focus is on what something *means* to a person. To achieve this, effort is directed at the phenomena themselves as they are experienced and as they present themselves to the person. According to Giorgi (1970), this represents an even more strictly empirical way of working than exists in natural scientific psychology. However, before investigating these claims more fully it may be helpful to examine the roots of existential psychology in greater detail and consider how it differs from some of the more familiar psychological paradigms and schools.

Existential psychology has been described by Giorgi (1985) as an approach which rejects the natural science orthodoxy that has dominated psychology since its earliest days. Particularly in the field of learning theory but also in much of experimental psychology as a whole, the discipline has modelled itself on the methods of physics. Giorgi has argued that it has often been an unwitting supporter of a rationalistic, materialistic and Lockean view of the world, where the person is viewed as exclusively a product of the environment. According to Fischer (1970), the clearest examples of this can be seen in psychoanalysis and behaviourism, in that both share a common view of the human being as a determined organism for whom notions such as *freedom*, *responsibility*, *anxiety* and *courage* are meaningless terms.

Existential psychology is primarily aimed at articulating psychology in such a way that human beings can be approached and studied as persons rather than as things, drive reduction organisms, or passive receivers of stimuli. The focus is on investigating how persons participate in and bring meaning to the situations experienced in their lives. In attempting to achieve this, existential psychology is often linked to phenomenological methodology where attention is directed at the *Lebenswelt* or 'the-world-as-lived'. The aim is to return to a consideration of things themselves; that is, focus must be on the phenomena and how these are experienced and appear to the person. In other words, this approach emphasizes that the starting point for all psychological enquiry must be with the subject's pre-reflective lived experience of the event and not with some idea of how the thing ought to be experienced or perceived.

(Nesti 2004, 20–21)

Interestingly, rather than being opposed to science and empirical approaches, the founder of phenomenology (Husserl 1970) claimed that this approach provided an even more strictly empirical method that could be used in all scientific disciplines. Existentialism and existential–phenomenological psychology is interested in describing reality as this is experienced by human persons. Interest is on 'things themselves' rather than hypothesized cause and effect relationships, theories or purely subjective reports. On this last point Valle and King (1978) have pointed that out existential psychology is not a subjective approach since it is based on a philosophy of science which rejects the whole idea of pure objectivity or pure subjectivity. This position has been described by Nesti (2004) in pointing out that existential approaches following Merleau-Ponty (1962) see human beings as an inseparable mix of subject and object, and to speak of one or other, or both combined, does not describe *reality* as such:

> Existential psychology and phenomenology are based on a common foundational philosophy, which rejects as its starting point the Cartesian dualism that separates subject from object. Whether it has been acknowledged or not, natural science based psychology has proceeded from the philosophical position that it is both possible and desirable to look for cause and effect relationships to explain people's behaviour and thoughts, and that these can in turn be categorized, measured and analyzed. In contrast, the existential–phenomenological approach eschews any interest in searching for causes and concentrates on identifying what an experience or situation means to a person. This approach denies that it is possible for us to carry out psychological research or therapy by attending exclusively to either objective data, or subjective reports. The existential–phenomenological position however is not merely equivalent to that proposed by those advocating an interactionist approach, where reality is conceived of as a mix of both the subjective and objective.
>
> (Nesti 2004, 21)

Existentialism claims that being aware that someday we will die is the most important fact of life. It may sound very strange to our ears to hear this statement; however, awareness of the inevitability of death is, according to this view, the ultimate question facing philosophy, theology and psychology. This relates to anxiety, which is the most important emotion according to existential psychology. This focus on death, dying and mortality can be understood both literally and symbolically (e.g. retirement in sport). The centrality of this fact of life found in existential writings has made it possible for this approach to psychology to study the importance of meaning. Faced with the inevitability of death, the question of what life means has implications for each individual in a variety of ways, including psychologically. Although referring to philosophy, the following could equally be understood from a psychological perspective:

> Existentialism lays particular emphasis on the fact that we are alone in being aware that we must ultimately die and that this unavoidable condition, which faces us all as individuals, is the most important point of our existence. According to the existential philosophers, that people at certain points in history and within their personal lives try to forget about or ignore this fact, does not diminish its centrality in understanding the human experience and ourselves. Indeed the existentialists are united in portraying the failure of people and societies to face up to the questions associated with an awareness of our mortality as deeply worrying and a sign of a profound imbalance in our mental outlook.
>
> In relation to this, most existential philosophers stress that philosophy should remain open to a consideration of the spirit and the transcendental

dimension in human existence. They are not claiming that philosophy must move into the area where the great spiritual and religious traditions operate, and neither do they feel it appropriate to engage in debates normally within the preserve of theology. However, they are highlighting in their view, any philosophy worthy of the name should have something to say on those aspects that are most unique to humankind. That this includes a consideration of topics that other philosophies often ignore makes their task even more necessary. For example, questions around love, freedom, whether there is meaning in our lives or meaninglessness, the necessity of choice and the degree of responsibility for our actions represent the main areas of interest. That each of these according to existential philosophy, provides a great challenge in terms of understanding because of their fundamentally ambiguous nature does not lessen the need to try to grasp their meaning for our lives.

(Nesti 2004, 26)

Finally, existential psychology places a special emphasis on anxiety and views this experience as something that can be either negative or positive. Most of psychology and sport psychology has tended to define anxiety as a negative and debilitating emotion, although research (Jones 1995) suggests that sport performers don't always see it that way. Existential psychology differs markedly in *starting* from a position where normal anxiety is viewed as a positive sign and something that should be welcomed. Existential accounts of anxiety relate closely to the issues of freedom, choice, responsibility and meaning, which are factors experienced by all human beings. At one level, the existential view argues that anxiety always accompanies recognition that we have some measure of freedom and choice in our lives. By repeatedly failing to face up to this responsibility and by avoiding the need to find some form of life goal, or *Logos* (Frankl 1984), individuals may experience neurotic anxiety.

This view suggests that normal anxiety is always present when we face up to new challenges, learn and grow. Unlike within much of psychology and sport psychology, normal anxiety is understood as something uncomfortable but potentially beneficial which should not be managed away, controlled by therapy or mental skills techniques. Existential psychology claims that the more mature a person's values are the more likely they will be able to accept and work through new and demanding tasks and experiences. May (1977) has claimed that mature values are those oriented to the common good. They have been assimilated after personal effort rather than being uncritically accepted by an individual; they are *won by* the person, rather than *imposed* on him or her. Of course these values could be very individual and unique or be identical to those held by other groups in society, including institutional religions.

It should be clear by now that existential psychology is significantly different from other approaches. For most psychologists and sport psychologists this is a very alien landscape. The mention of values, choice, freedom, death, responsibility, authenticity and meaning immediately conveys that at least some forms of existentialism can accommodate ideas relating to spirituality, transcendental dimensions and religious belief. The favourable view taken towards anxiety also suggests that existential psychology is unafraid to talk about courage, will, pain and suffering. This is fortunate for those psychologists interested in sport, since this activity provides an ideal vehicle to experience these elements, alongside more frequently discussed terms like achievement and joy.

The chapter now turns to consider some of the key existential themes and examines how these have been, or could be, applied to an understanding of sport.

Encountering the existential in sport

Irrespective of level, sport has the capacity to confront the person with clear challenges. These could be in terms of learning new skills, adapting to different tactics, maintaining standards under mental and physical stress and facing up to injury. This experience is common to all who play sport, although research (Nesti and Sewell 1999) supports the commonsense view that, at higher levels and in professional sport, there is a greater significance in failing to meet such demands. Whether competition is against self or others there is research evidence to suggest that those who participate in sport do so, in part at least, for reasons of intrinsic motivation. Deci and Ryan (1985) defined intrinsic motivation in sport as involving an innate desire to feel self-determined and to experience perceived competence. Perceived competence can be further divided in terms of task and ego goal orientations. Ego-involved individuals tend to view their ability relative to others. In contrast, those who are task-oriented view perceived competence as more related to the effort and motivation that an individual puts into an activity. In sport it is assumed that there is a strong negative relation between ego orientation and enjoyment, and a strong correlation between task orientation and enjoyment (Ntoumanis and Biddle 1999). Sport psychologists have advocated that focus on the task and on factors like effort, which are within the control of the individual, can be used to reduce the negative impact of anxiety on performance (Jones 1995). Nevertheless, the fact remains that, beyond this concern with pre-event anxiety, the experience of anxiety for those involved in sport will often relate to a much broader range of factors. For example, progressing in sport places the individual in a situation where defeat becomes a more frequently encountered experience, the pressure to perform at consistently high levels increases and the expectations of others rises. Although some athletes are able to maintain a strong task focus in these and other moments in their sport experiences, all will encounter feelings of doubt and anxiety as they move on to new challenges and face different demands. It is exactly because of this that sport has the potential to develop qualities of spirit, like self-knowledge, courage, personality and resilience. Anxiety pervades all of life but, for the sport psychologist drawing on existential principles, sport is uniquely attractive because it requires sustained commitment from our *whole* selves in a way that work and other areas of life rarely do. Sport has the capacity to draw equally on our mental and physical capacities, and to reward those at any level who hold nothing back of themselves time and time again. Sport at *all* levels requires discipline, dedication, sacrifice and love in equal measure!

One of the most important concerns of existential psychology is that of choice. Existentialism, in agreement with the main monotheistic religions, accepts that human beings possess individual freedom. In straightforward terms, we are able to select options and make decisions. Sartre (1956) expressed this even more clearly in pointing out that we are *condemned* to freedom. However, existentialism points out that we are never totally free to make any choice we wish; this is referred to as *situated freedom*. Some existential psychologists (Van Kaam 1975; Frankl 1984) claim that the existence of this type of freedom differentiates humans from all other creatures, whose actions are totally governed by their biological instincts and environment. For these writers, human freedom conceived in this way can only make sense if we are understood to be spiritual creatures. Finally on this point, it is important to grasp that existential psychology is not suggesting that we are completely free to do as we wish. Critics of humanistic psychology have claimed that it has tended to overstate the person's capacity for freedom and choice whereas existential perspectives highlight that choice is always (and should be!) constrained by responsibilities to self and others (Spinelli 1996).

In sport the performer must make choices and accept responsibility for the outcomes. For example, at elite levels an athlete may have to change coaches, clubs or teams to further his or her career, deal with family illness and relationship problems alongside preparing for a major competition, or set new goals and challenges after success or failure. Although the athlete may be supported in this by coaches, sport psychologists or mentors (Lavallee and Wylleman 2000), ultimately the decision to act and choose a particular path rests with individuals themselves. Mental skills like good goal setting and psychological qualities like motivation and mental toughness can often play an important role here. Existential sport psychology accepts that these techniques and skills may be able to assist the athlete especially in coping with stressful reactions to the choices made. However, uniquely in sport psychology, the existential approach claims that human spirit is developed when individuals are willing to confront the anxiety associated with freedom and choice, and to accept some measure of personal responsibility for the decisions they take.

The existential view claims that the concept of personality should include our psychological qualities, inclinations and tendencies, *and* include reference to the spirit. Within sport it is common to come across comments about performers showing 'great spirit' and producing 'spirited' performances. Of course, the main approaches in sport psychology have assumed that these phrases really refer to confidence, self-belief and team cohesion. As has been discussed previously this represents a scientifically weak perspective that is based solely on hypothesised constructs rather than empirical data. The phenomenological method used in existential psychology research in sport avoids this weakness by maintaining focus on the words and descriptions used by the research subjects. The radical empiricism of phenomenology reveals that sports performers and coaches often use other spiritual terms to describe experiences in sport, even where these do not fit the restricted underpinning philosophy of sport psychology. Some of the most frequently used words in sport such as 'character', 'courage', 'willpower' and 'resilence' have been largely cleansed from the extant literature in sport psychology. Although individual objections to each exist, there is an underlying set of reasons why these terms have been rejected. Arguably, the most important are that they cannot be defined adequately by methods derived from natural science and that they sound vague, almost religious and old fashioned! In opposing this, existential phenomenology in sport research allows the scientist to investigate spiritual notions like prayer (Czech *et al.* 2004), meaning (Nesti 2002) and contemplation (Ravizza 2002). These are important areas in all sport, and performance sport in particular, which have already been studied in a wide range of other human activities (Watson and Nesti 2005).

The important concept of self-awareness has been discussed in relation to developing mental skills and coping strategies in sport (Ravizza 2002). Existential psychology is more interested in helping athletes to grow in self-knowledge. With the exception of Corlett's (1996) outstanding and scholarly article addressing this topic, there are very few references to self-knowledge in the research literature. This is most likely because it is seen as a philosophical concept and as something connected to spirituality. The existential perspective argues that 'the greater the self-knowledge the more prepared the *self* is to approach another person in humility and openness' (Nesti 2004, 80). 'This process of self examination rather than the more detached and impersonal task of improving self awareness, is key, as it is about the growth and development of the deepest core of being' (Nesti 2004, 92). This is the centre of who we really are: the authentic self and most important element of our personalities. According to the existentialists, sport can provide opportunities for the individual athlete to confront and accept the challenges and anxiety inherent in this form of human activity. Encountering success and failure in competitive sport has the potential to educate the sport performer about where his or her limits are, what he or she is willing to go through and who he or she really is.

This account of self-knowledge links closely to ideas of courage, identity, meaning and values. Each of these words signifies that our personality can be seen as a spiritual entity which engages with the world around it through use of particular psychological skills and qualities. This view of human spirit is capable of reconciling the ideas that sport can simultaneously assist individuals to learn useful psychological skills *and* grow spiritually. It is very apparent in the work of Kierkegaard, and others who have stayed close to the founder's approach, that courage, self-knowledge and meaning are understood as spiritual and ethical categories. Existential psychology is quite prepared to mention values and ethics because these are part of human *being*. May (1975) has defined the human as the being who values. Sport psychology and most of psychology does not touch on this topic, seeing it as the preserve of philosophy and theology. Existential psychology has pointed out 'that anxiety is only possible because the human is a valuing being' (Nesti 2004, 100). This link to personal growth in and through the sport experience can be understood by considering how normal anxiety and values interact according to existential psychologists:

They contend that anxiety is experienced when something that is important and valued by us is threatened. According to this view, values are always under constant threat and gain in depth and maturity as we confront the choices and make decisions in our life. Such deeply held values are said to form the centre of a person, or their core self. Finally on this point, May (1967) has stated that an individual's capacity to meet anxiety positively is directly related to the adequacy of their value system. The individual without healthy and strong values will attempt to avoid anxiety by either falling into line with the views of others, trying to ignore their claims by engaging in constant activity, or by crystallizing their values into rigid dogma. All of these strategies can lead to a weakening of the core self and stagnation in terms of personal growth.

(Nesti 2004, 100)

Given this it is easier to understand why existential psychology should advocate that it is important to develop healthy, mature and ethically sound values in sports performers, if only because this helps them to deal with the normal anxiety deeply embedded in sport. May (1977) has observed that mature values may or may not be linked to religious belief systems, political groupings or specific ideologies. However, he has suggested that they must 'transcend also the immediate in-groups' (May 1967, 82) and that they should be freely chosen, bring responsibilities and allow the person to be 'inner directed and future oriented' (Nesti 2004, 101).

Existential psychology accepts that our values will be based on how we construct meaning in our lives. As an approach in psychology rather than theology or philosophy, the existential perspective is unable to put forward the case for a particular account, but it can state that the need to find meaning is a legitimate concern for each individual. Sartre famously declared that 'life is absurd', and his brand of existentialism has declared that there is no meaning in life beyond that which the individual creates for him- or herself. This view, which is the basis of postmodernism and is a totally relative account of values and ethics, has been criticised by Nesti (2004) within sport psychology. A more consistent existential psychology approach is that of the psychiatrist Viktor Frankl (1984). He contends that the most important challenge facing any person is to discover some form of ultimate meaning in their lives. His existential approach is called logotherapy – *Logos* being Greek for 'meaning'. Added to this, Frankl states that the human being is a physical, psychological and spiritual unity and that each of these elements must be nourished if we are to be fully human. This would suggest that in working only with physical, emotional and cognitive elements, some sport psychologists are missing out on helping their athletes to develop an important and integral part of themselves.

The final section of this chapter reviews how sport psychology could draw on existential psychology and phenomenology to investigate performance and spiritual notions in sport. The conclusion suggests areas where future work needs to focus.

Performing with spirit

Research during the past 30 years has studied the psychological factors associated with exceptional or peak performances in sport. Early work carried out by Ravizza (1977) identified that athletes tended to experience a number of common perceptions during their best performances. Several of these, such as feeling totally immersed in the task, experiencing time and space disorientation and sensing the world holistically, appear closely related to spiritual practices like contemplation. Probably the most extensive empirical work in this area relates to Csikszentmihalyi's (1975) account of *flow*. During the past thirty years there have been numerous studies into the relationship between flow and sport performance. Flow has been described by Csikszentmihalyi (1975) as the feeling that accompanies optimal performances when we are focused on an activity to the exclusion of everything else. This can occur to anyone in any task. For this to happen our skills must be adequate to meet the challenge of the task and, crucially, we should *perceive* that we have this necessary level of competence. In applied work, Gallwey's (1979) notion of *inner game* describes a very closely related phenomenon. His work draws on coaching in tennis, golf and skiing. According to Gallwey, peak performance and learning takes place best when the individual allows him- or herself to perform without the distractions and interference from the ego, or 'self 1' as he calls it. When 'self 2' is in control we tend to perform without fear and effortlessly and learn more quickly and easily. In this mental state, sports performers experience many of the same types of moments that Maslow (1968) and Ravizza (1977) called peak experiences, and Jackson and Csikszentmihalyi (1999) identified as the main dimensions of flow.

It is very tempting to define these 'pure' moments of absorption beyond the self as yet further examples of the spirit in sport. Flow, peak experiences and playing in the zone of 'self 2' sound much more 'spiritual' than goal setting, mental rehearsal and concentration training. Murphy and White (1995) have written a well researched and groundbreaking book in this area, pointing out that sports seem to be capable of providing mystical moments and transcendental encounters. This claim has been thoroughly examined and largely rejected within other chapters in this book. However, from an existential psychology perspective a more sympathetic view may be possible and desirable.

An existential analysis would highlight that phenomenologically derived terms like 'flow' (Csikszentmihalyi 1975) clearly show that our best performances often occur when we are prepared to give ourselves over to the task fully and without reservation. The accounts of mystics and contemplatives (Merton 1961) contain these ideas in terms of self-forgetfulness and loving union with God. Contrary to common sense and psychological skills training in sport, the best performances seem to take place just at that moment when control is 'handed over' to something other than the individual and his or her physical and mental capabilities. The paradox here is that, whereas mental skills training is about increasing perceptions of control, the best sport performances often occur just at that point where the self disappears, and the task and the individual seem to merge. In other words, it

appears that spiritual notions like selflessness, disinterestedness and passive recep-
tivity are the precursors to 'flow-like' peak performances. These ideas have been
linked to Eastern mystical traditions found in Zen, Buddhism and the martial arts.
Much less has been done to consider these elements in terms of Western spirituality and religious practices. This may be because, at least since the Reformation,
there has been a move towards a separation of spirituality from everyday life and
a conviction that authentic spirituality can only be found in religious belief and
practice. From an existential psychology viewpoint, this is an unfortunate split
because it ignores claims made by Marcel, Kierkegaard, Pascal and St Thomas
Aquinas. They argued that we can speak of human spirit and religious spirituality as intimately connected yet different aspects of *human being*. For existential
psychology, peak moments in sport could lead the individual to reflect on the
fact that performance can occur outside felt mental and physical control. The
religious athlete might interpret this as evidence of our religious spiritual natures
and reliance on God. This has been reported in research (Watson *et al.* 2004) with
off-piste expert skiers who were Christians. They used Christian belief to interpret
their experiences of peak experiences in sport.

The religious existentialism of Kierkegaard (1980/1844) left room for the idea
of human spirituality, whilst arguing that the self (and our spirit as the main part
of this) is ultimately grounded in God. For existentialists such as Marcel and Kierkegaard, human spirit is always oriented towards the infinite, the unfathomable
and non-material end or goal of man, which is God. However, they accept that
human spirit prepares the ground in advance of this end in being the home of
faith, hope and love. This last word cannot be fully understood as anything other
than the clearest example of spirituality. Love cannot be understood if it is reduced
to its psycho-physiological correlates or to an emotional response. The spiritual
and the spirit in sport could be seen in a similar way to love. For the religious
person all love culminates in love of God. This does not prevent the believer and
non-believer alike from encountering love in their lives. For one person love gives
meaning to life because it cannot be understood apart from God; for the other person love itself transcends any perceived need to search for a greater meaning. For
such individuals it is quite true to say that life is love and love is life! In sport there
are many examples of athletes whose relationship to their sport could be likened
to passionate love. The famous statement attributed to Bill Shankly, the hugely
successful Scottish manager of Liverpool Football Club, that 'Football is not about
life and death; it is more important than that!' powerfully expresses this love. The
passion of the committed fan and the lifelong supporter and the language used
by sports participants themselves often bear witness to this deep love. Again, the
existential view that we possess some measure of freedom or agency in our lives
connects to this. Love is impossible without free will; real love is given freely by
one person to another person, group or institution. Love is *the* testimony to human
freedom. It cannot be forced and to be love it must be offered voluntarily, without
compunction. This spiritual gift is seen in the lives of countless individuals taking
part in sport through their dedication, sacrifice and courage. At the highest levels
of sport performance, despite little formal research being carried out, the spiritual

human quality of love can be gleaned from the actions and words of the participants. For example it is not uncommon to hear athletes talking about the love for their sport, and willingness to accept pain, suffering and hardships as they search for superior performances. Unfortunately, sport psychology has dismissed these accounts and assumed that love equates to intrinsic motivation (Deci and Ryan 1985) and that sacrifice is fully accounted for by mental toughness and coping skills. These cognitive psychology constructs have arguably helped to advance understanding in sport psychology; however, they have proved incapable of dealing with the many spiritual terms that permeate the sports world. Existential psychology is able to consider the language used by sport performers that other psychological approaches either rephrase or ignore. Love, sacrifice, hope, joy, courage, anxiety (angst), freedom and responsibility, amongst others, can all be considered as they stand. The spiritual roots of these words does not lead to their exclusion from psychological research within existential psychology.

Existential approaches focus equally on despair, grief, elation and joy. Yalom (1999) pointed out that sport performers often face anxiety and doubt at boundary situations. 'This refers to those occasions where the athlete may be facing a major sports injury, significant change in personal circumstances or shift in responsibilities. Within team settings examples could include the threat of relegation, the introduction of new practices and major tactical alterations and changes in team managers or coaches' (Nesti 2004, 124). A number of applied sport psychologists (Ravizza 2002; Nesti 2004) have pointed out that for some athletes these moments are seen as a test of human spirit (Pieper 1989) in which their usual psychological and physical responses prove inadequate in the face of such *existential crisis*. It has also been reported that some sport performers interpret these difficult experiences through their own religious beliefs that provide a spiritual framework of meaning for them. This may in fact be the most frequently experienced opportunity for a spiritual encounter in sport. Given the wonderful capacity for sport to bring personal challenges and difficulties into sharp relief, and that defeat and loss are more common than victory and winning, the sport performer must find it within him- or herself to go on when the sensible option seems to be to give up hope and abandon the task. The existential psychology view of anxiety gives a glimpse of how the frequent encounters with failure in sport exposes the spirit, or lack of spirit in the performer. For those who claim that tough times can be dealt with through use of psychological techniques alone Kierkegaard offers a seething rejoinder. He contends that:

> Not being conscious of oneself as spirit – is despair, that is to say, spiritlessness, whether the state is one of total extinction, a merely vegetative life, or a life full of energy the secret of which is nevertheless despair.
>
> (Kierkegaard 1989/1849, 74)

This view argues that the athlete with spirit will differ from those lacking spirit. Performers with spirit will be resolute, selfless, courageous and authentic (*real*). They will have the resource of spiritual strength to stay in the battle to the end.

Spiritless individuals in contrast can be discerned because they use frenetic activity to avoid having to take a deeper look at themselves, or they abandon their existential freedom for the quiet life and merge into the crowd. According to this particular existential psychology view, these athletes have nothing to sustain them when their psychological skills and physical capacities are stretched to breaking point. It is for this very reason that so many coaches and managers at the highest level of sport have identified that team spirit and players with spirit are the most important personal qualities they look for.

Conclusion

Finally, it could be that existential psychology approaches to spirituality in sport might have encouraged much less emphasis on peak experiences and altered states of awareness, and more on spiritual strength and courage. The peak experience literature emerged out of humanistic psychology with its very positive view of human nature and personality. As has been discussed, it is not surprising that some writers (Murphy and White 1995) appear to have suggested that the shared language of exceptional athletic performances and spirituality means that peak experiences in sport and transcendental and religious accounts are synonymous. To say that flow sounds similar to religious ideas of spirituality is one thing. To argue that these experiences *are* examples of religious spirituality is quite another. This is not to say that, for some athletes, peak moments in sport cannot add to their established beliefs based on a particular religion. This chapter has suggested that following some approaches within existential psychology and those of the foremost Thomist philosopher of the twentieth century, Josef Pieper, could have been much more helpful. Pieper (1989) and Marcel (1948) both discuss the idea that human spirit is not just another name for religious spirituality and neither does it refer to a specific set of psychological attributes. The other clear advantage of such a perspective is that it supports the way that this term is most often used in the real world of sport. Putting this in a straightforward way, the interest of those at the highest levels of professional sport in the concept of spirit is not because of flow or altered states, but because it is associated with winning ugly and succeeding against the odds!

The increasing use of existential phenomenological methods in sport psychology research (Dale 2000) could lead to an increase in studies investigating spirit, spirituality and sport. Phenomenological interviewing and data analysis are based on a strictly empirical outlook that does not attempt to theorise and develop hypothetical constructs. Focus is on the descriptions provided by the participants in any research study; these convey the personal meanings that individuals attach to particular events and experiences. Kerry and Armour (2000) have suggested that phenomenology could facilitate the study of a number of important terms used by sports participants which do not fit into other quantitative or qualitative approaches. For example, courage, hope, passion and spirit are frequently referred to in sport but rarely examined within research.

Wertz (2005) has pointed out that phenomenology was the first qualitative method since it is derived from the work of Husserl in the nineteenth century. Nevertheless, it has only recently been employed in sport psychology research. This is most likely on account of the dominance of the natural attitude that prevails in most qualitative and quantitative research. This is based on the model of natural science that looks at relationships between factors, rather than *meaning*. Spirituality in sport and the descriptions of spirit provided by sport participants and coaches could be more easily captured when the researcher sets aside 'our natural attitude – that objects in the external world are objectively present in space and time – and instead focus solely on our immediate and present experience of them' (Cooper 2003, 10).

An existential phenomenological approach to sport psychology could mean that spirituality, suffering, sacrifice, joy, love and religious belief would no longer be mostly ignored in academic work. As has been highlighted throughout this chapter, these terms and ideas are worthy of study because they are found in the real world of sport. It is surely poor science to reduce the phrase 'team spirit' to mean group cohesion, or to deny that experiences in competitive sport can strengthen an individual's religious belief when an athlete has profound reasons for this claim. Maybe if researchers worked more closely with athletes in applied settings and with those who participate in sport, and listened more carefully to these individuals, the relationship between sport and spirituality would be harder to ignore. Then it might even be possible to understand why many Catholic professional footballers cross themselves as they come on to the field and some Muslim athletes pray in the changing rooms before sport competitions, and why most coaches claim that performers with spirit are so sought after. Finally, beyond competitive sport, research needs to take seriously those who claim that a brisk walk at lunchtime 'lifts the spirit' for the religious believer and non-believer alike!

Study questions

1 What differentiates existential psychology from humanistic psychology?
2 What evidence is there for the assertion that human spirit is related to, but different from, religious spirituality?
3 How does existential psychology view anxiety in sport?
4 Why would an existential–phenomenological psychology bring a more strictly empirical approach to the study of sport and spirituality?
5 Why does most research tend to describe flow and peak experiences as examples of the spiritual dimension in sport?
6 Explain why you think that the spiritual concept of love is, or is not, a suitable topic for research in sport.

8 Persons and players

A psychological perspective

Mark Nesti

Introduction

It can be argued that psychology should focus on the human person rather than on the behaviour and experiences of individuals. Unfortunately, since the arrival of Cartesian dualism, most of psychology has tended to emphasise the notion of individuals and societies over persons and communities. Related to this, Giorgi (1970) argued that the result of following the natural science model and its underlying assumptions has led to a significant restriction in which topics have been studied in the human science disciplines. Within psychology and sport psychology, the major challenge to this dominant paradigm has been provided by existential–phenomenological and transpersonal psychology. According to Valle, existential psychology is based on 'a critical stance towards the natural science conception of the person and the world and the technologically oriented culture that arises from this world-view' (1989, 255). Existential literature has attempted to investigate all aspects of human experience, including love, creativity and religious belief, which most other approaches in psychology have generally ignored. Within such a perspective, based as it is upon the lived reality of human persons, it has been possible to consider matters like spiritual awareness and transcendental belief. Behaviourist and cognitive psychologists have ignored these and other similar elements like will, courage and consciousness largely because the underpinning natural scientific foundations of their paradigm reject these concepts as unverifiable. What is really being said here is that, since the methods of natural science cannot accommodate these important human experiences, the solution has been to leave them to philosophy, theology and the arts. However, the difficulty with this is that psychology and sport psychology conceived as a natural science is forced to *reduce* human beings to something which fits neatly into its methods. The outcome of this is that science has *determined* its subject matter and presented a particular and restricted view of human beings when it should have changed its approach to meet the reality of the human person.

Arguably, the central issue in all of this is that of *free will*. The ideas of freedom and responsibility in terms of human agency have been central to the disciplines concerned with understanding human nature. However, whilst philosophers and to some extent theologians have had much to say on this matter, psychologists until the 1960s proceeded as though free will had long since been disproved. The development of humanistic psychology was a response to this materialist conception of human beings. It elevated the concept of free will to become our most distinguishing characteristic and it opened the door to the scientific study of unique human characteristics. This welcome change made it possible to study the whole individual again. However, by focusing mainly on our positive behaviours, capacity for growth, and by giving the message that personal freedom could be attained fully, some argued (Spinelli 1996) that it failed (as had psychoanalysis and behaviourism before it) to capture the reality of our human lives. Once again the fundamental difference between this approach and others related to competing views on what constituted human nature. Another way of expressing this is that humanistic psychology ushered in the return of the person. This is in sharp contrast to the understanding the individual as a drive reduction organism by Freud and his followers, or as a stimulus–response mechanism by Watson, Skinner and the behaviourists. However, this particular rehabilitation of personhood and the personal in psychology and other human sciences also led to some unforeseen and undesirable consequences. Spinelli (1989) has been a forceful critic, claiming that humanistic psychology has actually contributed to the cult of the individual rather than providing an authentic account of the person. The solution to this weakness has been to propose existential–phenomenological psychology as the best approach because it considers the human being as an 'inextricable intermixture' (Merleau-Ponty 1962, 518); that is, not fully free or completely determined.

What has this debate got to do with sport? A perusal of much of the sport-related literature to date would seem to indicate that researchers and writers in our field have failed to address this important issue. The work of some of those who have discussed the concept of the human person and sport will be considered in this chapter. In particular, we will assess how this could impact on the work of applied sport psychologists. This group has been at the forefront of mental skills training, sport psychology counselling and coach education, in which the issues of delivery philosophy and the applied approach taken with sport performers have been of central concern. Some applied sport psychologists (Ravizza 2002; Nesti 2004) and others from a more philosophical perspective (Corlett 1996a) have claimed that who they are is more important in their work than what they do. These individuals have emphasised the importance of person-to-person communication in their work with athletes, and are in agreement with Marcel (1948) that the idea of personality would be better understood as a spiritual concept instead of a purely psychological construct.

Special focus on existential and transpersonal psychology will be included in this chapter because each, in slightly different ways, argues that the spiritual is possible only because we are persons. The contrast between individualism and personalism is of great importance and has particular implications for sport as a whole. Whether we are described as merely raw material whose purpose in life is governed by utilitarian ends or as 'an embodied spirit that can never be reduced to mere matter' (John Paul II 1994, 55) is of huge importance for all of us. This chapter will discuss the implications arising from this spiritual account of the human person for those who participate and work in sport.

Persons

The notion of persons rather than individuals is something of profound importance for philosophy and the different sciences dealing with *human being*. From an anthropological perspective, any approach taken to the body that separates mind and spirit leads to a very different account of human nature from when the spiritual dimension is considered an integral part of who we are. In its opposition to the concept of spirit, modern rationalism has arguably led to a depersonalisation of human being in which we are measured in terms of a utilitarian ethic. All that really matters according to this view is our effectiveness, efficiency and production of goods for consumption. Detached from the spirit and therefore *spiritless* beings, we 'cease to live as a person and a subject. Regardless of all intentions and declarations to the contrary, we become merely an object' (John Paul II 1994, 56).

We have become so accustomed to using the words 'individual' and 'person' interchangeably that it is difficult to recognise that their meanings are quite different and distinct. However, it could be argued that when the terms used are 'individualism' and '*personalism*' we are somewhat more familiar with the fact that these represent related but ultimately opposing concepts. Individualism is centred on the self as something capable of *absolute freedom*. The individualistic person is a contradiction and, at a philosophical, anthropological and psychological level, an impossibility. Individualism and being individualistic is based on an ethic of self as totally sovereign in which, psychologically speaking, the only possible outcome is egocentricity. In stark contrast, the notion of *personalism*, which is related to the spiritual concept of the person, is based on an ethic of self-giving, altruism and a freedom bounded by responsibility to others. It is this final dimension that relates most closely to the idea of community. It is for this reason that some (Nesti 2004) have pointed out that, without an adequate idea of the person, a genuine community is impossible to achieve.

The existential philosophy of Marcel (1948) states that 'persons should be regarded as ends in themselves . . . and that the act whereby persons are regarded as ends in themselves is intrinsically communal' (Marcel, quoted in Kingston 1961, 316). An explanation of this statement draws upon the idea that freedom, which is something we possess by our existence as a person, is not about doing what the individual wants, but is about acting in hope beyond the environmental and biological constraints of our *being*. The ideas of freedom and hope will be discussed more fully later in the chapter in relation to sport; however, both concepts are of central importance to understanding *personhood*.

In addressing the topic of *being*, some philosophers have claimed that without a recovery of an authentic conception of human being we will continue to experience growing despair, alienation and anxiety. They have argued that when we see human beings as *only* an agglomeration of particular functions, we conceive of ourselves in a mechanical and impersonal way. The product of this shrinking of human beings to mere functionaries, according to Marcel, is that 'In the brave new world the person has disappeared and so has the sense of wonder. Existence is basically empty instead of full. The need for Being is a need to participate; as contrasted with fitting into a routine' (Marcel quoted in Kingston 1961, 283). This view argues that we are increasingly living isolated and self-absorbed lives, whilst denying the spirit of authentic participation with others and the world beyond ourselves. According to psychologists such as Fromm (1994), this has contributed to the increase in mental illness and psychological disturbance that is evident in modern life.

It is important to examine the ideas of freedom and the spirit at this point since each in its own way could be said to define the concept of person. Dealing first with spirit, Pieper has pointed out that 'Spirit by definition is ability to comprehend the world!' (1998, 87). By this he means that, unlike all other animals, human beings are not *merely* limited by their environment but can grasp the whole of *being*. That is, their awareness is comprehensive if not complete. The human person is aware of him- or herself, others and their environment, although it is true that none of these in themselves can answer the question (known as the philosophical act) of why there is something, rather than nothing. According to Pieper (1998) there is a ranking of 'worlds' based on the amount of inwardness present and the level of interrelatedness. The lowest of these 'worlds' is that of plants, whose 'relation' is restricted to those around them; animals are beyond this level; and finally, 'transcending all these partial worlds, is the world related to spirit, *the world* as the totality of being' (Pieper 1998, 89). Accordingly, the authentic essence of the human person is 'a being in whom the various realms of plant-animal-, and spiritual beings are bound into a unity' (Pieper 1998, 93). Following from this, the human person needs both the environment, such as food, shelter and role, and a 'world', which is something that is beyond 'pure' environment. This final element of the human person allows him or her to stand apart (from time to time) from his or her own self and the environment. Pieper claims that this final quality of human being is *the spirit* and it expresses itself in our freedom to act in a particular and personal way. Indeed, without this notion of the person as a unity of animal and spiritual, there is no possibility of freedom in thought or action. This has allowed some philosophers and psychologists to state that, the greater the level of inwardness, the less determined our actions are by our environment. This notion of independence, of being more than our genes (nature) and conditioning (nurture) or the influence of both combined (the interactionist view), relates to the earliest arguments around the important concept of freedom and the free will. Without recognising the possibility of some measure of freedom in human acts it is impossible to argue that the human being is unique, sovereign and worthy as an end in him- or herself. Without this notion of the person it is not possible to claim that the human is any different from an animal since both exist in their given environments and live in accordance with the specific demands met there.

This links closely to the relationship between *free will* and personhood. To be a person, and to have a personality, immediately conveys the idea that we have some choice in the matter. Personality can be conceived by thinking in terms of predetermined and narrow categories like introvert, extrovert, type A, type B, and so on. In sport psychology, personality has typically been studied through the use of specially adapted tests and questionnaires. Personality traits and dispositions have been investigated in an effort to identify particular personality types and their influence on success in competitive sport. However, personality can be understood in a way much closer to the everyday use of this term. For example, when we say that someone has a lot of personality, or that they are a *real personality*, we mean something quite different from the approach taken by sport psychology. Using the term in this sense immediately conveys the idea that our personality, and therefore what type of person we are, is partly our choice, and that the greater the level of *inwardness* we possess, which is the nature of spirit according to Pieper (1998), the more of *a personality* we will be. Of course, this says nothing about whether this will be a destructive and negative personality or a positive and constructive one. This matter is related to ethics and morality and is therefore very important in sport and elsewhere; however, a discussion of this is beyond the scope of this chapter. It has been suggested that the best means of preventing the heavily spiritualised personality from loosening itself from the bonds of reality and becoming a self-centred and debilitating force is to ensure that the person is deeply anchored in the ballast of real life. This could be important physical, biological and psychological factors and also include higher order demands, such as those emanating from our personal relationships, vocational responsibilities, goals and ideals. In sport this could relate to the need to adhere to training programmes, contribute to the team effort and sometimes sacrifice personal goals to help team mates, or support family and friends. In one sense, this point emphasises that personal growth and becoming a *personality* requires *both* a life rich in the things and experiences of the world and an ever-increasing openness to the spiritual dimension of human being.

Before leaving this consideration of what it means to be a person it is helpful to examine the idea of personhood. This term is particularly well known and familiar to person-centred approaches in psychology (Rogers 1961) and existential and transpersonal psychology (Valle and Halling 1989). These approaches have criticised the prevailing deterministic and mechanistic view of human beings. They accuse behavioural psychology, in particular, of reducing personality to a series of stimulus–response connections and ignoring 'what is essential in human beings, that is, their very *personhood*' (Valle and Halling 1989, 182). The reductionist account provided by much of natural science psychology has been challenged by human science psychology (see Chapter 7). The human science approach has focused on what they describe as the *person-in-the-world*. This means that their view of personality is grounded in questions surrounding 'what does it mean to be human?' (Fischer 1989, 164). Interest is directed at unique individual phenomena and at studying general patterns. However, arguably the most important point here is that, unlike the dominant natural science-based reductionist approaches like the behaviourist and cognitive, the human science psychologist is not content with unexamined philosophical accounts. In opposition to the main perspectives encountered in the relatively young discipline of academic psychology and sport psychology, they are prepared to confess to a philosophically derived account of what it is to be a human person before proceeding to discuss personality and its assessment.

The last word on this issue in many ways reveals both the challenge and the opportunity facing those hoping for a move towards persons and away from individuals and research subjects in psychology and sport psychology. In commenting on the excesses of the behaviourist approaches to the study of personality and therapy, Halling and Nill (1989, 182) have noted that 'Fortunately, in practice it is impossible to treat people as if they were mere stimulus–response configurations'. It seems that, despite the claims of behaviourists and other reductionist psychologists, when they work with clients and study subjects they inevitably develop rapport, respect for their individual autonomy, and include data from a broad range of life experiences which do not fit the neat and tidy model of stimulus–response behaviour. In other words, the person of the individual client, athlete or research subject continually bursts through the façade of the detached, impersonal and apparently objective world of the psychologist, sport psychologist or researcher!

Existential and transpersonal psychology

As has been discussed in Chapter 7, existential–phenomenological approaches in psychology developed as a reaction to the mechanistic, reductionist and narrow perspectives of natural science psychology. The aim was to bring theoretical understanding of human beings closer to the reality of how each one of us actually lives and experiences our lives. This meant that a fully holistic view was taken. The human person was seen as someone determined to some degree by biology, instinct, past experiences and future goals, *and* free to choose how to interpret and respond to these *givens of existence*. This account of our capacity to select a particular choice and act on it, despite our limited knowledge and control over the final outcome, has been referred to as *situated freedom*. From this description it is quite clear that freedom here does not equate to pure subjectivity and does not involve such idealistic notions as believing that a person is totally free to become whoever and whatever they wish. This last point relates to postmodernism and relativism, which is associated with certain strands of existentialism in which the one-sided position of the determinists has been replaced by the equally empirically false account of the total subjectivists. It is important to note that the modern founder of existentialism, Søren Kierkegaard, was not a subjectivist and held firmly to the idea that the human is a mixture of free will and determined being (Schneider and May 1995). This can be captured by Kierkegaard's (1980/1844) famous statement that *personhood is a synthesis of possibility and necessity*. Or, to express it in more modern language, we are more than our genes and we cannot be understood unless we are considered holistically. He contends that, if this presents a difficulty for the methods of science, then it is science that must change to fit the human being rather than persons being made to fit science. Kierkegaard's account of the person emphasises that many people do not in fact behave as though they are persons. One group of individuals are what he describes as excessively *infinitised*, who live their lives surrounded by abstraction, imagination, ideas and fantasy. The opposite of this are the *finitised* individuals who only accept what they can measure and quantify, living in a world of narrowness, social conformism and, having lost any knowledge of themselves, believe in whatever the majority believe in.

To many outside of the formal academic environment it may seem quite surprising to find that what was largely held to be true by Aristotle, St Thomas Aquinas and others has only recently been reconsidered by medicine, psychology, sport psychology and other disciplines. In their attempt to study human beings more scientifically, scientists reduced us to pure matter, or more recently to mere minds, and in the process lost their way. The subjects of the resulting academic research and investigations began to look less and less like real people and the environments from which they were drawn. Not surprisingly, this has led to a breakdown in public confidence in science broadly conceived and an inexorable undermining of the idea of the human person. This crisis of meaning in terms of what constitutes a human being has of course impacted on ethics, morality and what are referred to as the ultimate questions around the meaning of life and the transcendental.

Existential psychology has articulated this issue in claiming that, ultimately, psychology, sport psychology and psychotherapy cannot be based upon biology, the mind or the spirit alone but that 'It ought to include the whole human person; and might be described as personalist' (Caruso 1964, 122). However, the failure of psychology and sport and exercise psychology to fully embrace a personalist approach is due:

> to man having been considered by natural science as a being devoid of, and outside, transcendental links. His spiritual life, and his freedom as the proper sphere of that life, could not, as we have seen, be known by the means of natural science.
>
> (Caruso 1964, 122)

Psychoanalytic, cognitive and developmental psychologies do not accept that human persons have a transcendent element which is integral to the whole. However, humanistic, existential and transpersonal approaches recognise that there is a spiritual dimension in human personality and that this is being undermined by technological progress. Although technology if harnessed properly has been immensely beneficial, when its values (sic) of efficiency, functionalism and utilitarianism dominate all, it tends to undermine spiritual values and eventually annihilates the notion of spirit altogether. Existential perspectives claim that technology eventually degrades the human spirit and creates a de-personalisation because our values become centred on *doing* rather than *being*. That is, we view others and ourselves in terms of what we do, our roles and functions rather than (or as well as) who we are. Indeed, it has been argued that this process of adaptation has been so powerful that most in the scientific–technological societies of the world can think of themselves and others only in these terms. When these are removed from us through illness, retirement, unemployment or other structural change we lose our sense of identity and life becomes meaningless for many. This can be seen in retirement from sport and career-ending injury, when the athlete turns to alcohol and drug abuse and other harmful behaviours to numb the pain associated with the collapse of personal identity and feelings of meaninglessness and despair.

One of the most important existential psychologists (Van Kaam 1969) claimed that, without a conception of personality that includes the spiritual, the so-called transcendental life directives of faith, hope and love cannot be fully encountered or experienced. The question of hope is extremely important especially in relation to any discussion of sport performance. The uniquely human capacity 'to wish for something that may or may not happen' (i.e. to hope) reveals that the desire to think beyond the fully knowable is part of human nature. The transcendental refers to those ideas and thoughts beyond our normal day-to-day lives. Some existential and transpersonal approaches describe this in terms of the human capacity to think about why there is a world and life in the first place, what is the meaning of life and what will happen when we die.

One of the difficulties of discussing the transcendental dimension is that we are faced with the challenge of describing something deeply personal that is experienced holistically, when our mind, body and spirit act as one. However, studies employing phenomenological approaches have attempted to capture the essence of these experiences. In many ways similar to the sport research on peak experiences (Ravizza 2002) and flow states (Csikszentmihalyi and Csikszentmihalyi 1988) these investigations have identified that transpersonal and transcendental experiences often involve a number of very specific elements. For example, Valle (1989) has claimed that they involve a sense of calmness, stillness, a transformation of time and loss of self-awareness coupled with a feeling of being part of something much bigger than oneself and the world.

Finally, transcendental and transpersonal accounts in psychology most usually accept that, to be fully human, a person must remain open to the possibility that there is some form of ultimate meaning. Within existential traditions, Frankl (1984) has been an advocate of a related view which claims that we have a need to search for some form of ultimate meaning in our lives. Alsup (1995, 247) has gone a step further and sees the human personality as sacred, in which an 'encounter with the Supreme Personality of the Creator takes place' in our interactions with each other, the world and with our spiritual selves. Alsup's particular perspective is based on his psychotherapeutic work with Native American clients and their traditional approaches to spirituality. This idea of a personal relationship between God and individual human beings is central to the approach of transpersonal psychologists and others who have drawn on Christian, Jewish, Buddhist and other Eastern religious and spiritual perspectives in their work. For these psychologists and psychotherapists the person is understood as a *synthesis* between mind, body and spirit and as someone for whom the need to place all meaning into a final or *ultimate framework*, variously referred to as the supreme being, the ultimate source or God, is intrinsic to human being whether consciously accepted or not. Within sport, an increasing number of athletes have mentioned the importance of holding religious and spiritual beliefs that provide meaning and direction in their careers and broader lives. For example, recent research by Watson and Czech (2005) suggests that a number of athletes frequently use prayer and other religious practices to make sense of their experiences in competitive sport.

Sport and persons

Before considering the possible implications for sport arising out of this discussion on persons and personality it may be helpful to identify where this topic has been alluded to within sport literature. Although it could reasonably be expected that sport and exercise psychology would have had something to say on the matter given its early interest in sports personality research, that this did not occur is more likely on account of the failure of the discipline, until recently, to consider much beyond cognitive, behavioural and trait psychology. Miller and Kerr (2002) have suggested that during the 1960s and 1970s sport psychology researchers focused on the relationship between personality traits and sport performance. This body of work became known as sport *personology* research, despite the fact that very little discussion ever took place about the differing conceptual notions of personality and persons! Not surprisingly, this largely atheoretical research revealed very few interesting or useful findings. During the 1980s and 1990s sport psychology turned its attention to measuring specific personality traits rather than studying personality in more global terms, and began to concentrate on mental skills training.

However, outside of this particular scientific discipline, a disparate group of scholars had already been engaged in an analysis of the personal significance of sport, in American life at least. Possibly the most important and earliest work in this area was that of Michael Novak. Prebish (1993, 242) refers to Novak as:

> a highly respected Catholic theologian . . . His 1976 volume *The Joy of Sports* was one of the very first books to deal extensively with the topic of the relationship between religion and sport, thus providing a major impetus to the work of others that followed.

Although not dealing in any systematic way with the ideas of personhood, persons and spirituality, these terms and those of freedom, play, courage, sacred and spirit infuse his writing. One of the most stimulating chapters in Novak's book looks at the metaphysics of sport through a discussion around the depth and reality of sport. In a brilliant analysis and reverse of the commonly held beliefs of the past 300 years or so, Novak argues it is play that is serious and work that is an illusion! In developing ideas expressed by Aristotle, St Thomas Aquinas and Josef Pieper (whose approach we will consider later in this chapter), he points out that in Protestant and Marxist cultures there is a belief that progress is fully achievable through human effort and work. Novak challenges this particular prejudice by arguing that, despite organisational, educational and material improvements, humans are not morally and ethically any better now than in earlier times. We have been so conditioned to believe in the completeness of human progress that we tend to overlook uncomfortable facts; such as the two world wars in the last century which killed more people than all wars combined in the preceding centuries.

Novak claims it is this all-consuming belief in the myth of continual progress that gives work its elevated status. Work to survive and produce the basics of life, which was the view held by the ancient Greeks and in pre-Reformation Christendom, was informed by a particular account of the human person. As Novak makes clear, work was meant to serve play and it is when playing that the human being is most fully him- or herself. Play is such an authentically personal experience because, unlike work, its focus is not on ends but about means. In play the person experiences freedom within set constraints and limits; the output is, materially speaking, quite worthless. *Play, like the person, finds its full justification in and of itself.* This is why we can describe play as a truly holistic mode of being, involving a synthesis of mind, body and spirit. In more straightforward terms, we can say that, whereas individuals work, only persons can really play! The spirit of playfulness is only possible when we give ourselves wholly and completely over to the game, where the immediate focus is on the task itself and nothing beyond this. There is much similarity between this idea and Csikszentmihalyi's (1992) concept of flow in sport. Novak (1994/1967, 43) argues that 'Sports are the highest products of civilization and the most accessible, lived, experiential sources of the civilizing spirit.' The more that sport provides a vehicle for play the more it provides the environment to encounter the world beyond mere work, the world of utilitarianism, of projects and products. Of course for professional sport performers these experiences are compromised since their occupation *is* sport. However, the existence of *fair play, playing to win* and, at a more psychological level, peak experiences and flow states suggests that, even in elite and paid sport, moments of pure play are desirable and possible. Finally, and approaching the matter from a more sociological view, Novak (1994/1967, 21) claims that 'Sports are religious in the sense that they are organised institutions, disciplines, and liturgies; and also in the sense that they teach religious qualities of heart and soul'. It is this final quality that links sport to notions of the person as a being composed of body, mind and spirit, or, as Novak states, heart and soul. In this sense participation in sports could be said to nurture persons and develop personality.

Objections to these claims for sport tend to highlight that this activity is only another form of entertainment and is infected with corruption, greed and dishonesty like the rest of life. However, according to Pieper (1989), Novak (1994/1967) and Nesti (2004) these criticisms have missed a very important point, which is that sports are not merely entertainment for many people but represent something much more serious, and are imbued with *personal meaning*. Again, the fact that some sports have been over-commercialised, manipulated and abused does not mean that moments of courage, beauty, creativity and testimony to human resilience and spirit do not exist within them.

Playing sport

It may be helpful at this stage to offer a summary of the relationship between play, persons and sport. It appears that the concept of play is inextricably linked to the idea of human persons. Although it may sound unusual to those who see sport as just another means of entertainment, sport is ultimately based on play and this concept cannot be understood apart from human nature. *From an existential perspective, to be human is to play.* Play is purposive, directed and, simultaneously, spontaneous and free. Novak (1994/1967) and Pieper (1998) argue that it is a form of behaviour that only humans pursue and develop. This is because 'play is not tied to necessity, except to the necessity of the human spirit to exercise its freedom, to enjoy something that is not practical or productive, or required for gaining food or shelter' (Novak 1994/1967, 33). The person, as an embodied spirit, is capable of *playing* sport. This is because to be a person is to be someone beyond pure matter (Hume) or pure mind (Kant) and to be more than a psycho-physiological organism with a social identity! Slusher (1993) has claimed that sport allows the individual to enter into personhood because engaged in a spirit of play we come to know ourselves whole. This self-knowledge paradoxically reveals to the person that he or she can never completely understand or control everything. Within sport this can be seen when, despite training, planning and preparing methodically, competitive success is often attributed to something beyond each of these elements. 'They showed great spirit', 'put themselves on the line' and 'were prepared to die for the cause' are not simply melodramatic phrases used by coaches, fans and sport performers but convey that something else, which is not easy to express in words, contributed to the success. Slusher describes this in terms of the potential for a person playing sport to experience the transcendental and to be confronted with an awareness that we can never fully know anything. This relates to the idea of hope, which, as we shall discuss, is intrinsic to sport and personhood. Slusher (1993, 195–6) points out that:

> to achieve in sport man must achieve his own awareness of personal horizons. Anything requiring this depth assumes a communication with the self, requiring the utmost of silence in order to be really *heard*, to be heard by powers that, somehow, are more than human.
>
> (Slusher 1993, 195–6)

Sport offers the athlete an opportunity to participate holistically: mind, body and spirit in unison. Engaging in training and competitive games facilitates the development of courage (Corlett 1996b), self-knowledge (Corlett 1996a), awareness of the transcendental (Nesti 2004) and spiritual growth (Ravizza 2002). Each of these terms cannot be adequately explained apart from the idea of the person as a *unified entity* composed of mind, body and spirit.

Sport psychology

In their review of spirituality in sport psychology, Watson and Nesti (2005) have identified that other fields such as medicine (Bernardi *et. al.* 2001), psychotherapy and counselling (Richards and Bergin 1997) and psychiatry (Galanter *et al.* 1991) have begun to consider the importance of spiritual and transcendental issues in their work. Most of the research and practice investigating these topics draws on humanistic, transpersonal and existential psychology accounts of human being. Unfortunately, with the exception of Corlett (1996b), Ravizza (2002) and Nesti (2002) in terms of practice, and Fahlberg *et al.* (1992), Csikszentmihalyi (1992) and Dale (2000) in research, few in sport psychology have alluded to the spirit or spiritual concepts. The most likely explanation for this is because sport psychology has been based on a positivist natural science paradigm which does not recognise elements like spirit, will, courage and other related concepts. In contrast, existential–phenomenological psychology emphasises that personal meaning is an important dimension that must be acknowledged if we are to understand human being. The human person, as an *inextricable intermixture* (Merleau-Ponty 1962), capable of acting freely despite the limits set by individual biology and circumstance, must confront the ultimate question around the meaning of their lives and life in general. For some, meaning is found in God or commitment to a cause such as the environment or world peace. Others affirm that there is no meaning in life beyond the meaning they give it, and that this is always changing and individually chosen (this is known as the postmodern position).

Sport has been praised as something capable of confronting human beings with a reality beyond its very special physical and psychological demands. For example, Pope John Paul II in his address to the Council for the International Amateur Athletics Federation in 1987 stressed that sport, through its focus on developing harmony of movement and action, 'is also an important moment for guaranteeing the balance and total wellbeing of the person'. He added that sport:

> is an activity that involves more than the movement of the body; it demands the use of intelligence and the disciplining of the will. It reveals, in other words, the wonderful structure of the human person created by God as a spiritual being, a unity of body and spirit. If sport is reduced to the cult of the human body, forgetting the primacy of the spirit, or if it were to hinder your moral and intellectual development, or result in you serving less than noble aims, then it would lose its true significance and, in the long run, it would become even harmful to your healthy full growth as human persons. You are true *athletes* when you prepare yourselves not only by training your bodies but also by constantly engaging the spiritual dimensions of your person for a *harmonious* development of all your talents.
>
> (John Paul II, quoted in Feeney 1995, 67)

In the sport psychology literature there are few examples where writers have discussed the relationship between human persons, sport and the spirit in such clear terms. Clearly, these notions do not fit neatly into the dominant cognitive, behavioural and trait approaches, although it is surprising that recent work by Balague (1999) dealing with values, identity and meaning in sport avoids any in-depth discussion of persons and personhood. The exception to this is to be found in the work of Ravizza and Fazzio (2002) and Nesti (2002, 2004). That these three sport psychologists are writing about their applied work and drawing on humanistic, existential and transpersonal approaches in psychology is of considerable importance. Their work argues that it is within the experience of one-to-one work with sport performers in real sport settings that questions around what is personality and what constitutes the human person are most keenly felt.

From a different perspective, recent work by Miller and Kerr (2002), investigating excellence and sport performance, has highlighted that sport psychology consultants may be able to encourage personal development in athletes and coaches through improving their self-awareness and self-knowledge. According to Corlett (1996a, 88), self-knowledge and not mental skills training is the most important element, and too often sport psychology has been relying only on 'technique based symptomatic relief'. In building on this critique of sport psychology, Nesti (2004) claims that, through a process of self-examination, self-knowledge rather than the more superficial concept of self-awareness will be developed. He adds that 'it is about the growth and development of the deepest core of being. This is the base where our *authentic self* is located, this core must be constantly confronted and fed for its growth' (Nesti 2004, 91–92). Within sport, the athlete engages in a journey filled with elation, despair, and highs and lows. Unlike in most other areas of human activity, these experiences are equally felt physically and mentally. Ultimately, at least for those prepared to listen, these experiences can teach us something about ourselves as persons that assists us within sport and the rest of life.

Corlett (1996b) has claimed that courage is an important virtue, rather than a skill as such, which can be developed in sport. He views courage as did Aristotle, Plato and Aquinas before him, as something both rational and emotional. The courageous person tries to act in the best possible way to achieve desired ends despite being uncertain and feeling anxious about the outcome. Another benefit of increasing self-knowledge in the sport performer is that he or she learns about the experience of anxiety and hope in human being. Competitive anxiety in sport has received considerable attention within sport psychology, although most work (Jones 1995) has adopted a narrow cognitive–behavioural and trait psychology approach to the topic. Where sport anxiety has been conceived more holistically (Nesti and Sewell 1999) or from a more ecological perspective (Lazarus 2000), it is possible to understand how this concept relates to greater self-understanding. For example, an existential psychology perspective in sport states that persons expand and strengthen their sense of self by facing up to and moving through the normal anxiety accompanying a challenge. By repeatedly going through this process in sport the person learns more about him- or herself and grows in understanding. The competitive sport performer in particular will begin to recognise that 'knowing who they are and what they stand for' (i.e. their core values) is vital to being able to freely choose to subject themselves to the challenges and anxiety encountered in sport.

These ideas of self-knowledge and existential anxiety cannot be understood apart from a personalist account of psychology and sport psychology. The notion of courage, as described by Corlett (1996b), depends on a definition of the person as a spiritual being possessing free will. Again, sport performers experience anxiety because they have chosen to place themselves in the competitive event or challenge. If persons were not free then there could not be any experience of anxiety, although of course fear would be possible. Anxiety accompanies the possibility of choice and the act of choosing. In this sense only the human person, as a partially determined being with some measure of responsibility for his or her actions and thoughts, can experience anxiety.

Freedom and the concept of *free will* has received very little attention in the sport-related literature. Centrally to the idea of persons, scholars such as Clark (1973) have argued that personal freedom without responsibility to others does not represent true freedom but is licence. Within sport this position is represented by some strands of existential psychology, according to Nesti (2004). Another view of freedom and persons can be found in the sport research of Jackson and Csik-szentmihalyi (1999) and the peak experience literature (Privette and Bundrick 1997; Ravizza 1977). Hill (2001, 129) contends that peak experiences in sport have a mystical or transpersonal quality and 'include joyfulness, transcendence . . . that result in personal integration, growth, and expansion of personal identity'. Sport psychologists drawing on humanistic psychology have described the potential for sport to provide peak experiences or flow states. Usually associated with optional performance, athletes experience deeply enjoyable, absorbing moments accompanied by feelings of mind, body and spirit integration. The almost religious and transcendental accounts of climbers, runners and many other athletes in these states can only be adequately understood by researchers who conceive of human beings in terms of the person. However, for humanistic sport psychologists following the earlier work of Rogers (1961) and Maslow (1968), persons are understood as possessing complete freedom to become what they wish. This has been challenged by some existential approaches, pointing out that participants are fully aware from their engagement in sport that, although they have some measure of control over what they do, they are limited by others and by their own physical and psychological capabilities. A very important book by Murphy and White called *In the Zone: Transcendent Experience in Sports* (1995) includes chapters on mystical, transcendental, spiritual and philosophical accounts of exceptional occurrences in sport. Unfortunately, despite being one of the most comprehensive accounts of altered states and peak experiences in sport, this detailed and impressive work does not examine the key notions of personhood, persons and personality. Arguably, without this analysis it is difficult to convince the natural science and positivist sport psychologist that these experiences in sport are signs of our spiritual natures, rather than being merely examples of heightened emotional states.

Finally, the work of applied sport psychologists rests upon philosophical accounts of human being. However, very few writers on sport psychology seem aware of the need to articulate the underpinning philosophical assumptions of their work. This is most likely because of a reluctance to mix questions of philosophy with the (natural) science of sport psychology. This position has been challenged and criticised in the work of Corlett (1996a), Ravizza (2002) and Nesti (2002, 2004). They have pointed out that all techniques, for example mental skills training, also rest on a particular philosophical base whether explicitly recognised or not.

Conclusion

As has been discussed, the clearest example of an approach that focuses on links to philosophy is existential psychology. This is because it views psychology as a human science which can trace its lineage to philosophy and the natural sciences equally. Lavallee *et al.* (2000, 122) have noted that 'existential psychology has dared to declare its link with a school of philosophy and, by doing so, exposes other psychologies in their refusal to examine their own philosophical roots and metaphysical assumptions'. One such area where this has important implications for applied sport psychologists is how they view the relationship between themselves and the client–athlete. Goldenberg and Isaacson (1996) have highlighted that Buber's (1937) notion of I–*Thou* encounters is important in explaining the philosophy of persons and personhood that undergirds many approaches in existential psychology. When in the I–Thou mode the relationship between the sport psychologist and the sport performer is much more than an impersonal encounter. In contrast to the *I–It* mode, which involves personal distance and detached analysis, I–Thou communication is only possible where there is an 'open, unguarded self-giving of one person to another . . . a complete absorption and total focus in another person *as an end in themselves*' (Nesti 2004, 82).

Existential psychologists outside sport such as Spinelli (1996) stress that the encounter itself is the most important part of a counselling or therapeutic experience. Some applied sport psychologists (Andersen 2000) have made similar claims, although without providing a rigorous philosophical justification in support of this. A notable exception to this is Ravizza (2002), and Ravizza and Fazio (2002), who have claimed that their personal qualities and personalities have been a major factor in their successful activities as consultants. Their view supports the position advocated by existential psychology that authentic communication is only possible when a meeting takes place between persons rather than individuals. In order words, only when we approach the other as Thou (i.e. a person) can genuine empathy, spontaneity and passion exist in our dialogue with someone else. The idea is that the sport psychologist should 'bring their personality along' if they truly hope to meet the sport performer as a fully human person in an encounter that is *real!* This can be contrasted with an *impersonal* meeting, in which two individuals, carrying out their respective roles and functions as sport psychologist and athlete, discuss superficial, peripheral and often trivial matters.

Finally, it must be admitted that this emphasis on the person of the sport psychologist and their personality is a controversial one and can easily be misunderstood. This view is not an attempt to argue for a narrowly defined personality type. Nevertheless it *is* a demand that the sport psychologist has acquired personal qualities arising out of self-reflection, engagement with a wide range of different cultures and contextual settings, personal integrity, trust and a high level of self-knowledge. Although not a psychologist or writing specifically about sport, Berdyaev (1937) has explained why notions of the person, personhood and personality are so important. He 'contends that a person can only grow, develop and learn in relation to another personality' (Nesti 2004, 80–81). In echoing the idea that persons are integrated beings of mind, body and spirit, he claims that personality itself is holistic and that it 'is my whole thinking, my whole willing, my whole feeling, my whole creative activity' (Berdyaev 1937, 113). Such a spiritual view of persons and personality could have a new, exciting and positive impact on the playing of sport and our encounters with sport performers.

Study questions

1 What is the main difference between persons and individuals?
2 Try to summarise Pieper's (1998) account of spirit.
3 Give examples of sport performers who you feel have personality. Explain what it is about these performers that provides evidence of this.
4 How would a sport psychologist talk to an athlete when approaching them as Thou? Can you see any problems that might arise in this situation?
5 What methodological approach and research methods would you advocate for the study of personality in sport? How would your suggestions change if personality was conceived as ultimately a spiritual concept?
6 Briefly summarise why the notion of play is related to the idea of persons.
7 Argue for and against the claim that 'only persons can play to win in sport!'

9   Suffering, sacrifice, sport psychology and the spirit

Mark Nesti

Introduction

Sport undoubtedly provides a vehicle for participants and spectators alike to experience moments of pure elation, ecstasy and even self-fulfilment. Performers of varying levels and standards have reported positive mood states and emotions whilst engaging in sport tasks and events. Research suggests that many athletes discover a real sense of enjoyment through competitive sport (Balageur *et al.* 1999), develop higher levels of self-esteem and intrinsic motivation (Ntoumanis and Biddle 1999) and achieve deeply satisfying moments of flow (Jackson and Csikszentmihalyi 1999). Empirical evidence also exists to support the view that health enhancing physical activity and exercise programmes (Crone-Grant *et al.* 2005) are associated with improvements in a number of psychological factors. This tendency of sport and exercise psychology to emphasise the beneficial dimensions of sport participation is consistent with the tenor of the parent discipline of psychology during the past forty years. Following the acceptance and growth of humanistic psychology in the 1960s, many psychologists became more interested in positive concepts like love, creativity and self-actualisation, and there was less attention given to negative behaviours and destructive emotions.

According to Maslow (1968) this represented a much needed change of direction, since he argued that psychology, and the psychoanalytical tradition in particular, had concentrated excessively on the pathological and disturbing elements of mental life. The positive psychology approach advocated by Seligman and Csikszentmihalyi (2000) is the most recent attempt to counter the formerly pessimistic mood within much of psychology. This perspective claims to build on the vision of humanistic psychology but through use of more thorough empirical research than in the past. Although this assertion has been vigorously challenged by some within humanistic psychology, few voices have pointed out that, in not equally concerning itself with the negative side of life, positive psychology represents a one-sided account. This failure to consider the ugly and unattractive dimension of our existence is especially unfortunate when one considers sport and exercise as a whole and competitive sport in particular. For example, in Cockerill's (2002) applied text addressing the key areas facing sport psychologists there are chapters on mental toughness, coach–athlete conflict, rehabilitation and severe injury, therapeutic interventions and sport retirement. Other literature in the field deals with anxiety, fear of failure, coping strategies, adherence, drop-out, and clinical conditions such as burnout, eating disorders and depression. The need for this more balanced account of the positive and negative aspects of sport participation has been succinctly captured by Wolfson (2002). She has claimed that 'The world is a stimulating but puzzling place for sports participants, who regularly experience the joys of success and the pains of failure' (Wolfson 2002, 91).

Quite clearly then, sport and exercise cannot be understood as exclusively positive experiences. Coaches and sport performers appear much more aware than researchers that achievement in sport requires sacrifice, dedication, commitment and resilience. The concept of mental toughness in sport psychology relates very closely to this. Brennan (1998) has described mental toughness as involving, among other factors, the ability to withstand pain, to persist in the face of challenges and to accept responsibility for failures without excuses. Research by Clough *et al.* (2002) with coaches and elite level players identified that mental toughness is important in helping athletes deal with injuries, poor refereeing, aggressive spectators, performance mistakes, getting substituted, negative media and being dropped. These and several other uncomfortable moments and challenging experiences are as much a feature of sport as the more positive and uplifting ones. Given this capacity for sport to provide positive and negative elements in equal measure, it may seem surprising that so many continue to engage in it, and often for no obvious extrinsic reward.

This chapter intends to approach the problem of pain, suffering and sacrifice in sport beyond any account of the merely physical and mental aspects associated with this important cultural phenomenon. At one level it is possible to interpret the trials and tribulations of the mind and body in sport as being an unfortunate component; an unattractive obstacle on the way to achievement and success. However, by adopting a more holistic and broader conception of the human being as a person made up of mind, body and spirit, it is possible to view the anguish and disappointments of sport from a different philosophical and psychological framework.

The first section of this chapter will consider how researchers within sport psychology have generally treated this topic. Brief consideration will be given to studies investigating injury (Maddison and Prapavessis 2005) career transition, termination and retirement (Lavallee and Wylleman 2000), and stress and coping (Nicholls *et al.* 2005). The approach taken to anxiety in sport will also be discussed for two main reasons. First, the overarching theme of this body of research has been to conceptualise anxiety for the most part as a negative emotion (Nesti 2004). This will be contrasted with the existentialist position that highlights the potentially positive and constructive dimension of anxiety. Second, the experience of anxiety is common to all those activities, including sport, in which individuals strive to meet a challenge and achieve goals. Sport, whether explicitly competitive or not, provides a perfect vehicle to encounter the uncomfortable emotion of anxiety. This chapter looks at some of the implications of this for the sportsperson and examines how anxiety links to concepts like courage, destiny, self-knowledge and spiritual growth.

Courage is a very important and frequently used term in sport. Coaches often talk about courageous fight-backs, brave tackling, strength of character and team spirit. Unfortunately, with a few exceptions, these and other similar words are rarely discussed in the coaching or sport psychology literature. However, in the real world of sport, athletes and teams are lauded for their strong personalities and for never giving up no matter what. Clearly then, these more traditional terms and indeed that of personality itself, are connected to an individual's capacity to succeed in sport. Personality is a well-known topic in psychology and many different theories exist around this term. Very few approaches to personality theory acknowledge that we are spiritual beings possessing a mind and body. One such example that does conceive of personality in this way is the transpersonal existential psychology perspective (Valle 1989). This will be discussed and some suggestions made about how such a paradigm could add to our understanding of the role of suffering and sacrifice in sport.

Some writers and researchers have argued that sport psychology will remain largely unable to make sense of the place of pain, suffering and sacrifice in sport because of its inability to see these terms as anything other than negative. The dominance of positivism means that, whereas it is possible to acknowledge that the sport experience can lead to bad and difficult times, these can never be understood as something potentially beneficial. However, by concentrating on individual meaning (Nesti 2004) and the athletes' lived experience (Dale 2000) it is possible to generate data confirming that failure, loss, pain and hardship can help the overall development and spiritual growth of the person undergoing these experiences. According to applied sport psychologists like Ravizza (2002) and Watson and Nesti (2005) there are links between mental excellence, spiritual awareness and enhanced performance. These connections are beginning to emerge more clearly as the field increasingly adopts qualitative methodologies (Sparkes 2002) and existential–phenomenological methods (Czech *et al.* 2004) focusing on subjective accounts and personal meaning.

Despite these promising advances, the discipline of sport psychology may be unable to make any further headway without recognition that it should be based on a human science approach (Giorgi 1970) that can accommodate a transcendental and personalist philosophy. The ideas behind this and the implications for sport psychology research and practice have been addressed in an earlier chapter in the book. This chapter will examine how recent literature in sport psychology has dealt with such difficult terms for the contemporary individual as sacrifice, hardship and despair. One approach to understanding these concepts is by considering the idea of *catharsis*. Although commonly associated in modern times with Freud and psychoanalysis, catharsis has much older and more philosophical roots. Pieper (1995) has provided one of the most impressive and lucid accounts of catharsis. His work draws on the writings of Plato, Socrates and the medieval theologian and metaphysician St Thomas Aquinas. Beyond this, Pieper also considers the relation between courage and fear, and despair and hope. These important and familiar terms are scrutinised in this chapter alongside a Christian interpretation of anxiety. The final section considers what this all means for competitive sport and sport psychology. This chapter focuses on sport at all levels of performance to reveal how personal sacrifice and the frustrations encountered in this growing and important area of human activity can help develop the whole person, his or her personality, and the important spiritual qualities of courage, integrity and hope.

Painful moments in sport

One of the most studied areas in sport psychology relating to pain is that of physical injury in athletes. This is easy to understand since most competitive sport performers will be injured at some time in their playing career. Interestingly, whilst most focus has been on injury to the body there have been few examples addressing how injury is *experienced holistically*, that is mentally and physically. Consistent with the reductionist and positivist approach that still prevails in most of sport and exercise psychology, research has investigated the relationship between athletic injury and a range of psychological factors. Studies have looked at psycho-social factors and incidence of injury (Lysens *et al.* 1984), predictability of sport injury (Lysens *et al.* 1986), differences in pain response (Marsh and Kleitman 2003) and psychological support during injury rehabilitation (Gutkind 2004). A notable exception to this body is the work by Sparkes (2002) that provides an autobiographical account of a serious sport injury. This particular qualitative method allows for a discussion of the experience from a personal perspective and highlights that pain and injury cannot always be viewed as completely negative factors. Unfortunately, empirical studies to date have been less interested in the individual sport performer's *experience* of injury and *the meaning* they attach to it. The use of nomothetic methods and designs in sport psychology has helped to identify the important psychological antecedents of injury and the key variables in managing rehabilitation. Although this is valuable and important information it can be criticised for failing to provide an account of how different individuals, each in their own unique world, actually encounter and understand this experience. Such an approach could reveal, for example, that it may be possible for an athlete to be frustrated and upset about an injury and yet be capable of believing that they have developed greater self-awareness, mental toughness and courage in working towards their goal of regaining fitness.

The overarching approach to sport injury as a completely negative phenomenon represents a one-sided account that has more in common with research into clinical issues in sport and exercise. Studies on burnout (Gould *et al.* 1996) and anxiety and perfectionism (Hall *et al.* 1998) tend to emphasise that these experiences are completely negative and unappealing. Some psychologists have argued that depression can be a hopeful sign since it reveals that an individual is struggling to find meaning in their lives (Frankl 1984), or that they have rejected impersonal norms as a guide to their behaviour (Laing 1969). In general, though, most writers and researchers in psychology and sport psychology tend to view depression as an unwelcome and deeply unpleasant state.

A more promising account of the personal difficulties and painful challenges facing an athlete can be found in some of the 226 studies carried out from 1950 to 2000 on career transitions in sport (Lavallee and Wylleman 2000). This work fo-

cuses on coping mechanisms, adjustment problems, athletic identity, career-endi
injury and a range of other factors related to career termination and within-spc
transitions. Most of the literature examines the negative experiences of athlete
in transition, although some attempt has been made to look at transferable skills
(Mayocchi and Hanrahan 2000) and athlete lifestyle programmes (Petitpas *et al.*
1997). Lavallee *et al.* (2000) have revealed that mentoring, account-making and
existential psychology interventions can be used to help athletes deal with transitions. Evidence suggests that these and other models of intervention can help
sport performers negotiate difficult phases in their careers and begin to accept
some measure of personal responsibility for this. The existential approach differs
from the others by examining how the anxiety-producing steps towards transition
can benefit an athlete, especially when they confront the challenge and move
forward in spite of feelings of uncertainty and doubt. This final point highlights an
important difference between this perspective and the coping research in applied
sport psychology. Recent studies, such as Nicholls *et al.* (2005) on coping and elite
level golf, adopt a predominantly cognitive behavioural perspective that advocates
the use of mental skills training to deal with performance stress. Although the
work of Nicholls *et al.* represents a promising new development because it uses a
phenomenological method to allow a more person-centred account to emerge, it
remains wedded to the general idea that stress needs to be *managed away* rather
than accepted and even welcomed. This view of stress is even more prevalent
within the literature dealing with anxiety and sport, and is something that will be
considered in depth later in the chapter.

Finally, the topic of pain in sport has been described in most of the literature as something to be avoided and as a negative and unattractive by-product
of competitive sport. However, phenomenological research by Smith and Smith
(2004) has revealed that, at least for elite endurance athletes, physical and mental
pain can be viewed both positively and negatively. It seems that intense suffering
and personal sacrifice are accepted and may even be welcomed by some athletes
because they assist in the development of inner fortitude, courage and humility, all
of which relate to sporting performance. In addition, some accounts from athletes
refer to the *cathartic* or cleansing power of sacrifice and pain. This is especially
evident in the autobiographies and personal recollections of elite athletes like cy-
clist Lance Armstrong, and Olympic champions such as Kelly Holmes, Jonathan
Edwards and Steve Redgrave.

Anxiety and sport

One of the most studied concepts in sport is that of competitive anxiety. According to Jones (1995) this refers to the feelings of apprehension and nervousness felt
by performers before sport competition. Although this has generally been seen as
a negative emotion that undermines performance, empirical studies have failed to
support this view unequivocally. The reasons for this could be due to several factors
such as the use of inappropriate performance measures (Jones and Hardy 1990),
problems with competitive anxiety questionnaires (Lane *et al.* 1999), failure to

consider broader causes of anxiety in sport (Nesti 2002) and athlete perceptions of high levels of anxiety as being beneficial to sport performance (Jones *et al.* 1994). In relation to this, a significant number of studies with elite athletes (Lane and Terry 1998) and lower-level performers (Jones *et al.* 1996) have revealed that some interpret higher than normal levels of anxiety before competition as a good sign, and as something likely to assist them to perform well in the approaching event or match. Despite this, as Corlett (1996a) has pointed out, sport psychologists have been keen to use various forms of mental skills training to help sport performers reduce or completely remove any feelings of competitive anxiety. Given the potential for anxiety to be positively related to performance for some athletes, this strategy seems unhelpful. In addition, such a conceptualisation of anxiety in sport fails to consider that this uncomfortable emotion can be beneficial to the person beyond any immediate links to performance. A recent applied study by Nesti (2006) with an Olympic-level performer and former world champion highlighted that from an existential psychology framework it is possible to understand anxiety as being a disturbing and often very uncomfortable experience which nevertheless can be good for us. This challenges the notion of positive psychology and most forms of humanistic psychology whose exclusive focus is on pleasant emotions and positive affect. An important critique of positive psychology has been provided by Held (2004). She argues that reality is made up of positive and negative experiences and a more balanced and valid perspective would take this fact into account. She further challenges what she calls the 'tyranny of the positive attitude', pointing out that 'if people feel bad about life's many difficulties and they cannot manage to transcend their pain no matter how hard they try [to learn optimism] they could end up feeling even worse' (Held 2004, 12).

The existential view builds on this, going one step further, and claims that normal anxiety is healthy and it is often associated with personal growth. This conceptualisation of anxiety rests on the idea that a person is a spiritual being capable of making choices and acting freely. According to the existentialist perspective, anxiety results from and very often accompanies the awareness we have of our responsibility to grasp our freedom to do, think or feel something. Although existential philosophers (Marcel 1948) and psychologists (May 1995) emphasise that our behaviour is influenced by our genes and the environment, they argue that human beings are genuinely capable of making their own choices and decisions. For example, in sport an individual may have the ability (genes) and skills (environment) to allow him or her to move on to a higher level; however, ultimately the responsibility to pursue this path lies with him or her. Existential psychology would claim that the anxiety associated with facing new challenges should not be seen as a negative but as the inevitable, uncomfortable and even painful feeling that 'accompanies something that we simultaneously fear and yet desire' (Nesti 2004, 59).

This view of anxiety is impossible to understand without reference to spiritual ideas of the person. Human spirit has been identified with the notion of freedom. However, as Clark (1973) states, humans are not purely material or totally spiritual beings but, as the phenomenologist Merleau-Ponty (1962) argued, the person is an inseparable mix of matter and spirit. Within sport and exercise we often put ourselves in difficult situations where we may fail to achieve our goals. This uncertainty of outcome creates anxiety which is accepted and even embraced by sportspersons, especially where they have freely put themselves in this situation. From an existential view, the anxiety encountered in these moments develops the deepest core of who we are. This has been referred to as the *self* and according to the most important existential thinker (Kierkegaard 1980/1844) the spirit is at the centre of the self. In competitive sport it has been noted that those athletes with excellent self-awareness (Ravizza 2002) and deep self-knowledge (Corlett 1996a) are best able to successfully confront the stresses, challenges and demands of sport. Anxiety then is seen here as related to spiritual strength and growth of a person. The link to performance should be clear from this in that the greater the level of self-knowledge and the stronger the *person,* the more likely he or she will be able to fully utilise his or her physical and mental attributes. This is one of the reasons why experienced applied sport psychologists like Salter (1997), Ravizza (2002) and Nesti (2004) advocate the enhancement of performance through encouraging spiritual growth in the athletes they work with.

Kierkegaard has been identified as the first to investigate the concept of anxiety from a psychological rather than a philosophical position. Although not in any way addressing how this is experienced in specific activities in life like sport, his work is remarkably insightful. He claimed that 'Anxiety is freedom's possibility' and 'the more profoundly he is in anxiety, the greater the man' (Kierkegaard 1980/1844, 155). This relates to the idea that in freely choosing new challenges we inevitably experience anxiety. Kierkegaard states that this should not divert us from the task, no matter how much we would like to abdicate our responsibility and evade what he calls a dreadful torment! Sport is infused with the possibility of anxiety. Returning from injury, dealing with both victory and defeat, progressing to higher levels and remaining at the top for as long as possible are just some of the moments where anxiety pervades the sport experience. The choice facing the sport performer is to persist in spite of uncertainty over the outcome. This depends on a number of factors of which the spiritual concept of courage is the most important according to Corlett (1996b). This view of the person as a spiritual being endowed with some measure of freedom provides a different way for understanding the relationship between anxiety and courage in sport.

Finally, Kierkegaard (1980/1844) chides those who claim that they have never known anxiety in their lives. To such people he gives a stark explanation; it is because they are *spiritless!* This could be understood in a sporting context where a team continued to try to win a match during which they had been outplayed, or found themselves several goals or points behind their opponents. Coaches and players often refer to these fight-back moments as being evidence of *team spirit.* From an existential psychology view this demonstration of spirit occurs when individuals or teams refuse to hide from the anxiety of their perilous state by giving up. Instead, they accept the responsibility to do their duty, and to heroically continue to strive for the goals when the easiest and less painful option is to accept defeat and play out the rest of the game. Sport performances in which an athlete (irrespective of level) defies the odds, overcomes a superior opponent or puts up a great fight, are incredibly exciting and appealing. Arguably these are the clearest examples of spirit in sport and cannot be adequately understood without consideration of spiritual terms like courage, character, sacrifice and even personality itself.

Sporting courage

Courage has very rarely been discussed in the sport psychology literature. This may be because it is seen as more of a philosophical concept and a rather old-fashioned term. In contrast, sport psychology texts often include reference to mental toughness (Clough *et al.* 2002) and self-belief and self-confidence (Moran, 1996). Definitions of these and other similar constructs refer to resilience, commitment, motivation, focus and dedication. Although courage clearly involves most, if not all of these elements, it is not fully captured by this list. A further unusual aspect of the exclusion of courage from the literature is that it has always been understood in opposition to fear and anxiety. As has been discussed, anxiety in sport and fear of failure has been extensively studied in the discipline. This has almost invariably been done without any mention of the relationship between these terms and bravery and courage. Exceptions to this are Corlett's (1996b) philosophical work and Nesti's (2004) account from an existential psychology perspective. Corlett's work is especially important since it draws on the writings of Aristotle, Socrates and St Thomas Aquinas and reconnects courage to the notion of virtue. He points out that courage is not about 'overcoming fear, it is the transformation of fear into willing sacrifice' (Corlett 1996b, 51). In arguing that sport provides an ideal opportunity to act courageously he defines it as 'reason, passion and action in concert . . . in the face of threats to one's physical, mental, or social well being of the kind perceived regularly by competitive athletes' (Corlett 1996b, 52). Arguably, courage can only be understood holistically and therefore is as much a spiritual idea as it is psychological. The courageous athlete faces up to challenges, difficulties and pain rather than seeking to avoid these moments or experiences. This requires a high degree of self-knowledge and the capacity to suffer for some higher goal. The accounts of athletes overcoming serious injury, training towards major events and recovering lost form often reveal examples of courage in adversity. Courage is much more than motivation, confidence or mental toughness because it demands that the whole person place him- or herself 'on the line'. The courageous act is always deeply personal even though it may also help the team or squad in a sports situation. To act courageously means at least that the person wills him- or herself to do something for a greater good which may not be actualised in the end. Courage cannot be imposed on someone and is best seen in sport where the performer or team keeps doing the right thing even when they are vilified for this, or where the situation seems hopeless. In this sense courage in sport does not fully make sense in that it is the opposite of a clinical, calculating and utilitarian approach. In addition, the courageous act testifies to the mystery of human existence in that it is a clear example of voluntarily putting oneself in a difficult and even dangerous situation where failure may bring suffering, humiliation and even an end to a particular stage of life. For example, the amateur sport performer may accept the hardships and mental discomfort involved in trying to play within the rules in a team facing relegation from the division. This could be despite injunctions from the coaches and other players to win at any cost. Clearly this reveals, as Corlett (following Aquinas) has argued, that courage has a moral dimension and it is this which differentiates it from mere bravery and fearlessness.

It is quite common to hear coaches talking about the need to have courageous performers who will not wilt under the anxiety of competition and the demands of sport. In contrast, bravery is seen as an important attribute but one that is more instinctual, habitual and not as freely expressed and personal as courage. The courageous athlete is the one who keeps asking for the ball even after making a mistake, or trains hard despite no recognition from the coaches, or tries to give his or her best even in the worst moments, failures or defeats. In analysing the notion of courage, Pieper (1989) highlights that, unlike the techniques favoured by psychology and sport psychology, courage is not something we learn to allow us to banish fear and control anxiety. He remarks that neither should courage be equated with fearlessness. Particularly in its more extreme form this is the opposite of courage, in that like bravery it does not originate from our deepest core but is often more of a specific behaviour or psychological attribute.

In conclusion, it is possible to understand the reluctance of sport psychology to include courage as a topic worthy of study because it is quite clearly a spiritual category. Although a psychological investigation of its value, place in sport and connection to other constructs in sport psychology is possible and attractive, this is currently unlikely to occur because the discipline has largely removed all spiritual concepts from its lexicon. A challenge to this is slowly beginning to emerge within the work of Ravizza and Fazio (2002) and Watson and Nesti (2005), which calls for the inclusion of spirituality in sport psychology consulting. Arguably, a deeper understanding of courage as ultimately a spiritual idea cannot be developed in sport psychology without a truly holistic account of the person.

Personhood, personality and persons have been discussed in Chapter 8 and much of what was said there is equally important to a proper understanding of courage in sport. Without some recognition that the person is capable of acting freely beyond the constraints of his or her genes and particular environment, courage becomes a meaningless term. Approaches to personality such as those of Jung (1956) and Van Kaam (1969) include some reference to the transcendental dimension of human experience. In their work, personality is conceived as something forever unfinished and open. It is the core of who we are and is a dynamic, involving our daily battles of striving for the good against the limitations imposed on us by self and others. Courage has a special place in this since it is the self-conscious act of the whole person in freely putting him- or herself forward to grow in the many (often) small victories and (frequently) painful defeats of life. In sport the courageous personality would be the spiritually aware athlete who heroically holds nothing of him- or herself back and quite literally gives his or her all, time and time again. Such heroes exist at all levels of sport and across different nationalities, sex and age groups. In referring to heroic acts in sport, Saint Sing (2003) uses the phrase 'breakthrough kinesis' to describe those special moments when athletes somehow manage to overcome levels of performance previously thought of as insurmountable. Bannister's four-minute mile, the sub-ten-second 100 metres and, in football, Arsenal's unbeaten run of games in 2003/4 are examples of this. These and many other feats cannot be understood adequately without recourse to ideas of human spirit, courage and recognition of a transcendental element in personality formation. This final point relates to the idea that without the transcendental and spiritual notions of hope and love, ideas like sacrifice, suffering and even joy in sport are impossible to understand, especially when these are experienced by the millions of people who engage in sport without significant extrinsic rewards. Saint Sing (2004) captures this desire that athletes have to struggle to achieve their goals in spite of setbacks. As an Olympic rowing coach she points out that this spiritual task is not exclusive to the sport performer. She claims that a major reason why coaches, leaders and others get involved in sport is to help their athletes 'use the tools and techniques of sport and training to overcome the hurdles of life, to transcend' (Saint Sing 2004, 115). Transcendence describes the capacity to acknowledge that there will always be limits to human understanding and knowledge, and that human beings are always oriented towards something *not yet achieved* (Pieper 1989). The sport performer is a striking testimony to the reality of this particular spiritual notion of transcendence, through his or her relentless pursuit of the ultimate performance and by striving to achieve perfection on a task despite knowing that this is ultimately unattainable.

Religion and sacrifice in sport

At one level there appears to be a profound difference between the notions of sport and religious belief. Sport is often described as a form of bodily activity centred on physical achievement. Religion is most usually located in an altogether different realm where the main concern is with morality, mortality and the transcendental. Stripped down to the basics, sport is a vibrant testimony to our physical nature, whereas the religious impulse is oriented beyond our bodies to something spiritual and non-material. However, there have been a small number of writers who have challenged this restricted and narrow view and have sought to explain the deep connectedness between sport and religion. Some like Hoffman (1992) have discussed this from a philosophical perspective and others (Coakley 2003; Eitzen *et al.* 1993) have relied on a sociological account. The literature tends not to focus on issues like pain, suffering and sacrifice in sport and when these are considered it is almost uniformly negatively. A notable exception to this is the work of Morgan (1993), Novak (1994/1967) and Feeney (1995). Feeney and Novak consider the relationship between religious belief, sport and suffering by drawing on Catholic beliefs. Morgan has approached the topic from an existential–phenomenological perspective to explain how pain and failure in sport can bring deeply personal rewards. Although not a sport psychologist, Novak's (1994/1967) writing on this topic covers many of the key areas considered traditionally in psychology. For example, he refers to the athlete's need for dedication, preparation, focus and motivation. Beyond this, he incorporates language most usually heard within the great religious traditions to describe why sports share much common ground with religious and spiritual beliefs. Of particular interest, excellence, victory, community and spirit are mentioned alongside courage, battles, asceticism, sacred and sacrificial. Novak's account of sacrifice in sport powerfully expresses the idea that the athlete takes on a role similar in many ways to the priest celebrating Mass. Both priest and athlete offer a sacrifice on behalf of others. They approach the altar or the stadium alone but with the fears, desires and hope of the congregation or fans. At such moments, there is an almost tangible spiritual bond that exists between players and supporters, and priest and congregation. We participate in hope, ready to place ourselves on the line one more time despite our weaknesses, sufferings and thoughts of failure.

The willingness to be prepared to face up to demanding situations, to risk loss and defeat without the promise of any immediate material reward seems illogical. Psychologically speaking it makes little sense to knowingly place oneself in an uncertain and potentially painful situation where failure and defeat are ever present spectres. This cannot be understood from either a rationalist or a materialist view since there is always a good chance that the result of the effort and exertion will amount to nothing. However, from a spiritual perspective, sport sacrifice like the sacrifice of the Mass makes sense (to the believer at least). In both, the victor is the one who fully participates by putting his or her whole self in that arena where there is no hiding place and where ultimately success or failure is felt personally and deeply. This is one reason why sport (and religion) can be a source of great joy and at other times experienced as pain, suffering and even despair.

Novak (1994/1967) points out that competitive sport inevitably brings with it the experience of success and failure. Indeed he argues that a new approach to sport for women should provide games that 'demand high wit, arrogance, boldness, risk and the experience of many failures' (Novak 1994/1967, 211). He goes on to explain that, especially in the traditional team games, men have been fortunate to suffer together through their encounters with defeat and that this has given meaning to the claims that sport builds character, spirit and mental resilience. Defeat in sport can be turned into victory at the next competition or match. In this way, although the pain of defeat is often profoundly felt, it is transitory in sport because usually the chance to test yourself again arises quickly. To prepare for this requires discipline, focus, mental and physical preparation and *sacrifice*. This final quality is only fully possible where the person has developed a high degree of self-knowledge and spiritual awareness. Sacrifice involves giving up something for the sake of another or out of duty to a higher purpose. In other words, it is about *selflessness* and the courage to follow a path which involves *self-renunciation*, denial, hardship and *humility*. It is this last spiritual term that Novak highlights in claiming that sport provides the vehicle to learn to live 'gracefully with defeat, humiliation, or self betrayal' (1994/1967, 236). Humiliation when one has given one's all reminds the sport performer that one's destiny is not merely attained by following a rational and systematic plan of action. Fate or luck plays its part in all that we do alongside our own failure to perform as consistently well as we need to. Sport can remind the athlete that life itself is unfair at times but that our task is to keep playing the game with all we have at our disposal and hoping for a particular outcome.

Destiny is a very important word and yet it has very rarely been mentioned in academic sport literature. This is surprising since it refers to the end point or culmination of our efforts. Ultimately, our destiny is related to what we *hope* for. In the language of sport psychology destiny could be described as our goals; however, it is much more personal in its orientation because it relates to that which ultimately is not really in our control. According to this view, we are destined to become someone or something in the future but at best we can only guess at who or what this will be. Competitive sport requires that the athlete participate in their journey towards an unknown final destination even though the way is full of difficulties, frustrations and pain, alongside moments of joy and achievement. The sportsperson learns humility through the daily recognition that despite one's best efforts one can fail spectacularly, again and again. Mentally and physically exhausted and crushed, it is those with spirit who will find it within their selves to hope, and place themselves on the line one more time. In this way, sport failure can be embraced since it has the capacity to plumb our depths and test the very core of our being. This spiritual account of destiny, hope and the sacrifice inherent in sport are witness to a philosophy of life that is counter-cultural and politically incorrect! Novak expresses this very clearly, claiming competitive sport reveals that 'life isn't equal. Living with humiliation is part of not being equal to everyone. In few fields of struggle are the standards of excellence so clearly worked out for our humiliation. Being humbled is the name of – some game or other' (Novak 1994/1967, 236).

Feeney (1995) cites St Thomas Aquinas' account of fortitude as involving finding a reason to persist in spite of mental suffering and physical pain. Sport offers the athlete the chance to develop the virtue of fortitude; to acquire the strength of mind and patient courage necessary to repeatedly engage in sport competition. Feeney emphasises that the church has always taught that sport can be a form of education of the body and through our psychosomatic unity as human persons it can help develop virtues, spiritual strength and sound morals. He argues that, against the heresy of the Albigensians and the Jansenists and the more recent errors of the Puritans and Victorians, the Catholic Church (following St Augustine and St Paul) has stated that the body as the dwelling place of the Holy Spirit is not to be despised. Instead, according to Pope Pius XII, 'the prime purpose of sport, understood in a healthy and Christian sense . . . is to cultivate the dignity and harmony of the human body, to develop its health, strength, agility and grace' (Feeney 1995, 29). The account of this and other popes, as well as other spiritual and religious leaders, makes it clear that for them the arduous training regimes, physical and mental sacrifices and challenges encountered in sport can serve to strengthen the inner person. Sport, it seems, has been valued by the church throughout the past 2,000 years, on some occasions more explicitly than at other times. Rather than seeing the hardships of sport as an unfortunate by-product, this perspective has welcomed the elements of dedication, suffering and sacrifice engendered most clearly in competitive sport. These terms are found within many religious traditions and are valued because they can lead to an awareness by the athlete that goals are rarely achieved without some form of sacrifice. This does not mean that sport has become a new religion, despite what some writers such as Prebish (1993) appear to have argued. However, this *shared vocabulary* suggests that both religion and sport recognise that, beyond their different rituals and outward appearances, each is partly engaged in reminding us that the aim of life is more about developing our innermost being than acquiring external material success.

Meaning and suffering in sport

Much of the argument outlined above would be rejected by those following a postmodern approach. This view is based on the ideas of nihilistic existential thinkers like Sartre who considered life to be ultimately meaningless and absurd. In postmodern thinking values are portrayed as being completely relative, and questions around the meaning of life are considered futile and irrational. Likewise, following the 'philosophy of scientism' (John Paul II 1998, 129), which rejects the validity of any other forms of enquiry and knowledge other than those of the natural 'hard' sciences, tragedy, pain and suffering can never be understood, let alone welcomed. For the religious believer, especially the orthodox Christian, suffering has the potential to be transformed into something that connects us with others and is personally redemptive. Suffering can lead us to reassess our lives and dedicate ourselves to higher goals and more worthy aims. In sport, the performer may find that his or her most vivid memories and proudest moments were those in which achievement occurred after great discomfort, anxieties and mental suffering. This could be when a team has failed to win for a prolonged period of time and has unexpectedly moved into the relegation zone of a division. At an individual level, when a player has been criticised by the media and ignored by the team coaches and manager, the experience of suffering and fear can be quite overwhelming especially for the young athlete in elite professional sport. Athletes in these situations not unnaturally look to find an answer to their pain and for some this may be found temporarily by stoically 'putting on a brave face', or by refusing to accept some measure of responsibility for the position they find themselves in. For the Christian athlete this suffering can be mediated through prayer (Watson and Czech 2005), contemplation and an acceptance that bearing one's cross is the path to salvation. The athlete who is agnostic or atheist lacks a transcendental framework of meaning within which sacrifice and suffering can be viewed positively. Nevertheless, personal trauma and mental pain can be understood by anyone to some degree when through their own personal experience and reflection they are able to discern some level of meaning attached to these terms. Although it is more likely to be felt or sensed than precisely understood, sport performers, coaches and others involved in sport are capable of recognising that sometimes, as the philosopher Nietzsche put it, *the things which don't kill us make us stronger*. Indeed, some athletes and coaches may know more than a professional theologian about St Paul's maxim 'When I am weak, then I am strong' (2 Corinthians 12:10), having lived this repeatedly over their career in sport!

Psychology, suffering and sport

As has been pointed out earlier in this chapter from a psychological perspective, pain, sacrifice and personal suffering are most often seen as the unfortunate side effects of our actions in sport and as inherently undesirable experiences. The exception to this is uniquely found within existential psychology. This approach differs from others in claiming that moments of discomfort, anguish and angst are part of the human condition, *and because of this*, they should be fully accepted and even welcomed in some situations. At different times in the past 150 years, psychologists have criticised the existential approach for 'over emphasizing the ugly and tragic side of life . . . with a focus on death, freedom and responsibility, isolation and inauthenticity, it is easy to see how it has been described as an approach for the temperamentally gloomy' (Nesti 2004: ix). Advocates of some forms of humanistic psychology and positive psychology (Seligman and Csikszentmihalyi 2000) are now closer to the existential position in recognising that happiness, peak experiences and self-actualisation are rarely achieved without hard work, dedication and resilience. Nevertheless, it is only within existentialism that anxiety is praised as the best teacher (Kierkegaard 1980/1844) and remaining true to one's values (even if the cost of this is death!) is understood as genuine psychological health.

The most important contributor to this, within the existential and transpersonal psychology tradition, is Frankl (1984), whose work was strongly influenced by the years he spent in a Nazi concentration camp during the Second World War. His influential and profound work argues that suffering, sacrifice and the challenges of living make sense only against a backdrop of meaning. He contends that without finding an *ultimate source of meaning* an individual will be unable to begin to accept hardships and pain, and learn from these experiences. In sport, this is often seen when an athlete claims that he or she has discovered more about him- or herself and life during a long-term injury, prolonged drop in form or period of unfair media castigation, or when moving from hero to zero (Orlick 1998). For some sport performers this ultimate or highest level of meaning is linked to the discovery of spiritual values, belief in God, or even an awareness that life has a purpose beyond the here and now. Frankl's own approach, known as *logotherapy*, is based on the idea that humans are body, mind and spirit and that our spiritual self requires sustenance like the rest of our human nature. This of course has been vigorously rejected by most other approaches in psychology for a number of reasons (see Chapter 7). Despite this, a number of high profile athletes – such as the former England Rugby Union captain Jason Robinson; the cricketer Imran Khan; the boxer Mohammed Ali; the World Footballer of the Year Roberto Baggio; and the African Footballer of the Year Jay Jay Okocha – have highlighted that spiritual and religious beliefs have been important in helping them to make some sense of the often very great sacrifices and hardships they have encountered in their careers in sport.

Frankl (1984) observed that those who seemed best able to survive the horrors of life in the concentration camp without abandoning civilised values were those with personally strong spiritual beliefs. Such inmates seemed capable of maintaining some level of hope when all around them was resignation and despair. Although the world of sport does not place people in anything like these terrible conditions of evil, the athlete frequently faces the need to accept some measure of suffering and anguish on the journey to the top and during their inevitable decline. Research (Watson and Nesti 2005) is beginning to reveal that for a considerable number of sport performers it is their commitment to religious belief and practices that helps them to confront and make some sense of the difficult moments across their careers.

Maybe the most important contemporary view on existential psychology and suffering, at least in the English-speaking world, has been provided by the American therapist Rollo May. Drawing on the work of the great Italian writer Dante Alighieri and his account of the journey through hell contained in the poem *The Divine Comedy*, he points out that 'through history it is true that only by going through hell does one have any chance of reaching heaven' (May 1995, 28). He argues that therapy is not about curing but is about guiding and accompanying people to the point where they are ready to choose for themselves a path to follow, and to steadily pursue this in spite of difficult moments and anxieties. This connects strongly to the Christian notion of accepting your cross freely and progressing towards the goal of heaven and eternal life. May (1995) has been very critical of those who claim that suffering, sacrifice and pain should be avoided at all costs because nothing can be gained from these experiences. Sport performers, especially at the highest levels, represent the embodiment of these ideas. Their successes have not infrequently been achieved after facing up to and moving through physical pain and mental anguish time and time again. In elite competitive sport the athlete (and often the coach and manager) is required to maintain a high level of excellence over a season and during their entire career. This is clearly impossible for anyone to fully achieve. As a result the performer must deal with failed expectations, immense pressure, financial matters, such as contract renegotiations, wage cuts and being sold. These and many other sport-specific examples show that especially at the highest levels of professional sport the factors contributing to mental suffering and anxiety are unavoidable. Whereas the extrinsic rewards of money, fame and prestige are well known to all, it is easy (and convenient!) to ignore or forget the degree of sacrifice demanded to succeed. From an existential psychology perspective these painful experiences have the potential to develop the mental attributes and spiritual qualities of the athlete like courage and personality, which in turn makes them more likely to succeed in terms of sport performance. Until recently, most of the academic and scientific literature in the area tended to reject this interpretation of the potential for sport to develop character and courage. However, the testimonies of athletes, coaches, qualitative researchers (Dale 2000) and existential psychologists working in sport (Nesti 2004) are beginning to challenge these outdated views.

An important discovery of Freud, referred to as *catharsis*, described the release of tension that takes place in therapy when a person expresses his or her fears and concerns. This has been explained in terms of providing the opportunity for an emotional release through talking. Alternatively, catharsis has been referred to in sport psychology to describe how structured physical activity can be used to help dissipate aggression through a form of physical release. However, the term 'catharsis' was originally used in Platonic thought to describe the idea that pain, guilt and suffering can be healed by a *theia mania*, that is, through a divinely inspired cleansing. It is clearly evident that sport offers an opportunity to test oneself to the limit and make sacrifices in pursuing a focused, disciplined and arduous journey to personal excellence. Along the way most athletes will have moments of doubt, experience great frustrations and repeated failure. Much of this will be due to factors beyond their control. Nevertheless, sometimes the responsibility for failing to make the team, getting dropped, becoming injured or losing out on a professional contract, for example, is much more with the athlete's self. In relation to this the career transition literature (Lavallee and Wylleman 2000) in particular discusses the difficulties that athletes face upon termination of their sport careers, and the feelings of regret and even despair that accompany these traumatic moments. When the athlete acknowledges that he or she has been personally responsible for some of these failings, early departure from the sport or not achieving their goals, painful feelings of guilt and remorse can be intensified. The support of coaches, sport psychologists and others can assist performers to progress through these demanding phases of transition in a constructive and more positive way. However, frequently the athlete's feelings of regret and guilt cannot be completely removed through this support. It is at this stage that Plato's notion of catharsis can provide a possible explanation of how this type of mental suffering in sport links to spiritual and transcendental ideas. According to Platonic teaching, ultimately a person cannot simply rely on rational thought processes to 'explain away' feelings of personal guilt. These painful feelings of regret and guilt can only be removed fully by accepting some measure of responsibility for your failures and by accepting that it is right to feel regret. This final requirement is a challenge to the prevailing view of much of psychology and contemporary society, in which we are advised never to feel regret or guilt since this can undermine self-confidence and bring painful emotions. Pieper (1995) suggests that the ancient wisdom of Socrates and the dialogues of Plato are nearer to the truth, psychologically speaking, in reminding us that it is through *metanoia*, that is, by repentance and conversion, that the process of catharsis works fully. This cathartic cleansing necessitates 'that one surrenders and abandons the self-sufficiency of the mind that claims total independence', and 'that such emersion can never be fully decided by a mere act of will; rather it is bestowed on man as a divine favour' (Pieper 1995, 27–28).

Within a sporting context this more spiritual notion of catharsis can be detected in the lives of athletes who find the strength to continue on to glories after terrible misfortune and failure. Often, these sportsmen and -women claim that they have managed to pass through very difficult times by accepting that it is not always possible or desirable to seek to fully understand something. They describe how they eventually managed to accept that some things must be endured in a spirit of patient suffering. Typically this has only been learned after trying hard to take control and assume full responsibility for everything. Not infrequently athletes explain that their sufferings became bearable and even transformatory experiences only as they began to embrace these experiences. Cathartic moments have been vividly described in the autobiographies of sport performers like Lance Armstrong and Kelly Holmes. Although empirical research has not really investigated this phenomenon, there is an increasing body of sport-related literature that attests to its existence. These accounts are often infused with spiritual ideas and an acknowledgement that, although not completely understood, sacrifice and suffering have brought benefits to the person that they did not expect. Gains are often achieved by the athlete only after a period of despair and hurt, and when their normal responses and strategies have ultimately proved ineffectual.

For religiously minded athletes, and particularly if they are Christians, the anxiety that accompanies the frustrations and challenges of sport can lead to a very definite outcome spiritually speaking. Balthasar (2000) argues that Kierkegaard's (1980/1844) book *The Concept of Anxiety*, despite the intention of its author, is a psychological rather than a theological account. In contrast, Balthasar's theological approach to anxiety relies on a Catholic perspective to explain how, by remaining open to God's grace, a person can negotiate a path between the anxiety of the cross and the guilt of sin. This view would accept that through sport participation the athlete must face up to suffering, torments and failure but that *ultimately* these will make sense only when they are accepted as evidence of a mystical dimension in life. In other words, these experiences cannot be fully explained in rational terms and yet are much more than examples of irrational choices. Whereas no athlete deliberately chooses to encounter pain, failure and hardship in and through sport, at the same time they appear willing to voluntarily submit to the likelihood of this. At one level this paradox seems beyond comprehension. However, particularly for non-professional sport performers, that is, for the overwhelming majority who take part in sport, there is a preparedness to freely choose to engage in this form of human activity and accept (and even enjoy!) that this is accompanied by physical discomfort, frustration, challenge and psychological pain. The spiritually aware athlete possesses a framework of meaning that allows him or her to at least see that sport does not make complete sense when it is conceived in material and physical terms only. This spirituality may or may not be grounded in formal religious belief. What is becoming clear is that for an increasing number of sport performers and sport psychologists (Nesti 2004; Ravizza and Fazio 2002) there is a recognition that sport and spiritual awareness are intimately related. Flowing from this it follows that courage, character and personality formation can be enhanced through repeated encounters with the anxiety, mental trials and sacrifices woven into the fabric of sport.

Conclusion

Especially at the highest levels of competitive sport, coaches and managers constantly refer to words like 'character', 'spirit' and 'courage' when describing the qualities needed to achieve success. The famous American football coach Vince Lombardi captured this in his oft-quoted and frequently misunderstood claim that 'Winning isn't everything; it's the only thing.' Many sport sociologists, and others who have not bothered to find out what he actually meant, wrongly infer that Lombardi was calling for a 'win at all costs' mentality. In fact, his real point was that in sport, like in the great game of life, the only way to behave is to give everything of yourself every time and then victory even in defeat will be yours (Klein 1971). This of course quite logically requires the athlete to focus on winning the game but it says nothing about achieving it in any way possible! Such a victory would not represent winning according to the true Lombardian ethic since it is spiritually empty and morally and ethically wrong.

This connects with the experience of mental distress and suffering in sport. To be able to pass successfully through these difficult experiences the athlete needs to 'dig deep' and draw on his or her whole being. Put another way, winning in the tough world of sport, especially at elite levels, is rarely achieved by anyone not prepared to gather him- or herself up and unreservedly empty his or her self completely into the task. This takes courage, strength of character and *personality*. It is also conceivable that, without a pure focus on giving all one can to win, which in the final analysis is the reason for playing the game, the sport performer will be incapable of accepting the extremely demanding moments inherent in sport.

Murphy and White (1995) have managed to capture this link between sport and suffering in discussing the spiritual and mystical dimension of sport. They point out that:

> It is easy to see the love of play and adventure exemplified in sport. But the athlete's love of pain and ordeal is more mysterious. One key to the mystery comes with the ancient mystical insight that a fundamental delight exists within or behind all suffering.
>
> (Murphy and White 1995, 129)

This point highlights another important aspect of sport that defies rational explanation; victory tastes sweetest after overcoming intractable obstacles and apparently insurmountable challenges. If the aim is to win at all costs or in the easiest way possible, the elation and ecstasy at winning despite the odds would make no sense. The most striking testimony to this is that as sports fans, performers, or coaches we are most moved emotionally by teams or individuals who show a spirit of defiance to emerge as winners. This relates as much to world champions as to the 80-year-old completing his or her first marathon. The unifying bond between these and all other athletes is that, although most have not broken world records or set new standards of excellence, they have all passed by the way of sacrifice, suffering and pain. This willingness to undergo physical hardship and the mental torture of anxiety, stress and self-doubt clearly indicates that sport has the potential to test our mind and body. But sport also provides a chance for the person living in the apparently rational, planned and scientific modern world to experience that sometimes success happens to those we least expect. Although they may be physically and mentally shattered, great achievements are still possible for the athletes whose spirit is not broken. This chapter has argued that courage (Corlett 1996b), personality (Nesti 2004) and even some aspects of mental toughness (Clough *et al.* 2002) represent more than simply psychological skills that can be acquired through a mental skills training programme. These and other qualities of the person can only be understood as evidence of our deeper selves, our spiritual natures, and are best seen when the sport performer keeps going when all seems lost, powered by the spiritual fuel of hope!

Study questions

1 Consider your own experience of suffering in sport. How closely does this relate to the ideas on suffering and sacrifice discussed in this chapter?
2 How has the term 'catharsis' been used in psychology and sport psychology?
3 Why does this chapter argue that existential psychology allows for a more complete understanding of pain and sacrifice in sport?
4 How can anxiety in sport be said to help develop spiritual growth in athletes?
5 List three reasons why pain and suffering have been viewed negatively in sport psychology and sport research.
6 Explain why you agree or disagree with the idea that courage is as much a spiritual notion as a psychological construct.

Section IV

Ethics, Olympism and spirituality

Chapter 10 begins with Reid's explication of the Platonic virtues in relation to Olympic sport, and develops a wider account, including a consideration of theological virtues. It argues that virtues are central to any understanding of spirituality as well as morality, since they enable awareness and appreciation of the other, the capacity to respond, and the development of significant life meaning. Major themes are that virtues are internal to skills; that the virtues are developed through practice of the skills; and that, although embodied in individuals, virtues are realised in a social context.

Chapter 11 examines in particular the educational justification for sport and exercise on the school curriculum, arguing for a holistic concept of 'person' in the educational process, and the morally educative possibilities of sport. A sport may be characterised by its rules, but also by its ethos, and this is important in the educational setting, where qualities of mind and spirit are supposedly developed. The ideology of Olympism is presented as setting out an ethical ethos, based on fairness and equality, which embodies living ideas with the potential to cultivate virtuous dispositions.

The notion of a 'religion of athletics' was central to Pierre de Coubertin's project to revive the Olympic Games at the end of the nineteenth century. Chapter 12 explores the place of religious sentiment and ceremonial in ancient and modern sport, and extends the account of Olympism into the political arena through a discussion of its commitment to peace, inspired by the ancient idea of Olympic Truce. Sport is thus seen as a spiritual practising of our ethical and political values – as an embodiment and expression of holistic and value-based meaning, expressing a sense of value and purpose in relation to ourselves and others.

10 Spirituality, sport and virtues

Simon Robinson

Leeds Parish Church Rugby Club[1]

In March 1874 the vicar and church wardens of Leeds Parish Church (the main Anglican church in Leeds) decided that they would form a rugby team. Many present-day football and rugby clubs have their roots in similar developments, such as Aston Villa and Wakefield Trinity. The aim of this project was bring to the growing urban masses the virtues of Muscular Christianity, such as courage, honour and self-reliance. One clergyman wrote with great conviction, 'I believe in the value of Rugby in developing the physique, in influencing the character, and in improving the moral as well as the physical well being of the working man player' (quoted in Collins 2004).

The club grew and as it grew achieved success, buoyed by a boom in rugby and football teams. In one cup match in 1900 the crowd was over 20,000. But all was not well. Slowly but surely the original rules of the club, including church membership, age limits and abstinence from alcohol, were broken. The amateur code, forbidding payments and encouraging the virtues of the gentleman, began to erode, with players being subsidised in many 'creative' ways. The lowering of 'standards' began to spread to the field, where in the 1880s the team developed the reputation of being one of the most violent in the game. After one tour the Irish RU threatened to bring criminal changes, accusing the team of 'roughness, tripping, fighting and generally playing in a . . . manner that was "brutal in the extreme"'(Collins 2004). One of the curates at the time was one Cosmo Lang, who would be Bishop of Stepney within nine years, and Archbishop of Canterbury within 25. He too was hauled before the Yorkshire Rugby Union, charged with violent conduct.

And so it continued on to the terraces, where betting abounded and the response of the crowd to referees was so violent that some 15 local referees refused to officiate. One referee, at the end of a game in which Leeds lost to Castleford, had to shin over a wall and be rowed across the canal. Even then he could not escape the crowd, who pursued his bus down East Street.

Two final things caused the dream of character building through sport to evaporate. The first was the Russian pogroms at the end of the century. These led to an influx of Jews to that area of Leeds. And the Jewish community took the team to their hearts. One can imagine the feelings of the vicar and church wardens as they looked out on to the terraces, only to realise that not only did few supporters seem to embody the gentlemanly Christian virtues, but every other person was a Jew! The second problem was also cultural. In 1895 the Northern Union (Rugby League) broke away from the Rugby Union. This led to professionalism and a 'working-class ethic', which seemed to be a direct challenge to the ethos of the gentleman that the church wanted to encourage.

It is not surprising that in 1901, presided over by the Revd Sidney Gedge, the remains of Leeds Parish Church Rugby Club were quietly 'disposed of'.

The adventures of the Leeds Parish Church into sport and character were striking. First, there was a clear idea that virtues were developed through the practice of sport. Second, there was the idea of virtues finding meaning within a community. In this case the virtues would reflect the thought of the Christian church, which in turn had a particular view of what these might be. The virtue would be the embodiment of the ethos, and thus be connected to spirituality. Third, there were major questions about leadership and education. How do you actually develop virtues? Behind all this were also very big questions about purpose and culture. Clearly, there were other virtues vying with the middle-class Anglican views, ranging from professional virtues, focused on winning, to 'working-class' virtues, frowned upon by the church, and those of the Jewish community. No one seems to have asked the Jewish community what they thought.

In this chapter we will develop these issues, looking first at how the virtues relate to spirituality and sport, and then explore different developments.

Virtues and sport

The story of Leeds Parish shows an eagerness to develop virtues, without actually working though what these might be and how they relate to sport. The word comes from the Latin *virtus* which is in turn from *vir*, man. *Virtus* means 'the male function' expressed in terms of strength or the capacity to accomplish. In this sense virtues are the qualities of the person that enable something to be brought into being. Moral virtues are the qualities that enable moral meaning and purpose to be embodied. By extension they are the qualities that enable the spiritual ethos to be lived out in individual and corporate practice. Hence, we would normally refer to the virtues of the individual, but it is also possible to use the term in relation to a community or group. It is possible, for instance, to refer to the integrity of a profession (Robinson and Dixon 1997).

In relation to sport Heather Reid (1998) begins with the Platonic virtues. Plato suggested four core virtues, and that these enable one to achieve *areté* or human excellence. In his Socratic dialogues, Plato identified the particular virtues associated with *areté* to be piety, temperance, courage and justice. Piety involves awareness of or obedience to a god, or something or someone that is greater than oneself, and actions or rituals that demonstrate this awareness. Reid suggests that for the modern secular sportsperson this virtue can be recast as self-knowledge or awareness. This relates closely to the virtue of humility, defined as an awareness of the limitations as well as the strengths the self. The point about piety is that awareness of something greater than oneself puts the self into perspective, thus enabling a realistic assessment of the self. Reid argues that the winning athlete must recognise and confront his or her weaknesses, both as a learning point and also to see any achievements in perspective.

Plato's second virtue was *sophrosunê*, temperance or self-control. Reid suggests that this corresponds to the athletic ideal of discipline. Discipline, in the sense of keeping to training or eating regimes, is, however, only part of this virtue. It also includes a sense of balance, of not moving to extremes, and is therefore critical to the exercise of judgement. At the heart of such a judgement in sport is the idea of balancing limitations with the push to excellence, to be the best that the person can be. This is a critical moral balance. The push to be excellent, and thus pushing beyond boundaries, is central to excellence in sport. At the same time such a push that ignores limitations, be they physical, moral, social or legal, precisely moves into actions that in some way might adversely affect the person, from breakdown to drug-taking. Myths from Prometheus to Faust illustrate the absence of this basic attitude of spirituality, and the consequences. Plato's two virtues embody this attitude and ensure that the sportsperson stays with his or her feet on the ground. The problem is knowing what the limits are. Often it is not possible to work these through without reaching out beyond them.

Plato's third virtue is courage. Courage for Plato is quite a complex idea. It is not about thoughtless bravery. It includes a capacity to persevere with an aim, whilst also holding a critical relationship to that aim that enables one to modify it as and when it is right to do so. Again there is tension in this virtue, between the courage to stick something out, literally going the extra mile, surviving perhaps great suffering, and knowing when to stop. When is sport an obsession and when is it about courage? Deciding on this is once again a matter of judgement for the person. A good example of what seems at first sight to be obsessional courage is Jane Thompson, the remarkable marathon and triathlon runner with terminal cancer. She just keeps on running, cycling and swimming. It looks obsessional, but in the context of her illness and of the purpose, to raise money for charities, this is in fact a very thoughtful courage, and might have real benefit to her possible survival.

A different example is Paula Radcliffe, who broke down several miles from the end of the 2004 Olympic marathon, and withdrew rather than run to the end. She was accused by many of a lack of courage. However, in the context of her condition and career it could be argued that to complete would have been foolhardy. Both these cases show that it is not always simple to determine the nature of any virtue. This reinforces the need for virtues to be attached to good reflective judgement.

Plato's final virtue is *dikaiosune*, justice. The idea of justice pervades sport. At one level this is about equal treatment for the same groups, combined with justice as merit. Hence, for instance, in a league system all are subject to the same system of promotion and demotion. The governing bodies will agree on this treatment at the beginning of a season. In the case of UK Rugby League in 1994/5 this system was changed with two weeks to go before the end of the season, leading to no promotion for Keighley Cougars, a team who were crowned champions. In this case the financial concerns of the League and the money of the Australian millionaire Rupert Murdoch caused them to set justice aside. The question is, can there be any justification for setting justice aside in sport? Another example of justice is in terms of fairness, not least fairness of treatment by referees and umpires. A final example of justice is in equal opportunity to win. As Reid (1998, 4) puts it,

> When athletes take to a starting line, or during the opening kick-off, tip-off, or face-off of a game it is important that those athletes, their spectators, and the live television audience believe the outcome to be undetermined. The belief that an athlete can win is just as important as the knowledge that he or she might lose, because if the outcome were predetermined by anything other than a purely just god (as in the case of Odysseus), the purpose of the game (not to mention its entertainment value) would be null and void.

Hence, if a contest is fixed in some way then this is an abuse of justice. The virtue of justice involves something of these meanings focused in the character of the sportsperson. This includes the desire for fairness and equality in the pursuit of the sport and the capacity to embody that justice both by avoiding abuses and by treating others justly. Justice also relates for Plato to knowing one's place and worth in the community, and thus by extension within the sport or team.

Several things can be noted about these virtues. First, as McIntyre (1981) suggests of the virtues in general, they are embodied in the individual but have a social context. Community provides the shared meaning within which they are cultivated. Hence, it is important to have the stories, ritual and codes which provide that meaning. Second, actually determining whether one is living out a particular virtue in a situation is a matter of individual judgement. Most often, though, it requires the assistance of the community in some way to help that judgement. In sport this may well be the coach. The influence of coaches in matters of spiritual and moral meaning can be major. They can reflect back to the player how they see their behaviour in context, and thus reinforce and assist in any judgement about values and virtues. Third, and connected, the virtues reinforce each other at an individual and community level. It is important, for instance, for courage to operate with justice. Equally, different members of a team may well embody different virtues, reminding others of their importance in judgement.

Developments

These virtues begin to spell out some of the virtues in the Leeds Parish vision of sport. But there are problems, focused largely around the question of just what we mean by human excellence. Non-Western spirituality, religions and philosophies may have a very different view of the end or purpose of humanity. The Buddhist philosophy, for instance, values mutuality, based on a view of interdependence, and underlying empathy. Such a philosophy looks rather to develop spiritual meaning through the development of responsive virtues. Confucianism on the other hand (Twiss 1998) stresses communitarian values, including paternalism and respect for authority, over freedom and equality. This leads to a stress on virtues such as loyalty and the capacity to maintain face and stay in one's place. Similar virtues are at the base of some forms of judo, for instance (Carr 1993). Many religious thinkers suggest that much philosophy is eurocentric (Lovin 2005) and does not take into account these different visions of the good. Theologians such as Hauerwas and Wells (2004) argue for further differences. They suggest that reconciliation and peace making is the core moral purpose, and thus that 'peaceableness' is the core virtue.

Deciding what the value foundation of virtues might be becomes then quite important. Arnold (1999) suggests that some virtues are instrumental in that they are about enabling a purpose outside them and that others are not. However, it would seem that all Plato's are in fact instrumental. One can have courage, piety and temperance and still pursue a morally dubious end. Even justice can be used to bad ends, depending on where one draws the boundaries of the application of justice.

Sport can embody the basic moral good, as Reid notes, but the nature of that good still has to be articulated and the way in which sport can embody that good has to be clarified.

The fact that there may be different views of the end of humanity, and thus different views of the ground of any moral meaning, does not prevent reflection on that good and coming to some view of it. Hence, Aristotle argues that the most important virtue is *phronesis*. Aristotle refers to two intellectual virtues, *sophia* and *phronesis*. The first of these is scientific knowledge and the capacity to understand nature and the laws of nature. *Phronesis* involves the capacity to reflect on and decide what the good end (*telos*) is, and put that end into practice. *Phronesis* enables *eudaimonia*, happiness or well-being, to be embodied in the particular. Aristotle argues that *phronesis* is both necessary and sufficient for being virtuous, and that with that it is not possible to be *akratic* (intemperate or not in control).

Phronesis came to be included amongst the cardinal virtues, along with justice, temperance and courage. It is precisely this virtue that becomes critical for any sportsperson to ensure that winning does not become the only 'end' of sport, but rather that winning is seen as in the context of the wider spiritual perspective of an awareness and appreciation of the other, and the capacity to respond and find meaning in these relationships. Ironically, this was one virtue that was markedly missing from the endeavours of the Leeds Parish Church. They had above all an intellectual awareness of the good end but failed completely to articulate that in terms of sport or to find a practical way of embodying it. There was an assumption that the simple practice of sport would bring out the character development they so desired. They found, however, that the practice of sport was not necessarily the same as the practice of the virtues.

Arnold (2001) suggests that *phronesis* is important in relating core concepts of justice to practice. This involves both knowing how the rules apply to practice and what the good behind those rules is. He also notes that *phronesis* can apply to behaviour beyond rules and codes. There is no rule, for instance, behind the practice in soccer of kicking the ball out of play if a player is badly injured. From the subsequent throw-in the ball is given to the defensive side, so that no advantage is gained from the throw-in. The goods behind this practice are justice and care. In one famous case, in a football cup-tie between Arsenal and Sheffield United, advantage was taken from the throw-in by an Arsenal player that led to a goal. The player was from a different country and was not aware of the meaning behind this practice. Though Arsenal won, it was agreed to replay the game, precisely because unfair advantage had been taken.

Important as clear thinking about purpose and practice is, there are other candidates for virtues that would seem to be important. McIntyre (1999, 122ff) moves from Aristotle to Aquinas in suggesting the importance of *misericordia*. This involves an awareness of others and their needs, regardless of who they are or whether they are a member of the community. This seems to indicate a form of empathy, the capacity to identify with the other and so be aware of both the vulnerability and limitation as well as the potential of the other. In this sense it could be seen as an affective virtue that sits alongside *phronesis*, affective in the sense of awareness of the feelings of the other.

Empathy differs from sympathy in that it has a degree of distance that is essential in perceiving the other and being able to respond appropriately to them. In sport empathy enables sportspersons to see beyond the narrow circle of the team or core community and be aware of the need surrounding them. The work of teams and clubs in developing community work can enable the growth of such empathy. However, empathy can enable the awareness of limitations in the self and others and thus can be seen as a more worked out version of piety. Empathy comes into play especially in dealing with loss and failure experienced both by any sportsperson of his or her opponents. McIntyre suggests that *misericordia* includes a sense of responsibility that is inclusive, beyond the local community. Hence, as noted in Chapter 3, empathy requires the underpinning of *agape*. That sense of inclusivity, and even shared responsibility for the other, takes us into what have been referred to as the theological virtues.

Theological virtues

The so-called theological virtues are faith, hope and love (1 Corinthians 13:13). Arnold (2001) refers to them as supernatural virtues, i.e. virtues that arise from a relationship with part of the Christian godhead, the Holy Spirit. However, as noted above, they have a generic meaning (Fowler 1996). Faith as a generic virtue is about the capacity to have faith in a person, group, idea or thing such that one can base one's life or part of one's life on that. Hence, although faith involves trust it is more than that. Many people see sport itself as a ground of faith, or a way of life rather than simply discrete activity. How that is worked out will once more depend upon reflecting on the underlying good. Putting one's faith in that good or the person or group that embodies that good then takes its place alongside *phronesis*.

Hope involves the capacity to envision the future in a positive and creative way. Hope, in one sense, is important to that view of justice and sport that states that all teams have a chance on the day. Hope for most sportspersons has to operate in a difficult world that seems anything but hopeful, but can still provide significant meaning, even when the team has not won for most of the season. In all this the sportsperson and the club can still find hope even when relegated. Hope in all this is more profound and proactive than simple optimism.

The third spiritual virtue is love. In its Judaeo-Christian form this is known as *agape*, an unconditional love for all (Robinson 2001). It is this that provides the basis of inclusive concern. The great pull in any sports context, as supporter, club or sportsperson, is to focus purely on the solidarity of the club itself, viewing outsiders or other club members as adversaries. *Agape* is a virtue that accepts others regardless of their difference, and enables a continued commitment to the other. The anti-racist initiatives and community work that have swept sport in recent years both embody this attitude. They embody a sense that responsibility for the other is shared by everyone (Bauman 1993). This basic ethical stance is then seen as core to the meaning of sport. Of course, this is a key attitude that the Leeds Parish wanted to embed, but failed to articulate. As noted in Chapter 3, shared responsibility demands that shared responsibility is negotiated. This can lead to all kinds of interesting partnerships. At one level this relates strongly to the idea of sporting institutions as corporate citizens who work out their responsibility to society together with other stakeholders. At another level *agape* invites the individual sportsperson to view his or her life as beyond the pitch or the game, and consider what his or her responsibilities are in relation to the broadly defined 'other'. All this points to an experience of sport that both finds meaning in its community or practice but is also facing outward.

This also takes into account respect for sporting officials. As the Leeds Parish example amply showed, referees are everyone's favourite target. However, they attempt to administer justice, and also have their limitations. Respect for their decisions has to take into account those limitations.

Agape in all this can be seen as the core moral virtue (cf. Aquinas), providing both a baseline of moral value and meaning, and also the motivation to respond. However, once again there is need for balance, with a care for the other which is conditional.

Eros

This is summed up in another form of love, eros, which is based on the attraction of the other. Although eros is often seen in terms of the erotic, it is much broader than that. It has two dynamics. First, it involves existential joy and pleasure (Florman 1976). This could be in music, or art, or even engineering. In sport it is the delight:

- in experiencing sporting action, when all the training and planning comes together in creating something special;
- in succeeding, seeing the action achieved;
- in seeing the focused and harmonious action of another;
- in contributing towards a wider social well-being (Florman 1976).

For theologians it is based in the creative act of God who turned to his creation and saw that it was good. Once again this is an outward-facing virtue, because it recognises and appreciates excellence, ability and significant experience in the other, be that other the self, a team-mate or an opponent. Eros enables one to transcend a limited view of sport. Eros also balances *agape* in its concern for the self as much as the other, and thus for what the self needs.

Integrity

There is perhaps one virtue that needs to be mentioned, one that in some ways brings the others together, or provides a framework for them. That is integrity.

Integrity involves several aspects, such that Solomon (1992) suggests that it involves several virtues:

- Integration of the different parts of the person: emotional, psychological and intellectual. This leads to holistic thinking, and an awareness of the self alongside awareness and appreciation of external data.
- Consistency of character and operation between value and practice, between past, present and future, and in different situations and contexts. The behaviours will not necessarily be the same in each situation, but will be consistent with the ethical identity of the person.
- Taking responsibility for values and practice. Without accepting responsibility for ethical values and for response neither the individual nor the group can develop a genuine moral identity or agency.

Absolute integrity is impossible to attain. Hence, an important virtue is humility, the acceptance of limitations, of weakness as well as strengths (Robinson and Dixon 1997, 341). Equally important therefore is the capacity to reflect, to evaluate practice, to be able to cope with criticism and to alter practice appropriately. This capacity to learn means that integrity should be seen not as simply maintaining values and ethical practice, come what may, but as involving the reflective process, such that values can be tested in the light of practice and either appropriately maintained or developed. Integrity can therefore be seen as a virtue which embodies the learning process.

Integrity takes on a new light in professional sport with so much of the game and behind the game made transparent by the media. Millions of people watch the scrum half in rugby trip the loose forward, or the centre forward in World Cup soccer handle the ball into the net, or the winger who falls to the ground holding his head when an opponent has kicked the ball at his legs – all unnoticed by officials.

Yet these individuals behave as though Plato's ring of Gyges had been slipped on their fingers and made them invisible. Modern sport has in fact massively increased in transparency, such that the sportsperson must assume that all that he or she does can be seen, and therefore that integrity is a prized virtue. Once again, integrity can be seen as outward facing and as acting as an example not just to the sport and other sportspersons but beyond to society in general.

It is worth noting that the virtues relate closely to skills and that virtues which enhance awareness, such as empathy, will enhance skills in general (Robinson 2005). Moreover, virtues such as courage and temperance will reinforce the broader virtues of sport, such as resilience.

Humility

In his Socratic dialogues, Plato identified particular virtues associated with *areté* to be piety, temperance, courage and justice. Piety involves awareness of or obedience to a god, or something or someone that is greater than oneself, and actions or ritual that demonstrate this awareness. Reid (1998) suggests that this can be recast as self-knowledge or awareness. This relates closely to the virtue of humility, defined as an awareness of the limitations as well as the strengths of the self. The point about piety is that awareness of something greater than oneself puts the self into perspective, thus enabling a realistic assessment of the self. This also involves a proper appreciation and acknowledgement of the contribution of the group, the practice or the profession and of its authority.

The virtue of *humility*, often seen as irrelevant to professions, is tied to these. The virtue of humility in one sense is an important corrective if the expertise of the professional becomes a *raison d'être* or the basis of status or identity. Humility is often seen as a nervous doubting of competence, self-deprecation, quite the opposite of the professional image. Tangney, however, summarises a very different view of humility, reminding us that all virtues rest between extremes:

- accurate assessment of one's ability and achievements;
- ability to acknowledge one's mistakes, imperfections, gaps in knowledge and limitations;
- openness to new ideas, contradictory information and advice;
- keeping one's abilities and accomplishments – one's place in the world – in perspective;
- relatively low self focus, 'a forgetting of the self', while recognising that one is but part of a larger universe;
- appreciation of the value of all things, as well as the many different ways that people can contribute to our world (Tangney 2000, 74).

Underlying such virtues are the traditional virtues, associated with Aristotle and Plato (May 1994):

- *Temperance.* This does not involve abstinence – from drink or anything else

– but rather moderation, balance and self-control. This is important for effective judgement, self-reliance and the acceptance of responsibility. Plato's *sophrosunê*, temperance or self-control, Reid (1998) suggests corresponds to discipline. Discipline, in the sense of keeping to training or eating regimes, is, however, only part of this virtue. It also includes a sense of balance, of not moving to extremes, and is therefore critical to the exercise of judgement.

- *Justice*. This involves both the capacity to maintain contracts (commutative justice) and the capacity to give equal regard and respect for all groups and issues in any situation, but also includes restorative justice.
- *Fortitude/courage*. This involves courage and resilience and the capacity to withstand a variety of pressures. Like all Aristotle's virtues this involves the mean, in this case between the extremes of foolhardiness and cowardice. Courage for Plato is quite a complex idea. It is not about thoughtless bravery. It includes a capacity to persevere with an aim, whilst also holding a critical relationship to that aim, enabling one to modify it as and when it is right to do so. Again there is tension in this virtue, between the courage to stick something out, literally going the extra mile, surviving perhaps great suffering, and knowing when to stop.

The precise definition of any of the virtues may differ and an important part of professional training can be to invite the student and practitioner to reflect on these and describe their own. Several things are, however, clear:

- The virtues are not simply individualistic. They are related to the whole and thus can be used and practised only in the light of the support of the wider community. Similarly, no individual could embody all the virtues. Hence, team members might embody different ones, enabling the whole team to embody the virtues. This also means accepting the limitations of team members. It is also possible to see the community as a whole as the bearer of virtues. Hence, we can speak, for instance of structural or group empathy.
- Virtues need to be maintained, encouraged and practised. They do not develop without such disciplines. The development of virtues is a lifelong process. Hence the concern for continual professional reflection (Schoen 1983).
- Virtues are not context-specific. Nor are they the virtues of expertise. On the contrary, as we noted above, they are the virtues of humanity per se, which can then be applied to different contexts.
- Virtues are interrelated and interdependent. Hence, although no one person can embody all the virtues, Aristotle believed that one could not develop the virtues singly.
- The virtues tend to be the same across different disciplines, practices and professions. *Phronesis*, empathy, integrity and moderated love in particular are core to professional competence and care. Different professions will work these through in distinct intentional relationships, but they remain important to all.

- The development of virtues provides the balance between freedom and autonomy and acceptance of authority. The development of the virtues enables good decision-making and good practice, with the practitioner taking responsibility for both. They also enable balanced judgement and acceptance of the authority of the community, including coaching staff. Such authority is both institutional, involving a recognition of the role and skills of the coach, and also relational, involving recognition of qualities and virtues.

The relationship of virtues to skills

Virtues are often thought of as distinct from skills and issues of competency, be that in sport practice or sport management.

However, the work of Carter, for instance, suggests a direct connection. He developed a taxonomy of qualities and skills for professional education (Carter 1985) in Table 10.1.

The taxonomy sets out the different levels of qualities, skills and knowledge and suggests that they relate to each other. The qualities line involves virtues, including respect for the self and others and integrity, and spiritual qualities including awareness. Such virtues relate directly to skills. Information skills, for instance, operate in the context of respect, and remembering and communication can themselves express respect and care. The virtues of openness and imagination tie in directly to good organisational and planning skills. Indeed, creativity

Table 10.1 A summary of a taxonomy of objectives for professional education

Personal qualities	Skills	Knowledge
Mental characteristics:	Mental skills:	Factual knowledge:
Openness	Organisation	Facts
Agility	Analysis	Procedures
Imagination	Evaluation	Principles
Creativity	Synthesis	Structures
Attitudes and values to:	Information skills:	Concepts
Things	Acquisition	
Self	Recording	
People	Remembering	
Groups	Communication	
Ideas		
Personality characteristics:	Action skills:	Experiential knowledge:
Integrity	Manual	Experience
Initiative	Organising	Internalisation
Industry	Decision making	Generalisation
Emotional resilience	Problem solving	Abstraction
Spiritual qualities:	Social skills:	
Awareness	Cooperation	
Appreciation	Leadership	
Response	Negotiation and persuasion	
	Interviewing	

Source: (Carter 1985)

is precisely expressed in such skills. Without them it would not be clear what creative imagination was. As Mcintyre (1981) notes, virtues are internal to skills, and the virtues are developed through practice of the skills.

Yorke and Knight (2004) suggest a four-components view of employability that precisely links deeper meaning to competence:

- Understanding. This is intentionally differentiated from knowledge, signifying a deeper awareness of data and its contextual meaning.
- Skills. This refers to skills in context and practice and therefore implies the capacity to use skills in the context of professional values.
- Efficacy beliefs, self theories and personal qualities. These influence how the person will perform in work. There is some evidence, for instance, to point to malleable, as distinct from fixed, beliefs about the self being connected to a capacity to see tasks as learning opportunities rather than opportunities to demonstrate competence (Yorke and Knight 2004, 5). This in turn influences commitment to learning goals and the capacity to learn.
- Metacognition. This involves self-awareness, and the capacity to learn through reflective practice.

The first of these can involve both doctrinal and affective meaning. The second sets skills in their context of meaning. The third involves identity. The final category is precisely the reflective capacity that enables self-transcendence and with that the ability to see how one thinks, feels (in relation to thought) and learns.

These connections suggest that virtues such as empathy and *phronesis* look 'both ways', into underlying meaning and values but also that awareness is important for competent practice.

Conclusion

In this chapter we have suggested that virtues are central to any understanding of spirituality as well as morality. It is the virtues that enable awareness and appreciation of the other, the capacity to respond and the development of significant life meaning. It is they that enable settled characters than can continually learn and reflect on the good internal to practices. Such virtues are also the fruits of those practices and relationships. Mustakova-Possardt (2004, 245) refers to the idea of critical moral consciousness, which brings together much of these insights. She sums this up as involving four dimensions: 'A moral sense of identity, a sense of responsibility and agency, a deep sense of relatedness on all levels of living, and a sense of life meaning or purpose.'

It is precisely that critical moral consciousness based in spirituality that the Leeds Parish failed to focus on. For all their splendid intentions they did not enable real reflection, or responsibility for reflection. Indeed, far from enabling or empowering the 'working man' in this, they judged 'him' to be lacking in the virtues and in need of development. However, spirituality is based in the individual taking responsibility for critical reflection on his or her life meaning, in the context of his or her community and wider relationships. Hence, virtue development is about empowerment in their reflection and response.

Aristotle in particular associates virtues with the mean between extremes. This chapter suggests a more dynamic model in which the virtues are continuously holding together several different tensions, including:

- *agape* and eros;
- acceptance of limitations and the drive to excellence and victory;
- an inclusive acceptance of others and support for one's own team and club;
- a concern for universal values and a concern for value internal to the practice of sport.

It is precisely the virtues of *phronesis*, empathy, *agape*, eros and integrity that enable all those to remain in creative tension.

Study questions

1 Consider Plato's four virtues. How applicable do you consider them to be to modern sports participation?
2 What 'virtues' do you think are important to sport?
3 What kind of personal and 'spiritual' qualities do you think would contribute to success in sport, and to getting satisfaction from sport?
4 What was lacking in the approach of the Leeds Parish?
5 Explain the relation between the virtues and spirituality.

11 Sport, ethos and education

Jim Parry

The Sunday Times, 24 September 2006: **Investigation**

Left to die at the top of the world

The British climber David Sharp suffered a slow, painful death on Everest in May. As he lay dying, 40 climbers passed him by. Did their lust for the summit override their humanity? Peter Gillman investigates

A few days before Christmas last year, David Sharp sent an e-mail to a climbing friend in Kathmandu, saying: "I'm (stupidly) contemplating a final (final) attempt on Everest." The friend, the New Zealander Jamie McGuinness, had been on Everest with Sharp when he failed in an attempt in 2003. Sharp had failed again in 2004, vowing not to return. Yet McGuinness was not surprised that Sharp was intent on a third try: "David knew he could do it, but he still had to prove it." Another climbing friend, Richard Dougan, says that where Everest was concerned, "David had stars in his eyes."

For Sharp to consider a third attempt says much about both the lure of the world's highest peak and a streak of stubbornness in Sharp himself, particularly as frostbite had cost him several toes in 2003. In May, Sharp, 34, paid a far higher price. He almost certainly reached the summit. But during his descent he died of cold, exhaustion and lack of oxygen in the scant shelter of a rock alcove on the crest of the mountain's northeast ridge.

There have been numerous deaths on Everest – almost 200 at the last count – but this was a spectacularly public one. Some 40 climbers, bidding to reach the summit via the north side of Everest that day, all passed Sharp during their ascent and descent, stepping within a few feet of his prostrate but still sentient body. It was a desolate place to die, ravaged by wind and cold, overlooking the slopes of Everest's monumental northwest flank. The manner of his death was equally disturbing. Climbers describe how his hands and arms were deformed by frostbite; how, when he was hauled to his feet, he was unable to stand; and how he was finally left to die alone.

Sharp's death led to anguished debate in the climbing world and the international press. Mountaineers of the stature of Sir Edmund Hillary have weighed in, complaining of the "horrifying" attitudes it revealed. The 40 or so climbers involved stand accused of putting their own summit ambitions ahead of saving Sharp's life. Such is the draw of Everest that the climbers involved are drawn from nations across the world, including Australia, New Zealand, Lebanon, Turkey and the US. Interviews with many of them, however, present a more complex picture than the accusations allow.

From one interested party, meanwhile, there has been only pained silence. That is David's family – his parents, both in their sixties, and his younger brother, Paul – who have recoiled from the media furore as they contend with their grief. From the accounts of friends, David emerges as a personable young man, close to his parents. He relished new challenges and, crucially, he was a loner who backed his own judgments.

There are contradictions too: a trained scientist renowned for his analytical thinking who, despite himself, was lured back time and again to Everest. So is this a parable of climbers passing by on the other side? What do the climbers have to say for themselves? To those questions may be added a third: was Sharp so blinded by the stars in his eyes that he took a risk too far?

The story that Peter Gillman begins to tell was one that many found shocking, not least because there was amongst many climbers a view that there was a settled ethos in their community. Spirituality and ethics come together perhaps most strongly in the idea of ethos. Ethos can be summed up as the distinctive character, spirit and attitudes of a group or community. As such it is something about the distinctive values and meaning of that community, but also the actual practice of those values. It is thus summed up not just in concepts but also in how people behave to each other, including the tone of communication. The ethos is discovered in relationship; in attention given, or not given, to the other, in concern for key values and purposes in practice, and so on.

For the climbers the ethos was one that was worked out within and around an environment of risk shared by all. At its centre was the belief that, however good any climber might be, he or she might at any time depend upon other climbers to survive. From that awareness of physical vulnerability, danger and need came the core principle that one always helped another climber in need. Ethicists as different as McIntyre (1999) and Levinas (1998) both agree on this point, that concern for the other arises from an awareness of vulnerability. Hence, for Levinas ethics begins with the face of the other, that which sums up the limitations, and ultimately the mortality of the other.

Such was the strength of this ethos for the climbing community that figures such as Edmund Hillary immediately condemned what they saw as its erosion in the Sharp case. Two things seemed to threaten this ethos. The first was the quest for excellence and achievement. Why was Sharp so determined to make it by himself and with limited resources? The irony was that Sharp had more than enough money on him to have paid for a Sherpa to accompany him. The people who walked past did not even do so 'on the other side'. They had to unclip themselves from the safety line to get round Sharp. These included Mark Inglis, a remarkable New Zealand climber with two artificial legs. Inglis had himself suffered in climbing accidents and seems to have been driven in his desire to overcome his handicap.

The second challenge to the ethos was from the commercial operation. Everest increasingly represents significant financial opportunities, with companies providing Sherpa support, and even fixed safety lines most of the way up. The argument runs that this focuses the concern of the company on the profits, and purely the care of their clients, ignoring the wider ethos of inclusive care for fellow climbers. The Sharp case is complex, and many of the factual details are disputed. It is argued by some that the company who had climbers on Everest that day knew of the Sharp situation and had the capacity to effect a rescue, but did not.

Much analysis has followed this case, including the view that at such extreme heights exhaustion and lack of oxygen make it very difficult to think through ethical challenges. However, it is precisely the point of an ethos that it enables ethical response at a very basic level. In this case the inclusive concern would come first, provided that there were the resources to effect a rescue.

In relation to education ethos becomes central. Any corporate activity expresses value, tells us something about what that group or community find important. In the case of education, ethos will be connected to the core purpose of learning and the conditions that enable that learning, including mutual respect, a safe environment for mutual critique, and the practice of academic freedom. Education, however, can provide an ethos that has a much wider focus, and this chapter will explore first how the ethos of sport itself can be central to the education process and experience, and then will suggest that Olympism provides an ethos that connects to broader values, such as fairness, justice and peace. It will then focus on how such an ethos can be sustained and how this involves an ongoing development of meaning. In one sense this will move from the commitment to an ethos to the contract or compact that can articulate that ethos and sustain it. Finally, in relation to education, it will examine the ethos and spirituality of the learning organisation.

Moral education, sport and games

Jones (2005, 140–142) argues against the Kohlbergian cognitive development theory of moral education, on the grounds that it is primarily a theory of moral understanding, not of moral action. Instead, he suggests, the education of moral character is not essentially about the cognitive resolution of moral argument, but about the development of those moral dispositions or virtues that enable a person to act morally and to become a good person.

Jones's critique coheres with one view of the morally educative potential of sports and games:

> Games are laboratories for value experiments. Students are put in the position of having to act, time and time again, sometimes in haste, under pressure or provocation, either to prevent something or to achieve something, under a structure of rules. The settled dispositions which it is claimed emerge from

such a crucible of value-related behaviour are those which were consciously
cultivated through games in the public schools in the last century.

(Parry 1986, 144–145)

A good moral education, therefore, would involve the cultivation of an ethos
or a 'moral atmosphere' (Jones 2005, 145) that presents and nurtures examples of
good behaviour. Sport ought to be seen as 'a moral practice for the cultivation of
habits of virtue as well as habits of skill' (2005, 146). Sports and games are a form
of 'moral association' (Carr 2003, 266), and successful engagement in them is a
matter of learning how to cultivate those dispositions appropriate to the context,
and how to behave within it.[1]

However, we are confronted with the obvious fact that competitive games are
contests, which raises the possibility that their primary function is to establish
superiority over others, and that this feature presents the temptation to cheat or
behave badly in order to secure victory. Whence derives the 'moral push' towards
virtue?

Part of Fraleigh's answer (1984, 41ff) is that there are certain prerequisites for
a good sport contest.

- First, there is a presupposition of equality of opportunity to contest (equality
  under the rules), without which the game could not be demonstrated unless
  all other variables are strictly controlled.
- Second, no contest could exist without the opponent, which would seem
  to require at least the minimum respect due to a facilitator – to one whose
  own level of performance is a major contributor to the very possibilities for
  excellence open to oneself in that category of endeavour chosen by both.
- Third, although it is clearly possible to break the rules, to do so alters the
  conditions of the contest, so that a range of abilities not specified by the rules
  comes into play. A good contest will maintain the framework that secures the
  integrity of the contest, and this requires rules adherence and fair play.

In addition, there are other necessary features of a sports contest. So:

- Fourth, there is a knowledge of relative abilities, which is a necessary outcome.
  This might be construed as permitting a form of braggadocio, but Reddiford
  (1982, 115) reminds us that 'you win some, you lose some' and so to make the
  game the occasion for 'marking up superiorities and inferiorities' is a short-
  term and self-defeating attitude. We play to produce an outcome favourable
  to ourselves, but we should not allow the actual outcome to be of persisting
  importance. Humility and generosity are at least as likely an accompaniment
  to a demonstration of one's relative abilities as overweening pride and
  conceit.
- Fifth, I would add that in games there is a simple right and wrong, easily
  enforceable by a clearly identified authority. At the same time, there is
  some possibility of differing interpretation and judgement. In playing games,

students learn how to follow explicit rules, how to bend them and evade them, and how to operate within a system of penalties and consequences, both official and unofficial.

- Sixth, I would suggest that this application, interpretation and appreciation of rules returns us to the idea of ethos, which we shall now explore further.

Part of Fraleigh's case is that the internal values of sport itself, as exhibited by its rules, impose upon us certain ethical requirements for its successful practice. But this is only part of the story, since these rules are interpreted and applied from within a context of the more broadly understood values of a community which supports the practice. (Later we will look at the philosophy of Olympism as an example of a proposed set of such community values, which provides an account of sport at its best, together with an ethics and politics within which sport can flourish and to which it can contribute.)

The ethos of sport

Take the example of any team game, to begin with. There is an immediacy about this playing experience which focuses on several aspects of activity in relation to others. First, there is a build-up of trust within in any team, which is mediated by the physical experience. Not only do the team members have to be clear about roles and rely on each other fulfilling those roles, but they also have to rely on the physical presence and support of their team mates, since their own physical well-being (and even safety) depends upon the role and function of their team-mates. This suggests the kind of responsibility which team members owe to and feel for each other. In this sense, responsibility begins to emerge from the physical aware-ness of the other and the needs and concerns of the other in the context of risk.

Second, responsibility goes beyond the team. At one level the ethos of concern for all who are playing the game is embodied in the rules. Such rules look to a system of justice and respect. At another level, though, there is a sense of interde-pendence between teams. Although there may be intense rivalry, the wellbeing of the individual depends upon members of all teams playing fair, and respecting the rules and ethos of the activity. Hence, there is a major outcry whenever a player is injured by an intentional and career-threatening foul such as an elbow to the face. The responses to such outrages stress the common perspective of the professional sportsperson.

Third, all teams play in the context of a much wider community that includes both the fans in the ground and a wider audience reached by media who them-selves project certain values. At this point the ethos of the sport might be in con-flict with the values and concerns of media or related sponsors.

Fourth, sport beyond media communications becomes 'public property', not least as part of the identity of the local community, and partly through general interest that will from time to time examine and analyse the behaviour of the teams and individuals.

The ethos of sport, then, is:

- based on experienced interdependence, at team level or beyond;
- inclusive, moving out from the experience on the field to the wider community of supporters and stakeholders;
- always being tested, either by problems on the field or by potential value conflicts with related groups.

It could be argued that the idea of ethos is not in itself fixed or settled, but that it provides the basis of embodied values that are and always must be tested. In other words the testing is critical to sustaining the ethos. Indeed, it might further be argued that such critical testing is in itself a part of any ethos. An ethos that is not open to interpretation or dispute is one that embodies some form of exclusion.

Looked at in another way this begins to show the different ways in which spirituality and ethics relate. At one level ethics grows out of spirituality. Holistic awareness of the other leads to an awareness of the needs of the other, a sense of interdependence and with that a sense of shared responsibility (Robinson 2007). Hence, an irreducible moral concern grows from spirituality.

At another level, the development of life meaning is being constantly tested by a variety of things, from conflicting values to set ethical principles. The story of the Abraham's challenge of God in Genesis 18:25 illustrates this. God has determined that he will destroy Sodom. Abraham challenges God as to how he could kill the 'righteous with the wicked'. Abraham is challenging God based on a simple view of justice, or perhaps even on the basis of what he saw as God's inclusive spirituality. Fasching and Dechant (2001) suggest that this story illustrates a Jewish tradition of 'audacious' challenge, and how such challenge was a core part of spirituality.

So the ethos of the sport can embody core and settled dispositions, but it also takes place within the laboratory 'for value experiments' where individuals and the team as a whole have to continuously respond to challenges under great pressure.[2] The more the ethos is challenged through practice, the more it is articulated and clarified.

> [P]articular practices like sport can offer arenas where ethical discourse can flourish and where a morally and psychologically binding consensus, based on both tradition and the more or less tacit knowledge of how to play the game, can come under the scrutiny of all practitioners. Moreover, we believe that the morality of particular sporting games is being presented, challenged and negotiated, not always in articulate forms, but in terms of embodied interaction throughout sports performances.
>
> (Loland and McNamee 2003, 75)

Character education

The virtues are what constitute the so-called 'character', in the sense of a particular identity and the capacity to relate. How then are the virtues developed? Aristotle suggests that they have to be developed in practice, through habituation. This is not about mindless conditioning. On the contrary it involves getting used to, and practising, *phronesis*. This means that it enables the person to take responsibility for performing moral actions. As Burnyeat (1980) puts it, this is the sort of person 'who does virtuous things in full knowledge of what he is doing, choosing to do them for their own sake.'

As McIntyre (1981) notes, the virtues, such as justice and courage, are embodied as internal goods in a community of practice.[3] So it is through these practices that we learn just what the meaning of justice or courage is in the particular, and begin to embody it ourselves, simply in the doing. We can contrast that with didactic teaching that simply sets out rules or principles, known only in their generality. However, acquiring virtues through practice does not mean that we have to ignore the written articulation of meaning – on the contrary, as McIntyre argues, there is a need for stories and other discourses that can communicate meaning in the tradition of the community, and also for broad statements of value. Nor does it mean that we must reject reflection upon moral matters – on the contrary, it is the dialectic of 'testing' between practice and thoughtfulness that produces wisdom in virtue.

It must not be forgotten, however, that none of this is simply about getting across values accepted by the community, but about the individual developing a personal and practical understanding of those values and the capacity to respond to others in the light of them. The development of virtues looks to a settled character that can reflect on internal goods, and this takes place not just within the practice, but also through continued reflection and debate within the community. Moreover, such debate will not end simply where the community ends. If sport is an outward-facing community it will embody in its practices values and virtues that are more universal, and which resonate (or not) with wider communities.

Indeed, sport may contribute insights about values (such as equality, fairness, justice, respect for others) beyond sport itself. Hence, there is much talk of the example given by sportspersons to wider society and especially to young children. Important in the development of such awareness is inter-textual dialogue – dialogue that takes into account different views of the good. Van der Ven (1998) suggests that this is critical to moral development, not least because it causes one to look again more closely at one's own values and beliefs, and their coherence.

Modelling of the virtues is clearly an important part of learning in and through practice (and this should cause us to reflect upon the virtues-in-role of the PE teacher and the sports coach). However, such learning is not simply about discrete actions but rather about actions in relationship. It is the relationality of the practice that actually enables the development of virtues. Players and clubs develop relationships that build up an inclusive attitude. Players relate to each other in ways that develop trust and thus faith in each other, and in the club. Players feel valued through the response of the club. As such relationships build up, so the affective as well as cognitive awareness of moral and spiritual meaning is developed (Robinson 2001), and the person is empowered through developing their role and responsibility and the underlying meaning that they give to and find within their activity.

The Olympic ethos

Pierre de Coubertin, the founder of the modern Olympic Games, was very conscious of the way in which sport connected with wider society, and he developed the idea and practice of Olympism as a means of connecting with and actively influencing social development, especially through education. He argued for the revival of the Olympic Games as a means to the popularisation of his ideal of holistic education centred on ethical sport and active physical education for all.

We can briefly note two key Fundamental Principles from the Olympic Charter (International Olympic Committee 2006).

Fundamental Principle 2 states:

> Olympism is a philosophy of life, exalting and combining in a balanced whole the qualities of body, will and mind. Blending sport with culture and education, Olympism seeks to create a way of life based on the joy found in effort, the educational value of good example and respect for universal fundamental ethical principles.

Fundamental Principle 6 states:

> The goal of the Olympic Movement is to contribute to building a peaceful and better world by educating youth through sport practised without discrimination of any kind and in the Olympic spirit, which requires mutual understanding with a spirit of friendship, solidarity and fair play.

J.A. Samaranche (1995, 3), former President of the International Olympic Committee, has suggested that a modern Olympism can be described in six 'basic elements':

- tolerance;
- generosity;
- solidarity;
- friendship;
- non-discrimination;
- respect for others.

I have suggested elsewhere (Parry 2006, 191) that this echoes the basis of Olympism in liberal humanism, stressing as it does the values of equality, justice, fairness, respect for persons and excellence. Underlying such values and principles there is a holistic philosophical anthropology of sport, first sketched by Coubertin. He speaks (1966/1894a) of the human not as a simple dualism of body and soul, but as a more complicated mix of body, mind and character, with character seen as formed primarily by the body.

> [T]here are not two parts to a man – body and soul: there are three – body, mind and character; character is not formed by the mind, but primarily by the body. The men of antiquity knew this, and we are painfully relearning it.

And later (1918):

> I prefer to harness a foursome and to distinguish not only body and soul, . . . but muscles, intelligence, character and conscience.

Although this is not an entirely perspicuous account of the elements of person-hood, it is important in showing his concern for the whole person, the relation between sport and moral education, and the role of properly designed physical activity in character development. Coubertin often made the point that Olymp-ism seeks to promote moral sport and moral education through sport. Referring to the UK school reforms of 1840, he says:

> In these reforms physical games and sports hold, we may say, the most promi-nent place: the muscles are made to do the work of a moral educator. It is the application to modern requirements of one of the most characteristic princi-ples of Greek civilisation: to make the muscles the chief factor in the work of moral education.
>
> (Coubertin 1896, 11)

Sport, then, not only provides a context of equality and fairness within which the individual can strive for excellence, but also forms a community within which friendships are developed and sustained and through which a wider vision of peace is articulated and pursued. The idea of pursuing peace through the Olympic Movement will be more thoroughly explored in the next chapter, but it is partly about bringing together different nationalities and transcending different national concerns in collaborative endeavour. At one level this involves a concerted ef-fort by the Olympic Movement to bring nations together and to influence future generations through education.

Reid (2006) begins to focus this international framework into peace-making through sport in the community. She connects three elements to this peace-mak-ing in practice that sport provides. First, 'we must deliberately set aside a time and place' for sport. This is both a sanctuary and a truce, in which differences are put to one side and the focus of the activity is for that time shared. In spiritual terms this is an experience which enables the participants to transcend the particular in disputes and differences. Reid (2006, 208) suggests that the ancient Greeks associated a strong inclusive idea, with this coming together of difference, through the concept of *xenia*, or hospitality to the stranger. The practice of *ekecheiria*, a truce enabling safe travel to the Games, extends this hospitality to the enemy.

The second element is the establishing of equality and fair play. No matter what the differences, coming together in sport demands equality before the rules, or law, the Greek concept of *isonomia*. I would add to Reid that the experience of that equality is another part of the lived ethos of sport, and that the different contestants come together to share that meaning. It is thus both a lived experience of shared meaning, reinforced by the sporting rituals, and a lived experience of being perceived of as equal value. Hence, once more, the meaning operates cognitively, affectively and somatically. The true power of this lived experience comes when, as Reid suggests, sport can show aggression and even anger, expressed within a context of equality. As Robinson notes (2001), when equal respect is offered in the context of difference and emotion, this further develops awareness and acceptance of the other. Hence, in the relationships developed through sport, a level of empathy and commitment to the other can begin to emerge.

Reid's final element extends from this. The ethos of Olympism enables an evaluation of the other based on their personal qualities and how these relate to the situation. This develops respect for the other in the context of a shared community. At one level it focuses on personal and positive difference. At another level it enables the person to operate in the shared community which is different from his or her own. This can raise great challenges in terms of spiritual and moral development. In itself, it enables a transcendence of the community. However, this does not simply involve going beyond the community, it involves espousing values that either are in a very different context or may have points of direct difference from the home community. This sets up a real 'inter-textual dialogue' between different communities and thus the possibility of critique of the home or other community, which nonetheless respects differences globally. Handled properly this sets up the development of forms of internationalism or even cosmopolitanism, the possibility of a world community, which is aware of and appreciates differences.

Cosmopolitanism is about being aware of difference and being at ease with it. However, this does not mean that we must accept difference that is unjust, and the Olympic Movement has in the past challenged such behaviour. When the International Olympic Committee took action to withdraw the recognition of the South African Olympic Committee on 15 May 1970 (see Mbaye 1995, 116–117), it was not simply because the IOC disagreed with its government's politics. IOC President Avery Brundage's letter (reproduced in Mbaye 1995, 279) makes clear his view that the IOC could not penalise a National Olympic Committee simply because it disagreed with some policy or another of its government, otherwise 'we will not have any left.' Rather, it was because, in the case of the South African government, its policies produced an apartheid sport which was unjust sport – the laws and local rules of the apartheid system were racially discriminatory, making it impossible for different sectors of the community to compete fairly, and thus violating Article 1 of the Olympic Charter (Mbaye 1995, 115.)

All of this reinforces the ethic, espoused by Coubertin, that although winning is important it is taking part in fair and ethical sport that is critical.

This ethos fits well into the stages of spiritual development suggested by Fowler (1996). His first two stages involve a generic faith that is determined by the family. The next two are determined by the community. Stage 5 then has the individual taking responsibility for his or her own faith in relation to the communities of which he or she is a part. He or she is still part of a community but understands its limitations, and is also part of and appreciates other communities.

Two central ideas begin to sum up the virtues that Olympism strives for, *kalos k'agathos* and *areté*. Nissiotis (1984, 64) sees the Olympic ideal as a means of educating 'the whole man as a conscious citizen of the world'. He defines this ideal as:

> that exemplary principle which expresses the deeper essence of sport as an authentic educative process through a continuous struggle to create healthy and virtuous man in the highest possible way (*kalos k'agathos*) in the image of the Olympic winner and athlete.

Areté is the idea of excellence, with the Olympian striving to better him- or herself. If the focus of education is on the development of transcendence beyond one's home community, then *areté* looks at another aspect of transcendence, beyond physical and intellectual limits. Hence, Nissiotis (1984, 66) writes,

> The Olympic Idea is thus a permanent invitation to all sportsmen to transcend . . . their own physical and intellectual limits . . . for the sake of a continuously higher achievement in the physical, ethical and intellectual struggle of a human being towards perfection.

Of course, perfection cannot be achieved, and in falling short one becomes clearer about one's limitations. However, only through that striving can one be aware of and accept limits, and move beyond the self.

The underlying philosophical anthropology of Olympism may be summed up as:

- striving towards excellence and achievement;
- through effort in competitive sporting activity;
- under conditions of mutual respect, fairness, justice and equality;
- with a view to creating lasting personal human relationships of friendship;
- with international relations of peace, toleration, and understanding;
- and cultural alliances with the arts (Parry 2006, 199).

The Olympic ethos thus provides a real focus for wider education. With the core ideas of fair play, the value of competition, the nature of a good contest (including equality before the law and equality of opportunity), the very activity of sport in education provides a focus for the presentation of and reflection on values. This can be part of any school's approach to sport education. The pedagogy would focus on the ethical practice of sport, and there would also be opportunities for reflecting on its ethos and values, and how this allows us to connect with other groups.

Too often, sport or other activity at school is seen as meaningless beyond its simple activity. However, where a group, in school or higher education, is taken to outdoor activity weeks (for example), it is possible to begin the process of reflecting on the interdependence required for success and how this shapes core values of that community. Here we could see ethics and spirituality come together, focusing on meaning at cognitive, affective and somatic levels. There might also be a greater focus on Olympism per se. This can include:

- youth work, such as Young Olympians Clubs;
- involvement of Olympians as role models;
- special space and time, such as Olympic museums and heritage sites, and Olympic Day celebrations;
- arts-related events.

Education

There are, however, two issues that need to be noted with respect to education, spirituality and ethos.

First, no ethos can be set for all time and, as noted above, there has to be a continual reflection on and debate about the meaning and tone of the ethos. The very idea of generic spirituality is built around a learning or journey model which seeks to articulate meaning and to reflect on practice, both for the individual and the group. Hence, attention then has to be paid to what Hawkins (1991) refers to as the spiritual dimension of the learning organisation.

Hawkins argues that beyond the level of operations and strategy the developing organisation needs to attend to questions of underlying identity and purpose. At this level there is the development of 'integrative awareness' which ensures that there is transparency and participation such that all involved recognise shared life meaning and begin to accept mutual responsibility and interdependence. This may be the function of good planning, which allows wide participation in reflection on purpose aims and objectives. It may also enable the learning process to occur in any organisation. One example of this is the provision of whistle-blowing and anti-bullying procedures which enable transparency such that conflict can be dealt with constructively (Armstrong *et al.* 2006).

However this also raises the second issue, which questions how the ethos at the centre of sport might relate to the ethos of the wider learning organisation, for example the school or higher education institution. Should there be an effort to make them the same or, given the multicultural context of sport and the Olympic ideal, should the two be in dialogue? Should there be a stress on discourse which is not just within the sport, but also with the other institutions that sport partners? One way of setting this question is to ask how ethical principle and ethical practice can cohere in sports practice in an educational situation? At this point, let us remind ourselves of a thought of Coubertin's (1966/1894a):

> character is not formed by the mind, but primarily by the body. The men of antiquity knew this, and we are painfully relearning it.

And let us recall the idea of games and sports as laboratories for value experiments, in which participants are forced to react to opportunity and circumstance in the pursuit of some goal in a rule-structured environment. The idea here is that sport, properly conducted, might be capable of developing character, the virtues and moral behaviour, especially if we set out consciously to do so in pursuit of some rationale, or ideal, such as Olympism.

In discussing such a possibility (Parry 1988a, 117) I have argued that we should:

> seek to develop an account of culture and human experience which gives due weight to those forms of athletic, outdoor, sporting, aesthetic activities which focus on bodily performance, and which are generally grouped under the heading of physical education. Such an account, combining claims about human capacities and excellences with claims about the importance of a range of cultural forms, would seek to develop arguments which could justify the place of PE on the curriculum.

The suggestion here is that PE activities should be seen as 'practices' which act as a context for the development of human excellences and 'virtues', and the cultivation of those qualities of character which dispose one to act virtuously.

In an oft-quoted passage, MacIntyre (1981, 194) describes a 'practice' as:

> Any coherent and complex socially established co-operative human activity through which goods internal to that form of activity are realised in the course of trying to achieve those standards of excellence, and human conceptions of the ends and goods involved are systematically extended.

Carr (1987, 173) has applied the insights of MacIntyre to education:

> 'What is an educational practice?' The answer I have tried to provide is one which is firmly grounded in those developments in post-analytic philosophy which seek to re-establish the classical concept of 'practice' in the modern world.

Hirst, too, has picked up the theme:

> It is those practices that can constitute a flourishing life that I now consider fundamental to education

(1993, 6)

and he goes on to suggest that a curriculum should be organised in terms of 'significant practices'. However, just *which* practices constitute a flourishing life, or just which practices are to be deemed significant, remains opaque in his account. Above, I have tried to sketch out some considerations in favour of sport, under the umbrella of Olympism, as a significant practice.

Practices, then, promote those human excellences and values that constitute a flourishing life. But, more than that, practices are the very *sites of development* of those dispositions and virtues, for it is *within* practices that opportunities arise for (e.g.) moral education, including the nurturing and development of the virtues discussed in the last chapter. It is by *participating* in a practice (and by practising its skills and procedures) that one begins to understand its standards and excellences, and the virtues required for successful participation.

As Piers Benn puts it (1998, 167–168):

> we do not become virtuous . . . by learning rules . . . We gain virtue, and hence learn to make right decisions, by cultivating certain dispositions . . .
>
> . . . we can see the importance of the education of character – the acquisition of these firm dispositions . . . this does not come naturally but must be taught.
>
> . . . there is some similarity between acquiring virtue and acquiring skills such as the mastery of a musical instrument; both require practice before the appropriate habits are acquired. You get the dispositions by first of all acting as if you had them – you train yourself to do the right things, and gradually you gain a standing disposition to do them.

The suggestion here is that the practice of sport, informed by the philosophical anthropology and ethos of Olympism, offers a context and a route for us to achieve a number of important aims relating to moral education:

- to further our traditional concern for the whole person whilst working at the levels both of activity and of ideas (because the practical work can be seen as a kind of laboratory for value experiments);
- to show coherence between approaches to practical and theoretical work (because the physical activity is designed as an example and exemplar of the ideas in practice);
- to explore in later years ideas implicit in work in earlier years (because the practical work encapsulating the values and ideas can be taught well before the children are old enough to grasp the full intellectual content of the ideas).

I would wish to commend to teachers and coaches the values of Olympism, not just not just as historical anachronisms or moralising dogmas, nor as inert ideas to be passed on unthinkingly to students and athletes, but as living ideas which have the power to remake our notions of sport in education, seeing sport not as mere physical activity but as the purposeful physical activity of an educated and ethical individual, infused by an ethical ethos, and aiming at the cultivation of virtuous dispositions.

Study questions

1 Do you think that games and sports bring out the best of people? Do they have the capacity to make people morally better?
2 What are the 'internal' values of sport?
3 How would you describe the 'good sports contest'? (Think of the best games you have ever seen, or taken part in – what made them the best?)
4 What, if anything, is gained by seeing sports as social 'practices'?
5 What is the relation between practices and the virtues?
6 What is the ideology of Olympism, and how might it help us to view sports?

Acknowledgement

Thanks are due to Peter Gillman for permission to use the introduction to his extended and careful discussion of the issues surrounding David Sharp's death on Everest. The full article was published in *The Sunday Times*, 24 September 2006.

12 The *religio athletae*, Olympism and peace

Jim Parry

Introduction

> I therefore invite you . . . to come and sit on the wooded slopes of Mount Kronion at the hour when beyond the Alpheus the rising sun begins to touch the swelling hills with gold and to lighten the green meadows at their feet.
>
> I have drunk in this spectacle twice at an interval of thirty-three years. On a morning in November 1894 I became aware in this sacred place of the enormity of the task which I had undertaken in proclaiming five months earlier the restoration of the Olympic Games after an interruption of fifteen hundred years; . . . On a morning in April 1927 I waited there in a kind of devout contemplation for the hour when the hand of the minister of education would draw back the Greek and French flags veiling the dazzling marble erected to attest success.
>
> From this lovely pine forest which climbs Mount Kronion . . . it is possible to recreate in imagination the long avenues of plane trees along which there once came the athletes and pilgrims, the embassies and the commerce, all the traffic and all the ambition, all the appetites and all the vainglories of a civilisation both more complex and more strictly defined than any which have followed it.
>
> Altis – the sacred precinct – immediately reveals itself as a religious focus, the centre of a cult. Among this people and above all at this time it is difficult to imagine a religion not based upon a positive philosophical conception.
>
> Let us therefore look for this basis. And if there really was a religion of athletics . . . let us find out why it is in Greece that it took shape, and whether the Greek ideal . . . is still suited to the rest of humanity.
>
> (Coubertin 1966/1929, 107–108)

Whilst teaching at the International Olympic Academy some years ago I first accepted Coubertin's invitation, and jogged with other staff and students to the top of Mount Kronion, overlooking the archaeological site of Ancient Olympia, with the stadium in clear view, to wait for the dawn. I read out this passage from Coubertin's essay *Olympia* as the sun rose, and later the same day gave a lecture on ethical aspects of the Olympic Idea.

It is clear that Coubertin's 'devout contemplation' of the idea of a 'religion of athletics' (the '*religio athletae*') was central to his project to revive the Olympic Games at the end of the nineteenth century. The last chapter examined the ethical core of sport as exhibited by its rule structures and by the notion of ethos. This chapter will explore the place of religion, religious sentiment and ceremonial in ancient and modern sport, and will extend the discussion from ethical into political considerations.

Religion, myth and cult

The Olympic festival and the evolution of the Games

Olympia has been a sacred place since very early times. Thousands of votive offerings have been found there dating from at least the tenth century BC, left by a fertility cult associated with an oracle of Rhea, the earth goddess. But Zeus was the supreme Greek god, and the grove known as the Altis at Olympia became his most sacred precinct, beautifully situated at the foot of Mount Kronion (named after Kronos, the husband of Rhea and the father of Zeus). As the religious cult of Zeus gained ground, people used the grove for worship at altars and for hanging offerings from the trees: primitive figures of men and animals made from terracotta or even bronze.

However, local disputes interrupted celebrations, which some say included games and contests, until 884 BC, when the local rulers, King Iphitus of Elis, the lawgiver Lycurgus of Sparta and the Archon Cleosthenes of Pisa, made a truce and revived the festival. The terms of this sacred truce were engraved on a bronze disk, which still existed in the time of Pausanias the traveller and chronicler, who describes it to us from the second century AD, but we have no specific record of any games that might have taken place. The Olympic festival marked the beginning (and later also the middle point) of a Great Year of eight years. Thus an Olympiad was a period of four years, with each Olympiad celebrating one Games, and this became a standard way of marking the calendar in ancient times.

It was a festival of Zeus, held in early autumn, a season of rest from agricultural work and celebration of fertility – a sort of Harvest Festival. Gardner (1925, 76) also saw it as a festival of 'lustration', involving ceremonies of purification by making offerings to the gods. The ancient Olympic Games, so far as we know, began at Olympia in 776 BC. The first official event, a simple straight sprint race of about 192 metres, is the distance between the grooved starting blocks at either end of the stadium at Ancient Olympia, which modern visitors are tempted to run. Some authorities say that the 'stade' race originates in a race to light the flame that could be used for the sacrifice to Zeus.

This festival to the greatest of gods attracted athletes and citizens from all over the Greek city-states and colonies, which meant most of the known world at the time. It meant a truce from war and an opportunity for all Greeks to meet on neutral and sacred territory. This truce established Olympia not as one amongst many of the Greek city-states, but as a place apart – both neutral and sacred – a place where Greek society and culture could attain and represent its self-awareness and self-identity.

And of course the greatest of Games were held here, at which only free-born warriors of the Greek tribes might compete. As Swaddling (1980, 7) says, 'there is no modern equivalent for Ancient Olympia. It would have to be a site combining a sports complex and a centre for religious devotion – something like a cross between Wembley Stadium and Westminster Abbey.'

The Games were held every four years until they were banned by the Roman Emperor Theodosius I in AD 394. The last Games, the 293rd, were held in AD 393, and so they had been held continuously for 1,168 years. This astonishing record in itself demands the attention of students of history. Apart from the rituals of some of the major world religions, what other human institution has lasted as long?

The myth of Pelops

There are many myths that seek to explain the origin of the Olympic games, always with reference to events that occurred under the eyes of the gods. One is the myth of Pelops, after whom the peninsula is named.

The story is that Oenomaus, King of Pisa, challenged all suitors for his daughter Hippodaemia to a chariot race. During the race, he would kill each of his adversaries and then place their heads among his trophies. Naturally, this discouraged young men from seeking his daughter's hand. But then arrived Pelops, son of Tantalus, King of Phrygia. He was both fortunate, because Hippodaemia fell in love with him at first sight, and also clever, because he realised what was going on. He conspired with Oenomaus' charioteer, Myrtilus, and during the race managed to throw Oenomaus from his chariot. Oenomaus was killed and Pelops won both Hippodaemia and the kingdom, but he killed Myrtilus for his treason. To appease the Gods for his bold wrongdoing, Pelops established the Olympic Games.

The myth of Pelops echoes down to the twentieth century, when George Orwell described modern sport as 'war minus the shooting' (see Goodhart and Chataway 1968, 19) and Chris Chataway, an Olympic athlete, co-authored a book called *War without Weapons*. The earlier form of contest was that of mortal combat, in which the triumph of the victor meant the death of the adversary. In the Olympic Games, however, contest took on the nobler form of rule-governed and disciplined athletic competition. The instinct for murder was 'civilised' and became the drive for victory on the athletic field.

The chariot-race of Pelops and Oenomaus was to be the last deadly incident in the sacred site of Olympia. From then on in Olympia – after the death of the murderous and arrogant Oenomaus – a black ram was sacrificed instead of a human victim. This shift from primitive bloody antagonism to fair and peaceful competition constitutes the starting-point of the Olympic Games.

The myth of Hercules

Another myth sees Hercules as the heroic founder of the Games. Of the Twelve Labours of Hercules, six took place on the Peloponnese, and the next six all over the rest of the known world, including the underworld, where he wrestled Cerberus, the guard-dog, and brought him to Mycenae.

The fifth labour, the cleaning of the Augean stables, was staged in Elis. The King of Elis, Augeas, owned vast herds of cattle, but had been remiss in cleaning out their stables, full of the dung of thousands of animals. The problem was twofold: the local fields were becoming infertile because the dung had not been spread on them, and the filth of the stables threatened to pollute the whole of Elis. Hercules cleverly solved both problems by diverting the rivers Peneus and Alpheos, whose currents both washed out the stables and deposited the dung on the fields. However, Augeas did not keep his promise to Hercules to reward him with a tenth of his kingdom, so Hercules deposed him, gave his kingdom to his successor, and established the Olympic Games to celebrate his victory.

Notice that Hercules' labour was achieved not just by brute force, but also by intelligence: a marriage of muscle and mind. Also, his goals were honourable: the aim of his struggle was to serve the people of Elis. He represents the nobility of physical strength in the rational pursuit of the good: a model of the ideal Olympic hero. As Paleologos says (1982, 63):

> With the twelve labours depicted by the bas-reliefs on the two metopes of the Temple (of Zeus), the world is presented with the content of the moral teachings which Olympia intended with the Games.

The idea is that the sculptures of the demigod Hercules in Olympia performed a morally educative function, standing as role models, especially for the athletes who were there to train for the Games, of physical, moral and intellectual virtue:

> Hercules is shown bearded, with beautiful features, . . . a well-trained body, fine, proportioned muscles, . . . as a representative of the *'kalos k'agathos'* type, where the body is well-formed and harmonious, the expression of a beautiful soul, and the face radiates intelligence, kindness and integrity.
>
> (67)

Nissiotis concludes (1984, 66):

> The Olympic Idea is thus a permanent invitation to all sportsmen to transcend . . . their own physical and intellectual limits . . . for the sake of a continuously higher achievement in the physical, ethical and intellectual struggle of a human being towards perfection.

This prefigures the modern Olympic idea, which translates into a few simple phrases which capture the essence of what an ideal human being ought to be and to aspire to (see Parry 1998). The philosophical anthropology of Olympism promotes the ideals of:

- individual all-round harmonious human development;
- towards excellence and achievement;
- through effort in competitive sporting activity;
- under conditions of mutual respect, fairness, justice and equality;
- with a view to creating lasting personal human relationships of friendship;

• and international relationships of peace, toleration and understanding.

Restoration of the religio athletae

In his 1927 'Address from Olympia to the Youth of the World' Coubertin said:

> My friends and I have not laboured to restore the Olympic Games to you
> in order to make them a fitting object for a museum or a cinema; nor is it
> our wish that mercantile or electoral interests should seize upon them. Our
> object in reviving an institution twenty-five centuries old was that you should
> become new adepts of the religion of sports, as our great ancestors conceived
> it.
>
> (Coubertin 1966/1927, 100)

In an essay urging the reintroduction of the 'Oath of the Athletes' Coubertin
(1966/1906, 15) first explained what he meant by the 'religion of the athlete',
distinguishing religious observance from ethical participation:

> I must explain the term 'religious', which has here a special significance. The
> true religion of the athlete of antiquity did not consist in sacrificing solemnly
> before the altar of Zeus; this was no more than a traditional gesture. It con-
> sisted in taking an oath of honour and disinterest, and above all striving to
> keep it strictly. A participant in the Games must be in some manner purified
> by the progression and practice of such virtues. Thus were revealed the moral
> beauty and the profound scope of physical culture.

Now, there may well be a problem in translation from the French in these texts
(and the opening text of this chapter), but let us notice the references to both a
'religion of the athlete' and a 'religion of athletics', or a 'religion of sports'. The
first, of course, is translated as *religio athletae* – the second would be *religio ath-
letica*. (We should also notice, in passing, that perhaps the term is not Coubertin's,
but was in fact coined by an Irishman, A.A. Lynch, in 1895 – see Kruger (1993,
95–96).)

Coubertin did not distinguish the two, and uses them interchangeably. However, they bring with them different emphases. The first refers to the moral principles and precepts espoused by the athlete, and the virtues pursued and practiced.
The second refers to the moral basis, in principle and ethos, which is immanent in
sporting practice. The moral core of sport is exhibited both by the constitutive and
regulative rules from which each sport is composed, and also by the commitment
of athletes to the 'contract to contest', without which there could be no contest.
(This is what is formalised by the Olympic Oath.)

However, both are important to our understanding of the significance of sport
in culture, for it is the very nature of sport, as ethical and equal contest, that
provides the logical basis for the moral practice of the athlete.

Sport as a religion

On the question whether Coubertin saw sport as a 'modern religion', he is inconsistent on the matter. Occasionally he writes as if it were. In his *Olympic Memoirs*, Coubertin states that sports were 'a religion with its church, dogmas, service . . . but above all a religious feeling' (1997, 115).

And again in 1935:

> The first essential characteristic of ancient and of modern Olympism alike is that of being a religion . . . I therefore think I was right to recreate from the outset, around the renewed Olympism, a religious sentiment transformed and widened by the internationalism and democracy which distinguish the present age, but still the same as that which led the young Greeks, ambitious for the triumph of their muscles, to the foot of the altars of Zeus. The ideal of a religion of sport, the *religio athletae*, was very slow to penetrate the minds of competitors, and many of them still practise it only in an unconscious way. But they will come round to it little by little.
>
> (1966/1935, 131)

Certainly, too, some of his followers used similar language, and it might have seemed that the claim was being made that sport was set to take over from organised religion as a focus of spirituality for the masses. After all, scientism and secularism were beginning to make inroads into traditional forms of observance.

However, we should notice that both of the above quotes emphasise the importance for Olympism of religious feeling or sentiment, as distinct from religion itself. Roesch (1979, 199–200), argues that the 'pseudo-cultic' expressions of Olympism, consciously created by Coubertin, do not qualify Olympism (or sport) as a religion:

> Religious life and cultic expressions take part in other forms and contents, such as gesture, attitude, ritual dance, prayer, speech and rites. The individual athlete, no matter what his religion, denomination or ideology, lives and acts, according to his religious conviction as a Christian, Moslem, Buddhist, Jew and so on . . . 'Olympism' can't take the place of that.

He identifies the values of Olympism, which seem to be entirely secular: freedom, fairness, friendship and peace. This insistence on the secular nature of Olympic values seems to me entirely correct, and it concurs with Coubertin's more sober and settled view of the matter, as expressed in 'A Modern Olympia' (1910):

> But art will inhabit there continuously, and religion, too. We do not mean by this that a church must be erected there, or places of worship, or even one of those temples . . .
>
> In no case, therefore, should there be any question of providing any sort of building to be consecrated to the performance of religious rites. We have

used the term 'religious' in a different sense. Olympia derived this adjective not merely because it contained temples and altars and priests. The city drew its sanctity from the sentiment of patriotic piety that hovered over it, impregnating its atmosphere and investing its monuments.

(1966/1910, 22)

Roesch creates his contrast only by failing to take account of what Coubertin means by 'religion' in its wider senses, and of what he repeatedly says about 'the religio athletae', with its basis in both ethics and sentiment, which he sees as aspects of religiosity. Especially, we should notice that the core of Coubertin's concern here is the *moral* value of sport.

Sport and religiosity – ethics

Whereas Coubertin sometimes speaks of religion in its 'formal' sense, more often he does not. For example:

But first I must discuss this term 'religious', which has here a special meaning. The true religion of the classical athlete consisted . . . in the swearing of an oath of fidelity to the rules and unselfishness, and above all in compelling themselves to strict adherence thereto . . . We must find our way back to a similar phenomenon . . . firstly the acceptance of a wiser, wider, and above all more precise definition of the amateur; secondly the re-establishment of a preliminary oath.

(1966/1906, 17)

In distinguishing the Games from 'a mere series of world championships', Coubertin notes that:

The Olympiad calls for a solemnity and a ceremonial which would be quite out of keeping were it not for the prestige which accrues to it from its titles of nobility.
[. . .]
There is one which existed then and could be transposed almost unchanged. It is the oath. Before the opening of the Games those athletes who had been admitted as competitors went to the Temple of Zeus and vowed to observe in every particular the law of the Games. They declared themselves without taint and worthy to appear in the Stadium.

(1966/1910, 34)

It only enlarges our conception of the modern oath if we perceive it as deriving from such religious ideas of purification and sanctification (1966/1929, p. 109). Indeed, Coubertin thought that this would be a necessary condition of the moral success of the Games, and for sport to serve the purpose of moral education:

The moral qualification existed in antiquity in connexion with the religious requirements. We believe that it will impose itself again in our time. As the Olympiads grow in solemnity, so there will grow a movement to do homage to them . . . by purifying the participants and by creating a genuine elite worthy of so exceptional an occasion.

(1966/1910, 31)

The Olympic Oath was spoken for the first time in 1920 in Antwerp by Victor Boin, Olympic competitor in sword-fighting in Stockholm in 1912, and later President of the Belgian Olympic Committee. From 1920 to 1960 the wording of the oath was as follows:

We swear that we will take part in the Olympic Games in loyal competition, respecting the regulations which govern them and desirous of participating in them in the true spirit of sportsmanship for the honour of our country and for the glory of sport.

As Coubertin's collaborator, Carl Diem, remarked (quoted in Diem 1964, 126):

Coubertin introduced this Olympic oath with great deliberation and in the face of much criticism. Its aim was to announce that this Olympic contest arose from the most sacred feelings of youth and would be conducted with the highest moral seriousness in devotion to the most honourable sentiments that move young people.

Sport and religiosity – sentiment, ceremonial and symbols

As well as the seriousness with which the competitors were to take their ethical commitments and responsibilities, Coubertin also considers the importance of the role of ritual, ceremonial and symbolism in the Olympics, as establishing a kind of gravitas and religiosity.

The first essential characteristic of ancient and modern Olympism alike is that of being a religion. By chiselling his body with exercise as a sculptor chisels a statue the athlete of antiquity was 'honouring the gods'. In doing likewise the modern athlete exalts his country, his race, his flag. I therefore think that I was right to create from the outset, around the renewed Olympism, a religious sentiment (transformed and widened by Internationalism, Democracy and Science) . . . This is the origin of all the rites which go to make the ceremonies of the modern Games.

(1966/1935, 131)

Just as we understand the role of ceremonial events in the form of secular or religious events which mark rites of passage – ways of recognising important phases of life, such as birth, confirmation, marriage, death – so also we meet such ceremonies in the form of symbolic games, dances, and contests, both in ancient and modern times. In thus drawing attention to an event, we recognise its importance, and enable it to achieve dignity and solemnity. It is invested with meaning and significance.

As Carl Diem said (quoted in Diem 1964, 121):

> it is a festival in which man celebrates his humanity, that is the part of life which is not exhausted in the struggle for existence, but seeks to share in the transcendental and the spiritual, in that eternal forward movement by which we men become men.
>
> Ceremony characterises a solemn event, the presence of form, a religious content, a symbolic value. Ceremony is the governing framework of the . . . Olympic festival. Ceremony alone confers upon the event its inner consecration; it has the quality of a rite . . . The ceremony can still be understood today in its original sense as a compulsion to reflection, to dedication, and to participation.

As we have already seen, the Olympic Oath ceremony involves the personal commitment of each individual participating athlete. The medal ceremonies honour the victors by elevating them onto the podium into the public eye and heralding their achievement, and honour their countries by displaying their flag and anthem to the world.

These two ceremonies go back to ancient times, and so does the tradition of the torch relay. Diem, whose idea it was to take the Olympic flame, kindled by the sun's rays in the sacred Altis in Olympia, to Berlin in 1936, said in 1946 that this ceremony:

> should rank as a contribution to the symbolism of the Games. It forms a link with classical times, when an eternal flame was maintained in Olympia on the altar of the Hestia, and the privilege of continually renewing it fell to the victor in the stadium race. In this way the symbol-loving Greeks expressed the notion that youth has to take over the strength and spirit of its fore-fathers and hand them on to the next generation.
>
> (quoted in Diem 1964, 121)

The Olympic rings, the Olympic flag, the Olympic anthem, the Olympic address, the Olympic Oath, the carillon of bells, fanfares, ritual processions, choir-singing, banners, pigeons, symbolic light, architecture, and the opening and closing ceremonies, are all designed to heighten the feelings and experiences of participants and observers alike, to exploit symbolic meaning, and to elevate the importance and significance of the occasion.

In Chapter 2, Simon Robinson develops a working definition of spirituality, involving three elements: awareness and appreciation of the other, the capacity to respond to the other, and the development of significant life meaning based upon all aspects of awareness and appreciation of and response to the other. This section tries to show that Coubertin did not really see Olympism as a religion in the formal sense – as a competitor with Christianity and Buddhism for the allegiance of the people – but as a moral and spiritual movement in the above senses, with the capacity to promote moral commitment and communal seriousness of purpose in the significant effort to achieve human excellence.

In Olympic sport, we have the example of the ancient transition from barbarism to humanism – the civilising and unifying influence of sport for the ancient Greeks. We also see the athlete transcending himself in a performance which is both competitive and collaborative. And in the Olympic Games we see a festival of celebration which exhibits transcendent religiosity within an ethical structure of equal competition and mutual respect.

Truce and peace – a politics of Olympism

In order for this festival to take place in ancient times, over a period exceeding a millennium, an absolute prerequisite was the Olympic Truce (the *ekecheiria*), sanctioned under the auspices of Zeus. Thus, Coubertin's concern with the values of Olympism in modern times also extended beyond the narrowly ethical into the political arena.

Truce and peace

As we have already remarked, truce was the basis of the ancient Olympic Games. The Greek empire, which meant most of the known world at the time, was united in language, religion and ethics – and yet there was constant warfare amongst the different races and cities. It became necessary, then, to institute the *ekecheiria*, or truce, which guaranteed to all Greeks a meeting at a neutral religious site and competition under conditions of fairness, with justly administered rules.

In ancient times there were three conditions of truce:

- Elis (and the sanctuary) were declared neutral and inviolable;
- for three months competitors were allowed to travel;
- all Olympic states agreed to impose sanctions on violators.

Modern Olympism claims to further peace and international understanding, and it draws on the authority of such an alleged classical model. During the ancient Games, it is said, there was a general laying down of arms all over Greece. However, some writers have objected that this constitutes not peace, but only truce (see Lämmer 1982, p. 16). Furthermore, we should notice that the concept of truce is logically dependent on that of war, or conflict, since a truce is something that happens *between* hostilities, not instead of them. In ancient times, truce did not put an end to war – it simply ensured that the Games took place even if there was war.

However, we could argue that Olympia, with its mystic ceremonies, suspension of hostilities and gatherings of thousands on neutral territory, actually helped to neutralise political discord and led to the development of a common consciousness linking all Greek tribes (see Palaeologos 1965, 210). In the same way, it might be thought, the modern Olympic Games might stand as an example of global interaction and intercommunication the might lead to a common consciousness based on ideas of peace and internationalism.

That is to say, in time, this *ekecheiria* must have generated the conditions for peace, given its unifying function and its facilitation of supra-tribal contest under common rules – an example of multicultural cooperation and conflict resolution. As we shall see, this is also part of the modern case for truce – that it stands as an example of what might be possible in the field of human conflict, if only there were sufficient opportunity and motivation for a trucial pause.

Let us recall the myth of Pelops, who wins both Hippodaemia and the kingdom, but kills his helper, the charioteer, for his treason to the king. To appease the gods, he establishes the Olympic Games, and they become civilised, losing their murderous character, and taking on a nobler aspect, as a disinterested athletic competition, acknowledging of the value of the opponent, the reward of effort, and the devotion to moral ideals with a basis in truce.

Coubertin wanted to harness and extend these ideas to a modern concern with world peace, which Samaranche would later ally to the central mission of the United Nations, and the IOC would develop into the International Olympic Truce Foundation.

Quanz describes in detail the influence on Coubertin of the Paris-based peace movement of the late nineteenth century, which argued for human rights, international law and the cessation of war (1994, 122ff). But Coubertin further thought that the cultivation of international sports traditions would have an immediate, vivid and practical effect on people's desire to avoid war, which he thought a more realistic goal than to accomplish the end of war.

Just as the ancient Olympic Games united the Greek world, so the aim of the modern Games would be to enable us to raise our thoughts above the political differences of our age, to seek peaceful resolution to our conflicts, to achieve global human solidarity, and to reduce the possibility of war.

Modern truce

In pursuit of the aim, stated in the Olympic Charter, of promoting peace through sport and the Olympic ideal, the International Olympic Committee (IOC) decided to revive the ancient concept of the Olympic Truce.

The first initiatives were launched by the International Olympic Committee (IOC) in 1992. In order for the project to have a greater impact, the IOC relayed it to the United Nations (UN). Since 1993, the UN General Assembly has repeatedly expressed its support for the IOC by unanimously adopting, every two years, one year before each edition of the Olympic Games, a resolution entitled 'Building a peaceful and better world through sport and the Olympic ideal'.

Olympic ideals are also United Nations ideals: tolerance, equality, fair play and, most of all, peace. Together, the Olympics and the United Nations can be a winning team. But the contest will not be won easily. War, intolerance and deprivation continue to stalk the earth. We must fight back. Just as athletes strive for world records, so must we strive for world peace

(Kofi Annan, United Nations Secretary General, September 2000, quoted at: www.olympic.org/uk/organisation/missions/truce/)

Here are some important milestones in the first ten years:

1992   The IOC launched an appeal for the observance of the Olympic Truce and negotiated with the United Nations to allow individual athletes of the former Republic of Yugoslavia to participate as 'independent Olympic participants' in the Games of the XXIII Olympiad in Barcelona; and Croatia, Slovenia and Bosnia-Herzegovina could compete as separate nations for the first time.

1993   The first resolution on the observance of the Olympic Truce was adopted by the 48th session of the UN General Assembly.

1994   The year was proclaimed the International Year of Sport and the Olympic Ideal by the UN. The appeal for the observance of the Olympic Truce allowed the participation of athletes from the former Republic of Yugoslavia in the Olympic Winter Games in Lillehammer. An IOC delegation visited Sarajevo, which was at war, to extend its solidarity with the city that hosted the XIV Olympic Winter Games in 1984.

1995   The IOC president attended the UN General Assembly for the first time in history.

1998   The Olympic Truce was taken into consideration by member States during the Olympic Winter Games in Nagano and contributed, to a certain extent, to avoid war in Iraq and to set up a mediation mission by the UN Secretary General, which led to the signature of a memorandum of understanding between the UN and the Iraqi government.

1999   A record number of 180 member States were co-sponsors of the resolution on the Olympic Truce.

2000   The United Nations Millennium Summit, held in New York with the participation of more than 150 heads of state and government, adopted a Millennium Declaration that included a paragraph on the observance of the Olympic Truce. During the Opening Ceremony of the Games of the XXVII Olympiad in Sydney, the South and North Korean delegations paraded in the stadium together under the flag of the Korean peninsula.

2000   The IOC established an International Olympic Truce Foundation (IOTF), with the following objectives:

- to promote the Olympic ideals to serve peace, friendship and understanding in the world, and in particular, to promote the ancient Greek tradition of the Olympic Truce;

- to initiate conflict prevention and resolution through sport, culture and the Olympic ideals, by cooperating with all inter- and non-governmental organisations specialised in this field, by developing educational and research programmes, and by launching communications campaigns to promote the Olympic Truce.

2001 The 56th UN General Assembly adopted a resolution on the Olympic Truce as 'creating a better world through sports'. This idea is based on the core values of the United Nations, as Kofi Annan said (1999, 27):

> The flying of the United Nations flag at all Olympic events is a visible re-minder of the purpose shared between the UN and the International Olympic Committee ... I call upon all nations to observe the Olympic Truce. I am convinced that in this observance, and by working with the International Olympic Committee to promote the Olympic ideal, we will draw the world's attention to what humanity can achieve in the name of international under-standing.

Conclusion

Whether or not the Olympic Truce brings significant political change, we must further consider the educative value of example (as with all issues within sports ethics). As well as the idea of the moral laboratory, in which people, especially children, learn to consider moral choices and to act morally, Nissiotis raises the idea of a 'school of peace':

> It would, therefore, be a mistake to see the Olympic Truce as nothing but a passive pacifist attitude, or a fiction, or even a form of moral hypocrisy, because it is also an education, a training in view of permanent peace, a total negation of war and a victory over the feeling of hatred among people, who, in life, happen to be constantly competing. That is the reason why the Truce, in the final analysis, became a school of peace for the ancient Greeks.
>
> (Nissiotis 1985, 57)

Similarly, Reid notes that:

> Olympic-style sport can cultivate peaceful attitudes in three ways: first, by carving out space and time for putting aside conflicts ... ; second, by treating people as equals under the rules of the game ... ; and third, by tolerating and even celebrating differences ... The Olympic movement's contribution to peace comes at the grass-roots level – the conscious cultivation of peaceful attitudes through the image of its festival and the playing of its games.
>
> (2006, 207)

Importantly, too, Olympism aims at the political goal of a peaceful internationalism. We have already drawn attention to the emerging relationship between the Olympic Movement and the United Nations, two global organizations facing similar problems in regard to universality and particularity. The general problem faced by both is how they are to operate at a global (universal) level whilst there exist such differences at the particular level.

Sporting activity helps to overcome such difficulties, just because it presupposes the contract to contest, and the mutual rule-adherence that such a promise requires. And, not just in its sport, but in its principles as expressed in the Olympic Charter (International Olympic Committee 2006), Olympism itself seeks to be universal in its values: mutual recognition and respect, tolerance, solidarity, equity, anti-discrimination, peace, multiculturalism, etc. This is a quite specific set of values, which generate a set of universal general principles, but which also require differential interpretation in different cultures – *stated* in general terms whilst *interpreted* in the particular.

This search for a universal representation at the interpersonal and political level of our common humanity seems to me to be the essence of the optimism and hope of Olympism and other forms of humanism and internationalism. In the face of recent events in Europe and elsewhere it seems a fond hope and a naive optimism; but I don't see why we should not continue to argue for and work towards a future of promise, and I still see a strong case for sport as an efficient means. I believe that sport has made an enormous contribution to modern society over the past 100 years or so, and that the philosophy of Olympism has been the most coherent systematization of the ethical and political values underlying the practice of sport so far to have emerged.

Our commitment to the development of global forms of cultural expression such as sport, and to international understanding through ideologies such as Olympism is one way that we as individuals can express our commitments, ideals and hopes for the future of the world (see Parry 2006, 202–203).

Study questions

1 Some people say that sport is a kind of modern religion. What do you think they might mean by that? Are they right to say so?
2 To what extent might we take the ancient tradition of truce as an example of how sport could contribute to a better world?
3 What do you think of the ethical ideals of the Olympic Movement? Are they capable of being implemented in practice, or are they just empty words and slogans?
4 Do you think that sport is capable of helping us to see our way in the world – to develop ethical, political and spiritual ideas?

Notes

4 'Winning at all costs' in modern sport

1 The first major publication of the Church and Sport office is a collection of papers from an International Seminar on sport and Christianity that was attended by 45 people from 18 different countries. See Pontifical Council of the Laity (2006).

2 Although our discussion will focus on the competitive nature and pride of American professional sport and child and youth sport, many of our assertions could be applied to professional sport worldwide.

3 Readers should be aware that Lombardi's well-used (or abused) quote has oft been used out of context to justify simplistic arguments against competition per se. For a thorough history of this quote, see Overman (1999).

4 It is not our main task to examine the nature of, or theology of play and leisure, or the differences between sport, play and leisure. However, there is a significant literature that has developed from the seminal work of the Dutch historian Johan Huizinga (1950), the Catholic theologian Hugo Rahner (1972) and the Thomist philosopher Joseph Pieper (1998/1948). For a brief overview in relation to the sport–religion interface, see Mathisen (2005a).

5 Using Augustine's analysis of evil and immortality and his idea of 'disordered affections/loves', Hamilton discusses a number of issues intimately related to this chapter, such as the prevalence of sin, pride, shame and idolatry in modern competitive sport, while importantly championing the good of sport when played in the right spirit.

6 It is probable that in 'face-to-face' combative sports, such as American football, soccer, ice hockey etc. there is more potential for pride than in 'side-by-side' sports such as golf, or at least greater potential for the negative consequences of pride to manifest (e.g. alienation, violence). This said, pride is in essence a 'sin of the heart' (Proverbs 18:12) and thus it may be just as prevalent in non-contact, side-by-side sports such as golf, but will not necessarily be shown through behaviour.

7 Philosophers of sport have written extensively on the nature of competition in sport. For an accessible introduction see Kretchmar (2005). For more detailed analyses of competition in sport, see Simon (1991) and Hyland (1978, 1988).

8 Defining sport is a slippery challenge. We follow others in that play, games and sport are contiguous but as we move from play to sport we begin to introduce some important modifications: 'more restrictive rules, more difficulty in achieving goals, the development of physical skills and use of physical exertion, and the necessity of competition'. See Visker (1994, 174). For a more detailed discussion concerning the definitions see Loland (2002, 2–16).

9 For a scholarly but accessible analysis of the Greek concept of *agon*, see Pfitzner (1967).

10 Contrary to the competitive and status-driven ethos of the modern world shown

through this type of media advertising, at the heart of the gospel is the idea that God loves and cares for each and every person, regardless of social status, abilities, wealth or past wrongs. God's grace can *not* be earned on merit, it is a *free* gift to *any* person who asks and believes in his or her heart (Romans 10:8–10). For an accessible and heart-warming account of grace, see Manning (2004).

11 We see much fruit in Rene Girard's (1987) discussion about 'mimetic rivalry' and the application of this to competitive sports as a staging ground for violence.

12 For other and more specific examples and a greater analysis of the moral evaluation of this belief system, see Hughes and Coakley (1991) and Lumpkin *et al.* (2003).

13 For extensive documentation of most of these issues, see Howe (2004). Those wishing to explore what is arguably the most recent theological–ethical dilemma (alongside genetic enhancement) in professional sport, that is, surgical enhancement such as LASIK eye surgery for golfers and rotator cuff surgery (not corrective) for baseball players, we refer readers to Hamilton (in press).

14 In reviewing this chapter, Professor Scott Kretchmar pointed out that these immoral principals in sport are a kind of 'instrumental ethic', that is, things that used to be deemed as wrong in a moral sense are now considered largely (if not wholly) in terms of their efficacy – do they work? One of the outcomes of instrumental thinking is the loss of the notion of a 'meaningful victory' in the quest to 'win at all costs'.

15 There is no room here to develop this theme but it is important to note that Guttman emphasises that the *reasons* for the character of 'modern sports' 'are complex and much disputed' (1994, 4). For our purposes, however, it is sufficient to note that these socio-cultural developments emphasise the importance of 'achievement and winning' and thus provide increased *potential* for the sin of pride. We argue that this is the principal reason at the root of the many ethical and moral problems in modern sport.

16 For a thorough sociological analysis of this point, see Schmitt and Leonard (1986, 1088), who examine 'the processes through which Americans seek to leave their mark [identity] through achievements in sport'. This work adds support to our thesis and that of Grimshaw (2000), exploring the role of athletes' and fans' identity construction, the sports hero/idol, competition and the related economic and political drivers in modern sport.

17 This is comparable to states of flow and zen, deep play and peak experiences that are widely documented in the sports literature. See Chapter 6 below.

18 In their comprehensive book, *An Unholy Alliance: The Sacred and Modern Sports* (2004), Higgs and Braswell have provided a trenchant critique of the writings of a group of scholars they call the 'sport apologists', which for the most part supports many of the ideas in this chapter.

19 An idol can de defined as any object, idea or person that is worshipped in the place of God (Exodus 20:4). Idols may include money, human relationships, sport, religion, music, sex etc.

20 It is likely that this worldview may be entirely foreign to, or only partly understood by, some readers. It may be helpful to consider why Hollywood blockbusters such as *The Lord of the Rings*, *The Lion the Witch and the Wardrobe* and *Harry Potter* have such universal appeal. The central premise of all these films is an 'internal and external' battle between good and evil that we can all relate to in our daily existence. For an interesting take on this see Johnson (2005). For a brief and accessible account of evil (principalities and powers) from a mainstream Christian perspective see Banks and Stevens (1997).

21 Although we are focusing on what seems to be a generally 'explicit pride' in American culture/sport, this is arguably no worse, for example, than the 'defensive pride' that appears to be deeply imbedded in the British psyche. Of course, these cultural differences have historical determinants, not least in relation to a nation's past experience of invasion and wars and monarchical and constitutional/state structure and foundations.

22 Quoted in Overman (1997, 226).

23 'Showing off' often takes the form of athletes, coaches and parents *boasting* (and gossiping about others) about past achievements or their abilities and is arguably a very common form of pride. Let us consider the following proverbs: 'the tongue is a small part of the body, but it makes great boasts' (James 3:5) and 'where there are many words, sin is not absent, but he who holds is tongue is wise' (Proverbs 10:19). All biblical quotations are taken from the NIV (International Bible Society 2002).

24 Within his chapter *The Great Sin*, Lewis does differentiate between 'diabolical pride' and what I would term 'defensive pride'. Lewis defines 'black diabolical pride' as 'when you look down on others so much that you do not care what they think of you' (1997/1952, 104), which is often the root of power-mad dictators. Defensive pride is in some ways (however, a Christian should be able to forgive *all* sin, however despicable, by the grace of God) more forgivable, as it is normally rooted in unconscious emotional and spiritual wounds of the individual acting out of a proud heart, due to their need to appear *better than* their opponent, or whom they have *fantasised* as their opponent in some human endeavour. Also see footnote 36.

25 For documentation of the Puritan dislike for sport see Mathisen (2005a) and for discussion of the role of sport and play in medieval times see Hoffman (forthcoming). Hoffman makes the important point that medieval theologians, especially after Aquinas, were on the whole open to play and sport, with some strict provisos of course.

26 For a comparative analysis of 'identity' from a humanistic and Christian perspective that draws on the ideas of Augustine, Kierkegaard, Merton, Pascal, Rahner etc., see Morea (1997a).

27 The circumstances and reason for the crucifixion itself are an acute example of how pride in competitive sport situations, fuelled by the need to be 'number one' and feel and maintain power, can lead to alienation and the ultimate act of violence. Ultimately, it was the pride and fear of the Jewish and Roman leaders losing their power and social standing and traditions that led to the crucifixion of Jesus (John 11:47–48; Mark 15:15; Luke 22:2). If readers think this parallel is an exaggeration, consider the recent death of a young French tennis player who was drugged by the father of one of his opponents, in the desperate quest for his son to 'win at all costs'. Of course, acts of pride, alienation and violence in sport exist on a continuum and this is an extreme example.

28 Higgs and Braswell (see 2004, 97–115) make the important point, as have others (Weiss 1969), that sports stars do no wrong in earning large amounts of money but it does 'undermine the possibility of holiness in sports', i.e. the potential for corruption, greed and idolatry are increased if large sums of money are involved. As the Bible suggests, 'the love of money is the root of all kinds of evil' (1 Timothy 6:10a) *not* 'money is evil'.

29 Although Lofton's book review on religion and masculinity addresses Higgs' (1995) earlier book the tenor and method of the argument are very similar to his more recent collaborative work (Higgs and Braswell 2004).

30 It has long been debated whether sport can lead to character development, which is of course dictated by how one defines character and how one understands sport competition. See chapter 5, 'Does Competition Build Character?', of Kohn's (1992) book for a good overview, although we think he overstates the negative aspects of competition while giving little thought to potential positives.

31 Greek has four words for love that are important to understand in the context of relations in sport competition. These are: *storge* (affection), the love we have for family, especially parents to children, but also children to parents; *philia* (platonic), love expressed towards our friends; *eros* (sexual desire), the state of 'being in love', a healthy sexual desire toward one's partner; and *agape* (unconditional love or charity), the unconditional love of God for humanity (divine gift-love) and the unconditional (as far as it can be) and *willed* love of humans towards others without expecting anything in return, especially to those who do not deserve our love, our enemies, i.e. those

who annoy/offend us. Although all four aspects of love are interrelated and balance between them in relationships is vital, we would argue that *philia* and *agape* love are those most needed for virtuous and humble relations with others in sport competition, as often one would need to *willfully choose* to love others even when wronged or incited to retaliate verbally or physically. If sport had become an *idol* in an athlete's life leading to familial relational problems, then it would be *storge* that is being neglected. For an overview, see Lewis (1960).

32 The findings of Schroeder and Scribner's qualitative study examining the role of religion in American inter-collegiate athletics suggest that 'humility and graciousness' were values that were encouraged by coaching staff and administrators in a Christian college. Participants noted that the faith and skill of the staff were important in teaching; for example, being taught how to view winning as process oriented rather than outcome orientated and the values of perseverance and self-discipline. These findings cannot of course be generalised to the wider culture of professional sport, but they do suggest that through education and the example or witness of significant others (coaches etc.) athletes can learn about their faith and develop virtues from sporting competition.

33 This 'niceness' often manifests itself in the form of 'false humility' and a superficial and shallow understanding and practice of Christianity. Jesus and his followers are often viewed as 'weak' (e.g. needing an emotional crutch) and the teachings they follow (the Bible) as a type of 'fluffy spirituality' by the modern world. A cursory reading of the gospels and the book of Acts, however, should quickly dispense with any such sentimentally, demonstrating that Christ and to a lesser degree his disciples, although humble, meek and loving, were also 'masculine', courageous and willing to die for the love of God and his work in the world.

34 There are clear links here to the concept of Muscular Christianity and Plato's idea of *thumos* (a primal manly force involved in sex, morality and fighting) that was used by Charles Kingsley in developing his doctrine of Christian manliness. See Chapter 5 below.

35 This is most likely a psychological and behavioral manifestation of deep, probably unconscious, emotional and spiritual wounds that results in the athlete suffering from 'defensive pride/masks', or what Christian psychologists may call 'fig leaves' (Genesis 3:7), in order to hide from the 'real self' and feelings of shame and inadequacy. While there is no room here to expand upon this point, in brief the Christian story suggests that, in order to overcome the *false self*, a person can decide to allow the grace of the Holy Spirit to help them gradually surrender every dimension of their life into the care and guidance of a loving Father God. This results in the person's identity being rooted in the love of God, the source of their being (Ephesians 3:17b; Romans 8); thus they will have less need for 'fig leaves' and the obsessive striving to win at all costs that in turn alienates others and so on. For a short but incisive account of the idea of surrender in the Christian tradition, see Murray (2005). For a clear and detailed description of emotional and spiritual wounds, their consequences and the road to surrender and healing, see the Swiss psychiatrist Paul Tournier's work, especially *The Healing of Persons* (1965), and Frost (2002).

36 In light of the ongoing 'nature v. nurture' debate, although we provide a historical and cultural (i.e. institutional) basis for our argument in this section, we maintain that the temptation to be proud is inherent in our base nature (Romans 7:14–25) but this is fuelled by historical and cultural antecedents (nurture).

37 For a detailed analysis of the global sports economy and the aggressive market strategies imbedded in 'transnational corporate capitalism', which help promote this worldview, see Silk *et al.* (2005).

38 For further documentation of this point see Hoffman (2003).

39 For a scholarly analysis of the heroic in sport, see chapters 8 and 9, 'The Sports Hero'

and 'The Sports Fan and Hero-Worshipper' respectively, of Higgs (1982). The authors would like to thank Professor Higgs for his advice and guidance on relevant sources on this topic.

40 Interestingly, in his book *The Screwtape Letters* (1942), C.S. Lewis identifies the transient and repetitive fashions and 'ideas and philosophies' of humans, as a major strategy of the enemy (evil force) in deceiving and blinding humans to the real meaning of life, that is, accepting and living in the grace, love and guidance of an eternal God (John 1:4).

41 'Taking up one's cross' can legitimately mean many different things to different people; however, Higgs and Braswell's (2004, 236) proactive statement challenges us to consider what this means: 'Sports are about chosen ones, those who are able to make the team – the fit, the able, and the talented. All religions at their best are about caring for the unchosen, the rejects, those who don't qualify for any team.'

42 See the Centre for the Study of Sport and Spirituality, York St John University College, York, England (http://sportspirituality.yorksj.ac.uk) and the Centre for Sport, Spirituality and Character Development, Neumann College, Philadelphia, US (http://www.neumann.edu/academics/special/sscd.asp).

43 Think-Tank – *Lord of Sport: A Quest to Discover God's Wisdom for Sport*, 13–16 March 2005, Dayton, Ohio (sponsored and hosted by Athletes in Action). The authors of this chapter both attended the meeting alongside a number of leading academics and practitioners who have addressed this important area of study. These include the sport philosopher Professor Scott Kretchmar, the sociology professor James Mathisen, the kinesiology professor Shirl Hoffman, the Executive Director of Verité Sports (UK), Stuart Weir, and many other sports ministers and coaches.

44 See http://cskls.org.

45 Readers should note that this applies to Christians and the 'the worldwide Church' (2 Chronicles 7:14–15) as well as to those who perhaps have not considered the spiritual life to date.

46 The 'myths of progress' that Middleton and Walsh refer to come from the disciplines of anthropology (Feuerbach), psychology (Freud), sociology (Marx and Durkheim) and biology (Darwin). Following the 'Genome project' in 2000, genetic determinism has arguably become the latest mythic utopia for some. Undisputedly, all these ideas have in varying ways led to very positive scientific, technological, and some social, advancements that we should be most thankful for. However, the point is that the proponents and followers of these utopias have often slid into idolatry, seeing them as all-encompassing explanations for social and cultural existence and in turn ignoring God's guidance for how humanity should live. The history of the twentieth century and the *state of the modern world* clearly show the folly in this view, which we are warned about in the Bible (1 Corinthians 1:18–31; 2).

47 Closely related to the false myth of 'winning is everything' in big-time professional sports is our obsessively somatic culture, in which health clubs and gyms have to some degree become the new church. In his ironically titled book, *Working out My Salvation: The Contemporary Gym and the Promise of "Self" Transformation* (2005), William Hoverd uncovers what he calls a 'veritable Tower of Babel' in the sport and health industries, in which salvation (i.e. identity, recognition and significance) is often sought through bodily perfection and identification with cultural idols. See also Hoffman (1992a) for a similar analysis of what he calls *cultius aerobicus*, that is 'the horde of Sunday morning joggers . . . who claim to have found on the roads passing by the Church what they could never find within the walls' (1992a, 157). For an excellent, very practical and accessible account of how to keep a balance in both our physical and spiritual health see Hill (2005).

5 Muscular Christianity in the modern age

1 This holistic approach is often linked to the Ancient Greek concept of *mens sana in corpore sano* – sound mind in a sound body – and was used by Pierre Baron de Coubertin in developing the modern Olympic ethic. See Young (2005).

2 Ladd and Mathisen (1999) and Putney (2001) have provided comprehensive analyses with a more specific American focus.

3 Although most scholars date the origins of the movement from the New Testament, Eisen (1975) argues that Muscular Christianity can be traced back to the Old Testament. In addition to religious dancing at Jewish festivals he notes the Israelites' involvement in wrestling, military activities and archery. Ballou (1973) also suggests that an 'examination of the literature of the [Church] Fathers provides an indication that the relationship of Christianity to physical activity and sport was not as negative as the literature suggests' (196). Additionally, Higgs and Braswell (2004, 349) note that the roots of Muscular Christian ideas can be loosely linked to conceptions of medieval chivalry. All biblical quotations are taken from the NIV (International Bible Society 2002).

4 It would seem that the influence of Plato's mind–body dualism in Kingsley's seminal work has had a significant role in modern evangelicals' tendency to 'dichotomise' their faith and sport, a point which I critique in the final section of this chapter.

5 This is a theme picked up by Eldridge (2001), who argues that many men in the modern church have become emasculated, 'too nice' (often manifesting as false humility), with authentic masculinity being rare.

6 Owing to limited space, I will not discuss the YMCA or Olympic models. For further information, see Watson *et al.* (2005).

7 Although it is often termed a classic, Gay (1992, 110) notes that 'the "literary merits" of the book were scarcely formidable. What mattered more was that it gave the public what it wanted, an optimistic, breezy, "realistic" tale with moral attached.'

8 Quoted in Weir (manuscript in preparation).

9 Notably, the Marquis of Queensberry, the man who codified boxing, was also the man who instigated the prosecution of the aesthete Oscar Wilde (1854–1900) for homosexuality (Dobre-Laza 2003).

10 For an interesting historical account of 'manliness in Catholicism' that mentions Ampleforth College, see Chandler (2002). For a broader overview of Catholic perspectives on sport, see Feeney (1995) and Pontifical Council of the Laity (2006).

11 See www.neumann.edu/.

12 See www.christiansinsport.org.uk/.

13 For an in-depth analysis of this theme, see Chapter 4 above.

14 Key Pauline passages referring to the athletic: 1 Corinthians 9:24–27; Philippians 3:12b–14; 1 Timothy 4:7b–8, 6:11–12; 2 Timothy 2:5, 4: 7–8. Brief New Testament athletic references: Acts 20:24; Romans 9:16; Galatians 2:2, 5:7; Philippians 1:27c–30, 2:16; Colossians 1:29a, 4:12; Hebrews 12:1–3 (probably not Pauline). Possible additional athletic allusions: Romans 15:30; 1 Corinthians 4:9, 15:32; Ephesians 6:12; Philippians 4:1, 3; Colossians 2:18, 3:15; 1 Thessalonians 2:2, 19; 2 Thessalonians 3:1. Source of information: 'Biblical Foundations for Sports Ministry: The Key Pauline Passages', a conference handout received through a personal communication with Professor Mathisen.

15 Exegesis: the Greek verb behind the noun means to direct, to expound or interpret. Thus, biblical exegesis is the process of revealing and interpreting meaning in a text, which is of course determined by one's presuppositions (Richardson 1969, 123).

16 Although I wholeheartedly support the role of critical scholarship, I would suggest that perhaps individuals earn the right to be critical of others in matters of faith, only if they themselves have in some way 'put their hand to the plough for the Kingdom of God', i.e. are not peering down from the 'Ivory Tower'!

17 Mathisen (2002) suggests that any 'Muscular Christian preacher worth their salt' should access Pfitzner's (1967) scholarly but accessible analysis of the Greek concept of *agon*.

18 (1) *Pragmatic utility*: the worth of sport is essentially determined by its utilitarian effectiveness as a means of conversion. (2) *Meritocratic democracy*: the meritocratic nature of American sports is an appropriate model for the democratic appeal of Muscular Christianity. (3) *Competitive virtue*: competition and winning are consistent with the teachings of Jesus and the writings of the apostle Paul. (4) *Heroic models*: sport provides the predominant context for the heroes and role models American youth need, especially as a demonstration of Christianity's continuing relevance. (5) *Therapeutic self-control*: improved performance in sport is possible when one follows a disciplined regimen to achieve a level of self-control like a mature Christian (Mathisen 2002, 10–11).

19 I have no problem whatsoever with athletes trying their best to win in competitive sport (in a mutual and respectful quest for excellence with their opponent(s)) and glorifying God through their sport performance (1 Corinthians 6:20, 10:31). But it is what are arguably often crass, but I am sure well-meaning and genuine, post-game testimonies, where athletes 'spew references to their faiths during post-game jubilation . . . and from their celebrity pulpits . . . encourage their followers to subscribe to their faiths' (Elliott 2004, 1–2), that the 'winning a championship for Christ' syndrome, as Hoffman calls it, is most questionable and rooted in a 'work ethic' (i.e. the flesh or ego) rather than a 'play ethic'. In this context, would an athlete not be better to witness by 'the way they play' and gracious comments about opponents in victory or loss, unless specifically asked by the interviewer about religious faith? The witness of the German golfer Bernhard Langer comes to mind.

20 Karl Rahner is a Catholic theologian who has written on the spiritual aspects of play and leisure (*Man at Play*, 1972), as have others such as the Thomist scholar Joseph Pieper (*Leisure: The Basis of Culture*, 1998/1948), the theologian Jürgen Moltmann (*Theology of Play*, 1972) and perhaps what is the most well-known work from the Dutch historian Johan Huizinga (*Homo Ludens: A Study of the Play Element in Culture*, 1950). Protestant thinkers would do well to read these mostly Catholic writings, which provide a needed antidote to a 'work-based ethic' in competitive sports.

21 Plato's dualistic philosophy has of course been entrenched in the 'modern mind' by Cartesian–Kantian dualism from the Enlightenment period.

22 Marvin R. Wilson is a leading scholar on Christian–Jewish relations and is the Harold J. Ockenga Professor of Biblical and Theological Studies at Gordon College, Wenham, MA, USA. He recently delivered a keynote lecture at the 2006 annual conference of the Christian Society for Kinesiology and Leisure Studies (see http://cskls.org/) at Gordon College, in which he emphasised the *intrinsic value* of sport and exercise as a means of achieving and maintaining holistic health and well-being – *shalom* – and the important role that both scholars and practitioners in the field of sport and exercise have in offering this to others.

23 This quote comprises extracts from the following sections within various chapters of Wilson's text: 'Foundational not Optional', 131–132; 'Everything is Theological', 156–159; 'Dynamic Unity versus Dualism', 167–171; and 'Spirituality: Heavenly or Earthly', 174–178.

24 Dr Sara Savage provides an excellent account of dance in a Christian context and while focusing on 'dance as performance' provides many points that could be applied to sport, such as the error of mind–body dualism and prejudices against the body, intellectualism, and how we can experience glimpses of God through our embodiment (i.e. 'Personal Knowledge', as Polanyi termed it, through human movement) in dance and human movement as an individual can in music for example. Although the comparison between dance and sport is useful here, there are of course some limitations: for example, the highly competitive nature of sport and its rewards, different movement

forms and, perhaps most important, the focus and intentions (glory to God or to win personal status, money etc.) of the participant.

25 It could be argued that non-Christian sportspersons who are passionate about sport and 'just play' (an excellence of being) without the added baggage of 'winning for Christ' (an excellence of doing, a *works*-based and potentially analytical approach) probably *enjoy* participating more and *in one way* at *that moment* are living in a manner more pleasing to their Creator. Of course, this momentary experience may have no bearing on their inward spiritual journey.

26 A good example of this was a recent think-tank, in which a diverse group of individuals including theologians, sport chaplains and ministers, ex-professional athletes, coaches and philosophers met to explore ways in which to collaborate: Think-Tank – *Lord of Sport: A Quest to Discover God's Wisdom for Sport*, 13–16 March 2005, Dayton, Ohio (sponsored and hosted by Athletes in Action). A multi-authored book that is soon to be published was a major outcome of this meeting (Deadorff and White, forthcoming).

27 There are very positive examples of change in evangelical sport organisations, a good example being the Sport for Life conference that Athletes in Action run. Lectures and seminars include information on relationships in sport, the power, beauty and drama of sport, self-discovery and self-discipline, the damaging win at all costs myth of modern sport, fair play and character in sport competition, pursuing excellence, the balance between intrinsic and extrinsic motivators in sport etc.

28 I highly recommend Jeffrey Marx's book (2003) for readers wanting to explore how to disciple 'boys to become men' through the vehicle of sport. It is an inspirational semi-biographical and semi-instructional account of ex-NFL start Joe Ehrmann, who is now a high school football coach, ordained minister and leader of inner-city urban ministry programmes, such as the Building Men for Others Programme.

29 Quoted in Gire (1996).

6 Nature and transcendence

1 The word 'extreme' has been used to label an ever-increasing range of alternative sport forms, some of which are not high-risk and thus not really extreme. Examples of extreme sports, however, include big-wave surfing, solo rock-climbing, mountaineering, adventure racing, single-handed sailing, BASE jumping, ice-climbing, underwater cave diving, white and black water rafting, back-country skiing and snowboarding, and skydiving. For a comprehensive overview, see Tomlinson (1999). Many of the assertions I make throughout this chapter regarding extreme sports, excluding the elements of risk-taking and the role of the wilderness environment, I would argue can also be applied to 'mainstream sports'.

2 Quoted in Zaehner (1961, 199).

3 All biblical quotations are taken from the NIV (International Bible Society 2002).

4 Monotheism is a belief in *one* transcendent God and is a characteristic of the three Semitic religions, Judaism, Christianity and Islam. This is in contrast to polytheistic religions, whose adherents worship two or more deities, e.g. Hinduism.

5 This denotes a *general* acceptance of the biblical doctrines and usage of secondary sources, scholarly and biographical mystical writings, of both Catholic and Protestant mainstream denominations.

6 The terms 'soul', 'mind' and 'psyche' are often used interchangeably to collectively describe the 'will, intellect and emotions', which in modern psychology is commonly understood as *personality*. The *body* is viewed as the 'temple [vehicle] of the Holy Spirit' (1 Corinthians 3:16) and, as such, should not be subjugated to a lesser importance (i.e. mind–body dualism) than the other component parts, soul and spirit (i.e. holism). *Spirit* can have two meanings. First, as an 'animating' principle which creates and *gives* life (Genesis 2:7). Second, as the Spirit of God that came upon his prophets

and people in Old Testament times (e.g. 1 Samuel 10:10; Numbers 11:25; 2 Kings 2:9) and as the Holy Spirit that came in a new way at Pentecost (Acts 2:1–41) and which can redeem and guide human beings (Romans 8:1–17; 10:9–13). However, theologians, philosophers and more recently psychologists have long debated the *exact* composition of, and interrelationship between, these constituent dimensions of human personhood. For a scholarly analysis see McFadyen (1990).

7 The publication of books such as *Snowboarding to Nirvana* (1997) and *Surfing the Himalayas: A Spiritual Adventure* (1995), by Fredrick Lenz, further illustrates this point. See also Arytom (2005).

8 The relationship between spirituality and the wilderness (especially the mountains) has a clear historical lineage, dating back to some of the most significant stories of the monotheistic religions of Judaism, Christianity and Islam. More recent philosophical movements, such as British and German Romanticism and in America New England Transcendentalism (e.g. Emerson and Thoreau), have also promoted the spiritual and therapeutic value of the nature–person interaction. See Anderson (2001). For readers wanting a more in-depth analysis that could be applied to wilderness sports, I would recommend *Philosophy Gone Wild: Environmental Ethics*, by the 'founding father' of environmental ethics, Holmes Rolston III (1989).

9 The *flow* construct comprises nine dimensions: a balance between perceived challenges and skills, having clear goals, having a sense of control over one's actions, merging of action and awareness, receiving unambiguous feedback, being fully concentrated on the task, not being self-conscious, loss of time awareness, and the end result an *autotelic* experience (a high level of intrinsic satisfaction).

10 It is noteworthy that Maslow's understanding of human nature is based upon humanistic psychology/philosophy. In his classic critique of modern psychology, Paul Vitz (1994/1977) shows that the atheism and narcissism that characterise humanistic psychology are diametrically opposed to the Christian worldview.

11 See Higgs and Braswell (2004: chapter 10), who provide an incisive discussion of the similarities and differences between the experience of flow and the Holy Spirit.

12 Christian spirituality (*not* mystical/numinous experience per se, i.e. ecstatic experience of God) is the constant presence (Romans 8:9–11) and power of the Holy Spirit in the life of the believer. Based on Christian anthropological holism, any dimension of the believer's life may then be considered as having spiritual *potential*, especially in relation to creativity and the aesthetic in sport.

13 Of course, 'nature mysticism' can be a feature of undesirable even 'diabolical' human behaviour and ideology. An extreme example is 'Nazi mysticism', emanating from their power-crazed charismatic leader, Adolf Hitler. As Higgs (1992, 100) points out, this prideful and egotistical mysticism is the exact opposite of Christ's reverential qualities and humility.

14 See Dupré (1987) and, for a broad typology of 'introvertive' and 'extrovertive' mystical states, Stace's (1960, 131) classic study.

15 There is a significant controversy debating the roots of 'mysticism in the Bible', which revolves around the differences/similarities between 'prophetic and mystical' religion. Maquarrie provides a helpful discussion of this in chapters 2 and 3 of his book, arguing that although Christian mysticism can legitimately claim its roots in the Bible (based on the experiences of Moses and St Paul, e.g. Exodus 3; Acts 9:3–6; 2 Corinthians 12:1–5) it owes its modern form to classical Greek and medieval sources.

16 Quoted in Jones (1909) and Otto (1957, 73).

17 Antisocial and deviant behaviour have become widespread in both mainstream and alternative/extreme sports, which further questions the notion of religious and mystical experience per se in sport, especially when considering the 'fruits of the spirit' (Galatians 5:22–25). See Chapter 4.

18 James made no secret of his abhorrence for Christian orthodoxy, especially the 'institution' and corporate dimensions of organised religion. Christian theologians have been

quick to point out that James's pluralistic and finite conception of God (Lash 1988) results in what Stanley Hauerwas describes as an account of faith that is at best 'an expression of pietistic humanism' (2002, 44). Ironically, Lash notes, James's work has served as an important corrective for theologians wishing to develop a coherent and logical argument for theism.

19 Numinous and mystical experiences of the holy are certainly not restricted to biblical times or religious revivals of a bygone age. For an excellent auto-ethnographic analysis of modern mystical experience and manifestations of the holy see Poloma (2003).

20 In brief, there are two types of monism. First, a religious monism (a form of pantheistic belief, especially characteristic of Eastern religions), that God and the world are identical (Hinduism), or that the physical world is an illusion (Mahayan Buddhism) and the 'mystical oneness' is an experience of the void of 'nothingness'. Second, a monism that has *no* religious referent and can be classed as a 'nature mystical experience', in which an individual has a sense of oneness with self and/or objects.

21 There are of course historical antecedents that provide the basis of these spiritual sporting odysseys: in mountaineering, the birth of Alpinism within eighteenth-century European Romanticism; and in surfing, ancient Polynesian mythology in the birthplace of surfing, Hawaii.

22 Information sourced from Biblio.com, *Aldous Huxley*, online. Available at www.biblio.com/authors/ (accessed 2 May 2006).

23 Zaehner (1961, 50) was the founder of the term 'pan-en-hen-ism' (in English, all-in-one-ism): an experience of nature in all things or as all things being one, with no reference to God.

24 Another variation on pantheism (in English, all-God-ism) is pan-en-theism: God is *simultaneously* in the universe (immanent) but also above it (transcendent). The theologian John Macquarrie (2004) prefers to call pantheism 'dialectical theism', which he argues can never be free from some form of paradox, i.e. it implies a God that is both totally transcendent and totally immanent.

25 Even though Buber was more sympathetic to Christianity than some commentators would have us believe, he certainly did not support the mysticism of St Paul or Eckhart, whom he classed as Gnostics. See Bertman (2000).

26 On reading the biographies and poetry of mystics such as St John of the Cross, it is clear that mystical union and intimacy with God is anything but easy. See *The Ascent of Mount Carmel* and the *Dark Night of the Soul* if you want to be challenged!

27 It is important to stress that none of these great thinkers were 'pantheists', but rather saw how *contemplation* of the beauties of creation could touch the depths of the human soul and in turn point to the 'other'. For example, Thomas Merton sees such aesthetic responses to beauty as a form of 'active contemplation' that is *like* a 'mystical experience' but on a 'natural level' and which provides an 'intimation of God'. Importantly though, he stresses that this is not to be confused with 'infused mystical experience', which takes the experient to a much deeper level (Morea 1997, 82, 87).

28 Quoted in Dubay (1999, 117)

29 I realise that in many situations the two can never be clearly separated. For example, a surfer may experience exciting or even neurotic fear (accompanied by a release of adrenaline and endorphins) of 'wiping out' and at the same time encounter astonishment and awe in the soul at the size and power of the wave. This important distinction will be discussed in more depth in the next section.

30 Mainly under the influence of poststructuralist thinker Francois Lyotard, there are now many different definitions and usages of the term. See Fludernik (2001) for a brief historical account of the development of the idea of the sublime.

31 Although Kant did discuss the sublime in relation to the holy in religion and nature in his *Critique of Judgement*, it was the later Romantic theorists (especially Burke) who made this association more explicit.

32 For Kant, and others (e.g. Lewis and Tolkien), the faculties of *imagination* and *intuition*

were key in both appreciation of the sublime and the beautiful. For an in-depth discussion see the sections 'The Veil of the Sublime' and 'Beauty' in Hart (2003).

33 For examples of this work, see Bunting *et al.* (2000) and Ewert (1994).

34 The 'runner's high' has been immortalised by Dr George Sheehan's book *Running and Being* (1978).

35 Interestingly, there are millions of accounts of mystical and numinous experiences documented in the near-death experience literature, in which humans have *literally* faced death (*close* to clinical death) through illness, accidents and especially during cardiac arrest. See Fox (2003). Historically, it could also be argued that risk-taking as a vehicle for transcendence has been 'overplayed' by contemporary sports writers considering the role of risk-taking in our 'evolutionary heritage', i.e. risk-taking was a regular occurrence in our primitive ancestors through the need to hunt and battle for daily survival. For a relevant account, see Higgs (1986).

36 This is also a theme developed in the philosophy of Martin Heidegger (especially his idea of *Dasein*) and other existentialists, such as Sartre and Camus, and discussed in relation to sport by Reid (2002), Thomas (1996) and Standish (1998).

37 Developed from Stace's (1960) earlier work, the M Scale is a validated psychometric instrument for measuring various characteristics of mystical experience.

38 Although beyond the scope of this work, isolation in the wilderness and sensory deprivation (asceticism) have been used by religious mystics down the ages as a way of encountering the divine. The 'hermit' lifestyles of the Christian Desert Fathers and medieval monks, or the Aborigine practice of 'walkabout', are examples. Although mountaineering and single-handed sailing *may* include a degree of asceticism (see Hutch 2006), arguably activities such as adventure racing and arctic expeditions are more applicable here.

39 In support, the euphoria-inducing properties of endorphins have been shown to play a role in 'altered states of consciousness' through 'fear-inducing' religious practices. See Wulff (1991:81).

40 For a clear account of 'humanistic spirituality' (if this is not an oxymoron!) see Hamel *et al.* (2003).

41 Although writing from a Christian perspective I do not totally discount the philosophy of Nietzsche and the French existentialists on account of their atheism, as some themes in their work can help us to better understand ourselves and the human pursuit of excellence. It is however, ironic that the very honest, logically consistent and frightful conclusions of these existential philosophers were clearly articulated by the founder of existentialism, the Christian philosopher Søren Kierkegaard (1813–1855), and in biblical books such as Job and Ecclesiastes, penned thousands of years ago.

42 This quote originated from Greenfield (1999, 33).

43 See Stranger's (1999) study of surfing and my own study of surfing and snowboarding in which one participant reported the death of his friend in an avalanche (Watson *et al.* 2004).

44 Although speculative, it is interesting to consider that risk-taking for *some* in extreme sports may be actually an unconscious 'running away from the authentic life' (i.e. facing up to the existential predicament in a meaningless universe if one does not believe in God) rather than the oft-suggested deep quest for meaning through facing death in these activities. This is a central theme in the writings of Kierkegaard, what he called 'unconscious despair', the 'fictitious life', which has perhaps been most clearly articulated in chapter 5 ('The Psychoanalyst Kierkegaard') of Ernest Becker's book, *The Denial of Death* (1973).

45 The terms used by Slusher (mystical, ultimate reality and authentic self) and Reid (truth and encounters with reality) are not clearly defined or explained, thus I can only assume from their conclusions and the literature they cite that they are adopting a philosophy of humanistic existentialism (i.e. Know Thyself) as their start-point. If so,

truth and reality become 'relative', i.e. whatever individuals deem truth/reality to be 'for themselves'.

46   Following Slusher ('in a way'), I am *not* suggesting that all extreme athletes, or those who participate in 'alternative sports', are nihilists or narcissists or that they have a neurotic death-wish. However, authors seem to agree that there is an undercurrent of 'narcissism' and 'fatalistic risk-taking' in the extreme/alternative sports subculture, pointing to the meaningless culture of postmodernity as the origin. Themes such as the role of male and female egoism (bravado) in identity formation and the culture of risk-taking this may engender, the need for social prestige, the hedonistic search for the 'adrenaline rush' (i.e. thrills), 'at all costs', and superficial accounts of spiritual experience are discussed. See the introduction and chapters 3, 5, 6 and 7 of Wheaton (2004). For a good example of many of these themes, see also the mountaineering film *K2* (1991).

47   I am *not* suggesting that extreme athletes could not have a theistic mystical/numinous experience during their activities; I am sure a small number may have, as the contrary would be to deny the providential doctrine of God. However, based on this analysis, it is highly unlikely that the many so-called mystical and numinous experiences in the sports literature could be classified as Christian monotheistic in nature.

10   Spirituality, sport and virtues

1   I am grateful to Tony Collins, on whose paper about the club this case is based.

11   Sport, ethos and education

1   McFee (2004, chapter 8, and especially p. 140) further explores the notion of sport as a 'moral laboratory'.

2   So, an ethos account – following the spirit of the rules – 'can do justice to features of rule-following or rule-breaking not captured by a simple statement of the rules.' (For this, and a detailed discussion of ethos accounts, see McFee 2004, 56ff.)

3   For a concise discussion of internal and external goods, see Loland and McNamee (2003, 73).

Bibliography

Acevedo, E.O., Dzewaltowski, D.A., Gill, D.L. and Noble, J.M. (1992) 'Cognitive Orientations of Ultra-Marathoners', *The Sport Psychologist*, 6: 242–252.

Ackerman, D. (1997) *Deep Play*, New York: Vintage.

Agassi, J.B. (ed.) (1999) *Martin Buber on Psychology and Psychotherapy: Essays, Letters, and Dialogue*, Syracuse, NY: Syracuse University Press.

Aitken, B.W.W. (1992) 'Sport, Religion, and Well-Being', in S.J. Hoffman (ed.), *Sport and Religion*, Champaign, IL: Human Kinetics, pp. 237–244.

Albom, M. (1997) *Tuesdays with Morrie*, New York: Doubleday.

Alderson, D. (1996) 'An Anatomy of the British Polity: *Alton Locke* and Christian Manliness', in R. Robins and J. Wolfreys (eds), *Victorian Identities: Social and Cultural Formations in Nineteenth-Century Literature*, New York: St. Martin's Press, pp. 43–61.

Aldridge, D. (2000) *Spirituality, Healing and Medicine*, London: Jessica Kingsley.

Allen, D.W. (1994) 'Young England: Muscular Christianity and the Politics of the Body in "Tom Brown's Schooldays"', in D.E. Hall (ed.), *Muscular Christianity: Embodying the Victorian Age*, Cambridge: Cambridge University Press, pp. 114–132.

Alsup, R. (1995) 'Existentialism of Personalism: A Native-American Perspective', in K.J. Schneider and R. May (eds), *The Psychology of Existence: An Integrative, Clinical Perspective*, New York: McGraw-Hill, pp. 247–254.

Alves, C. (1991) 'Just a Matter of Words? The Religious Education Debate in the House of Lords', *British Journal of Religious Education*, 13 (3): 14–22.

American Association of Colleges of Nursing (AACN) (1986) *Essentials of College and University Education for Nursing*, Washington, DC: AACN.

Ampleforth College (2004) *Mission Statement: Ampleforth College*. Online. Available at: www.ampleforthcollege.york.sch.uk/ (accessed 5 April 2004).

Andersen, M.B. (2000) *Doing Sport Psychology*, Champaign, IL: Human Kinetics.

Andersen, M.B. (2005) *Sport Psychology in Practice*, Champaign, IL: Human Kinetics.

Anderson, D. (2001) 'Recovering Humanity: Movement, Sport, and Nature', *Journal of the Philosophy of Sport*, 27: 140–150.

Annan, K. (1999) 'Olympic Truce', *Olympic Review*, 26: 27.

Argyle, M. and Beit-Hallahmi, B. (1975) *The Social Psychology of Religion,* London: Routledge & Kegan Paul.

Armstrong, C. (2003) *College Sports: Prodigal Son of 'Muscular Christianity'*. Online. Available at: www.christianitytoday.com/history/newsletter/2003/ (accessed 3 September 2003).

Armstrong, J., Dixon, R. and Robinson, S. (2006) *The Decision Makers: Ethics in Engineering.* London: Telford.

Arnold, P. (1999) 'The Virtues, Moral Education and the Practice of Sport', *Quest*, 51: 39–54.

Arnold, P. (2001) 'Sport, Moral Development and the Role of the Teacher', *Quest*, 53: 135–150

Arytom, I. (2005) 'Philosophy of Extreme Sports', in Proceedings of the 33rd Annual Meeting of the International Association for the Philosophy of Sport: Palacky University, Olomouc, Czech Republic, 15–18 September. Online. Available at: www.iaps.paisley. ac.uk/

Ashley, M. (2000) 'Secular Spirituality and Implicit Religion: The Realisation of Human Potential', *Implicit Religion*, 3 (1): 31–50.

Avis, P. (1989) *Eros and the Sacred*, London: SPCK.

Baird, M. (2002) *On the Side of the Angels: Ethics and Post Holocaust Spirituality.* Leuven: Peeters.

Baker, W.J. (2000) 'Questioning Tom Brown: Sport and the Character Game', in J. Squires (ed.), *A Fair Go for All? Current Issues in Australian Sport Ethics*, Sydney: New College Institute for Values Research, pp. 7–18.

Balageur, I., Duda, J.L. and Crespo, M. (1999) 'Motivational Climate and Goal Orientations as Predictors of Perceptions of Improvement, Satisfaction and Coach Ratings among Tennis Players', *Scandinavian Journal of Medicine and Science in Sports*, 9: 381–388.

Balague, G. (1999) 'Understanding Identity Value and Meaning when Working with Elite Athletes', *The Sport Psychologist*, 13: 89–98.

Ballou, R.B. (1973) 'Analysis of the Writings of Selected Church Fathers to A.D. 394 to Reveal Attitudes regarding Physical Activity', in E.F. Zeigler (ed.), *History of Sport and Physical Education to 1900: Selected Topics*, Champaign, IL: Stipes Publishing, pp. 187–199.

Balthasar, H. (2000) *The Christian and Anxiety*, San Francisco: Ignatius Press.

Banks, R. and Stevens, P. (1997) *The Complete Book of Everyday Christianity*, Downers Grove, IL: Intervarsity Press. Available online at: www.ivmdl.org/

Barnes, L.P. (2003) 'Dispensing with Christian Mysticism', in C. Partridge and T. Gabriel (eds), *Mysticisms East and West: Studies in Mystical Experience*, Waynesboro, GA: Paternoster Press, pp. 278–305.

Barth, K. (1969/1933) *The Epistle to the Romans* (trans. E.C. Hoskyns), New York: Oxford University Press.

Bauckham, R. (2003) 'Creation Mysticism in Matthew Fox and Francis of Assisi', in C. Partridge and T. Gabriel (eds.), *Mysticisms East and West: Studies in Mystical Experience*, Waynesboro, GA: Paternoster Press, pp. 182–208.

Baudrillard, J. (1973) *Simulations*. New York: Semiotext.

Bauman, Z. (1989) *Modernity and the Holocaust*. London: Polity.

Bauman, Z. (1993) *Postmodern Ethics*. Oxford: Blackwell.

Beck, J. (1999) '"Spiritual and Moral Development" and Religious Education', in A. Thatcher (ed.), *Spirituality and the Curriculum*, London: Cassell, pp. 153–180.

Becker, E. (1973) *The Denial of Death*, New York: The Free Press.

Beckford, J. (1989) *Religion and Advanced Industrial Society*. London: Unwin Hyman.

Begbie, J. (ed.) (2000) *Beholding the Glory: Incarnation through the Arts*, London: Darton, Longman and Todd.

Bellamy, J. (1998) 'Spiritual Values in a Secular Age', in M. Cobb and V. Renshaw (eds), *The Spiritual Challenge of Health Care*, London: Churchill Livingstone, pp. 183–197.

Benn, P. (1998) *Ethics*, London: UCL Press.

Benner, D. (1998) *Care of Souls*, Grand Rapids, MI: Baker Books.

Benson, H. (1996) *Timeless Healing*, New York: Scribner.

Berdyaev, N.A. (1937) *The Destiny of Man*, London: Duddington.

Berdyaev, N. (1947) *The Divine and Human* (trans. R.M. French), London: G. Bles.

Berger, P. (1970) *A Rumour of Angels*, Garden City, NY: Doubleday.

Bernardi, L., Sleight, P., Bandinelli, G., Cencetti, S., Fattorini, J.W. and Lagi, L. (2001) 'Effect of Rosary Prayer and Yoga Mantras on Autonomic Cardiovascular Rhythms: A Comparative Study', *British Medical Journal*, 323: 1446–1449.

Berryman. J. (1985) 'Children's Spirituality and Religious Language', *British Journal of Religious Education*, 7 (3): 109–119.

Bertman, M.A. (2000) 'Buber: Mysticism without Loss of Identity', *Judaism*, 49 (1): 80–92.

Biggar, N. (1997) *Good Life*, London: SPCK.

Birrell, S. (1981) 'Sport as Ritual: Interpretations from Durkheim to Goffman', *Social Forces*, 60: 354–376.

Bloomfield, A. (1994) 'Muscular Christian or Mystic? Charles Kingsley Reappraised', *The International Journal of the History of Sport*, 11 (2): 172–190.

Booth, D. (2004) 'Surfing From One (Cultural) Extreme to Another', in B. Wheaton (ed.), *Understanding Lifestyle Sports: Consumption, Identity and Difference*, London: Routledge, pp. 94–109.

Boyd, J. (1995) 'The Soul as Seen through Evangelical Eyes, Part 1: Mental Health Professionals and the "Soul"', *Journal of Psychology and Theology*, 25 (3): 151–160.

Bradshaw, A. (1994) *Lighting the Lamp; The Spiritual Dimension of Nursing Care*, London: Scutari Press.

Brennan, S. (1998) 'Mental Toughness Wins Out', *Christian Science Monitor*, 90: 173.

Bridges, W. (1980) *Transitions: Making Sense of Life's Changes*, Reading, MA: Addison Wesley.

Brown, E. (1880) *True Manliness: From the Writings of Thomas Hughes*, Boston, MA: D. Lothrop.

Bruce, S. (1995) *Religion in Modern Britain*, Oxford: Oxford University Press.

Brueggemann, W. (1984) *The Message of the Psalms*, Minneapolis, MN: Augsburg.

Brueggemann, W. (1997) *Theology of the Old Testament*, Nashville, TN: Abingdon.

Buber, M. (1937) *I and Thou*, Edinburgh: T. and T. Clark.

Buber, M. (1952) *Eclipse of God*, Atlantic Highlands, NJ: Humanities Press.

Bunting, C.F., Tolson, H., Kuhn, C., Suarez, E. and Williams, R.B. (2000) 'Physiological Stress Response of the Neuroendocrine System during Outdoor Tasks', *Journal of Leisure Research*, 32 (2): 191–207.

Burke, E. (1990/1757) *A Philosophical Enquiry into the Origin of our Ideas of the Sublime and Beautiful*, Oxford: Oxford University Press.

Burleigh, M. (2000) *The Third Reich*, London: Macmillan.

Burnyeat, M. (1980) 'Aristotle on Learning to be Good', in A.O. Rorty (ed.), *Essays on Aristotle's Ethics*, Berkeley, CA: University of California Press, pp. 69-92.

Byl, J. and Visker, T. (eds) (1999) *Physical Education, Sports, and Wellness*: Looking to God as We Look at Ourselves, Sioux Center, IA: Dordt College Press.

Campbell, A. (1984) *Moderated Love: A Theology of Professional Care*, London: SPCK.

Campbell, A. (1995) *Health as Liberation*, Cleveland, OH: The Pilgrim Press.

Campolo, T. (1988) 'Should Preachers Start Preaching against Sports?', in T. Campolo,

20 Hot Potatoes Christians are Afraid to Touch, Nashville, TN: Word Publishing, pp. 122–131.

Camus, A. (1955) *The Myth of Sisyphus and Other Essays* (trans. Justin O'Brien), New York: Vingate.

Carey, P. (2004) 'Fixing Kids in Sport', *U.S. News and World Report*, 7 June: 45–54.

Carr, D. (2003) 'Character and Moral Choice in the Cultivation of Virtue', *Philosophy*, 78, 219–232

Carr, K. (1993) 'War, Philosophy and Sport in Japanese Judo', *Journal of Sport History*, 20 (2): 167–189.

Carr, W. (1987) 'What is an Educational Practice?', *Journal of Philosophy of Education*, 21 (2): 163–175.

Carroll, J.C. (1983) 'Two Sociological Perspectives on Sport Heroism', *American Baptist Quarterly*, 2 (1): 43–50.

Carter, R. (1985) 'A Taxonomy of Objectives for Professional Education', *Studies in Higher Education*, 10 (2): 135–149.

Caruso, I.A. (1964) *Existential Psychology: From Analysis to Synthesis*, London: Darton, Longman and Todd.

Caute, D. (1988) *Sixty-eight: The Year of Barricades*, London: Hamish Hamilton.

Chambers Dictionary (2004) Edinburgh: Chambers.

Chandler, T.J.L. (2002) 'Manly Catholicism: Making Men in Catholic Public Schools, 1954–80', in T. Magdalinski and T.J.L. Chandler (eds), *With God on their Side: Sport in the Service of Religion*, London: Routledge, pp. 99–119.

Clark, M.J. (1973) *The Problem of Freedom*, New York: Meredith Corporation.

Clark, S.H. (1996) *The Development of Leisure in Britain after 1850*. Online. Available at: www.65.107.211.206/history/ (accessed 25 January 2004).

Clifford, C. and Feezel, R.M. (1997) *Coaching for Character*, Champaign, IL: Human Kinetics.

Clinebell, H.J. (1968) *Understanding and Counseling the Alcoholic*, Nashville, TN: Abingdon.

Clough, P., Earle, K. and Sewell, D. (2002) 'Mental Toughness: The Concept and its Measurement', in I. Cockerill (ed.), *Solutions in Sport Psychology*, pp. 32–48.

Coakley, J.J. (2003) *Sport in Society*, eighth edition, Boston: Irwin McGraw-Hill.

Cobb, M. (2001) *The Dying Soul*, Buckingham: Open University Press.

Cockerill, I. (2002) *Solutions in Sport Psychology*, London: Thomson.

Cohen, S.R., Mount, B.M., Bruera, E., Provost, M., Rowe, J. and Tong, K. (1997) 'Validity of the McGill Quality of Life Questionnaire in the Palliative Care Setting: A Multi-Centre Canadian Study Demonstrating the Importance of the Existential Domain', *Palliative Medicine*, 11: 3–20.

Collins, T. (2004) 'How Muscular Christianity Met its Match: The Curious Rise and Fall of Leeds Parish Church', unpublished paper.

Comstock, G.W. and Partridge, K.B. (1972) 'Church Attendance and Health', *Journal of Chronic Diseases*, 25: 665–672.

Connor, S. (1989) *The Post Modern Culture*, Oxford: Blackwell.

Cooper, A. (1998) *Playing in the Zone*, Boston: Shambhala.

Cooper, M. (2003) *Existential Therapies*, London: Sage.

Corlett, J. (1996a) 'Sophistry, Socrates and Sport Psychology', *The Sport Psychologist*, 10: 84–94.

Corlett, J. (1996b) 'Virtues Lost: Courage in Sport', *Journal of the Philosophy of Sport*, 23: 45–57.

de Coubertin, P. (1966/1894) 'Athletics in the Modern World and the Olympic Games', in Carl-Diem-Institut (ed.), *The Olympic Idea: Pierre de Coubertin – Discourses and Essays*, Stuttgart: Olympischer Sportverlag, pp. 7–10.

de Coubertin, P. (1966/1896) 'The Olympic Games of 1896', in Carl-Diem-Institut (ed.), *The Olympic Idea: Pierre de Coubertin – Discourses and Essays*, Stuttgart: Olympischer Sportverlag, pp. 10–14.

de Coubertin, P. (1966/1906) 'Opening Address to the Conference of Arts, Letters and Sports', in Carl-Diem-Institut (ed.), *The Olympic Idea: Pierre de Coubertin – Discourses and Essays*, Stuttgart: Olympischer Sportverlag, pp. 16–18.

de Coubertin, P. (1966/1910) 'A Modern Olympia', in Carl-Diem-Institut (ed.), *The Olympic Idea: Pierre de Coubertin – Discourses and Essays*, Stuttgart: Olympischer Sportverlag, pp. 21–25.

de Coubertin, P. (1966/1918) 'Olympic Letters III', in Carl-Diem-Institut (ed.), *The Olympic Idea: Pierre de Coubertin – Discourses and Essays*, Stuttgart: Olympischer Sportverlag, p. 54.

de Coubertin, P. (1966/1927) 'Address from Olympia to the Youth of the World', in Carl-Diem-Institut (ed.), *The Olympic Idea: Pierre de Coubertin – Discourses and Essays*, Stuttgart: Olympischer Sportverlag, pp. 101–104.

de Coubertin, P. (1966/1929) 'Olympia', in Carl-Diem-Institut (ed.), *The Olympic Idea: Pierre de Coubertin – Discourses and Essays*, Stuttgart: Olympischer Sportverlag, pp. 106–119.

de Coubertin, P. (1966/1935) 'The Philosophic Foundations of Modern Olympism', in Carl-Diem-Institut (ed.), *The Olympic Idea: Pierre de Coubertin – Discourses and Essays*, Stuttgart: Olympischer Sportverlag, pp. 130–134.

de Coubertin, P. (1997) *Olympic Memoirs*, Lausanne: IOC.

Crepeau, R.C. (2001) *Playing with God: The History of Athletes Thanking the 'Big Man Upstairs'*. Online. Available at: www.poppolitics.com/articles/ (accessed 9 March 2004).

Crone-Grant, D., Smith, A. and Gough, B. (2005) 'I Feel Totally at One, Totally Alive and Totally Happy: A Psycho-Social Explanation of the Physical Activity and Mental Health Relationship', *Health Education Research*, 5: 600–611.

Csikszentmihalyi, M. (1975) *Beyond Boredom and Anxiety*, San Francisco: Jossey-Bass.

Csikszentmihalyi, M. (1990) *Flow: The Psychology of Optimal Performance*, New York: HarperCollins.

Csikszentmihalyi, M. (1992) *Flow: The Psychology of Happiness*, London: Rider Publications.

Csikszentmihalyi, M. and Csikszentmihalyi, I.S. (1988) *Optimal Experience: Psychological Studies in Flow Consciousness*, Cambridge: Cambridge University Press.

Cunningham, H. (1980) *Leisure in the Industrial Revolution c. 1780–1880*, London: Croom Helm.

Czech, D.R., Wisberg, C., Fisher, L. Thompson, C., and Hayes, G. (2004) 'The Experience of Christian Prayer in Sport – An Existential–Phenomenological Investigation', *Journal of Psychology and Christianity*, 2: 1–19.

Dale, G. (1996) 'Existential-Phenomenology: Emphasizing the Experience of the Athlete in Sport Psychology Research', *The Sport Psychologist*, 10: 158–171.

Dale, G. (2000) 'Distractions and Coping Strategies of Elite Decathletes during their Most Memorable Performance', *The Sport Psychologist*, 10: 17–41.

Davie, G. (1994) *Religion in Britain since 1945: Believing without Belonging*, Oxford: Blackwell.

Davie, G. (2004) 'A Reply to Francis and Robbins', *Implicit Religion*, 7 (1): 55–58.

Deadorff, D. and White, J. (ed.) (manuscript in preparation) A Christian Theology of Sport, Lewiston, NY: Edwin Mellen Press.

Deci, E.L. and Ryan, R.M. (1985) Intrinsic Motivation and Self-Determination of Human Behaviour, New York: Plenum Press.

Della-Fave, A., Bassi, M. and Massimini, F. (2003) 'Quality of Experience and Risk Perception in High-Altitude Rock Climbing', Journal of Applied Sport Psychology, 15: 82–98.

Department of Health (DOH) (2001) Your Guide to the NHS, London: Department of Health.

Diem, L. (1964) 'The Ceremonies – A Contribution to the History of the Modern Olympic Games', Proceedings of the International Olympic Academy, 4: 120–136.

Dobbs, B. (1973) Edwardians at Play: 1890–1914, London: Pelham.

Dobre-Laza, M. (2003) Victorian and Edwardian Sporting Values. Online. Available at: http://elt.britcoun.org.pl/ (accessed 5 February 2004).

Doyle, D. (1992) 'Have we Looked beyond the Physical and Psychosocial?', Journal of Pain Symptom Management, 7 (5): 301–311.

Dubay, T. (1999) The Evidential Power of Beauty: Science and Theology Meet, San Francisco: Ignatius Press.

Dupré, Louis (1987) 'Mysticism', in M. Eliade (ed.), The Encyclopaedia of Religion, New York: Macmillan, 245–247.

Edwards, D.L. (1999) After Death? London: Cassell.

Eisen, G. (1975) 'Physical Activity, Physical Education and Sport in the Old Testament', Journal of History of Sport and Physical Education, 6: 45–65.

Eitzen, D.S., Sage, C. and Brown, G.H. (1993) Sociology of North American Sport, Madison, WI: Brown and Benchmark.

Eldridge, J. (2001) Wild at Heart: Discovering the Secret of a Man's Soul, Nashville, TN: Thomas Nelson.

Elliott, P. (2004) Super God: 'Jock Idolatry' Gives Evangelical Athletes a Forum at the Super Bowl. Online. Available at: www.myinky.com/ecp/religion/ (accessed 30 March 2004).

Ellison, C. (1983) 'Spiritual Well-Being: Conceptualization and Measurement', Journal of Psychology and Theology, 11 (4): 11–21.

Erikson, E.H. (1964) Insight and Responsibility, New York: Norton.

Erikson, E. (1977) Toys and Reasons, New York: Norton.

Ewert, A.E. (1994) 'Playing the Edge: Motivation and Risk Taking in a High-Altitude Wilderness Like Environment', Environment and Behavior, 26(1): 3–24.

Fahlberg, L.L., Fahlberg, L.A. and Gates, K.W. (1992) 'Exercise and Existence: Exercise Behaviour from an Existential–Phenomenological Perspective', The Sport Psychologist, 6: 172–191.

Farmer, R.J. (1992) 'Surfing: Motivations, Values and Culture', Journal of Sport Behaviour, 15 (4): 241–257.

Fasching, D. and Deschant, D. (2001) Comparative Religious Ethics, Oxford: Blackwell.

Faulkner, T. (2001) 'A Puckish Reflection on Religion in Canada', in J.L. Price (ed.), From Season to Season: Sports as American Religion, Mercer Macon, GA: University Press, pp. 185–202.

Feeney, R. (1995) A Catholic Perspective: Physical Exercise and Sports, Minneapolis, MN: Aquinas Press.

Finch, J. and Mason, J. (1993) Negotiating Family Responsibilities, London: Routledge.

Firshein, J. (1997) 'Spirituality in Medicine Gains Support in the USA', The Lancet, 349: 1300.

Fischer, C.T. (1989) 'Personality and Assessment', in R.S. Valle and S. Halling (eds), *Existential–Phenomenological Perspectives in Psychology*, New York: Plenum Press, pp. 157–178.

Fischer, W. (1970) *Theories of Anxiety*, New York: Harper & Row.

Florman, S. (1976). *The Existential Pleasures of Engineering*, New York: St. Martin's.

Fludernik, M. (2001) 'Sublime (1650)', in Robert Clark (ed.), *The Literary Encyclopaedia*. Online. Available at: www.litencyc.com/ (accessed 21 December 2005).

Folley, M. (2001) *A Time to Jump: The Authorized Biography of Jonathan Edwards*, London: HarperCollins.

Fontana, D. (2003) *Psychology, Religion, and Spirituality*, Oxford: BPS Blackwell.

Forster, E.M. (1936) *Abinger Harvest*, New York: Harcourt, Brace and Co.

Fowler, J. (1990) 'Faith/Belief', in R.J. Hunter (ed.), *Dictionary of Pastoral Care and Counseling*, Nashville, TN: Abingdon, pp. 394–397.

Fowler, J. (1996) *Faithful Change*. Nashville, TN: Abingdon.

Fox, M. (2003) *Religion, Spirituality and the Near-Death Experience*, London: Routledge.

Fraleigh, W. (1984) *Right Actions in Sport*, Champaign, IL: Human Kinetics.

Frankels, B.G. and Hewitt, W.E. (1994) 'Religion and Well Being amongst Canadian University Students', *Journal for the Scientific Study of Religions*, 33: 62–73.

Frankena, W. (1986) 'The Relations of Morality and Religion', in John MacQuarrie (ed.), *A New Dictionary of Christian Ethics*, London: SCM, pp. 400–403.

Frankl, V. (1984) *Man's Search for Meaning: An Introduction to Logotherapy*, New York: Simon & Schuster.

Freeman, M. (1993) *Rewriting the Self*, London: Routledge.

Fromm, E. (1994) *The Art of Listening*, London: Constable.

Frost, J. (2002) *Experiencing the Father's Embrace: Finding Acceptance in the Arms of a Loving God*, Florida: Charisma House.

Gaita, R.(2000) *A Common Humanity*, London: Routledge.

Galanter, M., Larson, D. and Rubenstone, E. (1991) 'Christian Psychiatry: The Impact of Evangelical Beliefs on Clinical Outcomes', *American Journal of Psychiatry*, 148: 90–95.

Galli, M. (2005) *The Grace of Sports: If Christ Can't be Found in Sports, He Can't be Found in the Modern World*. Online. Available at: www.christianitytoday.com/ct/2005/ (accessed 8 April 2005).

Gallwey, T. (1979) *The Inner Game of Golf*, London: Random House.

Gardiner, N.E. (1925) *Olympia, its History and Remains*, Oxford: Clarendon Press.

Gay, P. (1992) 'The Manliness of Christ', in R.W. Davis and R.J. Helmstadter (eds), *Religion and Irreligion in Victorian Society*, London: Routledge, pp. 102–116.

Geertz, C. (1973) *The Interpretation of Cultures*, New York: Basic Books.

George, L. Larson, D. Koenig, H. and McCullough, M. (2000) 'Spirituality and Health: What we Know, What we Need to Know', *Journal of Social and Clinical Psychology*, 19 (1): 102–116.

Gibran, K. (1995) *The Prophet*, London: Penguin.

Gillham, J. (ed.) (2000) *The Science of Optimism and Hope*, Radnor: Templeton Foundation Press.

Giorgi, A. (1970) *Psychology as a Human Science*, New York: Harper & Row.

Giorgi, A. (1985) *Phenomenology and Psychological Research*, Pittsburgh, PA: Duquesne University Press.

Girard, R. (1987) *Things Hidden Since the Foundation of the World* (trans. Stephen Bann and Michael Metter), Stanford, CA: Stanford University Press.

Gire, K. (1996) *Windows of the Soul: Experiencing God in New Ways*, Grand Rapids, MI: Zondervan Publishing House.

Glasser, W. (1976) *Positive Addictions*, New York: Harper and Row.

Glatz, C. (2004) 'Sports Office Speeds Out of the Blocks', *The Catholic Times*, 15 August: 12.

Goddard, N. (1995) 'Spirituality as Integrative Energy', *Journal of Advanced Nursing*, 22: 808–815.

Goldenberg, H. and Isaacson, Z. (1996) 'Between Persons: The Narrow Ridge where I and Thou Meet', *Journal of the Society for Existential Analysis*, 7: 118–130.

Goodhart, P. and Chataway, C. (1968) *War without Weapons*, London: W.H. Allen.

Gould, D., Tuffey, S., Urdy, E. and Loehr, J. (1996) 'Burnout in Competitive Junior Tennis Players: III Qualitative Analysis', *The Sport Psychologist*, 10: 341–366.

Grace, D.J. (2000) 'Values, Sport and Education', *Journal of Christian Education*, 43 (2): 7–17.

Grainger, R. (2003) 'Believing and Belonging: A Psychological Comment on a Paper Given by E.I. Bailey at Windsor, 1990', *Implicit Religion*, 6 (1): 53–58.

Greeley, A.M. (1974) *Ecstasy: A Way of Knowing*, Englewood Cliffs, NJ: Prentice-Hall.

Greenfield, K.T. (1999) 'Life on the Edge', *Time*, 6 September: 29–36.

Grimshaw, M. (2000) 'I Can't Believe My Eyes: The Religious Aesthetics of Sport as Postmodern Salvific Moments', *Implicit Religion*, 3 (2): 87–99.

Gutkind, S.M. (2004) 'Using Solution-Focused Brief Counselling to Provide Injury Support', *The Sport Psychologist*, 18: 75–88.

Guttman, A. (1994) *Games and Empires: Modern Sports and Cultural Imperialism*, New York: Columbia University Press.

HM Government, England and Wales (1944) *Education Act 1944*, London: HMSO.

Hager, P.F. (2002) 'Can Athletic Actions be Heroic?', paper presented at the Thirtieth International Association of Philosophy of Sport Conference, Penn State University, PA, 23–27 October. Online. Available at: www.iaps.paisley.ac.uk/ (accessed 20 April 2006).

Haley, B. (1978) *The Healthy Body and Victorian Culture*, Cambridge, MA: Harvard University Press.

Hall, D.E. (1994) 'On the Making and Unmasking of Monsters: Christian Socialism, Muscular Christianity, and the Metaphorization of Class Conflict' in D.E. Hall (ed.), *Muscular Christianity: Embodying the Victorian Age*, Cambridge: Cambridge University Press, pp. 46–65.

Hall, H.K., Kerr, A.W. and Mathews, J. (1998) 'Precompetitive Anxiety in Sport: The Contribution of Achievement Goals and Perfectionism', *Journal of Sport and Exercise Psychology*, 20: 194–217.

Halling, S. and Nill, J.D. (1989) 'Demystifying Psychopathology: Understanding Disturbed Persons', in R.S. Valle and S. Halling (eds), *Existential–Phenomenological Perspectives in Psychology*, New York: Plenum Press, pp. 179–192.

Hamel, S., Leclerc and Lefrançois, R. (2003) 'A Psychological Outlook on the Concept of Transcendent Actualization', *The International Journal of the Psychology of Religion*, 13 (1): 3–15.

Hamilton, M. (2003) 'Disordering of Affections: An Augustinian Critique of our Relationship to Sport', paper presented at the Thirty-First International Association of Philosophy of Sport Conference, University of Gloucestershire, Cheltenham, UK, 18–21 September.

Hamilton, M. (2006) 'Elective Performance Enhancement Surgery for Athletes: Should it be Resisted?', *Gymnica*, 36 (2): 39.

Hargreaves, J.E.R. (1986) *Sport, Power and Culture: A Social and Historical Analysis of Popular Sports in Britain*, London: Polity Press.

Harrington, H.R. (1971) *Muscular Christianity: The Study of the Development of a Victorian Idea*, unpublished doctoral dissertation: Stanford University, CA.

Harris, S. (1990) 'The "Muscular Novel": Medium of a Victorian Ideal', *Tennessee Philological Bulletin*, 27: 6–13.

Harris, R.C., Dew, M.A. and Lee, A. (1995) 'The Association of Social Relationships and Activities with Mortality', *American Journal of Epidemiology*, 116: 123–140.

Hart, D.B. (2003) *The Beauty of the Infinite: The Aesthetics of Christian Truth*, Cambridge: William B. Eerdmans.

Hauerwas, S. (2002) *With the Grain of the Universe*, London: SCM Press

Hauerwas, S. and Wells, S. (eds) (2004) *The Blackwell Companion to Christian Ethics*, Oxford: Blackwell.

Hawkins, P. (1991) 'The Spiritual Dimension of the Learning Organisation', *Management, Education and Development*, 22 (3): 172–187.

Hay, M. (1989) 'Principles in Building Spiritual Assessment Tools', *American Journal of Hospice Care*, September/October, 25–31.

Heino, R. (2000) 'What is So Punk about Snowboarding?', *Journal of Sport and Social Issues*, 24 (2): 176–191.

Heintzman, P. (2003) 'The Wilderness Experience and Spirituality: What Recent Research Tells Us', *Journal of Physical Education Leisure and Dance*, 74 (6): 27–31.

Held, B.S. (2004) 'The Negative Side of Psychology', *Journal of Humanistic Psychology*, 44: 9–46.

Helminiak, D. (1998) 'Sexuality and Spirituality: A Humanist Account', *Pastoral Psychology*, 47 (2): 119–126.

Herrigel, E. (1999/1971) *Zen in the Art of Archery*, New York: Random House.

Herzog, R.J. (1953) *Annapurna*, New York: Dutton.

Hiatt, J. (1986) 'Spirituality, Medicine and Healing', *Southern Medical Journal*, 79 (6): 736–743.

Higgs, R.J. (1982) *Sports: A Reference Guide*, Westport, CN: Greenwood Press.

Higgs, R.J. (1986) 'The Sublime and the Beautiful: The Meaning of Sports in Collected Sketches of Thomas B. Thorpe', *Southern Studies: An Interdisciplinary Journal of the South*, 25 (3): 235–256.

Higgs, R.J. (1992) 'Muscular Christianity, Holy Play, and Spiritual Exercises: Confusion about Christ in Sports and Religion', in S.J. Hoffman (ed.), *Sport and Religion*, Champaign, IL: Human Kinetics, pp. 89–103.

Higgs, R.J. (1995) *God in the Stadium: Sports and Religion in America*, Lexington, KT: University Press of Kentucky.

Higgs, R.J. and Braswell, M.C. (2004) *An Unholy Alliance: The Sacred and Modern Sports*, Macon, GA: Mercer University Press.

Highfield, M. (1992) 'Spiritual Health of Oncology Patients. Nurse and Patient Perspectives', *Cancer Nursing*, 15 (1): 1–8.

Hill, D. (2005) *Walking with God: Physically and Spiritually*, Abilene, TX: Coach Book Company.

Hill, K.L. (2001) *Frameworks for Sport Psychologists: Enhancing Sport Performance*, Champaign, IL: Human Kinetics.

Hirst, P.H. (1993) 'Education, Knowledge and Practices', in Robin Barrow and P. White (eds), *Beyond Liberal Education: Essays in Honor of Paul H. Hirst*, London: Routledge.

Hoffman, S.J. (ed.) (1992) *Sport and Religion*, Champaign, IL: Human Kinetics.

Hoffman, S.J. (1992a) 'Sport as Religious Experience', in S.J. Hoffman (ed.), *Sport and Religion*, Champaign, IL: Human Kinetics, pp. 63–81.

Hoffman, S.J. (1992b) 'Recovering the Sacred in Sport', in S.J. Hoffman (ed.), *Sport and Religion*, Champaign, IL: Human Kinetics, pp. 153–159.

Hoffman, S.J. (2003) 'Toward Narrowing the Gulf between Sport and Religion', *Word and World*, 23 (3): 303–311.

Hoffman, S.J. (manuscript in preparation), *Unintentional Fouls: Christians and the Sport Problem*, Waco, TX: Baylor University Press.

Hollander, D.B. and Acevedo, E.O. (2000) 'Successful English Channel Swimming: The Peak Experience', *The Sport Psychologist*, 14: 1–16.

Hollander, Z., and Zimmerman, P. (1967) *Football Lingo*, New York: Norton.

Holt, R. (1990) *Sport and the British: A Modern History*, Oxford: Clarendon Press.

Hood, R.W. Jr (1977) 'Eliciting Mystical States of Consciousness with Semistructured Nature Experiences', *Journal for the Scientific Study of Religion*, 16: 155–163.

Hood, R.W. Jr. (1978) 'Anticipatory Set and Setting: Stress Incongruities as Elicitors of Mystical Experience in Solitary Nature Situations', *Journal for the Scientific Study of Religion*, 17: 279–287.

Hood, R.W. Jr. (1995) 'The Facilitation of Religious Experience', in R.W. Hood, Jr. (ed.), *Handbook of Religious Experience*, Birmingham, AL: Religious Education Press, pp. 569–597.

Hood, R.W., Spilka, B., Hunsberger, B. and Gorsuch, R. (1996) *The Psychology of Religion*, second edition, New York: The Guilford Press.

Hornby, N. (2000) *Fever Pitch*, London: Penguin.

Hoverd, William (2005) *Working out My Salvation: The Contemporary Gym and the Promise of "Self" Transformation*, Sydney: Meyer and Meyer Sport.

Howe, P.D. (2004) *Sport, Professionalism and Pain*, London: Routledge.

Hughes, T. (1861) *Tom Brown at Oxford*, London: Macmillan.

Hughes, Robert and Coakley, Jay (1991) 'Positive Deviance Among Athletes: The Implications of Overconformity to the Sport Ethic,' *Sociology of Sport Journal*, 8: 307–325.

Huizinga, Johan (1950) *Homo Ludens: A Study of the Play Element in Culture*, Boston, MA: Beacon.

Hull, J. (1991) *What Prevents Christian Adults from Learning?*, Philadelphia, PA: Trinity Press International.

Hull, J.M. (2001) 'Competition and Spiritual Development', *International Journal of Children's Spirituality*, 6 (3): 263–275.

Husserl, E. (1970) *The Crisis of European Sciences and Transcendental Phenomenology* (trans. D. Carr), Evanston, IL: Northwestern University Press.

Hutch, R. (2005) 'Under Sail Alone at Sea: A Study of Sport as Spiritual Practice', *Australian Religion Studies Review*, 18 (1): 3–24.

Hutch, R. (2006) *Lone Sailors and Spiritual Insights: Cases of Sport and Peril at Sea*, Lewiston, NY: The Edwin Mellen Press.

Huxley, A. (1954) *The Doors of Perception*, London: Chatto and Windus.

Hyland, D. (1978) 'Competition and Friendship', *Journal of the Philosophy of Sport*, 5 (Fall): 27–37.

Hyland, D.A. (1988) 'Opponents, Contestants, and Competitors: The Dialectic of Sport', in W.J. Morgan and K.V. Meier (eds) *Philosophic Inquiry in Sport*, second edition, Champaign, IL: Human Kinetics, pp. 177–182.

Idler, E. and Kasl, S. (1992) 'Religion, Disability, Depression and the Timing of Death', *American Journal of Sociology*, 116: 1052–1079.

Illich, I. (1977) *Medical Nemesis*, New York: Penguin.

Ilundain, J. (2002) 'Kant and his Philosophical Brethren Go Skydiving: Understanding

Extreme Sports and the Culture of Risk by Way of the Sublime', paper presented at the Thirtieth Annual Meeting of the International Association for the Philosophy of Sport, Penn State University, PA, 27–30 October. Online. Available at www.iaps.paisley. ac.uk/.

International Bible Society (ed.) (2002) *Bible: New International Version*, London: Hodder and Stoughton.

International Olympic Committee (2006) *The Olympic Charter*, Lausanne: IOC.

Jackson, P. (2006) 'My Rugby Obsession Has Left Me in Agony', *Daily Mail*, 7 March: 80.

Jackson, S.A. and Csikszentmihalyi, M. (1999) *Flow in Sports: The Key to Optimal Experiences and Performances*, Champaign, IL: Human Kinetics.

Jacobs, M. (1998) 'Faith as the "Space Between"', in M. Cobb and V. Renshaw (eds), *The Spiritual Challenge of Health Care*, London: Churchill Livingstone, pp. 57–72.

James, E. (ed.) (1968) *Spirituality for Today*, London: SCM.

James, W. (1902) *The Varieties of Religious Experience*, in R. Coles (ed.), *William James: Selected Writings*, New York: Book-of-the-Month Club, pp. 23–540.

Jantzen, G.M. (1990) 'Could There be a Mystical Core of Religion?', *Religious Studies*, 26: 59–71.

John of the Cross, St (1922) *The Ascent of Mount Carmel* (trans. David Lewis), Grand Rapids, MI: Christian Classics Ethereal Library.

John Paul II (1994) *Letter to Families*, Oxford: Family Publications.

John Paul II (1995/1979) 'Sport as Training Ground for Virtue and Instrument of Union Among People', in R Feeney (ed.), *A Catholic Perspective: Physical Exercise and Sport*, Minneapolis, MN: Aquinas Press, pp. 59–62.

John Paul II (1995/1980) 'Human and Sporting Qualities Make Men Brothers', in R Feeney (ed.), *A Catholic Perspective: Physical Exercise and Sport*, Minneapolis, MN: Aquinas Press, pp. 62–67.

John Paul II (1995/1986) 'Sports Can Help Spread Fraternity and Peace', in R Feeney (ed.), *A Catholic Perspective: Physical Exercise and Sport*, Minneapolis, MN: Aquinas Press, pp. 78–81.

John Paul II (1998) *Fides et Ratio*, Boston, MA: Pauline Books.

Johnson, K.K. (2005) 'Christian Theology as Depicted in *The Lord of the Rings* and Harry Potter Books', *Journal of Religion and Society*, 7. Online. Available at http://moses. creighton.edu/JRS/2005/.

Jones, C. (2005) 'Character, Virtue and Physical Education', *European Physical Education Review*, 11 (2): 139–151.

Jones, G. (1995) 'More than Just a Game: Research Developments and Issues in Competitive Anxiety in Sport', *British Journal of Psychology*, 86: 449–478.

Jones, G and Hardy, L. (1990) *Stress and Performance in Sport*, Chichester: Wiley.

Jones, G., Hanton, S. and Swain, A.B.J. (1994) 'Intensity and Interpretation of Anxiety Symptoms in Elite and Non-Elite Sports Performers', *Personality and Individual Differences*, 17: 657–663.

Jones, G., Swain, A. and Harwood, C. (1996) 'Positive and Negative Affect as Predictors of Competitive Anxiety', *Personality and Individual Differences*, 20: 107–114.

Jones, R. (1909) *Studies in Mystical Religion*, London: Macmillan.

Joseph, M. (1998) 'The Effect of Strong Religious Beliefs on Coping with Stress', *Stress Medicine*, 14: 219–224.

Jung, C.G. (1956) *Two Essays on Analytical Psychology*, New York: Meridian Books.

Jung, C.G. (1964) *Man and His Symbols*, New York: Doubleday.

K2 (1991) Frank Roddam, Trans Pacific Films.

Kant, E. (1952/1790) *The Critique of Judgement*, Oxford: Oxford University Press.

Kark, J., Shemi, G. and Friedlander, Y. (1996) 'Does Religious Observance Promote Health?', *American Journal of Public Health*, 86: 341–346.

Kelly, T. (1990) *A New Imagining: Towards an Australian Spirituality*, Melbourne: Collins Dove.

Kemp, D. (2001) 'Christaquarianism: A New Socio-Religious Movement of Postmodern Society', *Implicit Religion*, 4 (1): 27–40.

Kerry, D.S. and Armour, K.M. (2000) 'Sport Sciences and the Promise of Phenomenology: Philosophy, Method and Insight', *Quest*, 52: 1–17.

Kierkegaard, S. (1844/1980) *The Concept of Anxiety*, Princeton, New Jersey: Princeton University Press.

Kierkegaard, S. (1989/1849) *The Sickness Unto Death: A Christian Exposition of Edification and Awakening* (trans. Alastair Hannay), London: Penguin Books.

King, M and Dean, S. (1998) 'The Spiritual Variable in Psychiatric Research', *Psychological Medicine*, 28: 1259–1262.

Kingston, F. (1961) *French Existentialism: A Christian Critique*, London: Oxford University Press.

Klapp, O.E. (1962) *Heroes, Villains, and Fools: The Changing American Character*, Englewood Cliffs, NJ: Prentice-Hall.

Klein, D. (1971) *The Vince Lombardi Story*, New York: Lion Books.

Koenig, H. (1997) *Is Religion Good for your Health? The Effects of Religion on Physical and Mental Health*, New York: Howarth Press.

Kohlberg, L. (1984) *Essays on Moral Development Vol. 2: The Psychology of Moral Development*, San Francisco: Harper and Row.

Kohn, A. (1992) *No Contest: The Case against Competition*, revised edition, New York: Houghton Mifflin.

Kolb, D. (ed.) (1984) *Organisational Psychology*, New York: Prentice-Hall.

Kretchmar, S.R. (2005) 'Understanding Games, Competition, and Winning', in S. Kretchmar, *Practical Philosophy of Sport*, Champaign, IL: Human Kinetics, pp. 159–180.

Kruger A. (1993) 'The Origins of Pierre de Coubertin's "Religio Athletae"', *Olympika*, 2: 91–102.

Kung, H. (1991) *Global Responsibility*, London: SCM.

Ladd, T. and Mathisen, J.A. (1999) *Muscular Christianity: Evangelical Protestants and the Development of American Sport*, Grand Rapids, MI: Baker Books.

Laing, R.D. (1969) *The Divided Self: An Existential Study in Sanity and Madness*, Harmondsworth: Penguin.

Lämmer, M, (1982) 'The Peace Philosophy of the Olympic Movement: A Historical Perspective' [in German], *Stadion*, 8–9: 47–83.

Landis, B. (1996) 'Uncertainty, Spiritual Well-Being, and Psychosocial Adjustment to Chronic Illnesses', *Issues in Mental Health Nursing*, 17: 217–231.

Lane, A. and Terry, P. (1998) 'Mood States as Predictors of Performance: A Conceptual Model', *Journal of Sports Sciences*, 16: 93–94.

Lane, A.M., Sewell, D.F., Terry, P.C., Bartram, D. and Nesti, M.S. (1999) 'Confirmatory Factor Analysis of the Competitive State Anxiety Inventory', *Journal of Sports Sciences*, 17 (6): 505–512.

Larson, D., Koenig, H., Kaplan, B., Levin, J. (1989) 'The Impact of Religion on Men's Blood Pressure', *Journal of Religion and Health*, 28: 165–278.

Lartey, E. (1997) *In Living Colour*, London: Cassell.

Lash, N. (1988) *Easter in Ordinary: Reflections on Human Experience and the Knowledge of God*, London: SCM.

Lavallee, D. and Wylleman, P. (2000) *Career Transitions in Sport: International Perspectives*, Morgantown, WV: Fitness Information Technology.

Lavallee, D., Nesti, M., Borkoles, E., Cockerill, I. and Edge, A. (2000) 'Intervention Strategies for Athletes in Transition', in D. Lavallee and P. Wylleman (eds), *Career Transitions in Sport: International Perspectives*, Morgantown, WV: Fitness Information Technology, pp. 111–130.

Lazarus, R.S. (2000) 'How Emotions Influence Performance in Competitive Sports', *The Sport Psychologist*, 14: 229–252.

Leech, K.(1997) *Soul Friend*, London; Sheldon Press.

Leonard, G. (1974) *The Ultimate Athlete: Re-visioning Sports, Physical Education, and the Body*, New York: Avon.

Lesniak, V. (2005) 'Contemporary Spirituality', in P. Sheldrake (ed.), *The New Dictionary of Christian Spirituality*, London: SCM Press, pp. 7–12.

Lester, J.T. (1983) 'Wrestling with the Self on Mount Everest', *Journal of Humanistic Psychology*, 23 (2): 31–41.

Lester, J.T. (2004) 'Spirit, Identity, and Self in Mountaineering', *Journal of Humanistic Psychology*, 44 (1): 86–100.

Levin, J. and Vanderpool, H. (1989) 'Is Religion Therapeutically Significant for Hypertension?', *Social Science and Medicine*, 29: 69–78.

Levinas, E. (1998) *Entre Nous: On Thinking-of the-Other*. New York: Columbia University Press.

Lewis, C.S. (1942) *The Screwtape Letters*, London: The Centenary Press.

Lewis, C.S. (1988/1944) 'Myth Became Fact', in C.S. Lewis, ed. W. Hooper, *God in the Dock: Essays in Theology*, London: HarperCollins, pp. 31–37.

Lewis, C.S. (1960) *The Four Loves*, London: Fontana Books.

Lewis, C.S. (1997/1952) *Mere Christianity*, New York: HarperCollins.

Lewis, C.S. (2001/1946) *The Great Divorce*, New York: HarperCollins.

Lewis, C.S. (2001/1949) *The Weight of Glory*, New York: HarperCollins.

Lewis, C.S. (2001/1950) *The Lion the Witch and the Wardrobe*, London: HarperCollins.

Liddell, E. (1985) *The Disciplines of the Christian Life*, Nashville, TN: Abingdon Press.

Lipscombe, N. (1999) 'The Relevance of the Peak Experience to Continued Skydiving Participation: A Qualitative Approach to Assessing Motivations', *Leisure Studies*, 18: 267–288.

Lofton, K. (2004) 'The Man Stays in the Picture: Recent Works in Religion and Masculinity' (book review), *Religious Studies Review*, 30 (1): 23–28.

Loland, S. (2002) *Fair Play in Sport: A Moral Norm System*, London: Routledge.

Loland, S. and McNamee, M. (2000) 'Fair Play and the Ethos of Sport: An Eclectic Philosophical Framework', *Journal of the Philosophy of Sport*, 28: 63–80.

Lovin, R. (2005) 'Moral Theories', in W. Schweiker (ed.), *The Blackwell Companion to Religious Ethics*, Oxford: Blackwell, pp. 19–26.

Lumpkin, Angela, Stoll, Sharon Kay and Beller, Jennifer M. (2003) *Sport Ethics: Applications and Fair Play*, New York: McGraw-Hill.

Lyotard, J.-F. (1979) *The Postmodern Condition*, Manchester: Manchester University Press.

Lysens, R., Steverlynch, A., Van de Auweele, Y., Lefevre, J. Renson, L., Classens, A. and Ostyn, M. (1984) 'The Predictability of Sports Injuries', *Sports Medicine*, 1: 6–10.

Lysens, R., Van de Auweele, Y. and Ostyn, M. (1986) 'The Relationship between Psychosocial Factors and Sports Injuries', *Journal of Sport Medicine and Physical Fitness*, 26: 77–84.

McCullough, M.E. (1995) 'Prayer and Health: Conceptual Issues, Research Review and Research Agenda', *Journal of Psychology and Theology*, 23: 15–29.

McFadyen, A. (1990) *The Call to Personhood: A Christian Theory of the Individual in Social Relationships*, Cambridge: Cambridge University Press.

McFague, S. (1997) *Super, Natural Christians*, London: SCM.

McFee, G. (2004) *Sport, Rules and Values*, London: Routledge.

McGinn, B. (2005) 'Mysticism', in P. Sheldrake (ed.), *The New Dictionary of Christian Spirituality*, London: SCM Press, pp. 19–25.

McGlynn, H. (ed.) (1999) *The Hutchinson Encyclopaedia*, Oxford: Helicon Publishing Ltd.

McGown, L. and Gin, V.J. (2003) *Focus on Sport in Ministry*, Marietta, GA: 360° Sports.

McIntyre, A. (1981) *After Virtue*, London: Duckworth.

McIntyre, A. (1999) *Dependent Rational Animals*, London: Duckworth.

Macquarrie, J. (2004) *Two Worlds are Ours: An Introduction to Christian Mysticism*, London: SCM Press.

Maddison, R. and Prapavessis, H. (2005) 'A Psychological Approach to the Prediction and Prevention of Athletic Injury', *Journal of Sport and Exercise Psychology*, 27: 289–310.

Mangan, J.A. (1982) 'Philathlete Extraordinary: A Portrait of the Victorian Moralist Edward Bowen', *Journal of Sport History*, 9 (3): 23–40.

Mann, T. (1954) *The Magic Mountain* (trans. H.T. Lowe-Porter), New York: Random House.

Manning, B. (2004) *The Ragamuffin Gospel: Embracing the Unconditional Love of God*, Milton Keynes: Authentic Media.

Marcel, G. (1948) *The Philosophy of Existence*, London: Harvill.

Margulis, A. (1998) *The Empathic Imagination*, New York: W.W. Norton.

Markham, I. (1994) *Plurality and Christian Ethics*, Cambridge: Cambridge University Press.

Markos, L.A. (2001) 'Myth Matters', *Christianity Today*. Online. Available at: www.christianitytoday.com/.

Marlatt, G. and Kristeller, J. (2003) 'Mindfulness and Meditation', in W. Miller (ed.), *Integrating Spirituality into Treatment*, Washington, DC: American Psychological Association, pp. 67–84.

Marsh, H.W. and Kleitman, S. (2003) 'School Athletic Participation: Mostly Gain with Little Pain', *International Journal of Sport and Exercise Psychology*, 25: 205–228.

Martens, R. (1987) 'Science, Knowledge, and Sport Psychology', *The Sport Psychologist*, 1: 29–55.

Marx, Jeffrey (2003) *Season Life: A Football Star, a Boy, a Journey to Manhood*, London: Simon & Schuster.

Maslow, A. (1968) *Toward a Psychology of Being*, New York: Van Nostrand Company.

Mason, B. (2003) *Into the Stadium: An Active Guide to Sport Ministry in the Local Church*, Milton Keynes: Authentic Lifestyle.

Mathisen, J. (1994) 'Towards an Understanding of Muscular Christianity: Religion, Sport and Culture in the Modern World', in P. Heintzman, G.E. Van Andel and T.L. Visker (eds), *Christianity and Leisure*, Dordt, IA: Dordt College, pp. 192–205.

Mathisen, J. (1998) ' "I'm Majoring in SPORT Ministry": Religion and Sport in Christian Colleges'. Online. Available at: www.goodnewssports.com/support/.

Mathisen, J. (2002) 'Toward a Biblical Theology of Sport', paper presented at the Annual Meeting of the Association for Christianity, Sport, Leisure and Health (ACSLH), Wheaton, IL, 7–9 June.

Mathisen, J. (2005a) 'Sport', in Helen R. Abaugh (ed.), *Handbook of Religion and Social Institutions*, New York: Springer, pp. 279–299.

Mathisen, J. (2005b) 'The Paradox of Living in Culture while Transforming it: Meeting Needs of and Affecting Change within the World of Sport', paper presented at Think Tank on the Integration of Christian Faith and Sport, Sponsored by Athletes in Action, Xenia, OH, 13–16 March.

May, R. (1967) *Psychology and the Human Dilemma*, New York: Van Nostrand Company.

May, R. (1975) *The Courage to Create*, New York: Norton.

May, R. (1995) 'The Therapist and the Journey into Hell', in K.J. Schneider and R. May, *The Psychology of Existence: An Integrative, Clinical Perspective*, New York: McGraw-Hill, pp. 19–29.

May, W. (1994) 'The Virtues in the Professional Setting', in J. Soskice (ed.), *Medicine and Moral Reasoning*, Cambridge: Cambridge University Press, pp. 83–96.

Mayocchi, L. and Hanrahan, S.J. (2000) 'Transferable Skills for Career Change', in D. Lavallee and P. Wylleman (eds), *Career Transitions in Sport: International Perspectives*, Morgantown, WV: Fitness Information Technology, pp. 95–110.

Mbaye, K. (1995) *The IOC and South Africa*, Lausanne: IOC

Mbiti, J. (1990) *African Religions and Philosophy*, London: Heinemann.

Mead, M. (ed.) (1937) *Cooperation and Competition among Primitive Peoples*, New York: McGraw-Hill.

Mechikoff, R.A and Estes, S.G. (1998) *A History and Philosophy of Sport and Physical Education: From Ancient Civilisations to the Modern World*, second edition, London: McGraw-Hill.

Medalie, J., Kahn, H., Neufeld, H., Riss, E. and Goldbourt, U. (1972) ' Five Year Myocardial Infarction Incidence II', *Journal of Chronic Disease*, 26: 329–349.

Meehan, C. (1999) *'Spiritual Development' and 'Developing spirituality' in Relation to the Distinctiveness of Catholic Sixth Form Schools*, unpublished PhD thesis: University of Leeds.

Mendelson Center and Neumann College (2003) *Mendelson Centre: Ministry through Sports Initiative*. Online. Available at: www.nd.edu/ (accessed 12 August 2003).

Merleau-Ponty, M. (1962) *The Phenomenology of Perception*, London: Routledge.

Merton, T. (1961) *New Seeds of Contemplation*, New York: New Directions.

Metaphysical: Surfing on a Higher Level (1997) video, Sydney: Quicksilver International.

Miah, A. (2004) *Genetically Modified Athletes: Biomedical Ethics, Gene Doping and Sport*, London: Routledge.

Middleton, J.R and Walsh, B.J. (1995) *Truth is Stranger than it Used to Be: Biblical Faith in a Postmodern Age*, London: SPCK.

Miller, P.S. and Kerr, G.A. (2002) 'Conceptualising Excellence: Past Present and Future', *Journal of Applied Sport Psychology*, 14: 140–153.

Miller, W. and Thoresen, C. (2003) ' Spirituality and Health', in W. Miller (ed.) *Integrating Spirituality into Treatment*, Washington, DC: American Psychological Association, pp. 3–18.

Mitchell, R.G. Jr (1983) *Mountain Experience: The Psychology and Sociology of Adventure*, Chicago: The University of Chicago Press.

Moltmann, Jürgen (1972) *Theology of Play*, New York: Harper.

Moltmann, J. (1974) *The Crucified God*, London: SCM Press.

Moltmann, J. (1985) *God in Creation*. London: SCM.

Moore, C.E. (ed.). (1999) *Provocations: The Spiritual Writings of Kierkegaard*, Farmington, PA: The Plough Publishing House.

Moraglia, G. (2004) 'On Facing Death: Views of Some Prominent Psychologists', *Journal of Humanistic Psychology*, 44 (3): 337–357.

Moran, A. (1996) *The Psychology of Concentration in Sport Performances: A Cognitive Analysis*, Hove: Psychology Press.

Morea, P. (1997a) *In Search of Personality: Christianity and Modern Psychology*, London: SCM Press.

Morea, P.M. (1997b) 'Thomas Merton's Christian Self-Actualization', in P.M. Morea, *In Search of Personality*, London: SCM Press, pp. 63–92.

Morgan, W.J. (1993) 'An Existential Phenomenological Analysis of Sport as a Religious Experience', in C.S. Prebish (ed.), *Religion and Sport: The Meeting of Sacred and Profane*, Westport, CT: Greenwood Press, pp. 119–150.

Muirhead, D. (1962) *Surfing in Hawaii*, Flagstaff, AZ: Northland.

Murdoch, I. (1993) *Metaphysics as a Guide to Morals*, London: Vintage.

Murphy, M. (1995) 'Adventure and Sport', in M. Murphy, *The Future of the Body: Explorations into the Further Evolution of Human Nature*, New York: Jeremy P. Tarcher, pp. 415–447.

Murphy, M. and White, R.A. (1995) *In the Zone: Transcendent Experience in Sports*, London: Penguin.

Murray, A. (1982) *Humility*, New Kensington, PA: Whitaker House.

Murray, A. (2005) *Absolute Surrender*, Bridge-Logos Publishers.

Mustakova-Possardt, E. (2004) 'Education for Critical Moral Consciousness', *Journal of Moral Education*, 33 (3): 245–270.

Myers, B. (1997) *Young Children and Spirituality*, London: Routledge.

Nathanson, P. (1999) 'I Feel Therefore I Am: The Princess of Passion and the Implicit Religion of Our Time', *Implicit Religion*, 2 (2): 59–88.

Nesti, M. (2002) 'Meaning Not Measurement: Existential Approaches to Counselling in Sport Contexts', in D. Lavallee and I. Cockerill (eds), *Counselling in Sport and Exercise Contexts*, Leicester: British Psychological Society, Sport and Exercise Psychology Section, pp. 38–47.

Nesti, M. (2004) *Existential Psychology and Sport: Theory and Application*, London: Routledge.

Nesti, M. (2006) 'Existential, Humanistic and other Person Centred Approaches to Sport Psychology Consulting: Stories of Real World Practice and their Implications for the Discipline', workshop conducted at Second International Conference in Qualitative Research in Sport and Exercise, Liverpool, UK.

Nesti, M. and Sewell, D. (1999) 'Losing It: The Importance of Anxiety and Mood Stability in Sport', *Journal of Personal and Interpersonal Loss*, 4: 257–268.

Newman, J. (1989) *Competition in Religious Life*, Waterloo, Ont.: Wilfrid Laurier University Press.

Newsome, D. (1961) *Godliness and Good Learning: Four Studies on a Victorian Ideal*, London: Cassell.

Nicholls, A.R., Holt, N.L. and R.C.J. Polman (2005) 'A Phenomenological Analysis of Coping Effectiveness in Golf', *The Sport Psychologist*, 19: 111–130.

Niebuhr, R. (1964) *The Nature and Destiny of Man: A Christian Interpretation*, Vol. 1, New York: Scribner.

Nissiotis, N. (1976) 'Olympism and Religion', *Proceedings of the International Olympic Academy*, 16: 59–70.

Nissiotis, N. (1984) 'Olympism and Today's Reality', *Proceedings of the International Olympic Academy*, 24: 57–74.

Nissiotis, N. (1985) 'The Olympic Movement's Contribution to Peace', *Proceedings of the International Olympic Academy*, 25: 54–63.

Nordenfelt, L. (1987) *On the Nature of Health: An Action-Theoretic Approach*, Boston, MA: D. Reidel.

Norman, E. (1987) 'Victorian Values: Stewart Headlam and the Christian Socialists', *History Today*, April: 27–32.

Novak, M. (1994/1967) *The Joy of Sports: End Zones, Bases, Baskets, Balls and Consecration of the American Spirit*, New York: Basic Books.

Ntoumanis, N. and Biddle, S. (1999) 'A Review of Motivational Climate in Physical Activity', *Journal of Sport Sciences*, 17: 643–665.

Nye, R.D. (1973) *Conflict among Humans*, New York: Springer.

O'Connor, F. (1970) *Mystery and Manners*, New York: Noonday Press.

Odibat, A.A. (1989) 'The Mind–Body Relationship as Related to Theories of Sport and Physical Education: The Islamic Philosophy in Comparison to Others', *Islamic Quarterly*, 33 (4): 263–276.

Olivier, S. (2006) 'Moral Dilemmas of Participation Dangerous Sports', *Leisure Studies*, 25 (1): 95–109.

Orlick, T. (1998) *Embracing Your Potential: Steps to Self-Discovery, Balance and Success in Sports, Work and Life*, Champaign, IL: Human Kinetics.

Otto, R. (1968/1923) *The Idea of the Holy: An Inquiry into the Non-Rational Factor in the Idea of the Divine and its Relation to the Rational*, London: Oxford University Press.

Otto, R. (1957) *Mysticism East and West*, New York: Meridian Books.

Outka, G. (1972) *Agape: An Ethical Analysis*, New Haven, CT: University of Yale Press.

Overman, S.J. (1999) '"Winning isn't Everything. It's the Only Thing": The Origin, Attributions, and Influence of a Famous Football Quote', *Football Studies* 2 (2): 77–99.

Overman, S.J. (1997) *The Influence of the Protestant Ethic on Sport and Recreation*, Sydney: Ashgate.

Oxman, T., Freeman, D. and Manheimer, E. (1995) 'Lack of Social Participation or Religious Strength and Comfort as Risk Factors for Death after Cardiac Surgery in the Elderly', *Psychosomatic Medicine*, 57: 5–15.

Palaeologos, C. (1964) 'The Ancient Olympics', *Proceedings of the International Olympic Academy*, 4: 61–78.

Palaeologos, C. (1965) 'The Institution of the "Truce" in the Ancient Olympic Games', *Proceedings of the International Olympic Academy*, 5: 203–210.

Palaeologos, C. (1982) 'Hercules, the Ideal Olympic Personality', *Proceedings of the International Olympic Academy*, 22: 54–71.

Palaeologos, C. (1985) 'Olympia of Myth and History', *Proceedings of the International Olympic Academy*, 25: 64–70.

Palmer, C. (2004) 'Death, Danger and the Selling of Risk in Adventure Sports', in B. Wheaton (ed.), *Understanding Lifestyle Sports: Consumption, Identity and Difference*, London: Routledge, pp. 55–69.

Papadopoulos, I. (1999) 'Spirituality and Holistic Caring: An Exploration of the Literature', *Implicit Religion*, 2 (2): 102–108.

Parks, S. (1992) 'Fowler Evaluated', in Jeff Astley and Leslie Francis (eds), *Christian Perspectives on Faith Development*, Leominster: Gracewing, pp. 92–106.

Parry, J. (1986) 'Values in Physical Education', in P. Tomlinson and M. Quinton (eds), *Values across the Curriculum*, Brighton: Falmer Press, pp. 134–157.

Parry, J. (1988a) 'Olympism at the Beginning and End of the Twentieth Century', *Proceedings of the International Olympic Academy*, 28: 81–94.

Parry, J. (1988b) 'Physical Education, Justification and the National Curriculum', *PE Review*, 11 (2): 106–118.

Parry, J. (1998) 'The Justification of Physical Education', in K. Green and K. Hardman (eds), *Physical Education – a Reader*, Stuttgart: Meyer & Meyer, pp. 36–68.

Parry, J. (2006) 'Sport and Olympism: Universals and Multiculturalism', *Journal of the Philosophy of Sport*, 33: 188–204.

Parsons, G. (ed.) (1988) *Religion in Victorian Britain*, Vol. II, Manchester: Manchester University Press.

Pattison, S. (2001) 'Dumbing Down the Spirit', in H. Orchard (ed.), *Spirituality in Health Care Contexts*, London: Jessica Kingsley.

Perry, M. (1992) *Gods Within*, London: SPCK.

Perry, M. (1995) 'Idealism and Drift', in J. Watt (ed.), *The Church, Medicine and the New Age*, London: The Churches' Council for Health and Healing.

Petitpas, A., Champayne, D., Chartrand, J., Danish, S. and Murphy, S. (1997) *Athletes Guide to Career Planning*, Champaign, IL: Human Kinetics.

Pfitzner, V.C. (1967) *Paul and the Agon Motif: Traditional Athletic Imagery in the Pauline Literature*, Leiden: E.J. Brill.

Pieper, J. (1989) *Josef Pieper: An Anthology*, San Francisco: Ignatius Press.

Pieper, J. (1995) *Divine Madness; Plato's Case against Secular Humanism*, San Francisco: Ignatius Press.

Pieper, J. (1998) *Leisure: The Basis of Culture*, South Bend, IN: St Augustine's Press.

Piltz, G.A. (1995) 'Performance Sport: Education and Fair Play?', *International Review for the Sociology of Sport*, 30: 391–418.

Poloma, M.M. (2003) *Main Street Mystics: The Toronto Blessing and Reviving Pentecostalism*, New York: Altamira Press.

Pontifical Council of the Laity (ed.) (2006) *The World of Sport: A Field of Christian Mission*, Libreria Editrice Vaticana, *International Seminar*, Vatican, Italy, 11–12 November 2005.

Prebish, C.S. (1993) *Religion and Sport: The Meeting of Sacred and Profane*, Westport, CT: Greenwood Press.

Price, J.L. (1996) 'Naturalistic Recreations', in P.H. Van Ness (ed.), *Spirituality and the Secular Quest*, London: SCM Press, pp. 414–444.

Price, J.L. (2001) *From Season to Season: Sports as American Religion*, Mercer Macon, GA: University Press.

Privette, G. and Bundrick C.M. (1997) 'Psychological Process of Peak, Average, and Failing Performance in Sport', *International Journal of Sport Psychology*, 28: 323–334.

Putney, C. (2001) *Muscular Christianity: Manhood and Sports in Protestant America 1880–1920*, Cambridge, MA: Harvard University Press.

Quanz, D.R. (1994) 'The Formative Power of the IOC's Founding: The Birth of a New Peace Movement', *Proceedings of the International Olympic Academy*, 34: 121–129.

Quinn, C.H. (1965) 'The Readers Take Over', *Sports Illustrated*, 23 (18): 18.

Rahner, Hugo (1972) *Man at Play* (trans. B. Battershaw), New York: Herder and Herder.

Randels, G.D. and Beal, B. (2002) 'What Makes a Man? Religion, Sport and Negotiating Masculine Identity in the Promise Keepers', in T. Magdalinski and T.J.L. Chandler (eds), *With God on their Side: Sport in the Service of Religion*, London: Routledge, pp. 160–176.

Randolph-Horn, D. and Paslawska, K. (2002) *Spirituality at Work*, Leeds: Leeds Church Institute.

Ravizza, K. (1977) 'Peak experiences in Sport', *Journal of Humanistic Psychology*, 17: 35–40.

Ravizza, K. (1984) 'Qualities of the Peak Experience in Sport', in J. Silva and R. Weinberg (eds), *Psychological Foundations of Sport*, Champaign, IL: Human Kinetics, pp. 452–461.

Ravizza, K. (2002) 'A Philosophical Construct: A Framework for Performance Enhancement', *International Journal of Sport Psychology*, 33: 4–18.

Ravizza, K. and Fazio, J. (2002) 'Consulting with Confidence: Using Who You Are to Evoke Excellence in Others', workshop conducted at the Annual Conference of the American Association of Applied Sport Psychology, Tucson, Arizona.

Rawnsley, H.D. (1889) *Edward Thring, Teacher and Poet*, London: T. Fisher Unwin.

Reader, J. (1997) *Beyond All Reason*, Cardiff: Aureus.

Reddiford G. (1982) 'Playing to Win', *Physical Education Review*, 5 (2): 107–115.

Redmond, G. (1978) 'The First Tom Brown's Schooldays: Origins and Evolution of "Muscular Christianity" in Children's Literature', *Quest*, 30: 4–18.

Reed, P. (1987) 'Spirituality and Well-Being in Terminally Ill Hospitalised Adults', *Research in Nursing and Health*, 10 (5): 335–344.

Reed, P. (1998) 'The Re-enchantment of Health Care: A Paradigm of Spirituality', in M. Cobb and V. Renshaw (eds), *The Spiritual Challenge of Healthcare*, London: Churchill Livingstone, pp. 125–137.

Reid, H. (2006) 'Olympic Sport and its Lessons for Peace', *Journal of the Philosophy of Sport*, 33: 205–214.

Reid, H. (1998) 'Sport, Education, and the Meaning of Victory', in *Proceedings of the Twentieth World Congress of Philosophy*, Paideia.

Reid, H.L. (2002) 'Taking Responsibility for Life and Death', in H. Reid, *The Philosophical Athlete*, Durham, NC: Carolina Academic Press, pp. 97–117.

Ricoeur, P. (1992) *Oneself as Another*, Chicago: Chicago University Press.

Richards, P.S. and Bergin, A.E. (1997) *A Spiritual Strategy for Counselling and Psychotherapy*, Washington, DC: American Psychological Association.

Richardson, A. (1969) *A Dictionary of Christian Theology*, London: SCM Press

Rinehart, R. (2000) '~~Emerging~~ Arriving Sport: Alternatives to Formal Sport', in J. Coakley and E. Dunning (eds), *Handbook of Sport Studies*, London: Sage, pp. 504–519.

Robinson, S. (2001) *Agape, Moral Meaning and Pastoral Counselling*, Cardiff: Aureus.

Robinson, S. (2005) *Ethics and Employability*, York: Higher Education Academy.

Robinson, S. (2007) *Spirituality, Ethics and Care*, London: Jessica Kingsley.

Robinson, S. and Dixon, J.R. (1997) 'The Professional Engineer: Virtues and Learning', *Science and Engineering Ethics*, 3 (3): 339–348.

Robinson, S. and Katulushi, C. (eds) (2005) *Values in Higher Education*, Cardiff: Aureus.

Robinson, S., Kendrick, K. and Brown, A. (2003) *Spirituality and the Practice of Healthcare*, Basingstoke: Palgrave.

Robinson, S.J. (1998) 'Helping the Hopeless', *Contact*, 127: 3–11.

Roesch, H.E. (1979) 'Olympism and Religion', *Proceedings of the International Olympic Academy*, 19: 192–205.

Rogers, C. (1983) *Freedom to Learn for the 80s*, Columbus, OH: Charles E. Merrill.

Rogers, C.R. (1961) *On Becoming a Person: A Therapist's View of Psychotherapy*, Boston, MA: Houghton Mifflin.

Rolston, Holmes III (1989) *Philosophy Gone Wild: Environmental Ethics*, Buffalo, NY: Prometheus Books.

Rosen, D. (1994) 'The Volcano and the Cathedral: Muscular Christianity and the Origins of Primal Manliness', in D.E. Hall (ed.), *Muscular Christianity: Embodying the Victorian Age*, Cambridge: Cambridge University Press, pp. 17–44.

Ross, L. (1995) 'The Spiritual Dimension: Its Importance to Patients' Health, Well Being and Quality of Life and its Implications for Nursing Practice', *International Journal of Nursing Studies*, 32 (5): 457–468.

Ross, L. (1997) 'Elderly Patients' Perceptions of their Spiritual Needs and Care: A Pilot Study', *Journal of Advanced Nursing*, 26: 710–715.

Russell, J.S. (2005) 'The Value of Dangerous Sports', *Journal of the Philosophy of Sport*, 32: 1–19.

Ryan, T. (1985) 'Towards a Spirituality for Sports', *International Journal for Theology*, 5 (205): 110–118.

Saint Sing, S. (2003) 'Breakthrough Kinesis', *Quest*, 55: 306–314.

Saint Sing, S. (2004) *Spirituality of Sport: Balancing Body and Soul*, Cincinnati, OH: St. Anthony Messenger Press.

Salter, D. (1997) 'Measure, Analyse and Stagnate: Towards a Radical Psychology of Sport', in R.J. Butler (ed.), *Sports Psychology in Performance*, Oxford: Reed Educational and Professional Publishing, pp. 248–260.

Samaranche, J.A. (1995) 'Olympic Ethics', *Olympic Review*, 25 (1): 3.

Sartre, J.P. (1956) *Being and Nothingness* (trans. Hazel E. Barnes), New York: The Philosophical Library.

Saunders, M. (2003) 'New Course Combines Sport and Theology', *Christian Renewal*, May: 7.

Savage, S.B. (2000) *Through Dance: Fully Human, Fully Alive*, in J. Begbie (ed.), *Beholding the Glory: Incarnation through the Arts*, London: Darton, Longman and Todd, pp. 64–82.

Schleiermacher, F. (1928/1830) *The Christian Faith*, Edinburgh: T. and T. Clark.

Schmitt, R.L. and Leonard, W.M. II (1986) 'Immortalizing the Self through Sport', *American Journal of Sociology*, 91 (5): 1088–1111.

Schneider, K.J. and May, R. (eds) (1995) *The Psychology of Existence: An Integrative Clinical Perspective*, New York: McGraw-Hill.

Schoen, D. (1983) *The Reflective Practitioner*, New York: Basic Books.

Schroeder, P.J. and Scribner, J.P. (2006) 'To Honor and Glorify God: The Role of Religion in One Intercollegiate Athletics Culture', *Sport, Education and Society*, 11 (1): 39–54.

Schultheis, R. (1996) *Bone Games: Extreme Sports, Shamanism, Zen, and the Search for Transcendence*, New York: Breakaway Books.

Segrave, J.O. (1997) 'A Matter of Life and Death: Some Thoughts on the Language of Sport', *Journal of Sport and Social Issues*, 21 (2): 211–220.

Selby, P. (1983) *Liberating God*, London: SPCK.

Seligman, M.E.P. and Csikszentmihalyi, M. (2000) 'Positive Psychology: An Introduction', *American Psychologist*, 55: 5–14.

Sheehan, George (1978) *Running and Being*, New York: Warner books

Sherif, C.W. (1976) 'The Social Context of Competition', in Daniel M. Landers (ed.), *Social Problems in Athletics: Essays in the Sociology of Sport*, Chicago: University of Illinois Press, pp. 18–36.

Shuler, P. Gelberg, L. and Brown, M. (1994) 'The Effects of Spiritual/Religious Practices on Psychological Well-Being among Inner City Homeless Women', *Nurse Practitioner Forum*, 5: 106–113.

Shvartz, E. (1967) 'Nietzsche: a Philosopher of Fitness', *Quest*, 8: 83–89.

Siegel, A. (1986) *Love, Medicine and Miracles*, New York: Harper.

Silk, M.L., Andrews, D.L., and Cole, C.L. (eds) (2005) *Sport and Corporate Nationalisms*, New York: Berg.

Simon, B. and Bradley, I. (1975) *The Victorian Public School*, Dublin: Gill and Macmillan.

Simon, R.L. (1991) 'The Ethics of Competition', in R.L. Simon (ed.), *Fair Play: Sports, Values and Society*, Oxford: Westview Press, pp. 13–36.

Simpson, H.P. (ed.) (1970) *Selected Writings of Jonathan Edwards*, New York: Fredrick Ungar.

Sims, A. (1994) ' "Psyche" – Spirit as Well as Mind?', *British Journal of Psychiatry*, 165: 441–446.

Slusher, H. (1967) *Man, Sport and Existence: A Critical Analysis*, Philadelphia, PA: Lea and Febiger.

Smart, N. (1978) 'Understanding Religious Experience', in S. Katz (ed.), *Mysticism and Philosophical Analysis*, London: Oxford University Press, pp. 10–21.

Smedes, L.B. (1998) 'Stations on the Journey from Forgiveness to Hope', in E. Worthington (ed.), *Dimensions of Forgiveness*, Philadelphia, PA: William Templeton Foundation, pp. 341–354.

Smith, T. and Smith, A. (2004) 'Endurance Athletes in Pain: A Hermeneutic Phenomenological Inquiry', *Journal of Sports Sciences*, 2: 172–173.

Solomon, R. (1992) *Ethics and Excellence*, Oxford: Oxford University Press.

Speck, P. (1998) 'The Meaning of Spirituality in Illness', in M. Cobb and V. Renshaw (eds), *The Spiritual Challenge of Health Care*, London: Churchill Livingstone, pp. 21–34.

Spencer, A.F. (2000) 'Ethics, Faith and Sport', *Journal of Interdisciplinary Studies*, 12 (1/2): 143–158.

Spiegel, D. Bloom, J. and Kraemer, H. (1989) 'Effects of Psychosocial Treatment on Survival of Patients with Metastatic Breast Cancer', *The Lancet*, 142: 888–891.

Spilka, B. (1993) 'Spirituality: Problems and Directions in Operationalising a Fuzzy Concept', paper presented at the 101st American Psychological Association Annual Convention, Toronto, Ont., 20–24 August.

Spilka, B., Hood, R.W., Hunsberger, B. and Gorsuch, R. (2003) 'Mysticism', in B. Spilka, R.W. Hood Jr., B. Hunsberger and R. Gorsuch, *The Psychology of Religion: An Empirical Approach*, third edition, London: The Guilford Press, pp. 290–340.

Spinelli, E. (1989) *The Interpreted World*, London: Sage.

Spinelli, E. (1996) 'The Existential–Phenomenological Paradigm', in R. Woolfe and W. Dryden (eds), *Handbook of Counselling Psychology*, London: Sage Publications, pp. 180–200.

Spohn, W. (1997) 'Spirituality and Ethics: Exploring the Connections', *Theological Studies*. 58, 109–122.

Stace, W.T. (1960) *Mysticism and Philosophy*, Philadelphia, PA: J.B. Lippencott.

Standish, P. (1998) 'In the Zone: Heidegger and Sport', in M. McNamee and J. Parry (eds), *Ethics and Sport*, London: Routledge, pp. 256–269.

Steele, R.B. (2000) 'Devotio Post-Moderna: On Using a "Spiritual Classic" as a Diagnostic Tool in a Freshman Christian Formation Course', *Horizons*, 27 (1): 81–97.

Stern, D. (1985) *The Interpersonal World of the Infant*, New York: Basic Books.

Stranger, M. (1999) 'The Aesthetics of Risk: A Study of Surfing', *International Review for the Sociology of Sport*, 34 (3): 265–276.

Strawbridge, W., Cohen, R., Shema, S. and Kaplan, G. (1997) 'Frequent Attendance at Religious Services and Mortality over 28 Years', *American Journal of Public Health*, 87: 957–961.

Swaddling, J. (1980) *The Ancient Olympic Games*, London: British Museum.

Swinton, J. (2001) *Spirituality and Mental Health Care*, London: Jessica Kingsley.

Tace, D. (2004) *The Spirituality Revolution: The Emergence of Contemporary Spirituality*, New York: Brunner-Routledge.

Tangney, J. (2000) 'Humility: Theoretical Perspectives, Empirical Findings and Directions for Future Research', *Journal of Social and Clinical Psychology*, 19 (1): 70–82.

Taylor, C. (1996) *Sources of the Self*, Cambridge: Cambridge University Press.

Teasdale, J. (1997) 'Preventing Depressive Relapse', paper presented at the Twenty-Fifth Annual Conference of the British Association of Behaviour and Cognitive Therapy, Canterbury, July.

Theresa, St (1930) *Interior Castle*, London: Thomas Baker.

Thomas, C.B. (1982) 'Cancer in Families of Former Medical Students Followed in Midlife', *Johns Hopkins Medicine*, 151: 193–202.

Thomas, C.E. (1996) 'Sports', in P.H. Van Ness (ed.), *Spirituality and the Secular Quest*, London: SCM Press, pp. 498–519.

Thompson, D. (1997) *Beneath Mulhollan: Thoughts on Hollywood and its Ghosts*, New York: Alfred A. Knopf.

Thoresen, C.E. (1990) *Long-Term 8-year Follow up of Recurrent Coronary Prevention*, Uppsala: International Society of Behavioural Medicine.

Thoresen, C. and Hoffman Goldberg, J. (1998) 'Coronary Heart Disease: A Psycho-Social Perspective', in S. Roth-Roemer, S. Kurpius Robinson and C. Carmin (eds.), *The Emerging Role of Counseling Psychology in Health Care*, New York: Norton, pp. 94–136.

Tomlinson, J. (1999) *The Ultimate Encyclopaedia of Extreme Sports*, New York: Carlton Books.

Tournier, P. (1965) *The Healing of Persons*, San Francisco: Harper and Row Publishers.

Twiss, S. (1998) 'Religion and Human Rights: A Comparative Perspective', in S. Twiss and B. Grelle (eds), *Explorations in Global Ethics*, Boulder, CO: Westview Press, pp. 78–91.

UKCC (2000) *Requirements for Pre-registration Nursing Programmes*, London: UKCC.

Underhill, E. (1955/1911) *Mysticism*, twelfth edition, New York: Meridian Books.

Valle, R.S. (1989) 'The Emergence of Transpersonal Psychology', in R.S. Valle and S. Halling (eds), *Existential–Phenomenological Perspectives in Psychology*, London: Plenum Press, pp. 255–256.

Valle, R.S. and Halling, S. (1989) *Existential–Phenomenological Perspectives in Psychology*, London: Plenum Press.

Valle, R.S. and King, M. (1978) *Existential–Phenomenological Alternatives for Psychology*, New York: Oxford University Press.

Van Andel, G., Heintzman, P. and Visker, T. (eds) (2005) *Christianity and Leisure: Issues in a Pluralistic Society*, Sioux Center, IA: Dordt College Press.

Van Kaam, A. (1969) *Existential Foundations of Psychology*, New York: Image.

Van Kaam, A. (1975) *In Search of Spiritual Identity*, Pittsburgh, PA: Dimension Books.

Vance, N. (1985) *The Sinews of the Spirit: The Ideal of Christian Manliness in Victorian Literature and Religious Thought*, Cambridge: Cambridge University Press.

Vanier, J. (2001) *Becoming Human*, London: DLT.

Vanstone, W.H. (1977) *Love's Endeavour, Love's Expense*, London: Darton, Longman and Todd.

Veblen, T. (1970/1899) *Theory of the Leisure Class: An Economic Study of Institutions*, London: Allen and Unwin.

van der Ven, J. (1998) *Formation of the Moral Self*, Grand Rapids, MI: Eerdmans.

Visker, T. (1994) 'Play, Game, and Sport in a Reformed, Biblical Worldview', in Paul Heintzman, Glen A. Van Andel and Thomas Visker (eds), *Christianity and Leisure: Issues in a Pluralistic Society*, Dordt, IA: Dordt College Press.

Vitz, P. (1994/1977) *Psychology as Religion: The Cult of Self-Worship*, Grand Rapids, MI: Williams Eerdmans Publishing.

Volkwein, K.A.E. (1995) 'Ethics and Top-Level Sport – A Paradox?', *International Review for Sociology of Sport*, 30 (3/4): 311–319.

Walker, A. (1996) *Telling the Story: Gospel, Mission and Culture*, London: SPCK.

Walker, S.H. (1980) *Winning: The Psychology of Competition*, New York: W.W. Norton.

Watson, N., Smith, A. and Nesti, M. (2004) 'A Qualitative Investigation of the Psychological and Spiritual Dynamics of Surfing and Snowboarding', poster presentation at the First International Conference for Qualitative Research in Sport and Exercise, Liverpool John Moores University, 18–19 May.

Watson, N.J and Nesti, M. (2005) 'The Role of Spirituality in Sport Psychology Consulting: An Analysis and Integrative Review of Literature', *Journal of Applied Sport Psychology*, 17: 228–239.

Watson, N.J. (manuscript to be submitted for consideration) 'Identity in Sport: A Christian Theological Analysis', *International Journal of Religion and Sport*.

Watson, N.J. and Czech, D. (2005) 'The Use of Prayer in Sport: Implications for Sport Psychology Consulting', *Athletic Insight: The Online Journal of Sport Psychology*, 17 (4). Available at: www.athleticinsight.com/.

Watson, N., Weir, S. and Friend, S. (2005) 'The Development of Muscular Christianity in Victorian Britain and Beyond', *Journal of Religion and Society*, 7. Available at: http://moses.creighton.edu/JRS/.

Watt, J. (ed.) (1995) *The Church Medicine and the New Age*, London: The Churches' Council for Health and Healing.

Weir, S. (manuscript in preparation) *Christianity and Sport, 1830–2000*.

Weiss, P. (1969) *Sport: A Philosophic Inquiry*, Carbondale, IL: Southern Illinois University Press

Wenzel, D. and Allison, G. (1998) 'Teaching them Sports: An Evangelical Theology and Psychology of Sports', paper submitted for the Fiftieth Annual Meeting of the Evangelical Theological Society, 19 March. Online. Available at: http://sportsoutreachusa.com.

Wertz, F.J. (2005) 'Phenomenological Research Methods for Counseling Psychology', *Journal of Counseling Psychology*, 2: 167–177.

Wheaton, B. (ed.) (2004) *Understanding Lifestyle Sports: Consumption, Identity and Difference*, London: Routledge.

White, C. (2004). 'Kierkegaard and Sport: Willing One thing in Competitive Sports', paper presented at the First International Conference, Sport and Religion: An Inquiry into Cultural Values, St. Olaf College, MN, 24–26 June.

Wilkinson, R. (1964) *Gentlemanly Power – British Leadership and Public Schools Tradition*, London: Oxford University Press.

Williams, B. (2004) 'Competing Rightly: Applying Christian Ethical Thinking to Competitive Sport'. Online. Available at: www.sportsoutreachusa.com/ (accessed 2 May 2006).

Williams, B. (2005a) *Discipleship through Competitive Sport*. Online. Available at: http://sportsoutreachusa.com.

Williams, B. (2005b) *Theological Perspectives on Sport Parachurch Ministries and the Church*. Online. Available at: http://sportsoutreachusa.com

Wilson, M.V. (1989) *Our Father Abraham: Jewish Roots of the Christian Faith*, Grand Rapids, MI: Wm. B. Eerdmans Publishing Company.

Winn, W.E. (1960) 'Tom Brown's Schooldays and the Development of "Muscular Christianity"', *Church History*, 29: 66.

Wittmer, M. (2005) 'The Christian Perspective on Sport', paper presented at Think Tank on the Integration of Christian Faith and Sport, Sponsored by Athletes in Action, Xenia, OH, 13–16 March.

Wolfson. S. (2002) 'Sports Participants' Reflections on Past Events: The Role of Social Cognition', in I. Cockerill (ed.), *Solutions in Sport Psychology*, London: Thomson, pp. 91–107.

Woods, R. (1980) *Understanding Mysticism*, London: The Athlone Press.

Worthington, E. (1989) *Dimensions of Forgiveness*, Radnor: Temple Foundation Press.

Wulff, D.M. (1991) *Psychology of Religion: Classic and Contemporary Views*, New York: Wiley.

Wyschogrod, E. (1973) 'Sport, Death and the Elemental', in E. Wyschogrod (ed.), *The Phenomenon of Death: Faces of Morality*, New York: Harper and Row Publishers, pp. 166–197.

Yalom, I. (1999) *Momma and the Meaning of Life: Tales of Psychotherapy*, London: Piatkus.

Yancey, P. (2003) *Rumours of Another World: What on Earth are we Missing?* Grand Rapids, MI: Zondervan.

Yorke, M. and Knight, P. (2004) *Embedding Employability in the Curriculum*, York: LTSN.

Young, D.C. (2005) 'Mens Sana in Corpore Sano? Body and Mind in Ancient Greece', *The International Journal of the History of Sport*, 22 (1): 22–41.

Zaehner, R.C. (1961) *Mysticism: Sacred and Profane: An Inquiry into Some Varieties of Praeternatural Experience*, London: Oxford University Press.

Index